# QUESTIONS & ANSWERS:
# Constitutional Law

# QUESTIONS & ANSWERS:
# Constitutional Law

**SECOND EDITION**

*Multiple Choice and Short Answer*
*Questions and Answers*

**By**

**PAUL E. McGREAL**
Professor of Law
Southern Illinois University School of Law

**LINDA S. EADS**
Associate Professor of Law
Dedman School of Law
Southern Methodist University

ISBN#: 9781422417430

**NOTE TO USERS**
To ensure that you are using the latest materials available in this area, please be sure to periodically check the LexisNexis Law School web site for downloadable updates and supplements at www.lexisnexis.com /lawschool

Editorial Offices
744 Broad Street, Newark, NJ 07102 (973) 820-2000
201 Mission St., San Francisco, CA 94105-1831 (415) 908-3200
701 East Water Street, Charlottesville, VA 22902-7587 (434) 972-7600
www.lexis.com

(Pub.3174)

# DEDICATION

To Marianne — Wherever we go, you're my home

To Patrick — You'll always be a part of me

P.E.M.

To Madelyn — For all that she is and all that she will become

To Joan — My touchstone

L.S.E.

# ABOUT THE AUTHORS

**PAUL E. McGREAL** is Professor of Law at Southern Illinois University School of Law in Carbondale, Illlinois where he teaches (among other things) the Constitutional Law survey course as well as electives on the First and Fourteenth Amendments and National Security Law. He has written numerous law review articles on issues in constitutional law, and has spoken on these issues in various fora. Prior to entering teaching, Professor McGreal practiced in the litigation section of the Dallas office of the Baker Botts law firm.

**LINDA S. EADS** teaches at the Dedman School of Law, Southern Methodist University, in Dallas, Texas. She teaches and writes in the areas of evidence, legal ethics, constitutional law, and women and the law. From January 1999 to August 2000, Professor Eads served as Deputy Attorney General for Litigation for the State of Texas. In that position, she directed the State's civil litigation. Prior to joining the SMU faculty, Professor Eads served as a trial attorney with the United States Department of Justice, investigating and prosecuting tax evaders, tax protestors, and drug dealers throughout the United States.

# PREFACE

With two new justices recently joining the United States Supreme Court, the next few years may bring significant change in Constitutional Law. Indeed, the retirement of Justice Sandra Day O'Connor, who provided the deciding vote in many 5 to 4 cases, has cast doubt on a broad range of decisions. Seemingly settled doctrines on separation of powers, abortion, and establishment of religion are now up for grabs. So while our first edition arrived at a time of remarkable stability — the Supreme Court's membership had not changed for over a decade (a modern record!) — this edition hits during only the second full term of the Roberts Court. With so much at stake, lively debate and uncertainty are likely to be the rule, rather than the exception.

This book is written for students taking the basic survey course in Constitutional Law. In drafting questions, we have pitched the breadth, depth, and level of difficulty to those studying the subject for the first time. This approach led to several choices regarding coverage as well as the form of the questions and answers. To help the reader better understand our approach, and thus how best to use this study tool, we offer the following observations.

First, unlike hornbooks and treatises, our coverage is not encyclopedic. We expect that our readers will take a final exam in a general survey course, and so our coverage is that of virtually every introductory Constitutional Law course. Specialized issues within each topic are hit upon lightly, and esoteric wrinkles are omitted entirely.

Second, our topic selection is further influenced by the growing tendency to shrink the coverage of the basic Constitutional Law course. With the Court's recent revival of its federalism jurisprudence, and with many schools reducing their Constitutional Law survey courses from six to four hours, it has become impracticable to cram all of the structural and individual rights material into a single course. Consequently, many schools have shifted some topics from the basic survey course to upper level electives. For example, the First Amendment is increasingly covered in a separate course. Similarly, the Takings Clause is often covered in the Property survey course. For this reason, we offer only the type of broad-brush coverage of free speech, religious freedom, and takings that one might expect in the Constitutional Law survey course. More detailed coverage of those subjects appear in other volumes in the *Q&A* series.

Third, we caution the reader that this volume differs somewhat from others in the *Q&A* series. Users of other volumes will notice that our answers are longer than those in some of the other books. This is because most of the Constitutional Law questions worth asking, and thus worth your study time, cannot be answered and explained in a short space. So, while our multiple choice questions each list four (A), (B), (C), (D) one-sentence answer choices, the true answers — and the ones we would expect to see students produce on our exams — are the explanations we supply in the second half of the volume. Further, our "short answers" are likely longer than you will find in other volumes in the series. Again, the reason is that the types of questions that will best prepare you for a Constitutional Law exam are rarely susceptible to one-paragraph answers. In the end, we have tried to balance brevity with the need to provide the student with realistic, useful questions. Our practice has been to err on the side of usefulness, resulting in somewhat longer discussions.

While the answers to our short answer questions vary in length, none is more than three paragraphs. Unless otherwise indicated, the question can be answered in one paragraph. Do not fret if your answer comes in slightly longer or shorter than our answer. As long as the substance is the same, we would give full credit on an exam. If your answer is longer, however, our answer may show how to convey the same substance in fewer words. On time pressure exams, such brevity can be an asset.

Several of the questions in this volume do not have easy answers. When this is the case, we identify the question as a close call and then suggest which answer we believe is best. That does not mean our preferred answer is the "correct" one. Indeed, you or your professor may disagree with our chosen answer, and in a few instances we disagree between ourselves as to the better response. That said, we believe each answer discusses all of the relevant arguments, and this is what counts on our constitutional law exams. More important than merely choosing the "correct" or "best" answer is understanding *why* one answer is better than the others. If you reach this understanding and disagree with our choice, so be it.

As with all the subjects in the *Q&A* series, Constitutional Law undergoes periodic change. When those changes reach a critical mass, we will produce yet another volume. In the interim, we will make updates available on the *Q&A* section of the Lexis-Nexis website. The web address is www.lexisnexis.com/lawschool/study/texts/.

Last, as many of the questions are difficult and contestable, we are interested in hearing from you — our readers. We welcome any and all suggestions about alternate analyses, confusing discussions, or twists on various questions. We are grateful for the comments and questions that helped improve this edition, so please keep the feedback coming. You can reach us at the e-mail addresses listed below.

Best of luck in your studies!

Paul McGreal                      Linda Eads
Carbondale, Illinois              Dallas, Texas
pmcgreal@siu.edu                  leads@mail.smu.edu

# TABLE OF CONTENTS

# TABLE OF CONTENTS

# QUESTIONS

1.  In his opinion for the Court in *Marbury v. Madison*, 5 U.S. (1 Cranch) 137 (1803), Chief Justice John Marshall made which of the following assertions:

    (A)   Federal courts may never review actions of the President.

    (B)   Federal courts may exercise judicial review over the constitutionality of statutes enacted by Congress.

    (C)   Article III grants the Supreme Court original jurisdiction to issue writs of mandamus.

    (D)   All of the above.

2.  In his opinion for the Court in *Martin v. Hunter's Lessee*, 14 U.S. 304 (1816), Justice Joseph Story made which of the following assertions:

    (A)   Federal courts may exercise original jurisdiction over state law claims.

    (B)   Federal courts may exercise judicial review over a state court's interpretation of the state's constitution.

    (C)   Federal courts possess inherent power to hear cases that involve a state court's interpretation of the United States Constitution.

    (D)   Federal courts may exercise judicial review over a state court's interpretation of the United States Constitution.

3.  In *Cooper v. Aaron*, 358 U.S. 1 (1958), the Supreme Court made which of the following assertions:

    (A)   State government officials must follow the Supreme Court's interpretation of the United States Constitution.

    (B)   State courts must hear federal claims over which Congress has given state courts original jurisdiction.

    (C)   Federal courts need not defer to parallel state lawsuits over the same subject matter.

    (D)   Federal courts must follow a state's definitive interpretation of the state's law.

4.  Since Fidel Castro rose to power in Cuba over 40 years ago, Cuban nationals have consistently sought to migrate to the United States. Cubans who cannot meet the stringent requirements to enter the United States as "refugees" occasionally try to enter the United States by the extra-legal means of sailing private boats to the southeastern coast of Florida. Because of the trip's hazards, as well as the Cuban government's active discouragement, such attempts are rare enough that the United States allows survivors to legally immigrate, even if they do not qualify for refugee status.

In January 2002, the Cuban government announced that it would no longer forcibly prevent emigration from Cuba by boat. The announcement prompted a massive flow of Cuban nationals toward the United States. Later that year, Congress enacted the Cuban Immigration Act of 2002, which changed United States policy toward Cuban nationals. In addition to those already legally entitled to enter under current law, the United States would allow 20,000 Cuban nationals to legally enter the United States each year. Under the Act, the 20,000 eligible immigrants are selected by an annual lottery from those Cuban nationals who apply to immigrate under the program. The first lottery was held in January 2003.

The Act further alters prior practice by requiring repatriation of any Cuban national who reaches the United States by boat. The Act also provides, however, that if any section is held unconstitutional, the Act as a whole will be void, and United States immigration law will revert to the rules and practices in effect prior to the Act.

A lawsuit challenging the Act's lottery program has been filed against the United States in the federal District Court for the District of Columbia. The lawsuit seeks a declaration that the lottery violates the Due Process Clause of the Fifth Amendment. The Plaintiff is a Cuban national who participated in the January 2003 Cuban lottery. The Plaintiff was not selected for entry into the United States and does not qualify as a refugee under United States law. He claims, however, that under the pre-Act immigration laws, he would have entered the United States by sailing a private boat from Cuba to Florida.

Does the Plaintiff have standing?

(A)  No, because the Plaintiff has not suffered an adequate injury-in-fact.

(B)  No, because the Plaintiff's injury was not caused by the defendant's conduct.

(C)  No, because the Plaintiff's requested relief will not redress his alleged injury.

(D)  Yes.

5. Suppose the lawsuit described in Question 4 is brought by the Federation for American Immigration Reform (FAIR), which is an association of Florida citizens concerned about the domestic effects of United States immigration policy. As its injury, FAIR asserts that the lottery program will cause its Miami members to endure overcrowded public schools, decreased access to public medical facilities, reduced police protection, and diminished employment opportunities.

Does FAIR have standing to bring this lawsuit?

(A) No, because FAIR has not suffered an adequate injury-in-fact.

(B) No, because FAIR's injury was not caused by the defendant's conduct.

(C) No, because FAIR's requested relief will not redress its alleged injury.

(D) Yes.

6. The Appleknocker Society is an environmental advocacy group that draws members from several Missouri Valley states. The Society has filed a federal court lawsuit against the United States Army Corps of Engineers regarding the Corps' failure to prepare an Environmental Impact Statement (EIS) as required by the National Environmental Policy Act. The Society alleges that the Corps plans to build a dam along the Humongous Muddy River, and that federal law requires an EIS for such a project. The Society further alleges that many of its members live near and use the Humongous Muddy River for hiking, fishing, and canoeing; and that the proposed dam would drastically alter the river's aesthetics as well as its suitability for fishing and canoeing. The Society concedes that preparation of an EIS will not necessarily alter the Corps' decision to construct the Humongous Muddy River dam project. The Society further concedes that several procedural steps remain after an EIS and before construction of the dam, and that construction would likely begin no sooner than five years from now, if ever.

Can the Appleknocker Society allege sufficient injury to support standing?

ANSWER:

7. Consider the lawsuit described in the preceding Question.

Can the Appleknocker Society satisfy the standing requirements of causation and redressability?

ANSWER:

8. After a recent newspaper article disclosed its existence, the President announced that the United States National Security Agency has been operating a domestic foreign intelligence surveillance program without seeking prior judicial approval. The surveillance applies to communications into and outside the United States where at least one of the parties is known or suspected to have links to terrorism. Suspicion can be related to a person's country of citizenship or prior activities.

Greg George is a lawyer who represents clients in international financial transactions. Specifically, George advises clients on compliance with United States anti-money-laundering and foreign trade laws. George recently filed suit against the NSA for an injunction declaring the secret surveillance plan unconstitutional. George argues that the surveillance program violates both the Fourth Amendment and the separation of powers. In support of his standing, George claims that soon after the President announced the existence of the NSA's secret surveillance program, several of his clients terminated his representation. George claims that these clients all resided or did business in countries the President had identified as harboring suspected terrorists.

The NSA's strongest argument to dismiss George's lawsuit for lack of standing is:

(A) George has not alleged an actual injury.

(B) George has alleged a generalized injury shared by a large portion of the United States population.

(C) George's alleged injury does not have a sufficient nexus with the alleged constitutional violations.

(D) The causation and redressability of George's injury are speculative.

9. The Garden Park School District operates three public high schools. In fall 2006, the District abandoned its neighborhood school assignment plan, which assigned students to the high school closest to their home. In its place, the District adopted a plan that used a student's race as one of five factors in assigning students to a high school. In January 2007, a group of ten parents whose children were all freshman in the District's high schools filed a federal court lawsuit against the District seeking to have the plan enjoined as violating the Equal Protection Clause of the Fourteenth Amendment. Each of the parents' children had been assigned to a high school other than their first choice.

The District has moved to dismiss the parents' lawsuit for lack of standing. The District Court should:

(A) Dismiss the lawsuit because it is speculative whether the District's racial assignment plan caused the parents' children to be assigned to a school other than their first choice.

(B) Dismiss the lawsuit because it is speculative whether enjoining the District's racial assignment plan would redress the parents' alleged injury.

(C) Dismiss the lawsuit because state law does not guarantee a child assignment to the high school of her choice, and so the plaintiffs' children have not suffered an actual injury.

(D) None of the above.

10. How did the Supreme Court's decision in *Hein v. Freedom From Religion Foundation, Inc.*, 127 S. Ct. 2553 (2007), clarify the limits of the taxpayer standing doctrine recognized in *Flast v. Cohen*, 392 U.S. 83 (1968)?

11. The State of New Arkansas recently enacted the Later Term Abortion Liability Act:

> Any person who performs an abortion after the first trimester will be strictly liable to the biological father of the aborted fetus in an action for wrongful death. When the biological father is unknown, the Attorney General may bring suit to recover damages.

Dr. Janet Jones performs abortions in New Arkansas and is concerned about liability under the Act. Dr. Jones has filed a lawsuit against the New Arkansas Attorney General seeking an injunction against enforcement, as well as a declaration that the Act is unconstitutional. While the lawsuit is pending, the New Arkansas Medical Board suspends Dr. Jones' medical license for persistent failure to fulfill the Board's continuing medical education requirement. To regain her license, Dr. Jones must complete three months of continuing medical education courses and apply for reinstatement. Dr. Jones has submitted an affidavit stating that she is currently enrolled in the required courses. The Board must reinstate Dr. Jones' license if it finds that she has satisfactorily completed the courses. The Board's decision on reinstatement is unreviewable.

Does Dr. Jones' suspension moot her lawsuit against the Attorney General?

(A) Yes. Because Dr. Jones cannot practice medicine, and thus cannot perform abortions, she no longer faces liability under the Act.

(B) No. Because Dr. Jones will likely regain her medical license, the Act still threatens her with future liability.

(C) Yes. Because reinstatement is within the sole, unreviewable discretion of the State Medical Board, it is purely speculative whether Dr. Jones will ever practice medicine again.

(D) No, because Dr. Jones' injury is capable of repetition yet evading review.

12. Consider the lawsuit described above in Question 9.

Assume that while the lawsuit was pending, the District suspended the new assignment plan and decided to return to neighborhood high schools for the 2007-2008 school year. In September 2007, the District then moved to dismiss the parents' lawsuit as moot.

The federal court should:

(A) Grant the District's motion because the District's suspension of the racial assignment plan has mooted the parents' lawsuit.

9

(B) Grant the District's motion because the parents have not alleged a concrete injury that is traceable to the District's racial assignment plan.

(C) Deny the District's motion because it is not absolutely certain that the District will never reinstate the challenged racial assignment plan.

(D) Deny the District's motion because the issue of the constitutionality of the District's racial assignment plan is capable of repetition yet evading review.

13. Recalling the facts from Question 11, assume that Dr. Jones completes the required education courses, applies for reinstatement, and the Board restores her license to practice medicine. Is Dr. Jones' lawsuit ripe for adjudication?

   ANSWER:

14. The President recently negotiated a treaty that called for an immediate freeze of the tariff imposed on all steel imports. Without debate, the Senate ratified the treaty, and it went into effect. Several domestic steel companies, which will be financially disadvantaged by removal of the tariff, have filed suit to challenge the constitutionality of the treaty. They argue that by approving the treaty without debate, the Senate did not adequately perform its "Advice and Consent" role under Article II, Section 2. Specifically, while the Senate's vote was adequate "Consent," by failing to debate the treaty the Senate impermissibly withheld its "Advice."

Do the steel companies assert a non-justiciable political question?

ANSWER (two paragraphs):

15. The House of Representatives recently impeached the Vice President of the United States for allegedly providing false and misleading information to members of Congress during periodic intelligence briefings. Immediately after the House vote on impeachment, the Vice President files suit in the United States District Court for the District of Columbia to enjoin the upcoming trial in the Senate. The Vice President argues that the House impeachment is void because the House procedures violate the Constitution. Specifically, the Vice President argues that impeachment is the equivalent of an indictment by a federal grand jury, and so the House impeachment procedures must mirror those followed by federal grand juries. Because the House followed evidentiary and other rules that differ substantially from those used by federal grand juries, the impeachment violates Article I, Section 2, Clause 5. Counsel for the House files a motion to dismiss the Vice President's lawsuit because it poses a non-justiciable political question.

The Vice President's lawsuit likely poses a political question because:

(A) The issue of the proper procedures for impeachment is textually committed to the House of Representatives.

(B) Judicial resolution of the issue would interfere with the substantial need for finality in the matter.

(C) A and B.

(D) Neither A nor B.

16. The Democratic Party controls the Illanoy State House and Senate, as well as the governorship. After the last census, the State's delegation to the United States House of Representatives was split 18 Democrats to 12 Republicans, which was roughly proportionate to the party representation in the State House. When a Republican member

13

of the State's federal House delegation voted against an increase in the federal minimum wage, the Speaker of the State House announced, "This is a Democratic State, and we ought to have a Democratic congressional delegation. We need to go back to the drawing board."

In a fit of pique, the Illanoy Legislature re-districted the State to give Democrats a majority of registered voters in all but one of the 30 federal districts. The resulting map was composed of bizarrely shaped districts, some of which traveled for miles along interstates or State highways without capturing a single residence. When asked about the strange map, the Speaker of the State House explained

> Our only goal was to rid our federal delegation of Republicans. We didn't care about anything else — not geography, size, or whatever. And if there were enough Democrats in this State to go around, we might have got there. As it is, we will have to settle for 29 out of 30. For now.

When asked whether she agreed with the Speaker's view of the re-districting, the Illanoy Governor replied, "Yep — that's what we did." The legislative history of the new map does not reveal any other factors that determined the size or location of any of the congressional districts.

Several Illanoy voters brought suit to challenge the re-districting as an unconstitutional political gerrymander. The voters argued that a political gerrymander is unconstitutional when the State's *sole* motive is to *completely disenfranchise* the voters of a political party. The State moved to dismiss the case as raising a political question.

Should the court dismiss the voters' lawsuit as raising a political question?

ANSWER (two paragraphs):

17. In 2002, the First Church of God (FCG) purchased a five-acre plot of land in Middle County, where it intends to operate a church and a school. The property currently contains two buildings, a barn, and a house. FCG plans to construct two additional structures, one for the church and the other for the school. Middle County has zoned the land "agricultural," restricting its use to "cultivation of crops and the raising of livestock, and no other purpose." Middle County zoning ordinances, however, provide for special-use permits, which can authorize reasonable non-conforming uses. Granting special-use permits lies within the unreviewable discretion of the Middle County Zoning Commission.

FCG filed an application for a special-use permit that would allow construction and operation of the school and church buildings. The Commission rejected the application, explaining that the proposed new structures would greatly strain the existing sewer, water, and electrical infrastructure of the area. FCG asked its lawyers and architects to address the Commission's concerns. In addition, to begin operating a church on some scale, FCG filed a federal court lawsuit seeking a preliminary injunction ordering the Commission to issue a special-use permit that would allow FCG to operate a church in the property's existing buildings.

What is the Commission's best argument for dismissal of FCG's lawsuit?

(A) FCG does not have standing to seek an injunction ordering a special-use permit.

(B) FCG's request for a preliminary injunction is moot.

(C) FCG's request for a preliminary injunction is not ripe.

(D) The Eleventh Amendment bars this federal court lawsuit against the Commission.

18. Christopher Diaz is an American citizen who, as part of his business, imports books and other reading materials from other countries. This work entails periodic trips abroad to attend book fairs and other trade shows. Since 2000, Mr. Diaz has attended the Cuban International Book Fair each February in Havana. To travel to Cuba, he must obtain a license from the United States Department of the Treasury; the Department has issued Mr. Diaz a license each year since 2000.

In December 2007, Mr. Diaz applied for licenses to attend the Cuban International Book Fair for each of the next five years. The next Fair is to be held on February 12-15, 2008. On January 2, 2008, Mr. Diaz received a letter from the Department requesting further information to process his applications. Mr. Diaz sent this information on January 6, 2008. As of January 31, the Department had not acted on Mr. Diaz' applications, and inquiries with the Department only revealed that his applications were "open and pending."

On February 1, 2008, Mr. Diaz filed a lawsuit in federal district court seeking a writ of mandamus ordering the Department to act on his license application for the 2008 Cuban International Book Fair. The Department moved to dismiss Mr. Diaz' lawsuit. On March 1, while its motion was pending, the Department granted Mr. Diaz a license to travel to the 2009 Cuban International Book Fair.

What is the best ground for dismissing Mr. Diaz' claim regarding the Department's inaction on his license application for the 2008 Book Fair?

(A)  Mr. Diaz lacks standing to challenge the Department's inaction on his 2008 license request.

(B)  Mr. Diaz' challenge to the Department's inaction on his 2008 license request is not ripe.

(C)  Mr. Diaz' challenge to the Department's inaction on his 2008 license request is moot.

(D)  Eleventh Amendment immunity bars Mr. Diaz' federal court lawsuit against the Department.

19.  Assume the same facts as in the preceding Question, except that federal law prohibits filing a travel license application more than one year prior to the requested date of travel. An application filed prematurely is returned without a decision, and the applicant is instructed to file at a later date.

Explain whether the one-year filing window changes the mootness analysis.

ANSWER (two paragraphs):

20.  Assume the same facts as in the preceding two questions (including the legal bar on prematurely-filed travel license applications). Suppose that Mr. Diaz adds claims seeking a writ of mandamus regarding his applications for the 2010-12 Cuban International Book Fairs.

What is the best ground for dismissing these new claims?

(A)  Mr. Diaz lacks standing to bring the new claims.

(B)  Mr. Diaz' new claims are not ripe for adjudication.

(C)  Mr. Diaz' new claims are moot.

(D)  Eleventh Amendment immunity bars Mr. Diaz' from bringing these new claims in federal court.

21.  In the wake of string of terrorist attacks throughout Europe, Congress recently issued the following declaration:

Whereas, terrorism remains a method of attack by which enemies of the United States seek to destroy the American way of life by undermining citizens' confidence in their country's ability to protect them.

Whereas, terrorism is not perpetrated by any single nation-state, but rather through groups associated with and supported by sympathetic nation-states.

The United States declares war against all persons who perpetrate terrorist acts against the United States and its citizens, wherever they may be found, as well as all persons and nations who give aid and comfort to such terrorists.

Five members of the United States Army have filed suit challenging the constitutionality of Congress' declaration. These servicepersons allege that they have received deployment orders to Iran that are specifically pursuant to the above declaration. Their suit argues that Congress' power to declare war requires the national legislature to identify a specific nation against which the declaration applies.

What is the strongest argument against a federal court hearing this lawsuit?

(A) The servicepersons lack standing.

(B) The lawsuit poses a political question.

(C) The lawsuit is not ripe.

(D) The lawsuit is barred by the Eleventh Amendment.

22. Congress recently became concerned that American citizens face significant financial and other obstacles to adopting children. One such obstacle is the cost of taking time away from work to conduct and complete the adoption process. At a congressional hearing, several witnesses testified that lost wages pose a substantial financial hardship, and that some employers have threatened to terminate employees who take "excessive" time to participate in the adoption process. The issue came to a head when a Major League Baseball player was publicly chastised by his team's manager for missing a game for travel related to the adoption process.

To address this problem, Congress recently enacted the Adoption Assistance Act of 2008. The Act requires all employers with 50 or more employees to provide their employees with: (1) one week paid leave to undertake adoption-related activities, and (2) four weeks unpaid leave to undertake adoption-related activities. The Act applies to both public and private employers, and provides a cause of action for money damages to any employee who is denied the adoption-related leave to which they are entitled. The Act also specifically states that State employees may sue their employers in federal court for appropriate relief. Specifically, Congress invoked the Commerce Clause in passing the Act.

Paul Patterson is an employee of the State of Garyland who recently adopted a child. While the State allowed him four weeks of unpaid leave to participate in the adoption process, the State denied him the week of paid leave required by the Act. Paul has filed a lawsuit in the United States District Court for the District of Garyland against the Garyland State Treasurer. The suit is against the Treasurer in her official capacity, and Paul seeks an injunction that would order payment out of the State Treasury of the money he is owed for the week of paid leave. Garyland moves to dismiss based on state sovereign immunity.

The District Court should:

(A)  Grant the motion because, without the State's consent, a private litigant cannot sue a State in federal court.

(B)  Grant the motion because, without the State's consent, a private litigant cannot bring suit in federal court against a State official for an injunction seeking retrospective money damages.

(C)  Deny the motion because a private litigant may sue a State official for an injunction.

(D)  Deny the motion because the Act validly abrogates State immunity when it unequivocally states that a State employee may sue her employer for money damages.

23.  Paul Patterson's federal court lawsuit, which is described in the preceding Question, also alleges that Paul has begun the process of adopting a second child. On that ground, Paul also seeks an injunction ordering the State Treasurer to comply with the Act regarding any future adoption-related leave that Paul might take. Again, Garyland moves to dismiss based on state sovereign immunity.

The District Court should:

(A)  Deny the motion because a private litigant may sue a State official for an injunction ordering the prospective payment of money.

(B)  Deny the motion because the Act validly abrogates State immunity when it unequivocally states that a State employee may sue her employer for money damages.

(C)  Grant the motion because, without the State's consent, a private litigant cannot sue a State in federal court.

(D)  Grant the motion because, without the State's consent, a private litigant cannot bring suit in federal court against a State official for an injunction ordering payment of money.

24. In order to make the United States Postal Service more efficient and better able to handle the new technologies available to send messages, the Congress of the United States passed legislation — the United States Postal Modernization Act (USPMA) — giving the President of the United States the authority to do a number of things to modernize the postal service, including the authority to establish new post offices able to handle the new technologies. Under the USPMA, the President does not have to obtain the permission of Congress to establish these new post offices so long as the President declares that the new post offices are established under the USPMA. The USPMA also permits the President to transfer each fiscal year money appropriated by Congress to either the Commerce Department or the Interior Department for use in implementing the USPMA without prior Congressional approval of this transfer of funds from these other departments. One of the stated purposes for giving the President such authority is to provide for a quick response to technology developments so that the United States government will lose less postal revenue to private competitors. The President signed this legislation, and it became law.

Could the USPMA be held to violate the separation of powers doctrine?

(A) Yes. Under Article I, Section 8, Clause 7, only Congress is authorized to establish post offices.

(B) Yes. Allowing the President to create new post offices is not justified by a national emergency.

(C) No. It is a validly enacted law, passed by both houses of Congress, signed by the President, which has the purpose of making the federal government more efficient.

(D) No. A court could view this legislation as merely sharing or blending power between the legislative and executive branches, which is permitted under the separation of powers doctrine.

25. Referring to the same facts as in Question 24, could the USPMA be seen as *not* violating the separation of powers doctrine because:

(A) It is duly enacted legislation that was passed by both houses of Congress and signed by the President.

(B) It simply allows the President to execute the laws of the United States in a more efficient manner.

(C) The Constitution's textual commitment to Congress of the authority to establish post offices does not preclude the President having power to implement statutes passed by Congress under this power.

19

(D)  The fiscal parts of the USPMA allowing the President to reallocate budget appropriations are similar to the line-item veto statute, which the Supreme Court has held to be constitutional.

26.  Referring to the same facts as in Question 24, the authority given the President under the USPMA to transfer funds from one department to another may violate the separation of powers doctrine because:

(A)  The separation of powers doctrine, as stated in Article I of the Constitution, forbids disrupting the balance of power among the branches by delegating to the President power to alter authorized budget allocations.

(B)  It gives the President too much power over the federal government in these matters, violating the concept of checks and balances.

(C)  Article II of the Constitution does not give this power to the President.

(D)  The President cannot usurp the power given to the Departments of Commerce and Interior.

27.  In reviewing Question 24, how does the Supreme Court's decision in *Morrison v. Olson,* 487 U.S. 654 (1988), affect the likely outcome if the USPMA is attacked as violating the separation of powers doctrine?

ANSWER (three paragraphs):

28. Referring again to the same facts as in Questions 24 through 27 above, on the creation of the USPMA, assume that the Act also contains a provision requiring the United States Postal Service "to establish uniform standards by which the President is able to determine when technological changes require the creation of new postal facilities."

    Does this provision of the USPMA violate the non-delegation doctrine?

    (A) No. It provides an intelligible principle guiding the exercise of the delegated power given under the USPMA.

    (B) No. It is within Congress's power to decide what legislative prerogatives to delegate.

    (C) Yes. The federal courts have clearly held that Congress violates the separation of powers doctrine when it delegates this amount of legislative power.

    (D) Yes. Because the USPMA violates the principles of separation of powers, it also violates the non-delegation doctrine.

29. Last term, the United States Congress passed the Statute of Liberty Act (SLA). This Act is the most recent effort to stop illegal immigration into the United States. In one provision, Congress has given the Department of Homeland Security authority to bypass the rules that govern standard deportation proceedings in order to send out of the country any non-citizen who the Secretary of Homeland Security certifies to be on a terrorist watch list. The Act stays immediate deportation for one week upon the Secretary's certification. During this week the Chairs of the appropriate Congressional Committees are notified of the intention to bypass the rules of deportation for the terrorist-identified individual. Any Chair may then put a hold on the deportation for no longer than one month. If either the House of Representatives or Senate does not act within that month to veto the Secretary of Homeland Security's certification to immediately deport the individual, then the individual shall be deported immediately. However, if either the House or the Senate does use a legislative veto to stop the speedy deportation triggered by the Secretary of Homeland Security's certification, then the individual shall be processed in accord with standard deportation procedures.

A group called Protecting Our Borders brings a suit to declare the legislative veto provision of the SLA unconstitutional. The likely outcome of the lawsuit will be:

(A) The provision will be declared constitutional because it does not so interfere with the core functions of the executive branch as to impede that branch's ability to perform its constitutional duties.

(B) The provision will be declared constitutional because it is part of a duly enacted law—the SLA—passed by both houses of Congress and signed by the President.

(C) The provision will be declared unconstitutional because it is a violation of the non-delegation doctrine.

(D) The provision will be declared unconstitutional because it would permit one house of Congress to legislate in violation of the constitutional requirements of bicameralism and presentment.

30. The SLA, discussed in Question 29 above, also contained a provision to tighten border security. The provision creates a Commission, under the control of the President, to oversee the actions of various federal agencies, such as the Department of Transportation and the Department of Homeland Security that handle matters related to border security. This Commission has the authority to order these agencies to take action and also has the authority to order these agencies to cease activities. The SLA makes it clear that the purpose of this Commission is to guard against political influence in border security matters. The Commission has seven members. Four are selected by the President and

three are selected by the Congress. In its lawsuit, the plaintiff, Protecting Our Borders, also challenges this provision of the SLA as unconstitutional. The likely outcome of this part of the lawsuit will be:

(A)   The provision will be declared unconstitutional because Congress is not permitted under the Constitution to select members of this Commission.

(B)   The provision will be declared unconstitutional because the President is not permitted under the Constitution to select members of this Commission.

(C)   The provision will be declared constitutional because it does not violate the principles of separation of powers as both the executive and legislative branch are sharing power in the selection process.

(D)   The provision will be declared constitutional because it involves a matter of national security, and the courts always defer to legislative and executive branches in such matters.

31. Returning to the Statute of Liberty Act, (SLA), discussed in Question 29, Congress, in passing this Act, considered whether to authorize the erection of an electrified fence on the border between Texas and Mexico. Congress could not reach agreement on this issue and did not authorize this fence in the SLA. But it is debating whether to authorize the building of this fence in its current legislative session. Congress, in fact, has been considering such legislation for three years and has yet to vote the proposal out of committee. The debate in Congress has centered on: 1) humanitarian issues related to having an electrified fence; 2) the effect such a fence would have on United States-Mexico relations; and 3) the cost compared with whether the fence will do much to stop terrorists from entering the country.

Two weeks ago the President issued an executive order authorizing the erection of an electrified fence between Texas and Mexico, and he deployed 20,000 federal troops to the border area to begin the work. The President's executive order states that his action was necessary in order to protect the United States from possible terrorists entering the country at the border between Texas and Mexico.

The action of the President to begin the erection of the electrified fence is:

(A) Constitutional because Article II specifically gives the President authority to take any action he deems necessary to protect the United States from attack.

(B) Unconstitutional because the President has to wait to take action until Congress decides whether to pass the fence legislation it has been debating.

(C) Constitutional, if the President's action is necessary to protect the nation and is not forbidden by other law.

(D) Unconstitutional, if the analysis of Chief Justice Vinson's dissenting opinion in *Youngstown Sheet & Tube Co. v. Sawyer*, 343 U.S. 579 (1952), is followed.

32. Please discuss the differences in approach used by the Supreme Court in *Clinton v. City of New York*, 524 U.S. 417 (1998), and in *Youngstown Sheet & Tube Co. v. Sawyer*, 343 U.S. 579 (1952), in its analysis of Presidential power under the Constitution.

ANSWER:

33. Referring to the facts in Question 30, assume that the SLA has been amended so that four members of the Commission are appointed by the President and three are appointed by the Court of Appeals for the District of Columbia. The Commissioners are to serve for two-year terms, and the statute is silent as to any procedure for their removal.

   The appointment process for the members of this Commission is:

   (A) Constitutional, because the Commissioners are appointed only to two-year terms.

   (B) Constitutional, because the President is authorized to appoint officers of the United States.

   (C) Unconstitutional, because the statute is silent on the procedure for removal.

   (D) Unconstitutional, because it compromises the independence of the judiciary in involving it in the appointment process when some federal court may have to decide legal matters pertaining to the Commission at a later date.

34. Referring to the facts in Questions 31 and 33, assume that the Commission has been appointed and is proceeding under its statutory authority. Five months into the process, the President is dissatisfied with the commission's supervision of immigration matters. He removes from office four commissioners, two appointed by the Court of Appeals and two appointed by the President. In removing these officers, the President states that he has a constitutional duty to protect the nation, and the performance of these Commissioners is making it difficult for him to do this.

    The President's removal of these Commissioners is:

    (A) Unconstitutional, because the Commission is an independent agency, not a part of the Executive Branch, and thus the President cannot remove the Commissioners.

    (B) Constitutional, because this Commission engages in quasi-legislative and quasi-judicial tasks, which make it part of the Executive Branch.

    (C) Unconstitutional, because this Commission is not subject to the President's broad removal power due to its need for independence from political influence.

    (D) Unconstitutional, because the President cannot claim that restricting his authority to remove these Commissioners will impede his ability to perform his constitutional duty, and thus violates separation of powers principles.

35. Discuss how removal power under the Constitution was important to the Supreme Court decision in *Bowsher v. Synar*, 478 U.S. 714 (1986).

    ANSWER:

36. Assume that technology now exists making it possible for all telecommunications — television, telephone, computers, etc. — to be wireless. However, the crucial question is whether the new wireless utility should be regulated by the federal government or open to marketplace dynamics. The President of the United States engaged in a series of private meetings on this subject. Consumer advocates who are concerned about the price to consumers of such wireless service filed a properly prepared Freedom of Information Act request seeking the notes and minutes of the private meetings the President had on this matter.

   This Freedom of Information Act request should:

   (A) Be rejected, because the statements made at these meetings are protected by executive privilege.

   (B) Be rejected, because ordering the President to provide this material could violate separation of powers principles.

   (C) Be granted, because the Freedom of Information Act requires that such material be provided upon the filing of a properly prepared request.

   (D) Be granted, because no person, even the President, is above the law.

37. Referring to the facts in preceding Question, assume that allegations have been made that members of the telecommunications industry have paid money to members of the President's administration in order to receive favorable treatment. These allegations are under grand jury investigation by an independent prosecutor. The minutes of the President's private meetings discussed in the above Question are subpoenaed by the grand jury. The President has sought to quash this grand jury subpoena on grounds of executive privilege, stating that the minutes contain national security secrets.

   In ruling on this motion to quash the subpoena, a court:

   (A) Should quash the subpoena on separation of powers principles.

   (B) Should quash the subpoena because the information requested contains national security secrets.

   (C) Should quash the subpoena unless the prosecutor can show that the material subpoenaed is essential to do justice in the case being investigated.

   (D) Should quash the subpoena because the President has an absolute executive privilege.

38. A consumer group — Citizens for Cheap Access (CCA) — has sued the Federal Communications Commission to stop the implementation of new FCC rules regarding wireless transmissions. CCA is claiming that the new rules will create an oligopoly in the telecommunications industry. The case is in the discovery stage, and the CCA has subpoenaed the Vice President of the United States for any documents, recordings, or other written information pertaining to a meeting he had with leaders of the telecommunications industry three months prior to adoption of the challenged rules.

The Vice President:

(A) May be excused from complying with the subpoena if compliance would affect the separation of powers.

(B) May be excused from complying with the subpoena since he is not a party to the lawsuit.

(C) May not be excused from complying with the subpoena unless he establishes a valid claim of executive privilege.

(D) May not be excused from complying with the subpoena because separation of powers principles only protect from discovery communications with the President, not the Vice President.

39. Discuss whether the reasoning in *Marbury v. Madison*, 5 U.S. (1 Cranch) 137 (1803), supports the Supreme Court's holding in *United States v. Nixon*, 418 U.S. 683 (1974), that it was for the Supreme Court, rather than the President, to decide whether executive privilege protected the material requested by the prosecutor in *United States v. Nixon*.

ANSWER:

40. Assume that we are in the future and a former employee of the Department of Defense has sued the sitting President of the United States for money damages. This employee asserts that he was fired in violation of the federal whistleblower statute, claiming that he was dismissed after bringing to the President's attention kickback schemes that fraudulently increased the cost of military equipment.

In reviewing a motion to dismiss this lawsuit filed by the President, the lower federal court:

(A) Should dismiss the lawsuit against the President because the Secretary of Defense was the proper defendant, not the President.

(B) Should dismiss the lawsuit because the President has absolute immunity from suit for money damages for conduct while in office.

(C) Should not dismiss the lawsuit because the President does not have absolute immunity from a suit for money damages for conduct while in office if the suit alleges intentional violation of the law.

(D) Should not dismiss the lawsuit because Congress has authorized the cause of action in passing the whistle blower statute.

41. Referring to the facts in preceding Question, assume two additional facts: first, that the lawsuit filed against the President was not just for money damages, but also sought an injunction against the President to stop his use of the defense contractors who allegedly paid kickbacks to procure the contracts; and, second, that a parallel criminal investigation of this kickback scheme is being conducted by an independent prosecutor who is planning to seek an indictment against the President for participating in this illegal scheme.

Discuss whether a private litigant is able to enjoin a sitting President and whether a prosecutor can indict a sitting President.

ANSWER:

42. The Supreme Court's decision in *Clinton v. Jones*, 520 U.S. 681 (1997):

(A) Acknowledged that the President has a temporary immunity while President for lawsuits involving his or her actions prior to becoming President.

(B) Acknowledged that the significant burdens on the President's time require that he or she be freed from having to defend lawsuits while serving as President.

(C)   Rejected the possible application of separation of powers principles to reviewing the question of whether a sitting President can be sued for unofficial behavior while President.

(D)   Rejected the use of separation of powers principles to require federal courts to stay all private actions against the President until he or she leaves office.

43. Congress has passed, and the President has signed, a law that permits the sale of sophisticated computer technology to India. The statute give the United States Department of Commerce the authority to decide each year what computer technology may be sold to India and what technology cannot be sold to India. The Department of Commerce is to make this decision based on considerations of national security and protecting the United States economy.

Giving the Department of Commerce authority to suspend such sales:

(A) Is unconstitutional because the Constitution does not give the Department of Commerce power over foreign policy.

(B) Is unconstitutional because it violates the non-delegation doctrine.

(C) Is constitutional because the President is Commander-in-Chief.

(D) Is constitutional because the Executive Branch possesses great inherent power in matters of foreign policy.

44. During a prior presidential administration, the United States ratified the International Treaty on Gender Equality. The then-president negotiated and signed the treaty on the nation's behalf, and two-thirds of the Senate ratified the document. The current President concludes that the treaty is an impediment to his ability to carry out certain foreign policy initiatives. He, therefore, unilaterally rescinds the treaty.

May the President unilaterally rescind a treaty ratified by the Senate?

ANSWER:

45. Assume the President has, over a period of years, negotiated with many other countries on various aspects of global environmental protection. These aspects include regulation of ozone emissions, discharge of sewage into the ocean, etc. The President fears that if these agreements were submitted to the Senate for approval, it would not approve these measures. The President, therefore, signs an executive agreement between the United States and these other countries, committing the United States to take certain actions regarding aspects of global environmental protection, including regulating ozone emissions. Several years before the executive agreement on regulation of ozone emissions was signed, a federal statute went into effect that permitted much greater ozone emissions than does the executive agreement.

(A)   The executive agreement on ozone emissions takes control over the federal statute on ozone emissions because it was signed after the federal law went into effect.

(B)   The executive agreement should be held constitutional because the President has authority to commit the United States in its foreign affairs through executive agreements.

(C)   The executive agreement should be declared unconstitutional under separation of powers principles because such matters must be submitted to the Senate for its approval.

(D)   The executive agreement should be declared unconstitutional under separation of powers principles because there is no indication that the President had to take this action in order to avoid a crisis.

46. In an attempt to stop the growth of North Korea's nuclear capability, the President has placed a naval blockade around North Korea, halting all ships coming into or leaving North Korea and inspecting these ships for nuclear material. Under international law, a blockade is an act of war. The President did not seek Congressional approval of this blockade.

If a lawsuit is filed challenging the President's authority to impose a naval blockade without Congress first declaring war,

(A) The President's action will be declared constitutional because he is the Commander-in-Chief.

(B) The lawsuit will be dismissed as involving a non-justiciable political question.

(C) The lawsuit will be dismissed because the federal courts do not get involved in foreign policy matters.

(D) The President's action will be declared unconstitutional because he failed to get a war declaration from Congress before implementing the blockade.

47. Sadly, the United States suffers another attack by terrorists who seized a nuclear power plant and almost caused a deadly release of radiation. They were stopped and captured before achieving success. One of the terrorists is a United States citizen, and the others are foreign nationals. The President designates all as enemy combatants and orders that they be held at a United States military facility somewhere in the United States. The order denies them a hearing before a tribunal that would determine specific facts in support of continued detention. Each detainee files for a writ of habeas corpus in federal district court seeking release unless the government can show good cause for their continued detention based only on the President ordering their detention without a hearing by a judicial officer as to its legality. The President's order denying a hearing to all captured individuals is:

(A) Constitutional because the President has inherent power to protect and defend the United States, which power includes this order.

(B) Constitutional because the need to stop terrorist activity justifies taking action that is extraordinary under the Constitution.

(C) Unconstitutional, at least for the United States citizen, because separation of powers principles require that the citizen have access to the courts to challenge the detention.

(D) Unconstitutional because the President's power under Article II of the Constitution is limited by the text of the Constitution.

48. Discuss what the decisions in *Hamdi v. Rumsfeld,* 542 U.S. 507 (2004), and *Hamdan v. Rumsfeld,* 165 S. Ct. 2749 (2006), teach us about the President's war powers.

ANSWER:

49. Referring to the facts in Question 46, assume that the President and Congress take contrary positions with regard to the President's authority to impose this naval blockade, and that the President and Congress disagree on the wisdom of such a blockade. After months of intense debate on this subject, the President will not back down from his position. As a result of this impasse, the House Judiciary Committee is considering whether the President should be impeached for his decision to commit the United States to a war without congressional approval or declaration of war.

If a lawsuit is filed to stop the Judiciary Committee from voting out articles of impeachment against the President:

(A) The Supreme Court should declare those articles of impeachment to be unconstitutional as they violate separation of powers principles.

(B) The Supreme Court should declare those articles of impeachment to be unconstitutional as the President's actions do not constitute "high crimes and misdemeanors."

(C) The Supreme Court should declare those articles of impeachment to be within Congress' constitutional power.

(D) None of the above.

50. After reviewing the work of the 9/11 Commission, Congress passed the Safe Skies Act of 2008, which makes it a federal felony to assault or batter an airline pilot or flight attendant during a commercial domestic or international airline flight. The Act also imposes the death penalty for attempted murder of a pilot or flight attendant during a commercial domestic or international airline flight.

Barry Bentley has been arrested and charged under this new law for physically confronting a flight attendant during a flight from Dallas to St. Louis. In his defense, Barry argues that Congress lacked power under the Commerce Clause to pass the Act.

Barry's argument is:

(A) Correct because violent crime is a non-economic activity with only an attenuated link to interstate commerce.

(B) Correct because violent crime is a purely local activity that only the states may regulate.

(C) Incorrect because the costs associated with violent crime would, in the aggregate, have a substantial effect on interstate commerce.

(D) Incorrect because the Act protects the instrumentalities and people that move in interstate commerce.

51. Several years ago, two babies at a rural North Carolina hospital were switched at birth. The switch was discovered after a North Carolina couple learned that the five-year-old child they were raising was not their biological child. The child had gone in for surgery; and, in typing the parents' blood for a transfusion, doctors determined that neither parent was the child's biological parent. After an ensuing investigation, officials concluded that misidentification of the babies had occurred shortly after birth, when both arrived in the nursery at the same time. It was not determined whether the misidentification was inadvertent or intentional.

In the immediate aftermath of the media report, Congress passed and the President signed the Infant Protection and Baby Switching Prevention Act. The Act provides as follows:

Section 1. Whoever knowingly alters or destroys an identification record of a newborn patient with the intention that the newborn patient be misidentified by any person shall be fined not more than $250,000 in the case of an individual and not more than $500,000 in the case of an organization, or imprisoned not more than ten years, or both.

Section 2. As used in this section, the term "identification record" means a record maintained by a hospital to aid in the identification of newborn patients of the hospital, including any of the following:

(a) the footprint, fingerprint, or photograph of the newborn patient;

(b) a written description of the newborn patient; or

(c) an identification bracelet or anklet put on the newborn patient, or the mother of the newborn patient, by a staff member of the hospital.

The Senate Report accompanying the Act contained the following statement:

The birth of a child is one of the most sacred and emotional events in a family's life. The event is also fraught with financial consequences, as it changes parents' spending habits, investment strategies, and even career plans. The financial, emotional, and other commitment that this time symbolizes deserves the highest protection the law can provide.

The Report also states that Congress enacted the Act under its power to regulate interstate commerce.

Does the Commerce Clause empower Congress to pass the Act?

(A)   Yes, because hospitals are instrumentalities of interstate commerce.

(B)   Yes, because the delivery of a baby is an economic activity that has a substantial effect on interstate commerce.

(C)   No, because the Act regulates neither a channel of nor an instrumentality in interstate commerce, and a single baby-switching in a rural area has no substantial effect on interstate commerce.

(D)   No, because the Act regulates neither a channel of nor an instrumentality in interstate commerce, and baby-switching is not an economic activity or part of a larger economic activity.

52.   At a series of recent hearings, Congress heard testimony that the Internet has become a forum for posting and sharing digital images that contain child pornography. To address this problem, Congress enacted the Child Pornography Eradication Act (CPEA), which is a comprehensive federal criminal statute that prohibits the creation, distribution, purchase, or possession of child pornography. CPEA establishes substantial criminal fines and prison sentences for violations of its provisions, and creates a division within the Department of Justice to handle investigation and prosecution of child pornography cases. CPEA's legislative history makes the following statement about the statute's purpose:

With this statute, we take a strong stand against the burgeoning interstate market in child pornography. The Internet and digital media have made the creation, duplication, and transmission of images cheaper, easier, and harder to detect. To meet this threat, CPEA takes a comprehensive approach to the problem that attempts to stamp out this scourge wherever it exists. Any image that depicts child pornography poses a threat to our children and our society. As long as the image exists, it can all too easily enter the stream of commerce, regardless of how, why, or by whom it was created. That is why CPEA takes a zero tolerance approach to child pornography.

A separate portion of CPEA's legislative history noted that Congress enacted the statute under its Commerce Clause power.

Ron Ronald was recently arrested and indicted under CPEA for possession of child pornography. The indictment makes clear that Ronald is charged solely with possession, and that the government has no evidence that Ronald ever purchased, sold, or transmitted child pornography. The indictment further alleges that Ronald took non-pornographic pictures of his neighbor's children, and then used his computer to alter those pictures to make it appear that the children were engaged in pornographic acts.

In a motion to dismiss the indictment, Ronald has argued that Congress does not have power under the Commerce Clause to criminalize the personal creation and possession of child pornography. The court should:

(A) Grant the motion because Ronald's conduct is a non-economic activity with only an attenuated link to interstate commerce.

(B) Grant the motion because Ronald has not used an instrumentality of interstate commerce to obtain or distribute the pornographic images.

(C) Deny the motion because failure to regulate personal creation and possession of child pornographic images would undermine CPEA's comprehensive regulatory scheme.

(D) Deny the motion because the computer that Ronald used to create the child pornographic images was likely purchased in interstate commerce.

53. Congress has enacted the Prisoner Religious Freedom Act of 2008 (PRFA), which reads as follows:

No State shall impose a substantial burden on the religious exercise of a person confined in a correctional institution unless the government demonstrates that imposition of the burden:

(1) is in furtherance of a compelling government interest, and

(2) is the least restrictive means of furthering that compelling government interest.

In considering the bill, Congress made no relevant legislative findings.

Is PRFA constitutional under the Commerce Clause as a regulation of commercial or economic activity?

ANSWER:

54.   Analyze PRFA under the remaining factors that *United States v. Lopez*, 514 U.S. 549 (1995), *United States v. Morrison*, 529 U.S. 598 (2000), and *Gonzales v. Raich*, 545 U.S. 1 (2005), considered in deciding whether a federal law substantially affects interstate commerce.

      ANSWER:

55.   Recall the Adoption Assistance Act of 2008 discussed in Question 22 above. Assume that Congress claimed power to pass the Act under the Commerce Clause. The first section of the Act contains congressional findings, which include Congress' determination that family well being generally, and adoption specifically, are inextricably linked to an employee's productivity.

      The ABC Company challenges the constitutionality of the Act, arguing that Congress does not have power under the Commerce Clause to regulate adoption. The Act is likely:

      (A)   Constitutional because the Act promotes the general welfare.

      (B)   Constitutional because the Act regulates the terms of employment, which is an economic activity that has, in the aggregate, a substantial effect on interstate commerce.

      (C)   Unconstitutional because adoption is a matter of family law, which is a purely local matter that may be regulated only by the states.

      (D)   Unconstitutional because the connection between adoption and interstate commerce is too attenuated.

56.   Congress recently heard testimony that children exposed to second-hand smoke face an increased risk of a wide variety of health problems as an adult. Congress concluded that these increased health problems pose a possible $2 billion cost to the United States economy over the next ten years due to increased health care expenditures and lost work time. Also, Congress found that some of the second-hand smoke related health problems will decrease worker productivity, imposing an additional $500 million burden on the national economy over the same time period. To prevent these economic consequences, Congress enacted the No Smoking Near Our Precious Children Act of 2008, which makes it a federal crime punishable by up to a $1,000 fine to smoke any tobacco product in or near a "child-related facility." The Act is a stand-alone statute unconnected to any other federal regulatory scheme, and it defines "child-related facility" to include (among other things) schools, day care facilities, children's hospitals, and orphanages. Congress relied on its power under the Commerce Clause to pass the Act.

      Sarah Sanders was recently arrested and indicted for violating the Act by smoking a cigarette during the intermission of her child's school play. In her defense, Sarah argues that the Act exceeds Congress' power under the Commerce Clause. Sarah's argument is:

(A) Correct because Congress may not regulate intra-state non-economic activities.

(B) Correct because smoking near children is a non-economic activity with too remote a connection to interstate commerce and that is not part of a larger regulated activity.

(C) Incorrect because Congress has made congressional findings that support the connection between smoking near children and interstate commerce.

(D) Incorrect because while the effect of Sarah's second hand smoke alone will have little effect on interstate commerce, the aggregate effect of every person who smokes near a child would be substantial.

57. Congress has passed a law that conditions a state's receipt of federal highway funds on the state first passing a law that bans all post-viability abortions other than those necessary to protect the life or health of the mother.

May Congress do so?

(A) Yes, because the Due Process Clause of the Fourteenth Amendment does not independently bar state fulfillment of the condition.

(B) Yes, because the condition is rationally related to the purpose for which the federal funds have been allocated.

(C) No, because the condition is not rationally related to the purpose for which the federal funds have been allocated.

(D) Yes, because federal highways are instrumentalities of interstate commerce.

58. Suppose that instead of passing the Infant Protection and Baby Switching Prevention Act (described in Question 51), Congress conditioned receipt of 10% of federal law enforcement funds (including funding for local police forces and building state prisons) on a state's passage of an identical statute.

Does this condition satisfy the four-part Spending Clause test established in *South Dakota v. Dole*, 483 U.S. 203 (1987)?

ANSWER:

59. Consider the conditional spending law discussed in Question 58.

Even if the condition survives scrutiny under the four-part Spending Clause test of *South Dakota v. Dole*, does the condition nonetheless unconstitutionally coerce the states?

ANSWER:

60. Recall the Prisoner Religious Freedom Act of 2008 (PRFA), discussed in Question 53. Assume that instead of enacting PRFA, Congress enacts a statute that gives states the choice to enact a state law identical to PRFA or lose 4% of all federal prison funding.

Is this statute a proper exercise of Congress' power under the Taxing and Spending Clause?

(A) No, because the statute does not promote the general welfare.

(B) No, because the statute's condition is not reasonably related to the purpose of the federal funds.

(C) No, because the statute's condition violates an independent constitutional bar.

(D) Yes.

61. Suppose Congress enacts the same federal statute as in Question 60, except the condition is placed on the state's receipt of 100% of its federal prison funds. What is the best argument against the constitutionality of this statute?

(A) Conditioning receipt of 100% of federal funding is not reasonably related to the purpose of the funds.

(B) Congress is impermissibly coercing the states to legislate.

(C) Because Congress cannot enact PRFA itself, it may not use its Spending Clause power to do so.

(D) Operating prisons is a traditional state function, which Congress may not regulate either directly or indirectly.

62. Invoking its Spending Clause power, Congress has enacted the Federal Funds Anti-Embezzlement Act of 2008, with the purpose of preventing and punishing theft of federal funds. The Act makes it a federal felony for any "agent or employee of a state or local government, organization, or agency" to steal "anything of value" from a "designated state or local government, organization, or agency." A "designated state or local government, organization, or agency" is "any state or local government, organization, or agency that, in any one-year period, receives more than $15,000 under a federal grant, contract, subsidy, loan, guarantee, insurance, or other form of federal assistance." The Act does not require that the state official specifically embezzle federal funds. Rather, the government need only show that the state official embezzled from her employer, and that the employer had received more than $15,000 in federal funds.

Each year, the Public Safety Division of the Texana Department of Public Works (TDPW) receives $100,000 of federal funding for use in preventing forest fires. Amanda Andersen works in the Maintenance Division of the TDPW. The Department of Justice has indicted Ms. Andersen under the Act, alleging that (1) she embezzled from the Maintenance Division of the TDPW, and (2) the TDPW's Public Safety Division receives more than $15,000 a year in federal funds. Ms. Andersen moves to dismiss the indictment, arguing that the Act is not a proper exercise of Congress' Spending Clause power. Is Ms. Andersen correct?

(A) Yes, because the Act is not narrowly tailored to the government's compelling purpose of preventing and punishing theft of federal funds.

(B) Yes, because the Act lacks a jurisdictional nexus that ties the crime to federal funds.

(C) Yes, because the Act's criminal sanctions improperly coerce state and local governments.

(D)   No, because the Act is rationally related to ensuring honest use of federal funds appropriated to state and local governments.

63. Congress recently enacted the Religious Freedom Enforcement Act of 2008 (RFEA). RFEA's only provisions set forth remedies for state violations of the Free Exercise Clause. For example, RFEA authorizes federal courts to impose equitable remedies, such as injunctions, as well as legal remedies, such as actual damages for any harm caused, and punitive damages for any violation committed with common law malice. RFEA does not define what constitutes a Free Exercise Clause violation, leaving that to "existing case law." RFEA's legislative history indicates that Congress passed the statute pursuant to its enforcement power under Section 5 of the Fourteenth Amendment. Does Congress have the power to enact RFEA under Section 5 of the Fourteenth Amendment?

(A) Yes, because RFEA is appropriate remedial legislation.

(B) Yes, because RFEA is appropriate preventative legislation.

(C) No, because RFEA is neither appropriate remedial nor appropriate preventative legislation.

(D) No, because RFEA invades the traditional judicial function of interpreting the Free Exercise Clause.

64. Does Congress have power to enact the Prisoner Religious Freedom Act of 2008 (PRFA) (discussed in Question 53) under Section 5 of the Fourteenth Amendment? (Assume that there are no relevant congressional findings.)

(A) Yes, because PRFA is appropriate remedial legislation.

(B) Yes, because PRFA is appropriate preventative legislation.

(C) No, because PRFA is neither appropriate remedial nor appropriate preventative legislation.

(D) No, because PRFA invades the traditional government function of running prisons.

65. The United States recently concluded the International Treaty on Gender Equality. The President negotiated and signed the Treaty on the nation's behalf, and two-thirds of the Senate ratified the document. One provision of the Treaty requires all signatories to enact legislation that provides a national civil and criminal remedy for gender-motivated violence. In implementing this Treaty obligation, Congress passes, and the President signs, a federal statute modeled (without material alteration) on the Violence Against Women Act, which establishes federal criminal and civil sanctions for gender-motivated violence.

Is this statute constitutional?

(A) No, because the statute is beyond Congress' Commerce Clause power.

(B) No, because the statute is not within Congress' power to enforce the Fourteenth Amendment.

(C) Yes, because the statute is within Congress' treaty power.

(D) Yes, because the statute is within Congress' power to regulate commerce with foreign nations.

66. The United States recently concluded a treaty called the International Agreement on the Protection of the Unborn. The President negotiated and signed the Treaty on the nation's behalf, and two-thirds of the Senate ratified the document. One provision of the Treaty requires all signatories to enact legislation that prohibits all abortions except those absolutely necessary to save the life of the mother. In implementing this Treaty obligation, Congress passes, and the President signs, a federal statute that criminalizes all abortions except those necessary to save the life of the mother.

Is this statute constitutional?

ANSWER:

67. Congress has declared war on a nation it identified as an aider and abettor of terrorist organizations. In less than a month, the United States military has achieved its objectives and the President has declared that hostilities have ceased. During the hostilities, Congress considered a series of laws intended to prepare the United States for domestic acts of retaliatory terrorism. Given the war's short duration, however, none of the laws went into effect until after cessation of the hostilities.

Invoking its War Power, Congress passed the Antibiotic Preservation Act of 2008, which criminalized the possession or consumption of listed antibiotics. Congress' stated concern was that the listed antibiotics were the best known therapy for biological agents likely to be used in a terrorist attack, and that those antibiotics currently were in limited, though sufficient, supply. But if doctors and patients hoarded those antibiotics, the United States would lack an adequate supply in the event of a terrorist attack. Further, given the known side-effects of the listed antibiotics, the government feared that widespread prophylactic use of the antibiotics (out of an unjustified paranoia) would cause great harm with little benefit.

Is the Act a valid exercise of Congress' War Power?

(A) No, because Congress is regulating conduct outside the theater of war.

(B) No, because Congress is regulating activity that occurs after the cessation of hostilities.

(C) Yes, because Congress is regulating an economic activity with a substantial affect on interstate commerce.

(D) Yes, because Congress is addressing a direct and immediate effect of the recent war.

68. Congress continues to be frustrated by the incidence of violence near schools. Noting that such violence is higher in states that do not prohibit the possession of firearms in a school zone, Congress enacted the Gun-Free School Zones Tax Act of 2003. The Act imposes a $1,000 tax on any person who possesses a firearm in a school zone. The tax is imposed each time a person enters a school zone while possessing a firearm. Further, the tax applies only in those states that do not have a criminal law punishing possession of a firearm in a school zone. Congress hopes that the tax will decrease violence near schools.

Can Congress use its Taxing Clause power to pass the Act?

(A) No, because Congress is commandeering the states into regulating.

(B) No, because Congress is using a punitive tax to achieve a regulatory purpose.

(C) Yes, because the Act does not contain provisions extraneous to any tax need.

(D) Yes, because the Act taxes an economic activity with a substantial effect on interstate commerce.

69. Congress has recently enacted the Physician Discipline Transparency Act, which aims to provide patients with better information about their doctors. The Act imposes reporting requirements on all hospitals, both public and private. The reporting obligation is triggered whenever a hospital either (1) receives a complaint against a physician for services provided at the hospital, or (2) initiates its own disciplinary proceeding against a physician. Upon either event, the hospital shall, within 60 days of completing internal action regarding the physician, report the following information to the state's physician licensing body:

   (1) A copy of the complaint filed against the physician or, if none, a written summary of the misconduct leading to the hospital's investigation.

   (2) A written summary of the hospital's actions taken in response to the physician's actual or alleged misconduct.

   (3) A copy of the hospital's written decision, if any, or written summary of the hospital's disposition of the matter.

   The Act directs the United States Department of Health and Human Services to draft regulations prescribing the form for reporting the above information. Failure to make a timely report results in a $1,000 civil fine for the hospital.

   The Act provides that each state's physician licensing authority shall retain all materials gathered from hospitals under the Act. Further, on a quarterly basis, each state authority shall forward a copy of the information to the Department of Health and Human Services for inclusion in a national database.

   Does the Act violate the Tenth Amendment?

   (A) No, because it merely requires the states to comply with a generally applicable law.

   (B) Yes, because it commandeers state hospitals to enforce a federal statute.

   (C) Yes, because it commandeers the state physician licensing authority to enforce a federal statute.

   (D) Yes, because Congress cannot regulate the traditional government function of physician licensing.

70. Congress recently enacted the Infant Protection and Baby Switching Prevention Act. The Act provides:

   Whoever being in interstate commerce knowingly alters or destroys an identification record of a newborn patient with the intention that the newborn patient be misidentified by any person shall be fined not more than $250,000 in the case of an individual and not more than $500,000 in the case of an organization, or imprisoned not more than ten years, or both.

Can Congress constitutionally apply such a statute to a state hospital?

(A)  No, because Congress may not commandeer state legislatures into regulating state hospitals' handling of newborns.

(B)  No, because Congress may not commandeer state executive branch officials into enforcing a federal regulatory scheme.

(C)  No, because the Commerce Clause does not grant Congress power to regulate the states.

(D)  Yes, because Congress is regulating the state on the same terms that it regulates private actors.

71.  Suppose that, instead of enacting the Infant Protection and Baby Switching Prevention Act, Congress passed a statute that gave states the following choice: (1) enact the Act into state law, or (2) assume all tort liability for baby switching that occurs at private hospitals in that state. Does the Constitution limit Congress' power to enact such a law?

ANSWER (two paragraphs):

72.  Suppose, instead, that Congress put the states to the following choice: (1) enact the Act into state law, or (2) forfeit all Medicaid funding (which can be as much as $1 billion annually for a state). Does the Constitution limit Congress' power to enact such a law?

ANSWER:

73.  Suppose, instead, that Congress directs states to enact laws ensuring the proper identification of newborns at hospitals within the state, leaving the precise content of that law to the state legislatures. If a state does not pass such a law within two years, all hospitals within that state will be subject to the federal Infant Protection and Baby Switching Prevention Act. Does the Constitution limit Congress' power to enact such a law?

ANSWER:

74.  Congress has recently enacted the Integrity in Physician Discipline Act, which aims to regularize the process of physician discipline. Congress was concerned with the degree to which disciplinary practices varied among the states, with some states lagging far behind others. Also, Congress was concerned that physicians whose licenses were revoked in one state have too easily moved to another state to continue their practice without obstacle. Congress invoked the Commerce Clause for its power to enact the Act.

The Act has three parts: the physician discipline provision, the reporting provision, and the due diligence provision. The physician discipline provision directs each state to enact physician disciplinary procedures that comply with guidelines set forth in the Act. Within one year of the Act's effective date, the head of the state's physician licensing authority must certify to the United States Department of Health and Human services that the state has enacted the required procedures. Failure to certify is punishable by a $5,000 fine, and filing a false certification is punishable by a $50,000 fine.

The reporting provision requires the state's physician licensing authority to notify the United States Department of Health and Human Services within thirty days of suspending or revoking a physician's license to practice medicine. The Department is then to enter this information into the National Physician Disqualification Database, which is to be available to the physician licensing authorities in each state.

The due diligence provision requires the chief official of each state's physician licensing authority (or her designee) to annually check the name of each physician licensed to practice in her state against the National Physician Disqualification Database. If, through this check, the chief official learns that a physician licensed in her state has been suspended or barred from practicing in another state, the chief official shall immediately suspend that physician's license. Then, the chief official shall begin license revocation proceedings in accordance with procedures set forth in the Act. Failure to abide by the due diligence provision is punishable by a $5,000 fine.

Does the physician discipline provision of the Act violate the Tenth Amendment?

(A) No, because it merely requires the state to comply with a generally applicable law.

(B) No, because Congress can regulate even traditional government functions such as physician licensing.

(C) Yes, because it commandeers states legislatures to make law.

(D) Yes, because it commandeers the state physician licensing authority to enforce federal statute.

75. Does the due diligence provision of the Act violate the Tenth Amendment?

(A) Yes, because it commandeers states legislatures to make law.

(B) Yes, because it commandeers the state physician licensing authority to enforce federal statute.

(C) No, because it merely requires the state to comply with a generally applicable law.

(D) No, because Congress can regulate even traditional government functions such as physician licensing.

76. Suppose that instead of directing the states to enact the physician discipline provisions of the Integrity in Physician Discipline Act, Congress gives states the following choice: (1) enact the physician discipline provisions of the Integrity in Physician Discipline Act,

or (2) forfeit all federal Medicaid funds. The State of Texana has sued to challenge the constitutionality of this law under the Tenth Amendment. Texana receives a little over $1 billion annually in federal Medicaid funds.

Does the Tenth Amendment prohibit Congress from posing this choice to the states?

(A)  Yes, because Congress is commandeering states to make law.

(B)  Yes, because Congress is commandeering states to enforce federal law.

(C)  No, because Congress has placed a permissible condition on the state's receipt of federal funds.

(D)  No, because Congress has validly preempted state law.

77.  Suppose that instead of directing the states to enact the physician discipline provisions of the Integrity in Physician Discipline Act, Congress gives states the following choice: (1) enact the physician discipline provisions of the Integrity in Physician Discipline Act, or (2) the United States Department of Health and Human Services will conduct physician discipline within the state pursuant to rules established by the Department. Does the Tenth Amendment prohibit Congress from posing this choice to the states?

(A)  Yes, because Congress is commandeering states to make law.

(B)  Yes, because Congress is commandeering states to enforce federal law.

(C)  No, because Congress has placed a coercive condition on the state's receipt of federal funds.

(D)  No, because Congress may preempt state law.

78.  Consider once again the due diligence provision of the Integrity in Physician Discipline Act. Suppose that the Act imposes civil liability on a state for each instance of non-compliance with the due diligence provision that causes physical injury to a person. Earlier this year, in conducting the review mandated by the due diligence provision, the chief physician licensing official for the State of Texana failed to detect that Dr. James Jameson, who is licensed to practice in Texana, had been suspended from practicing medicine in another state. Texana did not suspend Dr. Jameson as required by the Act's due diligence provision. Dr. Jameson subsequently committed medical malpractice in caring for Peter Peterson, which caused Mr. Peterson severe physical injury. Mr. Peterson has sued the State of Texana in federal court, seeking compensation under the Act for the physical injuries caused by the state's failure to suspend Dr. Jameson.

Would the Eleventh Amendment bar Mr. Peterson's federal court lawsuit against the State of Texana?

ANSWER (two paragraphs):

79.  Would the Eleventh Amendment bar Mr. Peterson's state court lawsuit to recover for the state's violation of the Act's due diligence provision?

ANSWER:

80. Recall the Adoption Assistance Act of 2008 discussed above in Question 22. The State of Garyland claims that the Act's adoption leave requirement is unconstitutional as applied to state employers. Garyland's argument is:

    (A) Incorrect because Congress has the power to provide for the General Welfare.

    (B) Incorrect because Congress may regulate both private and state actors under the Commerce Clause.

    (C) Correct because Congress may not use its Commerce Clause power to commandeer the states.

    (D) Correct because Congress may not use its Commerce Clause power to interfere with integral operations of traditional state functions.

81. Instead of passing the Adoption Assistance Act of 2008, Congress passes a law that gives states the following choice: (1) enact a state law that provides employees with one week paid and four weeks unpaid adoption leave, or (2) lose 5% of federal funding for state operated foster care and adoption services. This law would be:

    (A) Unconstitutional because the condition commandeers the states into making law.

    (B) Unconstitutional because adoption is a purely local matter that Congress may not regulate.

    (C) Constitutional because Congress may validly regulate the terms of employment under the Commerce Clause.

    (D) Constitutional because the law promotes the General Welfare by imposing an unambiguous condition that is logically related to the purpose of the federal funds.

82. Instead of passing the Adoption Assistance Act of 2008, Congress passes a law that gives states the following choice: (1) enact a state law that provides employees with one week paid and four weeks unpaid adoption leave, or (2) assume liability for all adoption-related expenses incurred by all residents of the state who adopt a child. This law would be:

    (A) Unconstitutional because it commandeers the states into making law.

    (B) Unconstitutional because adoption is a purely local matter that Congress may not regulate.

    (C) Constitutional because Congress may validly regulate the terms of employment under the Commerce Clause.

    (D) Constitutional because the law does not interfere with the integral operations of a traditional state function.

83. The State of Arkabama has passed a law providing that all retail sales of automobiles or light trucks to persons located within Arkabama shall be made from a physical location within the state that has been licensed to do so. Sales in violation of this statute are a crime punishable by jail time and a substantial fine. The law's preamble states:

> The distribution and sale of motor vehicles in this State vitally affects the State's economy and the public interest and welfare of its citizens. This Act is an exercise of the State's police power to ensure a sound system of distributing and selling motor vehicles. Licensing only those firms with a physical location within the State serves to prevent fraud and unfair practices by ensuring that all sales transactions are negotiated and completed face-to-face.

Cars.com, Inc. is a firm that takes Internet orders for automobiles and light trucks. Cars.com acts as a broker, taking orders from customers and matching them with car manufacturers or distributors. The manufacturers or distributors then ship the vehicle directly to the purchaser. Cars.com has no physical retail location in any state, does not sell through any retail outlets, and does not have any operations in Arkabama. Arkabama's law effectively prohibits Cars.com from selling to consumers in that state.

Does Arkabama's law violate the Dormant Commerce Clause?

(A) Yes, because the statute discriminates between in-state and out-of-state commerce without adequate reason.

(B) No, because Arkabama has a valid reason to treat in-state and out-of-state commerce differently.

(C) Yes, because the statute places an unreasonable burden on interstate commerce.

(D) No, because the state's interest outweighs the federal interest in interstate commerce.

84. The State of Texana has the following tolling provision for its statutes of limitations:

> The applicable statute of limitations shall be suspended for any period that a person is outside the State of Texana.

The provision was enacted in 1880 in response to the Supreme Court's decision in *Pennoyer v. Neff*, 95 U.S. 714 (1877). *Pennoyer* held that a state could only assert personal jurisdiction over civil defendants served with process while physically present in the state. The Texana legislature feared that a potential civil defendant might flee the state to avoid service of process, returning only after the statute of limitations had run. In doing so, the prospective defendant could rob injured Texana residents of their rightful, legal compensation. To prevent this abuse, Texana passed the above tolling provision.

Does Texana's tolling provision violate the Dormant Commerce Clause?

(A)  Yes, because the statute discriminates between in-state and out-of-state commerce without justification.

(B)  No, because the statute treats in-state and out-of-state commerce evenhandedly.

(C)  Yes, because the statute substantially burdens interstate commerce without advancing a legitimate state interest.

(D)  No, because the state interest outweighs any burden on interstate commerce.

85.  A Jibbs County ordinance establishes several mandatory provisions that must appear in any contract between the county and a general contractor working on a county project. One provision states that the general contractor will receive a $1,000 bonus for each county resident it employs to work on a county-funded project. The county enacted this ordinance to address the runaway unemployment in its region of the state, which has caused loss of business for local merchants, reduced sales tax revenue, and prompted middle class families to move to other parts of the state.

Does the ordinance's resident hiring bonus violate the Dormant Commerce Clause?

(A)  No, because the Dormant Commerce Clause does not apply to municipal ordinances.

(B)  Yes, because the ordinance discriminates between in-state and out-of-state commerce without justification.

(C)  No, because the county is acting as a market participant.

(D)  Yes, because the county's contract with the general contractor imposes a discriminatory restraint on downstream conduct.

86.  This past summer saw the arrival in the southern United States of a rare termite previously found only in South America. It is believed that the insect was accidentally transported to the United States in a cargo shipment to the State of Texas. One casualty of this epidemic is the mulch business, which saw much of its supply infested with this rare termite. Once the mulch is spread into an area, the termites can rapidly infest plants, trees, and structures in the surrounding areas. Before the termite had been detected, some of the infested mulch was transported to other states for use in landscaping, which spread the termite infestation north. Unfortunately, there is no feasible method for screening mulch for the presence of the rare termites.

As of October 2007, there were no reports of the rare termite in the State of Minnesota. To prevent infestation, the Minnesota legislature passed a statute that banned the importation of mulch from any state where there was the confirmed presence of the rare termite.

A Texas mulch distributor challenges the Minnesota law as unconstitutional under the Dormant Commerce Clause. The Minnesota mulch law is likely:

(A) Unconstitutional because the law discriminates against out-of-state commerce and in favor of in-state commerce.

(B) Unconstitutional because Congress has the exclusive power to regulate interstate commerce.

(C) Constitutional because possession of mulch is a purely local matter committed solely to the states.

(D) Constitutional because the import ban is necessary to achieve the state's legitimate interest in protecting its ecosystem from the rare termites.

87. For this question, consider the Jibbs County ordinance described in Question 85. What is the strongest argument that the ordinance does not violate the Article IV Privileges and Immunities Clause?

   (A) The Privileges and Immunities Clause does not apply to local ordinances.

   (B) The ordinance does not burden a privilege or immunity of state citizens.

   (C) The county is acting as a market participant.

   (D) The county has a legitimate reason to treat non-residents differently, and the ordinance is substantially related to the county's reason for doing so.

88. Bountiful Bay State Park is located on the southern shore of the State of New Island. The Park is widely known for its pristine beaches and diverse marine life, which makes it a popular recreation spot for both residents and non-residents of the state. The most popular activities at the Park include sun-bathing, picnicking, row boating, snorkeling among the diverse marine life, and guided hiking tours of the Park's ecosystem. Admission to the Park is free for all. Snorkeling, row boating, and guided hiking tours are free to state residents, and $20.00 per person for non-residents. The fee is imposed so that non-residents who use the Park contribute to its maintenance. Residents already do so through their tax dollars.

   Does the Park's $20.00 fee for non-residents violate the Article IV Privileges and Immunities Clause?

   (A) Yes, the fee is not rationally related to a legitimate government interest.

   (B) Yes, because it discriminates against a non-resident regarding a privilege and immunity of state citizenship without adequate justification.

   (C) No, because New Island is not burdening a privilege or immunity of state citizens.

   (D) No, because the fee on non-residents is substantially related to a difference between residents and non-residents.

89. Congress has recently passed the Smallpox Vaccine Administration Act of 2003. Under this statute, Congress limits distribution and administration of the smallpox vaccine to health care providers licensed to administer the vaccine. To obtain a license, a health care provider must meet a list of requirements and must make a series of promises regarding handling and administration of the vaccine. One of the required promises is that the provider obtain a patient's "informed consent" prior to the vaccination. The Act defines "informed consent" to require the provider to "communicate to the patient the risks regarding the vaccine as set forth in this Act." A section of the Act specifically lists the risks that the provider must communicate to the patient. The Act, however, does not specify whether the communication must be written, oral, or both, and does not indicate whether the list of risks is exclusive.

The House Report for the Act contains the following statement regarding the informed consent provision.

> In the event of mass vaccinations, localities need to have specifically identified health care providers with a known supply of the vaccine. With such vaccinations, time will be of the essence. We know that health care providers will be concerned about their civil liability for informed consent, and so the Act provides guidance regarding those risks that should be communicated. This list will allow doctors to focus on doing their jobs for patients instead of tending to legal technicalities. Also, to allow doctors adequate flexibility under extreme circumstances, we do not specify whether the risks must be communicated orally, in writing, or both.

The Act's legislative sponsors made similar statements during floor debates.

In response to a suspected smallpox breakout, the City of Los Arkansas ordered vaccination of its 60,000 residents. While no one died of smallpox, James Jeffreys died from a reaction to the vaccine. Mr. Jeffreys' family has filed a wrongful death action against the health care provider that administered the vaccine. Before administering the vaccine, the provider orally communicated the risks set forth in the Act. The provider then asked each patient to sign a statement that said:

> The risks of the smallpox vaccine have been explained to me, and I was given an opportunity to ask questions about what I was told. I understand the information provided and voluntarily consent to administration of the vaccine.

Mr. Jeffreys orally received all the information required by the Act and signed a copy of the above statement. The lawsuit, however, claims that the applicable state tort law regarding informed consent required the health care provider to also provide a written summary of the risks for patients to examine. The family argues that the excitement, confusion, and distractions of mass vaccinations made oral disclosure an unreliable means of communication.

Does the Act's informed consent provision preempt the Jeffreys family's claim for lack of informed consent?

ANSWER (three paragraphs):

90. The State of New Island imposes an annual tax on the income of its residents. As New Island residents, the judges on the United States District Court for the District of New Island are subject to the state's income tax. Does the Constitution allow New Island to impose its income tax on the wages of a federal judge?

ANSWER:

91. Suppose that New Island law imposed a substantially lower income tax rate on the salaries of all elected state officials, including the state's elected judges. Does this change your answer to the preceding Question?

ANSWER:

92. Congress has just passed the Anti-Terrorism Efforts Liability Act of 2008 (ATELA). One section of the Act provides:

> Any manufacturer of an anti-terrorism vaccine approved for human administration by the United States Food and Drug Administration shall be immune from civil liability on account of use of the vaccine.

The Act defines "anti-terrorism vaccine" to include the smallpox vaccine.

As part of recent anti-terrorism preparedness measures, cities and counties in the State of New Arkansas have been requiring "first responders" to be vaccinated against smallpox. "First responders" include all doctors, nurses, and emergency medical personnel who would be the first to respond to a biological attack. One doctor who received the vaccine suffered a severe reaction and ultimately died. His family has filed a civil lawsuit against DrugVac, Inc., the vaccine's manufacturer, under the New Arkansas wrongful death statute. (The FDA had approved DrugVac's smallpox vaccine.) DrugVac is incorporated and has its principal place of business in another state.

What is DrugVac's best constitutional argument for dismissal of the family's wrongful death claim?

(A) The New Arkansas wrongful death statute places a burden on interstate commerce that far outweighs the state's interest.

(B) ATELA preempts the New Arkansas wrongful death statute.

(C) The New Arkansas wrongful death statute violates the Article IV Privileges and Immunities Clause.

(D) The New Arkansas wrongful death statute impermissibly discriminates between in-state and out-of-state commerce.

93. The State of New Arkansas has just passed a law imposing a 5% sales tax on all sales of goods to customers located within the state. The tax applies regardless of where the seller is located. Further, the law requires all vendors, wherever located, to collect the tax and remit it to the state on a periodic basis. BuyBooks.com, Inc. is an Internet bookseller that has no operations or personnel in New Arkansas, but that ships over $1,000,000 worth of merchandise annually to purchasers within the state.

What is BuyBooks.com's best constitutional argument against applying the New Arkansas sales tax to its sales?

(A)   The sales tax violates the Article IV Privileges and Immunities Clause.

(B)   The sales tax is an impermissible discrimination against out-of-state commerce under the Dormant Commerce Clause.

(C)   The sales tax violates the Dormant Commerce Clause because BuyBooks.com has no substantial nexus with the State of New Arkansas.

(D)   The sales tax violates Due Process because BuyBooks.com does not have a sufficient relationship with New Arkansas.

94. Jane Doe was lured to the United States by the promise made by a business that she would be employed at a wage much in excess of what she could earn in her native land. When she arrived in the United States, she was imprisoned by the owner of this business and forced to work 18 hours a day without pay. She eventually escaped.

    She has now sued the employer alleging, among other things, that he violated her rights under the Thirteenth Amendment of the Constitution.

    (A)  This part of her suit should fail because her claim should have been brought under the Fourteenth Amendment based on the infringement of her liberty during her captivity.

    (B)  This part of her suit should succeed because she received no pay for her work.

    (C)  This part of her suit should not succeed because the employer was a private individual, and the Constitution only prohibits government, not private, behavior.

    (D)  This part of her suit should succeed because the Thirteenth Amendment reaches private as well as government behavior.

95. In executing a search warrant, several police officers brutally beat an alleged lawbreaker found at the premises. An internal police investigation found that the officers' behavior violated several police regulations and state law. The police officers were dismissed from the police force. The victim of this police brutality filed a suit against the city's police department alleging that this beating violated the victim's right to liberty under the Fourteenth Amendment.

    In this lawsuit:

    (A)  The victim should not prevail because the action of the police officers was outside their official duties, and therefore, their behavior did not constitute state action.

    (B)  The victim should prevail because the police officers' actions constitute state action even though this beating was against the law, because the officers were acting in their official capacity at the time of the beating.

    (C)  The victim should not prevail because the lawsuit is not against the state but against the city, and the state action doctrine is satisfied only when it is state behavior, not local government behavior, at issue.

    (D)  The victim should not prevail because this beating did not violate his constitutional liberty interests.

96. Explain why private entities such as restaurants, hotels, and private employers are forbidden by law to discriminate on the basis of race when, on its face, the Fourteenth Amendment only prohibits state action.

    ANSWER:

97.   ABC Company purchases a large tract of land and builds houses for its employees. It also builds shopping centers, which contain all essential goods and services needed by the employees who live in this area. The company owns the land, the houses, and the business premises, and rents these out. The tract of land is not incorporated into any city. ABC Company considers all this to be its private property. ABC Company forbids any religious or political literature from being distributed anywhere on its property, even though there is general public access to its shopping centers and other retail establishments. An anti-abortion activist is stopped from distributing literature at a clothing store in this ABC Company-controlled area. The activist brings a lawsuit alleging violation of the Fourteenth Amendment because ABC Company violated his First Amendment rights.

The lawsuit:

(A)   Should be dismissed because there is no state actor involved in stopping the distribution of this literature.

(B)   Should not be dismissed because running a city is a public function, and in so doing ABC Company cannot violate the Constitution.

(C)   Should not be dismissed because the activist has a First Amendment right to distribute such information.

(D)   Should be dismissed because the First Amendment only applies to the federal government.

98.   Assume a change in facts from the preceding Question. This time the ABC Company sells, rather than rents, its homes to employees. Also it does not build retail and commercial sites. Rather, ABC Company decides to provide its own electric service to these homes. This ABC-owned electric company is regulated by the state's public utilities commission, as is every electric company. Eventually, it terminates the service of John Green for non-payment. Green files a lawsuit complaining that his service was terminated without an opportunity for hearing and notice. Therefore, he claims the ABC-owned electric company violated his procedural due process rights under the Fourteenth Amendment. Green's lawsuit:

(A)   Should be dismissed because there is no state actor involved in the termination of Green's electric service.

(B)   Should not be dismissed because running a public utility is a public function, and in so doing ABC Company cannot violate the Constitution.

79

(C)   Should not be dismissed because the Fourteenth Amendment applies to private behavior as well as state action.

(D)   Should be dismissed because the Constitution does not protect those who do not pay their debts.

99.   The Supreme Court has held that a privately-owned shopping center can regulate speech within its space. *Hudgens v. National Labor Relations Board*, 424 U.S. 507 (1976). Reconcile this with the Court's decision in *Marsh v. Alabama,* 326 U.S. 501 (1946).

ANSWER:

100.  A private school, Hopkins Academy, receives 90% of its funding from the State of Oregon through state education grants to the school and financial aid to the students. Hopkins dismissed a teacher for wearing a button in support of protecting wildlife refuges in the state. Hopkins has a policy against any display of political views or affiliation. The teacher sued Hopkins claiming this policy violates his Fourteenth Amendment rights.

The teacher:

(A)   Is likely to prevail as the school will be seen as performing a public function.

(B)   Is likely to prevail as the school will be seen as equivalent to a public school given the fact that it receives 90% of its funds from the state.

(C)   Is unlikely to prevail as the school will not be seen as performing a public function.

(D)   Is unlikely to prevail because teachers are not protected by the Constitution when they advocate political positions in the classroom.

101.  Ruth Adams owns a business that sits on land subject to a private, restrictive covenant signed in 1900. The restrictive covenant forbids the sale of any property to anyone who speaks Spanish. Ruth wants to sell her property to Jean-Paul Girard, a Frenchman who speaks French, English, and Spanish. Other property owners bring an action in state court to enforce the restrictive covenant and are successful.

State court enforcement of the restrictive covenant:

(A)  would simply be enforcement of a private contract and thus lawful.

(B)  would be state action to further private discrimination and thus subject to constitutional limitations.

(C)  would be erroneous because it interfered with the private contract rights of Ruth Adams.

(D)  would not be unconstitutional because it did not enforce a racially restrictive covenant.

102.  The State of New Jersey has a contract with WasteAway, a private waste management company. Under the terms of the contract, WasteAway is to supervise the state's landfill sites to ensure the state's compliance with federal environmental laws. The state recently was fined millions of dollars for its failure to comply with federal environmental laws that regulate landfills, and the state does not want this problem to reoccur. WasteAway is paid handsomely under this contract. The contract was in effect for six months when WasteAway was sued under the Fourteenth Amendment based on its alleged refusal to hire members of a particular religious sect to work under this contract.

If WasteAway asks to have the case dismissed because as a private company, it is not bound to comply with the Fourteenth Amendment, how should the lower court rule on this motion to dismiss?

(A)  The court should grant the motion because a private company is never obligated to comply with the Fourteenth Amendment.

(B)  The court should grant the motion because WasteAway does not have a sufficiently interdependent relationship with the State of New Jersey to make WasteAway's actions those of the state.

(C)  The court should not grant the motion because WasteAway does have a sufficiently interdependent relationship with the State of New Jersey to make WasteAway's actions those of the state.

(D)   The court should grant the motion for the reasons stated in both (A) and (B).

103.   Women want to join a famous golf club that restricts its membership to men. This club is licensed by the state in which it is located to sell liquor and sporting goods. The state receives sales tax from the sale of these items as well as from the sale of food and other drinks. Several women sue the club under the Fourteenth Amendment for gender discrimination. They:

(A)   Will likely succeed, because the relationship between the state and the club is interdependent and symbiotic, thus converting the club's private action into state action.

(B)   Will likely succeed, because the state collects sales tax from the activities that it licenses.

(C)   Will likely not succeed, because private clubs are permitted to discriminate.

(D)   Will likely not succeed, because state regulation or state licensing will not suffice to transform private action into state action.

104.   A privately-operated hospice for terminally ill children receives payments from the State of Pennsylvania under Medicaid. In addition, the hospice is highly regulated by the state. Would these facts be sufficient to convert the hospice's actions into state action?

ANSWER (two paragraphs):

105. For several decades the State of Texas has provided financial assistance to residents who want to attend state universities. Eighty percent of this state assistance has been in the form of grants and twenty percent in the form of loans. During the last legislative session Texas discovered that it would have a budget deficit if it continued to provide this financial assistance. It decided to change the assistance program to offer only loans and to provide only one-quarter as much in state funding as in prior years. Several high school students who are residents of Texas, and have been accepted to a Texas State university, have brought a law suit challenging this reduction in financial assistance the state offered for college education. The facts clearly show that these students will not qualify for a state grant under the new program, but they would have qualified for a grant under the prior program. The facts also clearly show that without state financial assistance these students will be unable to attend the state universities to which they have been accepted.

This lawsuit:

(A) Will likely succeed because these students, as citizens, have a fundamental right to education that can only be regulated if the state has a compelling reason for the regulation and if the means chosen for regulation are necessary.

(B) Will likely succeed because these students, as citizens, have a fundamental right to rely on the continued existence of government entitlement programs once a program has been made available to the public.

(C) Will likely not succeed because citizens do not have a fundamental right to education, and as such, the government may change this financial assistance program without having a compelling reason to do so.

(D) Will likely not succeed because these students do not have standing.

106. Sarah Smith has an illness that will cause her death within the next two years. No cure exists for this illness. However, a new drug is in the experimental stage and could provide a cure. The drug is currently being tested on animals, and if that part of the medical protocol is successful, the next stage will permit testing on human volunteers. The human testing stage will not begin for three years, at the earliest, well past the time for it to help Sarah. Sarah has petitioned all the federal government agencies involved with testing this drug to obtain permission to receive the drug earlier than the medical protocol would allow because it is her only chance of surviving. Sarah is willing to waive all her legal rights and sign an informed consent to obtain this drug. She has been denied permission to take this drug by every government agency because of the safety concerns.

Sarah sues the United States asking the court to order the government to give her permission to take the drug even though it is not yet proven safe for human testing.

This lawsuit:

(A)  Will likely succeed because Sarah has a fundamental right to life that cannot be abridged by the federal government under the Due Process Clause of the Fourteenth Amendment without a compelling reason for limiting this right and without using only necessary means to achieve the government's goal.

(B)  Will likely not succeed because Sarah's fundamental rights are protected from state interference but not from federal interference.

(C)  Will likely succeed because Sarah has a fundamental right to receive medical treatment if she provides informed consent.

(D)  Will likely not succeed because Sarah does not have a fundamental right to receive a drug that has not been tested and certified as ready for human testing.

107. In an effort to stop the so-called "medical malpractice crisis," the State of Illanoy passes legislation that requires all lawsuits filed containing any medical malpractice claims be decided by a board comprised of three doctors and three lawyers rather than by a civil jury. The head of the Illanoy Department of Health and Human Services will appoint the members of the Board for terms of four years. A Board decision on the merits of the lawsuit is to be by majority vote, with tie votes deemed a decision for the defendant(s). Appeals from Board decisions are to be handled as other appeals from administrative decisions under the state's Administrative Procedure Act. This legislation:

(A) Violates the Due Process Clause of the Fourteenth Amendment of the United States Constitution by failing to provide a civil jury trial for plaintiffs who file suits with medical malpractice claims.

(B) Does not violate the Due Process Clause of the Fourteenth Amendment of the United States Constitution by failing to provide a civil jury trial for plaintiffs who file suits with medical malpractice claims.

(C) Violates the Seventh Amendment to the United States Constitution because it denies these plaintiffs a state civil jury trial.

(D) Violates the Due Process Clause of the Fifth Amendment to the United States Constitution.

108. Discuss the major arguments advanced by those Supreme Court justices who have favored total incorporation of the Bill of Rights into the Due Process Clause of the Fourteenth Amendment.

ANSWER:

109.  For purposes of this Question, you should assume the year is 1910. The State of Nebraska, in an effort to bolster the economic position of its wheat farmers, who have fallen on hard times, has passed legislation that creates a pricing structure for the purchase of wheat, setting a minimum price per bushel for wheat produced and sold solely within the borders of the state. Farmer Jones, a Nebraska farmer who wants to sell his Nebraska-grown wheat in Nebraska, brings a lawsuit asking that the legislation be declared unconstitutional under the United States Constitution. Farmer Jones:

(A)  Is likely to prevail because this legislation might well be seen as an infringement on Farmer Jones' liberty of contract and thus in violation of Farmer Jones' liberty and property interests protected by the Due Process Clause of the Fourteenth Amendment.

(B)  Is unlikely to prevail because this legislation is within the legitimate police powers of the state to regulate the economic conditions of the farm industry and rationally relates to its purpose.

(C)  Is likely to prevail because this might well be seen as unfair to the general consumer in Nebraska, as it is likely to cause an increase in the price of various goods, including bread.

(D)  Is likely to prevail because this legislation might well be seen as an infringement on Farmer Jones' liberty of contract and thus in violation of the Privileges and Immunities Clause of the Fourteenth Amendment.

110.  Assume the same facts as in the preceding Question, except change the date. Nebraska passed the legislation in 2007. Farmer Jones now:

(A)  Is likely to prevail because this legislation might well be seen as an infringement on Farmer Jones' liberty of contract and thus in violation of Farmer Jones' liberty and property interests protected by the Due Process Clause of the Fourteenth Amendment.

(B)  Is unlikely to prevail because this legislation is within the legitimate police powers of the state to regulate the economic conditions of the farm industry, and rationally relates to its purpose.

(C)  Is likely to prevail because this might well be seen as unfair to the general consumer in Nebraska, as it is likely to cause an increase in the price of various goods, including bread.

(D)  Is likely to prevail because this legislation might well be seen as an infringement on Farmer Jones' liberty of contract and thus in violation of the Privileges and Immunities Clause of the Fourteenth Amendment.

111.  The State of New York passes legislation that requires automobile inspections be performed only by licensed inspection stations and further requires that only businesses independently owned may obtain such a license. This has the effect of cutting out of the automobile inspection business most gas stations because they are not independently owned businesses. In the legislative history, one lawmaker stated that this law is intended to help small businesses. The data shows, however, that in the State of New York only four companies qualify under this licensing law, all of which are multimillion-dollar businesses. Several gas station operators, who want to perform automobile inspections but cannot obtain a license under the law, file a lawsuit to declare the law unconstitutional as a violation of the Due Process Clause of the Fourteenth Amendment. What is the likely outcome of this lawsuit?

      ANSWER (two paragraphs):

112.  Explain how decisions such as *Twining v. New Jersey,* 211 U.S. 78 (1908), on the incorporation of portions of the Bill of Rights into the Due Process Clause of the Fourteenth Amendment, are important to understanding the Supreme Court's holding in such cases as *Lochner v. New York,* 198 U.S. 45 (1905).

      ANSWER (two paragraphs):

113. In *Griswold v. Connecticut,* 381 U.S. 479 (1965), the Supreme Court:

(A) Rejected Connecticut's ban on the use of contraceptives by married persons because it violated the right of privacy as found in the penumbra of privacy surrounding the various provisions of the Bill of Rights.

(B) Rejected Connecticut's ban on the use of contraceptives by married persons because it violated the Due Process Clause of the Fourteenth Amendment.

(C) Affirmed Connecticut's ban on the use of contraceptives by married persons because its purpose was legitimate (reinforcing the ban on illicit sexual relationships) and its means rationally related to its purpose.

(D) Rejected Connecticut's ban on the use of contraceptives by married persons for the reasons stated in both A and B.

114. A year after the Supreme Court's decision in *Griswold v. Connecticut,* 381 U.S. 479 (1965), the State of Connecticut arrests an unmarried couple for their use of birth control during times of intimate contact. This arrest was made under the same statute at issue in *Griswold.* You are asked to defend Connecticut's action before the appellate court.

Your best argument will be:

(A) The Court's decision in *Griswold* has no effect on the outcome of this case because it involves different parties.

(B) The Court's decision in *Griswold* has no effect on the outcome of this case because *Griswold* involved assisting in the use of contraception devices while this case deals with the actual use of such devices.

(C) The Court's decision in *Griswold* has no effect on the outcome of this case because the State of Connecticut has not yet repealed the statute so it continues to be a valid criminal law.

(D) The Court's decision in *Griswold* has no effect on the outcome of this case because *Griswold* only affects the state's power to interfere with marital privacy.

115. Recently, stem cell research indicates it may provide a cure for Parkinson's disease or at least the ability to slow the rate of physical deterioration from it. All this research is being conducted in other countries. The United States has passed a law that forbids the use of embryos in stem cell research. Without embryonic stem cells, the research is not useful. This ban applies to all states as well as the federal government and to

all private research laboratories. Several individuals with Parkinson's disease have formed a group that wants to create embryos from members' eggs and sperm for the specific purpose of using the stem cells from these embryos for research on Parkinson's disease. These individuals have brought a law suit to declare this federal ban on the use of embryonic stems cells for research violates their fundamental rights under the Constitution.

In pursuing this law suit, their best argument is to rely on *Roe v. Wade*, 410 U.S. 113 (1973), and argue:

(A) An individual has a fundamental right under the Fifth and Fourteenth Amendments to personal autonomy.

(B) An individual has a fundamental right under the Fifth and Fourteenth Amendments to procreate or not procreate.

(C) An individual has a fundamental right under the Fifth and Fourteenth Amendments to pursue research for health reasons.

(D) An individual has a fundamental right under the Fifth and Fourteenth Amendments to be free from government interference in life and death decisions, provided others are not endangered.

116. Considering the holding in *Roe v. Wade*, 410 U.S. 113 (1973), that a woman has a fundamental right to terminate a pregnancy, explain why *Roe* also holds that a state can ban abortions during the third trimester of a pregnancy.

ANSWER (two paragraphs):

117. *Planned Parenthood v. Casey,* 505 U.S. 833 (1992), changed the decision in *Roe v. Wade,* 410 U.S. 113 (1973), by:

(A) Holding that a woman does not have a constitutionally-protected liberty interest in her choice to terminate a pregnancy.

(B) Holding that prior to fetal viability the state may regulate abortions so long as such regulations are not an undue burden on the woman's decision whether to abort.

(C) Holding that after fetal viability a state may ban abortions.

(D) Holding that fetal viability is measured by whether the woman is in the second trimester of her pregnancy.

118. The Court's decision in *Planned Parenthood v. Casey*, 505 U.S. 833 (1992),

(A) did not change the compelling state interest test applied by lower federal courts after the decision in *Roe v. Wade,* 410 U.S. 113 (1973), in reviewing pre-viability state regulation of abortions.

(B) did not cause lower federal courts to apply the undue burden test, because only three justices adopted that test in the *Casey* decision.

(C)  caused lower federal courts to apply the undue burden test in reviewing pre-viability state regulation of abortions.

(D)  caused lower federal courts to apply the rational basis test in reviewing pre-viability state regulation of abortions.

119.  In 2007, the State of Ohio is considering adoption of legislation that would require every woman who is to receive an abortion to submit to a sonogram that shows the fetus. Further, the legislation would require that the woman receive the picture of the fetus produced from the sonogram. And, the legislation would require a 24-hour waiting period between the time the woman received the sonogram picture to the time of the abortion. The legislation provides for an exception to both the sonogram procedure and the waiting period if the life of the woman is at risk, but it does not provide an exception if the health of the woman is at risk.

This legislation, if passed:

(A)  Will likely be declared unconstitutional because it does not provide an exception to the law if the woman's health would be at risk by either the waiting period or the sonogram requirement.

(B)  Will likely be declared constitutional because the state is permitted to impose regulations on abortions that do not permit an exception for the health of the woman.

(C)  Will likely be declared unconstitutional because it imposes a waiting period on the woman prior to the abortion.

(D)  Will likely be declared unconstitutional because it imposes a medical procedure—the sonogram—on the woman that the woman may not have requested.

120.  Assume you are a legislative aid to a state legislator. It has been suggested that population control is one way to preserve the natural resources of the state. For example, a study shows that the available potable water could be in jeopardy in twenty years and that urban expansion is likely to pose a danger to some of the natural wildlife habitats. Legislation has been proposed that would require every citizen who has two natural born children to show evidence that they have been sterilized before they will be issued a driver's license. The legislator for whom you work has asked you to comment on the constitutionality of this proposed legislation. You will tell her:

(A)  The Due Process Clause of the Fourteenth Amendment has, since 1937, been interpreted to prohibit only procedural irregularities and to have no substantive content. Therefore, the proposed legislation would not violate the Due Process Clause of the Fourteenth Amendment.

(B)  Since 1937 the Supreme Court has used the rationality test in reviewing whether legislation violates the Due Process Clause of the Fourteenth Amendment. Because protecting the state's resources is a legitimate purpose and the method proposed by the legislation — population control — rationally relates to that purpose, the Court is likely to uphold the constitutionality of this legislation.

(C)   This legislation would violate the fundamental rights protected by the Due Process Clause because it involves procreation and contraception. As such, the legislation would likely be held to be unconstitutional as it violates the Due Process Clause of the Fourteenth Amendment.

(D)   This legislation violates the Ninth Amendment because it pertains to a right — the right to procreate — that, while not enumerated in the Constitution, is still retained by the people, and thus the legislation likely would be held unconstitutional because it violates the Ninth Amendment.

121.   In *Washington v. Glucksberg,* 521 U.S. 702 (1997), the majority held:

(A)   Even if a competent, terminally ill adult is greatly suffering and in pain, there is no fundamental right to physician-assisted suicide.

(B)   On its face, the Washington statute making it illegal to assist someone in committing suicide is not unconstitutional.

(C)   There is a fundamental right to die with dignity.

(D)   There is no fundamental right to physician-assisted suicide under the facts of this case.

122.   The Court's decision in *Lawrence v. Texas*, 539 U.S. 558 (2003),

(A)   rejected extension of the liberty protected by the Due Process Clause to consensual, private homosexual conduct.

(B)   recognized that a fundamental right to liberty included consensual, private homosexual conduct.

(C)   rejected the argument that the Texas sodomy statute violated the Equal Protection Clause.

(D)   rejected Texas' argument that it had a legitimate interest for its sodomy statute.

123.   Referring again to the creation of embryos in Question 115, assume that legislation now would prohibit the artificial creation of embryos for any purpose including in vitro fertilization. Consequently, married couples who cannot conceive a child through natural means would not be permitted to use in vitro fertilization for the purpose of having a child. In deciding whether individual liberty includes the right to use artificial means for conception, such as in vitro fertilization, the methodology most likely to be used by the Supreme Court to decide whether this is a fundamental right:

(A)   Will look to our nation's history and tradition in deciding the issue.

(B)   Will ignore history and tradition in deciding the issue.

(C)   Will require that the tradition relied upon be described at the most specific level of generality.

(D)   Will use a restrained common law method in deciding this issue.

124. Big Box Realty, Inc. operates the Tatum Mall, a shopping center in the Town of Plainview. Plainview is the northernmost commuter suburb of York City. When the Mall was built twenty years ago, Plainview and its neighboring communities were mostly rural, and the Mall was relatively small. As York City grew, however, newly-arrived residents settled north of the city, in formerly-rural areas. As Plainview's population increased, the Mall expanded on its north and south sides. The expansion, however, greatly reduced available Mall parking. When the Mall tried to purchase land to expand its parking, neighboring landowners refused, as they believed the Mall was partly responsible for eroding Plainview's rural character. Due to the parking shortage, Mall patrons began parking illegally on nearby side streets and vacant lots. The illegal parking, in turn, diverted police resources from ordinary law enforcement and increased local traffic hazards.

The town retained a consulting firm to analyze the traffic problem. After studying the local traffic patterns and other data for three months, the firm reported that the only feasible solution was for the town to condemn three acres of land adjacent to the Mall and pay the owners just compensation. The town then sold the land to Big Box Realty for a price equal to the compensation it paid the landowners. The deed to Big Box Realty contained a covenant requiring Big Box Realty to use the land for parking so long as the Mall is in operation.

Did Plainview's condemnation and transfer of the land violate the Takings Clause?

ANSWER: (two paragraphs)

125. The Town of Dixon is a growing commuter suburb in a major metropolitan area. About twenty years ago, Dixon was a rural area where most land was used for hunting and fishing. Recent development has pushed into areas formerly used for seasonal hunting, drastically reducing the habitat of the local bear population. Over the last year, with the habitat shrinkage reaching a critical point, bears have come into residential areas looking for food and shelter. To stem this threat, the Dixon Town Council has passed an Ordinance banning all further development of land that lies within a designated bear habitat. According to the Ordinance, the only permissible use of such land is seasonal hunting and fishing.

Ronald Roberts owns a three-acre lot covered by the Ordinance. He purchased the lot for $80,000, planning to build a home there. After the Ordinance, he can no longer build his home, and the lot is worth only $10,000.

What is the best argument that the Ordinance has taken Ronald's property without just compensation?

(A)   The Ordinance prohibits all economically viable uses of the land, making the land valueless.

(B)   The Ordinance goes too far in regulating the land because it substantially reduces the value of Ronald's land, destroys his investment-backed expectations for the land, and gives him little reciprocal advantage.

(C)   The Ordinance is an impermissible development exaction.

(D)   The Ordinance impermissibly forces Ronald to endure a physical invasion of his land by hunters.

126.   Instead of a permanent ban on development, suppose that the Town of Dixon enacted an Ordinance that imposes a six-month moratorium on use of land located within the bear habitat. During that time, the Ordinance prohibits all activities on the land (including hunting and fishing), except those activities necessary to exclude trespassers, maintain or repair existing structures, prevent a public or private nuisance, or comply with applicable laws. The moratorium is intended to preserve the status quo while the town studies solutions to the bear problem.

How do these changes to the Ordinance affect your analysis under the *Penn Central* factors?

ANSWER:

127.   Consider the Ordinance described in Question 126. After the six-month moratorium ends, the Town of Dixon decides to end the land-use ban and relocate the bear population to a nearby state park.

Assuming that the six-month moratorium was a taking, would the town owe Ronald Roberts compensation?

(A)   No, because the taking was not permanent.

(B)   No, because the taking still allowed some economically viable use of the land.

(C)   Yes, because taking prohibited all economically viable use of the land.

(D)   Yes, because the government must pay just compensation for temporary takings.

128.   In 1990, a movie western was filmed in the small, rural Town of Gorse, which is located in the State of West Arifornia. To promote the movie, the studio purchased the surface rights to 25 acres of land in Gorse and divided some of that land into 1,000,000 square-foot parcels. The studio duly recorded this subdivision in the appropriate local land records, and executed a deed for each of the 1,000,000 square-foot lots. The deeds were then used as promotional gimmicks, offered on a first-come-first-served basis at theaters

showing the movie. The deeds were valid in all respects and entitled the holder to a fee in the described square foot in Gorse.

When the studio purchased its 25 acres, the land was exempt from local property taxes. Recently, with dwindling local revenues, the town would like to extend its property tax to formerly exempt land, including the 25 acres. Doing so, however, would be an administrative nightmare. The cost of separately assessing and taxing 1,000,000 square-foot parcels would greatly exceed any tax revenue derived from the property. Further, buying back the land is not feasible, as identifying and contracting with 1,000,000 separate owners would far exceed the land's value.

To solve the problem of the fractionated 25 acres, the town proposed legislation with two key provisions. First, any interest in a parcel of land measuring one square foot or less would escheat to the town upon the owner's death. Second, to prevent conveyances that would avoid the escheat rule, the bill prohibited any person owning a parcel of one square foot or less from transferring any interest in that land.

Would the proposed escheat statute take private property?

(A) Yes, because the statute eliminates the rights of transfer and inheritance.

(B) Yes, because the government cannot offer a compelling government interest for the escheat statute.

(C) No, because the escheated land was of little value to its owners.

(D) No, because the escheat statute is rationally related to the legitimate government interest of promoting the productive use of land.

129. Suppose that the State of West Arifornia enacts the proposed escheat statute described in the preceding Question, and that some owners of one-square-foot parcels sue for just compensation. After an evidentiary hearing, the trial court finds that, prior to enactment of the escheat statute, none of the square-foot parcels had any market value. A single one-square-foot parcel was completely useless to its owner, and transaction costs were too high to make sale or consolidation of several square-foot parcels feasible.

Are the holders of the one-square-foot lots entitled to any compensation?

(A) Yes, because the government will obtain land with substantial value.

(B) Yes, because the government has taken essential sticks in the bundle of property rights.

(C) No, because, prior to enactment of the escheat statute, the land was valueless to its owners.

(D) No, because the escheat statute is narrowly tailored to the government's compelling interest in promoting the productive use of land.

130. The small Village of Brainia is home to Groton College. The College recently installed equipment that provided wireless Internet access throughout the campus. Students with

an appropriately-equipped laptop computer can access the Internet and e-mail without a cable or other physical connection. The College wants to extend wireless Internet access to businesses that border the campus. When approached by the College, however, some local businesses resisted installation of the necessary equipment. In response, the Village passed an ordinance requiring all public accommodations located within one mile of the Groton College Campus to allow College officials to enter the premises to install and maintain equipment necessary for wireless Internet access. It is undisputed that such equipment will not interfere with the operation of any businesses affected by the Ordinance. Further, the availability of wireless Internet access would likely increase patronage at many of the businesses.

Does the Village Ordinance take private property?

(A)   No, because the Ordinance may increase the value of the regulated property.

(B)   No, because the Ordinance does not defeat the investment-backed expectations of the regulated property owners.

(C)   Yes, because the Ordinance allows a third party to physically invade the regulated property.

(D)   Yes, because the Ordinance is not rationally related to a legitimate government interest.

131.   Suppose that instead of the Ordinance described in the preceding Question, the Village of Brainia makes installation of wireless Internet equipment a condition of obtaining a permit to build, alter, or improve any structure located within one mile of the Groton College campus. Café Ole, a coffee shop covered by the Ordinance, recently applied for a permit to build a screened enclosure around the seating located in front of its store. Pursuant to the Ordinance, the Village approved the permit on the condition that Café Ole permit installation and maintenance of the wireless Internet access equipment. In its permit decision, the Village noted that the Café's proposed development would reduce sidewalk space in front of the store, hindering the flow of pedestrian traffic.

Does this permit condition take private property?

(A)   Yes, because the condition prohibits all economically viable use of the land.

(B)   Yes, because the condition is not rationally related to a legitimate government purpose.

(C)   Yes, because the condition is not roughly proportional to a legitimate government purpose.

(D)   No, because the condition is roughly proportional to a legitimate government purpose.

132.   In 2006, the City of Timson enacts an environmental Ordinance that restricts the use of certain property within the city. James Johnson is a landowner in the city, and the

Ordinance effectively prohibits any economically viable use of his land, making the land valueless. In 2007, James sells his land to Kirk Kendall for fair market value. In 2008, Kirk sues the city to recover just compensation on the ground that the Ordinance has taken the property he purchased from James.

Can Kirk sue the city for just compensation?

(A) Yes, because the Ordinance has rendered his land valueless.

(B) No, because the Takings Clause will not protect those who buy a lawsuit.

(C) No, because, at the time Kirk purchased the land, the Ordinance was a background principle of law that inhered in his title.

(D) No. By purchasing after the Ordinance took effect, Kirk purchased the property at a price that reflected the Ordinance. Allowing just compensation would provide Kirk with an unjust windfall.

133. WasteCo, Inc. is in the business of solid waste disposal. It recently purchased property in the Town of Condot that it plans to use as a landfill. State and local regulators, however, denied WasteCo's request for a landfill permit, finding that operation of the landfill would pose a grave and imminent threat of flooding to area residents. WasteCo believes that there is no other economically viable use for the land, and thus denial of the landfill permit renders its land valueless.

Is the permit denial a taking?

(A) Yes, because the permit denial effectively prohibits all economically viable use of WasteCo's land.

(B) Yes, because the permit denial substantially reduces the value of WasteCo's land, destroys its investment-backed expectations for the land, and gives it little reciprocal advantage.

(C) No, because the permit denial was roughly proportional to a legitimate government interest.

(D) No, because WasteCo's proposed landfill would have been a public nuisance.

134. In *Home Building & Loan Association v. Blaisdell*, 290 U.S. 398 (1934), the Supreme Court,

    (A) followed the original intent of the drafters of the Contract Clause in reaching its decision.

    (B) followed its pre-1934 reliance on substantive economic due process in reaching its decision.

    (C) accepted the argument that only a substantial impairment of a contractual obligation violated the Contract Clause.

    (D) accepted the argument that a valid exercise of police power was a limitation on the scope of the Contract Clause.

135. Several years ago, the State of Nevahoma issued bonds in order to pay for new road construction. In offering these bonds for sale, Nevahoma stated in its public offering material that tolls collected from the roads built with these bonds would not be used, by statute, for any purpose other than repayment of the bonds or for general improvement of state roads built with the bonds. Nevahoma knew this limitation on the use of tolls was important to bond holders because it protected state revenue designated for repayment of the bonds. Several years later, but before the bonds had been repaid, Nevahoma repealed the statute discussed above, and passed new legislation that allowed use of the tolls for a light rail project. At that time, other methods of financing the light rail were available and feasible that would not impair contracts, but the legislature rejected these other alternatives. This action by Nevahoma:

    (A) likely violates the Contract Clause because it alters the underlying assumptions relied upon by the bond holders.

    (B) likely violates the Contract Clause because the statutory change does not seem necessary or to be the only alternative to funding a light rail project.

    (C) likely does not violate the Contract Clause because the Clause only applies when a contract is between private parties, and does not apply when, as here, the contract is between a state and private party.

    (D) likely does not violate the Contract Clause because the Supreme Court has displayed great deference in allowing states to exercise their police power without running afoul of the Contract Clause.

136. National Express, one of the largest credit card companies, has in its agreements with consumers a provision that allows it to charge interest at 12% above the prime interest

rate. National Express has included this contract provision in every contract with every consumer for the last ten years, and plans to continue to include this provision in future contracts. Assume that sometime later the national economy enters a downturn. To encourage consumer spending, several states pass legislation prohibiting credit card companies from charging interest in excess of 5% above the prime interest rate. National Express files lawsuits seeking to enjoin these state statutes as being in violation of the Contract Clause in Article I, Section 10 of the Constitution.

(A)  National Express may not succeed because the states are sovereign, and cannot be sued.

(B)  National Express may not succeed because this legislation is within the police power of the states and does not violate due process.

(C)  National Express may succeed, but only as to currently-existing contracts.

(D)  National Express may succeed, but only as to future contracts.

137.  On the same facts as in Question 136, a trial court has ruled against National Express, deciding that the legislation is not a substantial impairment of National Express's contractual relationship with consumers. This ruling:

(A)  likely will not be reversed because the legislation is not a substantial impairment of National Express's contract rights.

(B)  likely will not be reversed because the statute is a valid exercise of the state's police powers.

(C)  likely will be reversed because the Contract Clause is violated if there is any impairment of a contract right.

(D)  likely will be reversed because the legislation is a substantial impairment of National Express's contract rights.

138.  After graduating from law school and before taking the state bar examination, Jane Jones begins working at the County Attorney's Office as a paralegal. At the time she was hired, the County Attorney informed Jane that once she passed the bar examination, and became a member of the state bar, she would be promoted to the position of attorney. Nothing was said about what would happen if she failed the bar examination, but other law students hired under the same circumstances in the past who had failed the bar were allowed to stay as a paralegal while they waited to take the bar examination again. Jane failed the bar examination and was promptly fired. She comes to you for legal advice. She claims that she would gladly have remained as a paralegal while waiting to take the bar examination again, but she was not given this opportunity as she was dismissed the day after the bar results were posted without being offered an opportunity to discuss other options with the County Attorney.

If Jane sues the county:

(A)  She likely will not prevail because she failed the bar examination.

(B)  She likely will be unable to establish a property interest in her paralegal position because it was privilege and not a right.

(C)  She likely will be able to establish a property interest in her paralegal position.

(D)  She likely will prevail because she was dismissed without an opportunity for a hearing prior to dismissal.

139.  Assume the same facts as in Question 138, except this time no prior recent graduates had failed the bar examination, so there was no history of recent-graduate paralegals retaining their jobs under similar circumstances. Add to the facts that all county employees are hired under an employment-at-will contract that permits the county to dismiss any employee without cause, provided no other state or local law, such as a whistleblower statute, is violated by the dismissal.

Given this new information, if Jane sues the county:

(A)  She should not prevail because she was an employee-at-will, and no facts indicate that any other law was violated by her dismissal.

(B)  She should not prevail because she was not entitled to any other procedural due process under the terms of her contract.

(C)  She should not prevail because the actual terms of her contract make it clear that she did not have a property interest in her job.

(D)   She should not prevail because a court cannot alter the procedures agreed upon by the parties when they signed the employment contract.

140.   Several people who live close to the James River died as a result of the discharge of toxic chemicals by a private company. The company is bankrupt. The families have brought suit against the State of Virginia, claming that the individuals who died had a property interest in the having Virginia enforce its environmental laws, which would have prevented the discharge and their deaths. Further, these environmental laws required Virginia to closely monitor the James River to stop such discharges.

(A)   This suit will not be dismissed because the Due Process Clause protects life as well as liberty and property.

(B)   This suit will not be dismissed because Virginia violated its duty to protect its citizens.

(C)   This suit will be dismissed because the individuals who died did not have a sufficient property interest in Virginia's decision on how best to monitor environmental compliance.

(D)   This suit will be dismissed as non-justiciable under the political question doctrine.

141. Assume the same basic facts as in Questions 138 and 139, but add information different than what was added in Question 139. Assume again that county employees are typically at-will. However, Jane's employment contract stated that prior to dismissal, she was entitled to a written statement as to why she was dismissed, but that she was not entitled to any type of hearing prior to dismissal. Jane did receive a written statement informing her that she was dismissed because she had failed the bar examination and thus could not immediately assume the position of assistant county attorney.

Given this new information, if Jane sues the county:

(A) She should not prevail because the county followed its established procedure — to which Jane contractually agreed.

(B) She should prevail because the county's reasons for dismissal are unfair, as the county did not give her another opportunity to pass the bar examination.

(C) She should prevail because the county's procedures prior to dismissal do not satisfy the legal requirements of procedural due process.

(D) She should not prevail because under these facts she is not entitled to a hearing prior to dismissal.

142. Several alleged terrorists have been captured and are being held in a military prison in Seattle, Washington. Some are American citizens. They have been incarcerated for ten months and have not been informed of the charges against them, except the United States has informed them that they are being held under the Authorization for Use of Military Force (AUMF). This Act was passed by Congress in 2001 and gave the President broadly defined authority to use force against terrorists. Relying on the authority given to him under the AUMF, the President has classified these prisoners held in Seattle as "enemy combatants." Further, the President has stated that an enemy combatant is not entitled to access to civilian courts or to established criminal procedures in attempting to challenge incarceration under the AUMF. One of the citizens being held has filed a writ of habeas corpus asking for release because he is being held without making available to him traditional criminal procedures such as notice of the charges against him, the right to a speedy trial, the right to see the evidence against him, etc. The court reviewing this challenge:

(A) Will require the prisoner be accorded the same criminal procedures as used in any criminal proceeding against a citizen.

(B) Will not require the prisoner be accorded the same criminal procedures as used in any criminal proceeding against a citizen.

(C)   Will dismiss the case because the President has plenary authority under Article II to detain individuals who the President finds are a threat to the safety of the nation.

(D)   Will order the President to cease detentions under the AUMF.

143.   A prisoner attacks another prisoner. The victim sues the state for depriving him of his liberty under the Fourteenth Amendment by failing to take steps to stop the attack. Prior to the attack, he had informed the prison guards, orally and in writing, that his attacker was threatening him. Prison officials had inadvertently forgotten about the warnings, and the trial court agreed that the prison officials were negligent in failing to take action. What result?

ANSWER:

144. The State of Michigan passes a law that permits the state to take a child from parents for a period of two weeks if the child has witnessed an incident of domestic abuse in the home. During this two-week period, the parents can see the child every day, and the parents and child have to attend weekly counseling sessions. After the two-week period, a court determines whether it is in the best interest of the child to be returned to the parents.

This law is:

(A) Unconstitutional because it infringes on the parents' liberty interest without sufficient procedural due process protections.

(B) Unconstitutional because it infringes on the child's best interests without sufficient procedural due process protections.

(C) Constitutional because parental rights are not liberty, property, or life interests and therefore are not protected against deprivation by the Due Process Clause.

(D) Constitutional because sufficient due process is provided by the court hearing at the end of the two-week period.

145. In an effort to stop the so-called "medical malpractice crisis," the State of Illanoy passes the legislation described in Question 107. This legislation:

(A) Violates the Seventh Amendment to the United States Constitution because it denies Illanoy medical malpractice plaintiffs a civil jury trial.

(B) Does not violate the United States Constitution because none of the Bill of Rights, including the right to a jury in a civil case under the Seventh Amendment, applies to the states.

(C) Violates the Privileges and Immunities Clause of the Fourteenth Amendment of the United States Constitution by failing to provide a civil jury trial for plaintiffs who file suits with medical malpractice claims.

(D) Does not violate the Privileges and Immunities Clause of the Fourteenth Amendment of the United States Constitution by failing to provide a civil jury trial for plaintiffs who file suits with medical malpractice claims.

146. The State of Ventura recently enacted the Newborn Protection Act of 2008, which, among other things, mandates that a newborn infant receive its first feeding from a bottle containing a specified formula. The feeding must be administered under the direct care and observation of hospital staff. This procedure allows hospital staff to determine whether the infant has developed the proper swallowing reflex, as well as whether the baby's digestive tract has fully formed. The Act applies to both private and public hospitals, and it provides that the state will reimburse the costs of the required initial bottle-feeding for indigent mothers who have been a Ventura citizen for their entire pregnancy. The state claims that this limitation is intended to discourage women from moving to Ventura simply to obtain the reimbursement, as well as to preserve money in the state treasury.

Does the reimbursement provision violate the right to travel protected by the Privileges and Immunities Clause of the Fourteenth Amendment?

ANSWER: (two paragraphs)

147. The State of New Roark recently enacted the Responsible Gambling Act of 2008. The Act legalizes gambling on professional sporting events, but retains the state's prohibition of gambling on all other sporting events. The Act also makes it a state crime for any person involved in a professional sporting event to accept money (other than compensation from their employer) in exchange for affecting or influencing the outcome of that sporting event.

What level of scrutiny should the Act receive?

(A) Rational basis review.

(B) Intermediate scrutiny.

(C) Heightened scrutiny, because the law discriminates regarding a fundamental right to carry on one's livelihood or profession.

(D) Strict scrutiny.

148. The New City Council adopted an ordinance establishing a dress code for taxi drivers. The dress code provides:

> All taxi drivers shall wear appropriate attire while in their vehicles. "Appropriate attire" includes, but is not limited to, shoes (excluding sneakers, slippers, sandals, and similar footwear), long pants or skirts (excluding jeans), and shirts or blouses with a collar (shirts and blouses shall be tucked in). No hats shall be worn.

In a statement accompanying the new ordinance, the City Council offered two reasons for the dress code: (1) improve public safety, and (2) promote a clean, safe, and professional image of New City to visitors. As to the second purpose, the City Council explained that some tourists had been "turned off" by the appearance of "those people" who drive New City taxi cabs.

After being cited for a violation of the new ordinance, Mohammed Bahman, a New City taxi driver, filed a lawsuit challenging the dress code. His complaint contends that the dress code violates the Equal Protection Clause by forbidding him from wearing ethnic garb at work.

What level of scrutiny should the ordinance receive?

(A) Rational basis review.

(B) Intermediate scrutiny.

(C) Heightened scrutiny, because the law discriminates regarding a fundamental right to carry on one's livelihood or profession.

    (D)   Strict scrutiny, because Mohammed Bahman is a member of a suspect class.

149.   Under the laws of the State of Arkabama, certain groups of people are automatically excluded from jury service. Specifically, convicted felons, non-residents, people with certain mental impairments, people who are not United States citizens, and people under the age of 18 are not allowed to serve on juries. Otherwise, all adult Arkabamans are eligible to serve on a jury.

Recently, the Arkabama Legislature passed the Jury Integrity Act, which adds the following provision to the state's juror qualification statute:

> No person for whom English is not their first language may serve on a jury in the State of Arkabama.

The legislative history expressly states two purposes for the statute. First, because virtually all trials are conducted in English, it is imperative that *all* jurors understand that language. Based on the information before it, the legislature concluded that, on average, those whose first language was other than English had greater difficulty understanding English and, thus, would be less likely to adequately perform their duties as jurors. Second, in some trials, a witness may testify in a language other than English. In these cases, the court provides an interpreter who translates the witness' testimony for the jury. The judge then instructs the jury to rely *solely* on the interpreter's translation as the official version of the witness' testimony. In these cases, the state fears that a juror who is proficient in the language spoken by the witness might rely on her understanding of the witness' testimony instead of the official translation.

What Equal Protection test applies to the Arkabama Jury Integrity Act?

(A)   The Act must be narrowly tailored to serve a compelling government interest.

(B)   The Act must be substantially related to an important government interest.

(C)   The Act must be supported by an exceedingly persuasive justification.

(D)   The Act must be rationally related to a legitimate government interest.

150.   How did the Supreme Court's application of rational basis review in *City of Cleburne v. Cleburne Living Center*, 473 U.S. 432 (1985), arguably differ from the Court's application of that standard in traditional rational basis review cases, such as *F.C.C. v. Beach Communications, Inc.*, 508 U.S. 307 (1993), and *Railway Express Agency, Inc. v. New York*, 336 U.S. 106 (1949)?

ANSWER: (two paragraphs)

151. Consider the New City ordinance in Question 148. Would the ordinance survive scrutiny under rational basis review?

ANSWER:

152. Consider the Arkabama Jury Integrity Act described in Question 149. Suppose that rational basis review is applied to the Act. What is the strongest argument that the Act is unconstitutional?

(A) The Act discriminates against a discrete and insular minority.

(B) Arkabama does not have a legitimate government interest for the Act.

(C) The Act is not reasonably related to Arkabama's legitimate government interests.

(D) In a trial on the constitutionality of the Act, evidence is offered that contradicts the Arkabama legislature's evidence that the Act is rationally related to the state's purpose.

153. Consider the Responsible Gambling Act of 2008 described in Question 147. The preamble to the Act contains the following legislative finding:

> One historical rationale for banning gambling on sporting events is that such gambling creates an incentive for those in the gambling industry to bribe athletes to "fix" some aspect of an athletic event, thereby corrupting the competitive process. We find that the extravagant salaries earned by modern professional athletes eliminates this temptation, thereby removing the main reason for the historic prohibition on wagering on professional sporting events.

You Betcha, Inc., which is a bookmaking business, claims that the state's discrimination between professional and all other sporting events violates the Equal Protection Clause. Would that Act survive scrutiny under rational basis review?

(A) Yes, because regulation of gambling falls within the state's inherent police power.

(B) Yes, because the Act is rationally related to a legitimate government purpose.

(C) No, because the law is under-inclusive, as it allows gambling even on professional sports where athletes earn relatively modest salaries.

(D) No, because the law is over-inclusive, as it prohibits gambling even on amateur sporting events where athletes will soon earn extravagant salaries, such as certain college basketball and football games.

154. Would the answer to Question 153 change if You Betcha, Inc. offered evidence that (1) many professional athletes earn relatively modest salaries (e.g., players on

independent, minor league baseball teams), and (2) even in major professional leagues, those officiating the games (e.g., umpires and referees) would be vulnerable to influence by gambling interests?

ANSWER:

155. Atlantic State University (ASU) is a public university whose sports teams compete in Division III of the National Collegiate Athletic Association. ASU policy strictly prohibits female students from trying out for or playing on the University's football team.

Does this policy violate the Equal Protection Clause?

(A) No, because men and women have real, biological differences regarding the physical demands of football.

(B) No, because the University has an important interest in protecting the safety of its female students.

(C) No, because the University has an important interest in promoting *esprit de corps* among the members of the football team.

(D) Yes, because the policy is not substantially related to an important government interest.

156. The State of New Island provides health benefits for its employees. As part of those benefits, the state reimburses its male employees for birth control measures but does not do so for its female employees. The state claims an important interest in preventing unwanted pregnancies. The different treatment is meant to do so by equalizing incentives for men and women regarding the use of birth control. The state argues that women have an inherent incentive to avoid unwanted pregnancies (and thus seek birth control) because they bear the physical brunt of childbirth. Because men do not have the same incentive, the state encourages them to do so by providing a financial incentive through health benefits.

Does New Island's birth control reimbursement scheme violate the Equal Protection Clause?

(A) Yes, because the state does not have an important interest.

(B) Yes, because the state's policy is not substantially related to its important interest.

(C) No, because the state's policy is justified by real differences between men and women.

(D) No, because the state's policy serves an important government interest.

157. The City of Los Arkansas, located in the southeastern United States, has established a new hiring policy for the Los Arkansas Police Department (LAPD). The policy sets a goal for the number of African-American entry-level patrol officers based on the percentage of African-Americans residing within the city. Because African-American residents make up 20% of the city's population, the ordinance establishes a target of 20% African-American patrol officers. Until the target is met, the policy requires the LAPD to give hiring preference to "qualified" African-American applicants.

All applicants for the LAPD participate in the same hiring process. Applicants take a written exam followed by a face-to-face interview. The LAPD's Hiring Committee then reviews the test results and interview evaluations and assigns each applicant a score from 1 to 100. Any applicant scoring below a 65 is deemed "unqualified" and thus ineligible for hiring. Before the new hiring policy, applicants were hired in rank order of their score. Under the new hiring policy, however, qualified African-American applicants (even with lower scores) must be hired until the 20% target is met.

The LAPD hopes the policy will remedy past race discrimination in hiring. The LAPD points to two pieces of evidence of past discrimination. First, while a full 20% of the city's residents are African-American, only 4% of the patrol officers are African-American. Second, data shows race discrimination in police hiring in other major cities in the southern United States, such as Atlanta, Houston, and Miami. Third, the LAPD is concerned that the current lack of minority patrol officers could be linked to an educational disadvantage that African-American children suffered due to the racially segregated Los Arkansas public schools up through the late 1970s.

Does the LAPD promotion policy violate the Equal Protection Clause?

(A) No, because racial classifications that benefit minorities receive deferential rational basis review.

(B) Yes, because the policy does not serve a compelling government interest.

(C) Yes, because the policy is not narrowly tailored.

(D) No, because the policy survives strict scrutiny.

158. Suppose that the LAPD implemented the promotion policy described in the preceding Question, but offered a different purpose in its defense: Protecting the safety of its citizens by increasing the LAPD's effectiveness. The LAPD concluded that the best way to achieve this goal was to implement a program of community policing. The idea behind community policing is that the police should be familiar, active members of

a neighborhood, rather than distanced authority figures that randomly impose the law. Police should be seen as respected neighbors, not outsiders or enemies. To implement an effective community policing program, the City Council concluded that the LAPD should reflect the racial and ethnic make-up of the different neighborhoods that it serves. Due to the shortage of African-American officers, predominantly white patrol officers currently serve the city's substantial African-American community. The promotion policy is aimed at changing this imbalance.

Does this purpose change your answer to Question 157?

ANSWER:

159. The University of Orabama is the flagship school in the State of Orabama university system. A group of rejected applicants have sued the University of Orabama School of Law over the use of race in its admissions process. The School's admissions process has three steps. First, the Law School's Admissions Committee (which has nine members) meets at the beginning of the academic year to establish two sets of parameters — the "automatic admit" and "automatic deny" criteria. The automatic admit criterion establishes an LSAT/GPA index above which an applicant is automatically admitted without further review. Conversely, the automatic deny criterion establishes an LSAT/GPA index below which an applicant is denied without further review. The remaining files move to the next step of the process.

In the second step, the remaining files are circulated to three Committee members for substantive evaluation. Each member is to review the entire file, including college transcript, personal statement, LSAT, and recommendations, and evaluate the applicant's likelihood of success in law school. The Committee member assigns each file a score of one to ten — one for the weakest files, and ten for the strongest files. After this round of review, all files with a cumulative score of twenty-seven or higher are admitted.

In the third step, the remaining files are reviewed for several categories of "additional criteria" that might increase an applicant's score. Any increase due to these additional criteria is limited to five points. The first category is for children, grandchildren, spouses, and siblings of alumni, who are given one additional point. Second, the Dean is given discretion to add an additional point for "institutional reasons." The Dean has tradition-ally done so on account of an applicant's relationship to a major donor or prominent member of the local bench or bar. Third, the Chair of the Committee may add a point for each achievement or characteristic that would "increase the diversity of the student body." The Law School's admissions policy states that "diversity includes, but is not limited to, an applicant's state of residence, socio-economic status, life experience, work experience, expertise, unique talents, race, or ethnicity." The admissions policy further states: "Any member of a racial or ethnic minority group shall automatically receive one point during the third stage of admissions review." "Racial or ethnic minority" is defined as a member of one or more "groups that have historically been victims of discrimination, like African-Americans, Hispanics not of European descent, and Native Americans."

After awarding points for all "additional criteria," the Law School offers admission on a rolling basis, starting with the highest scores.

The rejected students challenge the constitutionality of the Law School's practice of awarding one point for race or ethnicity during the third stage of its admission process. The Law School defends this practice as necessary to achieve the educational benefits of a diverse student body. Specifically, the benefits of racial or ethnic diversity cannot be achieved unless an "essential minimum" number of minority students enroll at the Law School. Automatically awarding one point to racial or ethnic minorities helps achieve that essential minimum of minority students.

Does the Law School violate the Equal Protection Clause by automatically awarding racial or ethnic minorities one point during the third stage of its admissions process?

(A) No, because this admissions practice is a benign use of a race classification.

(B) No, because this admissions practice is narrowly tailored to the Law School's compelling purpose.

(C) Yes, because the Law School does not have a compelling government purpose for this admissions practice.

(D) Yes, because this admissions practice is not narrowly tailored to the Law School's compelling purpose.

160. *Parents Involved in Community Schools v. Seattle School Dist. No. 1*, 127 S. Ct. 2738 (2007), held that which of the following is a compelling government interest that will support the use of race in assigning students to local public elementary and high schools?

(A) Achieving the educational benefits that flow from diversity broadly defined, as in *Grutter v. Bollinger*, 539 U.S. 306 (2003).

(B) Remedying the past effects of intentional race discrimination in the local public schools.

(C) Remedying the racial isolation caused by de facto segregation of local public schools.

(D) All of the above.

161. The State of New Island has the following statutes of limitations that apply to suits to establish paternity:

> Eighteen years for a child support action by a child seeking to establish paternity of a man married to the natural mother at the time of birth.

> Ten years for a child support action by a child seeking to establish paternity of a man not married to the natural mother at the time of birth.

> No statute of limitations for a child seeking to establish paternity for purposes of inheritance.

> No statute of limitations for a man seeking to establish paternity to a child.

Further, New Island law tolls the statute of limitations for tort and contract actions while a minor is under the age of eighteen. The relevant legislative history says the following about the shorter, ten-year statute of limitations for establishing paternity in a child support action brought by a child born out of wedlock:

> Paternity actions, especially when the child is born out of wedlock, pose special proof problems that warrant a shorter statute of limitations. While the natural mother is easily determined at the moment of birth, society has no similar, reliable means to instantaneously identify the natural father. Other methods of proof must be adopted, and, as all statutes of limitations recognize, proof deteriorates over time. Thus, the ten-year statute of limitations serves our state's crucial interest in ensuring accurate paternity determinations, and avoiding stale and fraudulent claims.

Does New Island's ten-year statute of limitations violate the Equal Protection Clause?

(A) No, because it is rationally related to a legitimate government interest.

(B) No, because it is substantially related to an important government interest.

(C) Yes, because it is not rationally related to a legitimate government interest.

(D) Yes, because it is not substantially related to an important government interest.

162. The New City council recently passed an ordinance revising the hiring criteria for public transportation workers. The criteria apply to those who operate and maintain public transportation equipment, but not to those on the City's Public Transportation Board, which sets policy for the transit system. One criterion is that transportation employees be United States citizens. The council defended the citizenship requirement as serving the city's interest in having workers of undivided loyalty.

Does the city's citizenship requirement violate the Equal Protection Clause?

(A) No, because the affected employees perform a governmental function.

(B) No, because the citizenship requirement is rationally related to a legitimate government purpose.

(C) Yes, because these employees do not perform a governmental function.

(D) Yes, because the citizenship requirement is not narrowly tailored to a compelling government purpose.

163. Suppose that New City passed an ordinance imposing a United States citizenship requirement on members of the Public Transportation Board. The Board has five members, each popularly elected from a separate district within the city. (The ordinance does not apply to support staff and others who work with the Board.)

Would this ordinance violate the Equal Protection Clause?

(A) No, because these employees perform a governmental function.

(B) No, because the citizenship requirement is rationally related to a legitimate government purpose.

(C) Yes, because these employees do not perform a governmental function.

(D) Yes, because the citizenship requirement is not narrowly tailored to a compelling government purpose.

164. Suppose Congress passed a statute requiring all federal employees who operate and maintain public transportation equipment in the District of Columbia be United States citizens.

Would this statute violate the Equal Protection Clause?

(A) No, because these employees perform a governmental function.

(B)   No, because the citizenship requirement is rationally related to a legitimate government purpose.

(C)   Yes, because these employees do not perform a governmental function.

(D)   Yes, because the citizenship requirement is not narrowly tailored to a compelling government purpose.

165.   The Los Arkansas Independent School District (LAISD) operates the public elementary and secondary schools for the City of Los Arkansas. For the past five years, the LAISD has offered a term of voluntary summer courses. Summer courses consist of subjects not taught in the regular curriculum, such as additional foreign languages (*e.g.*, Polish, Portuguese, and Italian) and science classes (*e.g.*, astronomy). Because LAISD teachers are on a ten-month contract, the District must pay summer teachers extra for that session. Due to budget restrictions, the District can only afford to hire a small fraction of its teachers for the summer term. So, whereas the LAISD ordinarily handles 50,000 students, the summer program can only accommodate 500 students.

All students attending an LAISD school are eligible for the summer program. Registration for the summer term is on a first-come-first-served basis, and usually commences twelve weeks before the summer term begins. Students who are "undocumented aliens" may not register until the last two weeks of registration, and then only if spaces remain open. Each year the summer program has operated, all spaces have filled within the first three weeks of registration, and thus no undocumented student has been enrolled.

What equal protection standard of review would apply to the LAISD's summer program registration process?

ANSWER (two paragraphs):

166. The State of Arkabama recently experienced a string of automobile accidents in which the party at fault was an octogenarian. In each case, a condition related to the aging process caused the driver to lose control of the vehicle. The local press has dubbed these older drivers the "Gray Menace." In response to the perceived safety risk posed by older drivers, Arkabama amended its motor vehicle code to provide:

> 1. Upon the date that a person attains the age of eighty years, his license shall be revoked unless, within the six months prior to that date, he shall have passed the State Driving Competency Test. If the person passes the Test, his license shall be valid for two years.

> 2. A person obtaining a license under section one may renew that license for successive two-year terms by passing the State Driving Competency Test within six months of the expiration of the two-year term. If the person does not do so, his license is revoked.

> 3. A person whose license has been revoked under section 1 or 2 may obtain a new license by passing both the Written Driving Knowledge Test and the State Driving Competency Test. Renewal of any license obtained under this section shall be governed by section 2.

The Written Driving Knowledge Test and State Driving Competency Test are the written and road tests, respectively, administered when a person obtains their first driver's license.

Does this amendment to the Arkabama Motor Vehicle Code violate the Equal Protection Clause?

(A) No, because the amendment is rationally related to Arkabama's legitimate interest in public safety.

(B) Yes. Because many octogenarians can drive safely, the amendment is not narrowly tailored to serve Arkabama's compelling interest in public safety.

(C) Yes. Because many octogenarians can drive safely, the amendment is not substantially related to serve Arkabama's important interest in public safety.

(D) Yes. Because many octogenarians can drive safely, the amendment is not rationally related to Arkabama's legitimate interest in public safety.

167. Mark Mater has been a very active (and vocal) critic of lawyers who represent persons who have been designated as unlawful enemy combatants by the President of the United States. Mr. Mater maintains a web site that contains a page that lists lawyers known to represent such clients. For each attorney, the web page provides a recent picture, work and home addresses, and work and home phone numbers. The list is entitled "Traitors to the Republic."

About a month ago, Mr. Mater gave a speech with inflammatory anti-lawyer rhetoric. A newspaper account had him saying the following:

> Lawyers who represent terrorists are as good as terrorists, which makes them traitors. But they are lawyers, and the legal system will protect them to the ends of the Earth. When faced with a similar threat, our Founding Fathers took up arms. Lest we invite another 9/11, it is the responsibility of true Americans, like yourselves, to do whatever you can, by any means available, to stop this grave threat to our nation's future.

The day after the speech, someone shot and killed Nancy Norbert, who was one of the attorneys listed on Mr. Mater's web site. The local district attorney plans to prosecute Mr. Mater for inciting murder; Mr. Mater objects that any prosecution would violate his First Amendment right to freedom of speech.

Which of the following is the government's strongest response to Mr. Mater's First Amendment challenge?

(A) Mr. Mater's speech is unprotected because it was obscene.

(B) Mr. Mater's speech is unprotected because it was hate speech.

(C) Mr. Mater's speech is unprotected because it was likely to incite imminent lawlessness.

(D) Mr. Mater's speech is unprotected because it had the tendency to incite an immediate breach of the peace.

168. The Rev. Sid Sanders and his Church of the First Prophet are well known for the anti-war protests they have conducted over the last five years. Specifically, Rev. Sanders and his followers hold demonstrations at the funerals of United States servicepersons. During these protests, Rev. Sanders preaches, often within earshot of the mourners, that American soldiers are dying around the world due to divine intervention to punish the arrogance of American aggression. His past demonstrations have included the following:

Banners and placards reading "Praise the Lord for 2,010 Dead Soldiers in Iraq," "We humbly pray to God to please kill many more," and "God Sent the IEDs.".

Rev. Sanders shouted in the direction of the mourners: "I'm glad your son is dead" and "Thank God for Dead Soldiers."

A local community has warned Rev. Sanders that he faces arrest for holding such a demonstration at an upcoming military funeral. Rev. Sanders replied that he is simply exercising his First Amendment right to freedom of speech.

Which of the following is the government's strongest response to Rev. Sanders' First Amendment challenge?

(A)   Rev. Sanders' speech is unprotected because it is obscene.

(B)   Rev. Sanders' speech is unprotected because it is hate speech.

(C)   Rev. Sanders' speech is unprotected because it is likely to incite imminent lawlessness.

(D)   Rev. Sanders' speech is unprotected because it has the tendency to incite an immediate breach of the peace.

169. The Federal Communications Commission recently promulgated a rule that prohibits daytime (from 6 A.M. to 8 P.M.) radio or television broadcast of "patently offensive material dealing with sex that demeans women." The Commission's chair explained the rule's purpose as follows:

> We must protect children from sexist and misogynistic media messages that will warp the minds of our next generation of leaders. Children are far too impressionable, and do not have the social experience or maturity, to put such messages in context. Further, the government has the highest interest in preventing children from viewing indecent material.

Does this prohibition violate the Free Speech Clause of the First Amendment?

(A) No, because the rule covers only low value speech that is unprotected by the First Amendment.

(B) No, because the rule is adequately tailored to protect children and unwilling adult listeners from exposure to patently offensive material.

(C) Yes, because the rule discriminates based on the speaker's viewpoint.

(D) Yes, because the rule is not narrowly tailored to serve a compelling government interest.

170. Suppose the FCC promulgates a rule that prohibits daytime (from 6 A.M. to 8 P.M.) television broadcasts of "patently offensive material dealing with sex." The rule is intended to protect children from exposure to indecent material without their parent's consent. Would this rule violate the First Amendment?

ANSWER (three paragraphs):

171. The State of Michinois recently passed a law that enhances the punishment for any violent crime when commission of the crime was "motivated by the gender of the victim." Does the Michinois law violate the First Amendment's guarantee of free speech?

    (A) No, because the law is narrowly tailored to serve the government's compelling interest in protecting public safety.

    (B) No, because the law targets violent conduct unprotected by the First Amendment.

    (C) Yes, because the rule discriminates based on the speaker's viewpoint.

    (D) Yes, because the rule is not narrowly tailored to serve a compelling government interest.

172. Last year, the State of West Dakota experienced the most expensive campaign for Governor in its history. By the end, the reputation of both candidates had been heavily tarred by their perceived link to campaign contributors. To restore faith in the state's chief executive, the state legislature recently enacted one of the nation's strictest campaign finance laws. The law prohibits any individual or organization from making a contribution directly to a candidate for Governor over the amount of $50. The law also places a $1,000 limit on independent expenditures by individuals. The legislative history explains that these limits are needed to eliminate both actual and apparent corruption of the state's top law enforcement officer. The legislative history relies on public news accounts and newspaper editorials expressing outrage over contributions made during the last Governor's race.

What is the strongest argument that the $50 spending limit is unconstitutional?

(A) The spending limit is not closely drawn to the state's interest in preventing corruption.

(B) The spending limit is not narrowly tailored to the state's interest in preventing corruption.

(C) The spending limit regulates political speech.

(D) The spending limit discriminates based on viewpoint.

173. Is the $1,000 independent expenditure limit constitutional?

ANSWER:

174. The State of West Maine has enacted the Clean Up Politics Act of 2008. Section 1 of that law that provides:

> A political party, whether by national, state, or local committee, may not solicit or receive a contribution, donation, or transfer of funds, or any other thing of value, or spend any funds, that are not subject to the limitations, prohibitions, and reporting requirements of Section 2 of the Act.

Section 2 of the Act places the following restrictions on political party fund-raising and spending: (1) no contribution may be more than $1,000 per election cycle, and (2) for each contribution, the party must collect and maintain records of the contributor's name, address, and contribution amount. In sum, Section 1 prohibits political parties from receiving or spending so-called "soft money" on campaign activities calculated to affect the outcome of an election for state office. The legislative history for that provision says the following:

Having reviewed the recent federal campaign legislation, the Legislature of West Maine believes that it is appropriate for this state to experiment with such legislation. We charge the State Election Commission to study the next elections for state and local office to determine whether this law serves any need in this state's electoral system. The Commission shall file a report with the Legislature not more than 90 days after the next elections for state and local office.

Does the West Maine law banning soft money contributions to political parties violate the First Amendment?

(A) No, because the state has a sufficiently important interest in preventing political parties from influencing their candidates.

(B) No, because the state has a compelling interest in preventing contributors from using a political party to influence a candidate.

(C) Yes, because a political party has a constitutionally protected interest in influencing its candidates.

(D) Yes, because the state has not shown a sufficiently important interest in preventing corruption.

175.  About five years ago, the City of Los Arkansas passed an ordinance requiring a permit for any "group gathering" in the city's main public park (City Park). The ordinance defined "group gathering" as any event:

1.  at which the organizers either have invited or expect attendance by fifty or more people;

2.  advertised to the general public; or

3.  at which sound amplification equipment will be used.

To obtain a permit, the event's organizer must file a permit request no later than thirty days before the scheduled date of the event, at which time a $25 permit processing fee is charged. The city's Planning Manager reviews the permit request and must reach a decision within two weeks of receiving the application. The ordinance provides that "a permit shall be issued if the Planning Manager determines that conducting the proposed event in City Park would serve the public interest." The Planning Manager's decision is issued in a one-sentence statement that does not set forth the Planning Manager's reasons, and the decision is final. In the five years the ordinance has been in effect, the Planning Manager has never elaborated on the reasons for granting or denying a permit.

Another portion of the ordinance authorizes the Planning Manager to impose an additional "public reimbursement fee" as a condition of granting a permit. The purpose of the fee is to recoup the additional law enforcement and sanitation costs incurred by the city due to large public gatherings. In setting the public reimbursement fee, the Planning Manager must follow guidelines set forth in the ordinance:

1.  No fee shall be imposed on an event at which the organizers either have invited or expect attendance by less than 500 people.

2.  At any event to which the organizers have invited the general public, a fee of $2,000 shall be assessed.

3.  For an event organizer who has conducted one or more previous events in City Park, the fee shall be set consistent with the additional law enforcement and sanitation costs incurred by the city regarding those prior events.

4.  For an event organizer who has not conducted a previous event in City Park, the fee shall be set consistent with the additional law enforcement and sanitation costs incurred by the city regarding events of a similar size.

5.  In making the above determinations, the Planning Manager shall calculate the cost of law enforcement personnel based on a ratio of one police officer for every 50 people attending the event.

The amount of the reimbursement fee must be set forth in the decision granting the permit, and the Planning Manager must list the specific aspects of the planned event that led to imposition of the fee. If the event organizer promises to eliminate those aspects of the planned event that caused imposition of the fee, the fee is waived if the event organizer actually eliminates those aspects in holding the event. The Planning Manager's failure to make a timely decision waives the fee.

An event organizer who disagrees with the assessed fee has one week to appeal that decision to the three-person City Planning Board, which must rule on the appeal at least 48 hours prior to the event's start time. In ruling on the appeal, the Board is bound by the same criteria applied by the Planning Manager. Failure to timely rule on an appeal waives the fee. There is no provision of judicial or other review of the Board's decision.

Does the city's permit process violate the First Amendment's guarantee of free speech?

(A)   Yes, because it is a prior restraint of speech.

(B)   Yes, because it delegates the Planning Manager overbroad discretion without adequate procedural safeguards.

(C)   No, because it is a valid time, place, and manner regulation.

(D)   No, because the permit process is narrowly tailored to serve the city's compelling purpose.

176.   Assume that the Planning Manager's decision in the preceding Question denying a permit is immediately reviewable in the state trial court of general civil jurisdiction, and that the state rules of civil procedure are modeled on the Federal Rules of Civil Procedure. How does this change your analysis for the preceding Question?

ANSWER (two paragraphs):

177.   Does the "public reimbursement fee" violate the First Amendment's guarantee of free speech?

(A)   Yes, because it is a prior restraint of speech.

(B)   Yes, because it delegates the Planning Manager overbroad discretion without adequate procedural safeguards.

(C)   No, because it is a content-neutral time, place, and manner regulation that is narrowly tailored to serve a significant governmental interest, and leaves open ample alternatives for communication.

(D)   No, because the permit process does not discriminate based on the viewpoint of the permit applicant.

178.  Each year, the National Golfers Association (NGA) plays one of its most prestigious tournaments at the Adesta Regional Golf Club, located in the State of New Island. In the last year, it was widely reported that Adesta Regional has no women members and does not accept membership applications from women. Women are allowed to play the Club's two golf courses as guests of a member, and may use some of the Club's facilities, such as the pro shop and dining room, when in the presence of a member. Otherwise, women are excluded from the Club.

In response to negative national attention, New Island passed the Recreational Facility Anti-Discrimination Act prohibiting all "private recreational facilities" within the state from membership discrimination based on "race, gender, ethnicity, or religion." "Private recreational facility" is defined as "any facility where members are provided the opportunity to engage in golf, tennis, basketball, volleyball, aerobics, strength training, or other similar athletic activity on the premises." In lobbying against the Act, Adesta Regional argued that the anti-discrimination provision violates the Club's First Amendment right to expressive association.

Is the Club correct?

(A)  No, because the Act is narrowly tailored to serve New Island's compelling interest in eliminating gender discrimination.

(B)  No, because Adesta Regional Golf Club is not an expressive association.

(C)  Yes, because the Act's prohibition of discriminatory motive burdens the Club's members because of their viewpoint.

(D)  Yes, because the Act is not narrowly tailored to serve a compelling state interest.

179. The news media has recently reported a series of high profile deaths involving the use of ephedra by professional and recreational athletes. Ephedra is a stimulant marketed as a weight loss and energy boosting supplement. Some doctors, however, fear that regular ephedra use by those playing sports may lead to heatstroke and other potentially life-threatening conditions due to the combination of ephedra's stimulant effect with the stress of vigorous physical activity. Further, sports officials are concerned that professional athletes are misusing the product, taking much more than the recommended dose in hopes of obtaining a heightened energy and performance effect. Because of its performance-enhancing potential, ephedra is a banned substance in many amateur and professional sports.

Professional baseball players, at both the major and minor league levels, are permitted to use ephedra. The City of Los Arkansas is home to a minor league team, the Los Arkansas Arrows. A member of the Arrows recently died during a workout, and the city's coroner reported that the death was "related to" the player's use of a supplement containing ephedra. Local newspaper stories later reported that ephedra use by high school and college athletes in the city's schools, while strictly prohibited by league rules, was surprisingly widespread. Local law enforcement officials explained that they had no jurisdiction over the matter, as neither state nor local law bans the use of such supplements by either minors or adults.

To discourage ephedra use by local college and high school athletes, the city passed an ordinance that banned all advertising of products containing ephedra at sporting events held within the city. The ban applies to all media at the event, including billboards and other signs at the venue or on vehicles used at the event, print advertising in programs and other materials distributed at such events, and logos on uniforms and other attire worn by participants.

Does the city's advertising ban violate the First Amendment?

(A) Yes, because it is not narrowly tailored to serve a compelling government interest.

(B) Yes, because it does not directly advance a substantial government interest.

(C) Yes, because it is more extensive than is necessary to achieve the government's substantial interest.

(D) No, because it is rationally related to a legitimate government purpose.

180.  The United States Department of Justice is considering a program for prisoners in federal prisons that would allow certain privileges to those who actively engage in some type of religious worship during the week. This program is the result of a five-year study indicating that prisoners who engage in religious practices on a regular basis are less violent while in prison and have a lower rate of recidivism. You are advising the Attorney General of the United States on whether such a program would be constitutional. He has asked you to comment on what the Framers intended when they adopted the Religion Clause of the First Amendment.

You will tell him:

(A)  It is clear from the relevant history that the framers intended a strict separation between church and state.

(B)  It is clear from the relevant history that the framers intended that religion be part of civic life.

(C)  It is clear from the relevant history that the framers acknowledged that government could favor the monotheism of the Judeo-Christian religious tradition.

(D)  It is clear from the relevant history that the framers were Deists who did not favor organized churches.

181.  Assume the Attorney General in Question 180 decides to implement a program that does not give benefits to prisoners who engage in religious practices while confined. Rather, he decides to send orders to wardens of federal prisons that they are not to substantially burden religious worship or practice by prisoners. Several wardens are troubled by this order based on certain religious practices they see in their prisons, including a group who claims its White Supremacist views are religious. The wardens do not want to be seen as accepting in any way this position because they fear prison violence as a result. The Attorney General:

(A)  Should repeal his order because it violates the Establishment Clause.

(B)  Should not repeal his order because it is required by the Free Exercise Clause.

(C)  Should repeal his order if he concludes it will lead to more prison violence.

(D)  Should not repeal his order even if he concludes it will lead to more prison violence because a repeal, after the order was issued, will violate the Free Exercise Clause.

182.    After a spate of drunk driving incidents involving drivers of all ages, the Town of Paulsville passed an ordinance banning the sale and consumption of alcohol. Upon an inquiry from the Paulsville Catholic Church, the Town Attorney clarified that the ordinance has no exceptions, and that the town would expect to seek prosecution of any person who violated the ordinance. The Church had made its inquiry because sacramental consumption of alcoholic wine is an accepted, essential part of the Catholic mass. Thus, the ordinance effectively prohibits the Church from holding services within the town.

Does the Paulsville ordinance violate the Free Exercise Clause?

(A)    No, because the ordinance is narrowly tailored to the town's compelling interest in public safety.

(B)    No, because the ordinance is not targeted at religiously motivated activity.

(C)    Yes, because the ordinance burdens a core religious practice.

(D)    Yes, because the ordinance violates a hybrid constitutional right.

183.    Suppose that the Town of Paulsville enacts an ordinance banning the consumption of alcohol in designated portions of the town. The designated portions are identified as follows:

> All land that meets the following criteria: (1) zoning classification 5 — Special Public Accommodation Use; (2) an improved structure of 10,000 square feet or more with an adjacent residential structure; and (3) served by Public Utility District 8.

After working through the three criteria, one discovers that only one plot of land in the entire town meets the designation. That land is the site of the Paulsville Catholic Church, the only Catholic Church in Paulsville. Consequently, sacramental (as well as all other) consumption of alcohol is prohibited on the Church's property, effectively barring the Church from holding services on its land. The Church had purchased the land from a secular private school and converted the buildings to church purposes; the ordinance was passed about three months after the Paulsville Catholic Church purchased the property.

Does the Paulsville ordinance violate the Free Exercise Clause?

(A)    No, because the ordinance is narrowly tailored to the town's compelling interest in public safety.

(B)    No, because the ordinance is not targeted at religiously motivated activity.

(C)  Yes, because the ordinance burdens a core religious practice.

(D)  Yes, because the ordinance does not serve a compelling government purpose.

184.  You work for a state legislator who is concerned that the state is not doing enough to make religion a part of every day life. You have been asked to review all laws to see whether any law displays an animosity toward religion. You find a law that prohibits the awarding of state money for college scholarships to anyone who is studying to become a minister, rabbi, imam or other type of religious leader in a theological school or seminary. The law does not prohibit the awarding of scholarships to those who are studying religion generally so long as they are not studying to become a religious or spiritual leader. Your boss, the legislator, believes this law is unconstitutional because it targets those training for religious leadership, and thus, it will be easy to have the law removed from the state's statutes based on its unconstitutionality. In response to this:

(A)  You will tell her that the statute is likely constitutional because it does not display the degree of hostility toward religion or a particular religion required for a violation of the Free Exercise Clause.

(B)  You will tell her that the statute is likely constitutional because the Free Exercise Clause prohibits the spending of any government money on sectarian education.

(C)  You will tell her that the statute is likely unconstitutional because it targets those who want to become religious leaders in violation of the Free Exercise Clause.

(D)  You will tell her that the statute is likely unconstitutional because the Free Exercise Clause prohibits any law that has an effect on someone's religious liberty.

185.  Did the Supreme Court's decision in *Employment Division, Dept. of Human Resources v. Smith*, 494 U.S. 872 (1990) overrule its prior decision in *Sherbert v. Verner*, 374 U.S. 398 (1963)? If not, how much of *Sherbert* survives?

ANSWER: (three paragraphs)

186. Consider the Paulsville Town ordinance discussed in Question 182. Suppose that the Town of Paulsville enacts exceptions to its ordinance banning the sale and consumption of alcohol. The town explains that the exceptions, such as for medicinal use under a prescription from a licensed physician, do not pose a threat to the town's purpose of reducing the incidence of drunk driving. Another exception allows purchase and consumption for religious purposes. Because religious use is unlikely to threaten its safety interest, the town sought to accommodate affected religious practices.

Does the exception for religious uses of alcohol violate the Establishment Clause?

ANSWER (three paragraphs):

187. Suppose that the religious purposes exception allowed purchase and consumption solely for use in a Roman Catholic mass. Does this exception violate the Establishment Clause?

ANSWER:

188. The City of Los Arkansas recently adopted a new City Seal in celebration of its centennial. The seal's design was selected in a contest open to all students in public or private elementary schools located in the city. Members of the City Council judged the contest.

Cathy Croft, a sixth grade student at St. Mark's Elementary School, a private, Episcopalian school, submitted the winning design. Cathy's design was a four-leaf clover, with each quadrant containing an item that Cathy saw on her way to school each day. The quadrants contained the following items:

   1.  Left quadrant: the city water tower.

   2.  Top quadrant: City Hall.

   3.  Right quadrant: St. Mark's Elementary School, with a Latin Cross on the front lawn of the school. A "Latin Cross" is a cross whose base stem is longer than the other three arms. It is a symbol clearly identified with Christian denominations. The school's name does not appear on the seal.

   4.  Bottom quadrant: St. Mark's Episcopalian Church, adjacent to St. Mark's Elementary School. The seal does not identify the Church's name or denomination.

The City Seal is displayed on the City Flag (which is flown at all official city buildings and all public schools in the city), the city water tower, all city street signs, and all city-owned vehicles, including police patrol cars. The seal is also found on city letterhead, on the shoulder patches on city police uniforms, on city residents' trash barrels, on automobile registration stickers, and in the City Council meeting hall.

John Jones, a resident of Los Arkansas, has filed suit against the city, claiming that inclusion of the St. Mark's Elementary School and Episcopalian Church on the city's new seal violates the Establishment Clause of the First Amendment. Jones is an atheist and complains about being constantly confronted by the offensive and gratuitous religious images on the City Seal.

What is the strongest argument that the new Los Arkansas City Seal violates the Establishment Clause?

(A)   The city's design is not narrowly tailored to serve a compelling government interest.

(B)   The Seal impermissibly endorses religion.

(C)   The Seal creates an impermissible entanglement between government and religion.

(D)   The Seal incorporates overtly religious imagery.

189.   The new mayor of Brentwood has come to you as City Attorney for your legal advice. She wants to post in the center hallway of City Hall the third verse from the Battle Hymn of the Republic. This verse says:

> In the beauty of the lilies, Christ was born across the sea,
>
> With a glory in his bosom that transfigures you and me,
>
> As he died to make men holy, let us die to make men free,
>
> And God is marching on.

She noticed this third verse of the Hymn in a display at the Smithsonian Museum in Washington, D.C. celebrating the Emancipation Proclamation. At the Smithsonian, the verse was displayed along with the Emancipation Proclamation, the text of the Fourteenth Amendment and Lincoln's Second Inaugural Address. Her purpose in wanting to display this third verse, and no other verse, of the Battle Hymn of the Republic and with no other documents relevant to the Civil War, is to remind all who come to City Hall that human freedom is God's intention for the world. May the third verse of the Battle Hymn of the Republic be displayed in City Hall in the way the Mayor wants?

(A)   No, the reasonable observer would see this as an endorsement of Christianity in violation of the Establishment Clause.

(B)   No, it cannot be displayed alone but must be displayed with other items about the Civil War.

(C)   Yes, the reasonable observer would see this as an endorsement of human freedom and not as a religious statement.

(D)   Yes, government is permitted to invoke the image of God without violating the Establishment Clause.

190.    Jefferson High School is a public school in the City of New Houston. At the end of each school year, the seniors spend the last week of classes participating in a variety of pre-graduation activities. The week culminates with Senior Day, held on Friday, and graduation, held on Saturday. Senior Day is the creation of the High School's principal, Raphael James, and consists of a series of award ceremonies for outstanding achievement in various aspects of High School life. Each year, Mr. James convenes a faculty committee to choose the award recipients as well as set the agenda for the various award ceremonies. Attendance at Senior Day is purely optional. The students' families are invited to attend.

This year, Senior Day began with the presentation of academic awards, including awards for overall academic performance and achievement in specific subjects. Next, the athletic department gathered to present awards for achievement in team and individual sports. The middle of the day consisted of the class picnic, which included a variety of outdoor activities. The day ended with an awards ceremony recognizing service to various student organizations. Each ceremony was opened by a non-denominational prayer recited by Mr. James. The prayers were composed by members of the school's various religious student organizations (*e.g.*, Jewish Students Organization, Students Christian Bible Study Group, Islamic Students Association).

Did Jefferson High School violate the Establishment Clause by opening each award ceremony with a non-denominational prayer?

(A)    No, because the prayer is private religious speech, authored by the students, and not public religious speech.

(B)    No, because the prayer is not offered during a school function at which attendance is mandatory.

(C)    Yes, because the prayer coerces students into religious practice.

(D)    Yes, because the prayer is not narrowly tailored to a compelling government interest.

191.    Referring to Question 189, may a school teacher who teaches choir to high school students require them to sing all verses of the Battle Hymn of the Republic, including the third verse?

ANSWER: (two paragraphs)

192.    The various religious student organizations mentioned in Question 190 receive support from a Student Activity Fund maintained by Jefferson High School. The fund is taken from the general tax revenue appropriated to the High School, and the money is allocated equally among all eligible student organizations. Specifically, the High School allocates the money to reimburse organizations for reproduction of signs and fliers announcing meetings as well as limited refreshments served at the meetings. To pay a covered expense, a student organization files a disbursement request with the principal's office, and the High School pays the vendor directly. No money is disbursed directly to either the student organization or its members.

Does distribution of public funds to religious student organizations violate the Establishment Clause?

ANSWER (three paragraphs):

# PRACTICE FINAL EXAM: QUESTIONS

# PRACTICE FINAL EXAM

Instructions: This exam consists of two parts. The first part contains 20 multiple choice questions. You should allow no more than 60 minutes to complete these questions. The second part consists of four short answer questions. Try to answer these questions in no more than 60 minutes. For the short answer questions, we have allocated ten minutes per paragraph required to answer the question. So, a one-paragraph question is allocated ten minutes, and a two-paragraph question is allocated twenty minutes.

## PART 1:                                    PRACTICE FINAL EXAM
## MULTIPLE CHOICE QUESTIONS

193. The Commonwealth of Illanoy recently enacted a law prohibiting the importation and disposal of hazardous waste from outside the state. Disposal, Inc. is in the business of transporting hazardous waste across state lines, including carriage of waste into and out of the state. Illanoy's State Attorney General has sent Disposal a letter directing it to cease and desist importation of hazardous waste into Illanoy. Believing that Illanoy's import ban violates the Dormant Commerce Clause, Disposal filed suit against the Illanoy Attorney General in federal court. Illanoy's suit seeks an injunction against enforcement of the state's hazardous waste import ban.

The Illanoy Attorney General moves to dismiss Disposal's suit for lack of justiciability. Should the court grant the Attorney General's motion?

(A) Yes, because Disposal does not have standing.

(B) Yes, because Disposal's claim is not ripe.

(C) Yes, because the Eleventh Amendment bars this suit against a state official.

(D) No, because there is no constitutional bar to Disposal's suit in federal court.

194. The State of Texana recently enacted the Parental Abortion Liability Act, which provides:

Any person who performs an abortion on a minor without obtaining the prior written consent of both of the minor's parents will be strictly liable to the minor's parents for all medical expenses attributable to the abortion, including expenses incurred for follow-up care.

151

The Pregnancy Assistance Center, an abortion clinic located in Texana, sued the Governor and Attorney General seeking an injunction on the ground that the Act violates a minor's right to choose an abortion.

Does the Pregnancy Assistance Center have standing to bring this suit?

(A)   No, because the Pregnancy Assistance Center may not litigate the rights of the minors, who are not parties to the lawsuit.

(B)   No, because the Pregnancy Assistance Center has no concrete injury.

(C)   No, because the Pregnancy Assistance Center's injury is not actual or imminent.

(D)   No, because the lawsuit cannot redress any threatened injury to the Pregnancy Assistance Center.

195.   At a gathering of supporters, Sarah Simpson, a candidate for a seat on the Texana Supreme Court, gives a speech during which she says, "I am a proud Republican." Her statement violates the Texana Code of Judicial Ethics, which prohibits any candidate for judicial office from making a public statement identifying that candidate's political party affiliation. Texana's ban on identifying party affiliation, as well as its other ethical restrictions on judicial campaign speech, apply only once a person is an official candidate for judicial office. The commentary to the Code explains the provision's purpose:

> The judicial power rests solely on the confidence of the people that judges will discharge their duties with the utmost impartiality. Campaign statements that suggest bias or prejudice in later judicial service slowly erode that confidence. To protect the state's judiciary as a bulwark of liberty and justice, we must bar such candidate speech.

When the Texana State Bar brings disciplinary charges against her, Ms. Simpson asserts that the Code's prohibition on identifying a candidate's party affiliation violates her First Amendment right to free speech.

What is Ms. Simpson's best argument that the Code provision is unconstitutional?

(A)   The party-affiliation provision discriminates based on viewpoint.

(B)   The party-affiliation provision burdens political speech.

(C)   Texana has no compelling interest for the party-affiliation provision.

(D)   The party-affiliation provision is not narrowly tailored to serve Texana's compelling purpose.

196.   The State of New Island recently enacted the Homeless Shelter Bolstering Program, which appropriates $10 million for the provision of food service to organizations that operate homeless shelters. The appropriation funds Food for the Poor, a public agency that travels to homeless shelters and provides meals and meal service to the patrons.

With the recent economic downturn, New Island found that the homeless population has begun to rise. Further, private charitable giving has decreased, squeezing the budgets of many organizations that operate homeless shelters. Growing demand and dwindling resources have stretched existing shelters to their limits, leaving the possibility that many homeless will soon have no safe place to seek food and shelter. To avoid the serious health and safety consequences this situation would entail, New Island created the Program to carry homeless shelters through these difficult times.

Under the Program, Food for the Poor is to provide food and service to organizations that operate homeless shelters in cities with a population exceeding 500,000 people. The amount of food and service provided is determined solely by the number of persons assisted by the shelter in an average month. The Program does not restrict the type of organization that may receive such grants, so both public and private organizations are eligible. Further, churches and other religious organizations that operate qualifying homeless shelters are eligible for the grants. Available statistics show that approximately 60% of the eligible organizations are religiously-affiliated.

Would distribution of grant money to a church or religious organization violate the Establishment Clause?

(A) Yes, because New Island is awarding public assistance to a church or religious organization.

(B) Yes, because state assistance awarded to a church's homeless shelter allows the church to reallocate funds from its shelter to overtly religious functions.

(C) No, because New Island provides assistance to religious organizations on the same terms as secular organizations and solely through independent private choice.

(D) No, because the Program is narrowly tailored to a compelling government interest.

197. Congress has passed the following statute:

A person who knowingly discharges a firearm at a person from a motor vehicle while traveling along a public roadway shall be punished by imprisonment for not more than 25 years, and if death results, shall be punished by death or by imprisonment for life.

Does Congress have power under the Commerce Clause to enact this statute?

(A) No, because the regulated activity is neither economic nor commercial.

(B) No, because Congress may not aggregate the economic effects of violent crime.

(C) Yes, because Congress is regulating a channel of interstate commerce.

(D) Yes, because drive-by shootings substantially affect interstate commerce by discouraging interstate travel.

198. Congress recently passed the Keep Smokes from Our Kids Act of 2008, which is a comprehensive federal law that regulates the marketing, distribution, and sale of tobacco

products to minors. The law bans all tobacco advertising that targets minors, bans all sales of tobacco products to persons under the age of 18, and makes it a crime for an adult to purchase tobacco products for someone under the age of 18. The law also requires retail stores that sell tobacco products to follow stringent age verification procedures when selling tobacco products to persons who appear to be underage. One subsection of the law makes it a federal crime punishable by up to a $1,000 fine to possess any tobacco product in or near a "child-related facility." The Act defines "child-related facility" to include (among other things) schools, day care facilities, children's hospitals, and orphanages. Congress made findings that (1) children and teenagers often obtain tobacco from adults, and (2) the presence of tobacco products in child-friendly settings socializes children to believe that tobacco use is fun and safe, thereby undermining the Act's ban on advertising to minors. Congress relied on its power under the Commerce Clause in passing the Act.

Sam Samson was recently arrested and indicted for violating the Act by smoking a cigarette during the half-time of his child's high school basketball game. In his defense, Sam argues that the Act exceeds Congress' power under the Commerce Clause. Sam's argument is:

(A)   Correct because Congress may not regulate an intra-state non-economic activity.

(B)   Correct because smoking near children is a non-economic activity with too remote a connection to interstate commerce.

(C)   Incorrect because "child-related facilities" are within the channels of interstate commerce.

(D)   Incorrect because Congress rationally concluded that regulation of tobacco possession in or near a child-related facility is necessary to the success of Congress' larger statutory scheme regulating the marketing, distribution, and sale of tobacco products to minors.

199.   Congress recently enacted a law that conditions a state's receipt of federal maternity care funds on the state banning all abortions other than those necessary to protect the life or health of the mother. May Congress do so?

(A)   No, because abortions are not an economic activity.

(B)   Yes, because abortion regulation is rationally related to maternity care funds.

(C)   No, because the Due Process Clause of the Fourteenth Amendment prohibits states from banning pre-viability abortions.

(D)   No, because the Due Process Clause of the Fifth Amendment prohibits Congress from banning pre-viability abortions.

200.   Congress recently enacted the Family Legal Services for the Poor Act. The Act establishes a Poverty Law Office in every state that is responsible for representing indigent clients in family law matters, such as divorce, child custody, and child support

matters. The Act funds these new offices by imposing an occupation tax on every attorney licensed to practice in a state, territory, or possession of the United States. To facilitate collection of the attorney occupation tax, the Act requires every law firm or other organization, public or private, that employs lawyers to register with the Department of Labor, and to report quarterly the names and wages of each lawyer then employed. The Act places a similar reporting requirement on solo practitioners.

A national association of state Attorneys General recently spoke out against the law, arguing that the Act's registration requirement and occupation tax violate the residue of state sovereignty protected by the Constitution and Bill of Rights.

Does the Act's registration requirement violate the Tenth Amendment?

(A)   Yes, because it commandeers the state legislature into making laws that bring the state into compliance with the registration requirement.

(B)   Yes, because it commandeers the state agencies that employ lawyers into complying with the registration requirement.

(C)   No, because the Act merely requires states to comply with a generally-applicable registration requirement.

(D)   No, because the practice of law is an economic activity with a substantial effect on interstate commerce.

201.   Does the Act's attorney occupation tax violate the states' intergovernmental tax immunity?

(A)   Yes, because the Act impermissibly taxes the states.

(B)   Yes, because the Act impermissibly taxes attorneys engaged in the traditional government function of law enforcement.

(C)   No, because the Act taxes state employees and not the state itself.

(D)   No, because the Act imposes a nondiscriminatory tax on those who deal with the state.

202.   In your capacity as a legislative aide, your legislator asked you to review proposed legislation. This legislation relates to the Human Genome Project, which has isolated several genes that, if present, will absolutely result in serious illness and quite possibly death in adulthood. However, it is the nature of these illnesses that if they can be treated during childhood, the prognosis is greatly improved. The proposed legislation would mandate genetic testing for these genes of every child born in the state. The procedure for testing involves taking a small amount of blood; thus, it is minimally invasive. Each person tested will receive the results of the test with directions on how to proceed if they tested positive for the presence of the genes causing the diseases. The state's records of the results of these tests would be destroyed every six months to protect the privacy of the person tested. The legislator has asked you to comment on the constitutionality of this proposed legislation. What will you tell her?

(A)  The Due Process Clause of the Fourteenth Amendment has, since 1937, been interpreted to prohibit only procedural irregularities, but to have no substantive content. Therefore, the proposed legislation would not violate the Due Process Clause of the Fourteenth Amendment.

(B)  Since 1937 the Supreme Court has used the rationality test in reviewing whether legislation violates the Due Process Clause of the Fourteenth Amendment. Since the state has an interest in the health of its citizens, its purpose for testing to enhance the population's health is a legitimate purpose and the method proposed by the legislation — genetic testing — rationally relates to that purpose. Thus, the Supreme Court is likely to uphold the constitutionality of this legislation.

(C)  This legislation would violate the fundamental right of privacy protected by the Due Process Clause because it violates personal autonomy.

(D)  This legislation violates the Ninth Amendment because it pertains to a right — the right to personal autonomy and the right of privacy — which, while not enumerated in the Constitution, is still retained by the people.

203.  You are still working for our friend, the state legislator. This time she asks you to review some old statutes that are candidates for recission. One statute forbids the cohabitation of heterosexual, adult couples who are not married to each other but who are sexual partners. The legislation states that its purpose is to encourage marriage. The legislator wants to know if this statute would withstand constitutional scrutiny if challenged today. What do you tell her?

(A)  It is likely that the statute will pass constitutional scrutiny because it does not infringe on a fundamental right.

(B)  It is likely that the statute will pass constitutional scrutiny because it does not involve discrimination against homosexuals.

(C)  It is unlikely that the statute will pass constitutional scrutiny because it limits the freedom of individuals to make personal choices as to intimate associations without any legitimate justification.

(D)  It is unlikely that the statute will pass constitutional scrutiny because it favors marriage.

204.  Prior to the great Chicago fire, the City of Chicago relied on a volunteer fire department, but after the fire, in the late 1890s, and ever since, the Chicago Fire Department has been a branch of the city government. Last year, because of budget pressures, Chicago contracted out to a private company, Fire Safety, Inc., some of the firefighting duties previously handled by the Fire Department. These include paramedic duties, fire engine maintenance, and computer maintenance. Fire Safety dismissed an employee working under this contract without a hearing or explanation. The employee has filed a suit under the Fourteenth Amendment claiming that Fire Safety violated constitutional guarantees of procedural due process by failing to give reasons or a hearing after the termination. The employee:

(A)   Will likely prevail because the work of Fire Safety under this contract is a public function; and, therefore, Fire Safety must follow the constitutional requirements of due process.

(B)   Will likely prevail because the work of Fire Safety under this contract makes its relationship with the City of Chicago sufficiently interdependent to convert Fire Safety's private activities into public activities.

(C)   Will not likely prevail because the Supreme Court's decisions in *Jackson v. Metropolitan Edison Co.*, 419 U.S. 345 (1974), and *Blum v. Yaretsky*, 457 U.S. 991 (1982), appear to limit the situations in which a private entity is subject to the state action doctrine.

(D)   Will not likely prevail because the Fourteenth Amendment does not apply to private activity.

205.   Assume we are in the future and that a former President has been sued for money damages under the federal False Claims Act for official behavior while he was President. In the same case, the plaintiffs also sue a former Secretary of Commerce for money damages under the federal False Claims Act for official behavior while she was Secretary of Commerce. The President and the Secretary of Commerce both ask the trial court to dismiss the suit against them on grounds of absolute immunity for their official conduct while President and Secretary of Commerce. The trial court will likely:

(A)   reject the President's assertion of absolute immunity, because no one in the United States is above the law.

(B)   reject the President's assertion of absolute immunity, because the President is no longer in office.

(C)   dismiss the lawsuit, because it involves a political question.

(D)   dismiss the lawsuit as to the President, but not the Secretary of Commerce, on grounds of absolute immunity.

206.   The United States and several European nations have entered a treaty, negotiated by the President and ratified by the Senate, that requires the registration of handguns. The treaty, known as the Responsible Firearms Treaty (RFT), requires each nation to have registration accomplished by specified political subdivisions. In the United States, the RFT requires each state to register these handguns. Several states bring a lawsuit seeking to enjoin the enforcement of this Treaty. The states cite the Supreme Court's decision in *Printz v. United States*, 521 U.S. 898 (1997), which held that the federal government could not force state officials to provide background checks for firearm registration under the Brady Handgun Violence Prevention Act. According to the Supreme Court in *Printz*, the federal government could not force the states to provide their resources to implement a federal program. This commandeering violated the states' sovereignty and was unconstitutional. In their case against the RFT, the states argue the same principles declared in *Printz*: that this treaty amounts to forcing the states to provide resources to implement a national program and thus violates the states' sovereignty.

The likely outcome of this lawsuit will be:

(A)    the states will not prevail, because *Missouri v. Holland*, 252 U.S. 416 (1920), rejected a state sovereignty limitation on the treaty power of the federal government.

(B)    the states will not prevail, because the *Printz* decision involved only background checks rather than the actual act of firearm registration.

(C)    the states will prevail, because *Missouri v. Holland* has been overruled by the Supreme Court in its recent decisions on state sovereignty, including *Printz*.

(D)    the states will prevail, because states can never be forced to comply with treaty provisions unless the states agree to be bound by such treaties.

207.    By its nature, the phone service industry poses significant barriers to competition. The most severe barrier is the substantial capital investment required to enter the industry. For example, in the market for local phone service, a firm must establish a network of phone lines connecting each customer to the firm's transmission equipment. Existing local phone companies already have such networks in place. To compete, new entrants must either construct their own network or gain access to an existing network.

To promote competition in its local phone market, the Public Utilities Commission of the State of Arkabama (PUC) has promulgated a series of rules mandating cooperation between existing local carriers and new entrants. One rule requires existing carriers to provide new entrants access to their networks at a fair market price and on non-discriminatory terms. Another rule requires existing carriers to allow collocation, which means that the existing carrier must set aside space in its facility for a new entrant to install equipment needed to access the existing carrier's network.

Is the PUC's collocation requirement a taking of private property?

(A)    Yes, because the collocation requirement is not roughly proportional to a legitimate government interest.

(B)    Yes, because the collocation requirement forces landowners to endure a physical invasion by a third party.

(C)    No, because the collocation requirement is roughly proportional to a legitimate government interest.

(D)    No, because the collocation requirement does not prohibit all economically viable use of the land.

208.    Tennessee has passed legislation making it more difficult for employers to leave the state. The law requires employers to pay retirement benefits to certain employees even when the benefits have yet to vest under an employer's retirement plan. For example, under the law, an employer moving its entire operation out of state must pay a "pension funding charge" to cover the retirement benefits due any employee who has worked for the employer for at least ten years, even if the employee's right to retirement benefits

has not vested in this ten-year period. Tennessee has not previously regulated retirement benefits offered by private employers. ABC Company seeks legal advice as to whether this Tennessee law violates the Contract Clause.

(A)   ABC Company will be told that a claim under the Contract Clause is unlikely to succeed considering the Supreme Court's decisions in *General Motors v. Romein,* 503 U.S. 181 (1992); *Energy Reserves Group v. Kansas Power & Light,* 459 U.S. 400 (1983); and *Home Building & Loan Association v. Blaisdell,* 290 U.S. 398 (1934).

(B)   ABC Company will be told that a claim under the Contract Clause is unlikely to succeed because it will be dismissed under the Eleventh Amendment.

(C)   ABC Company will be told that the federal employee benefit laws preempt the Tennessee law.

(D)   ABC Company will be told that a claim under the Contract Clause is likely to succeed because the state did not pass this law to deal with a broad economic problem, the law was totally unanticipated by ABC, and the law is not temporary.

209.   The State of Texana has established a public agency — the Texana Employment Agency for the Blind (TEAB) — that identifies employment opportunities within various state offices for visually-impaired persons. The agency defines "visually-impaired person" as any person who is (1) totally blind or (2) legally blind. At work sites where TEAB has made employee placements, visually-impaired persons work alongside sighted employees.

TEAB has placed employees in various state departments. Each department is responsible for the design and manufacture of a different product. The departments include Uniforms, Janitorial Supplies (such as mops and brooms), and Furniture (such as chairs, desks, tables for office workers, and bed frames and mattresses for prison cells). Many of these goods are sold to private purchasers. While TEAB receives public funding, the compensation of the TEAB supervisors and management is determined in part by revenue received from private purchasers.

Offices working with TEAB try to maximize visually-impaired employees' participation in work tasks. TEAB has identified certain job tasks in each department that must be performed by sighted employees. These tasks involve use of heavy machinery deemed too dangerous for visually-impaired employees to operate. All other job tasks are open to visually-impaired persons.

TEAB has recently implemented a new promotion policy that forbids visually-impaired persons from holding supervisory or management positions in any department. TEAB claims that its promotion policy is supported by concern for the safety of its employees. Specifically, TEAB believes that safety requires that all managers and supervisors be able to perform all job tasks within the department they are supervising. Because TEAB disqualifies visually-impaired employees from certain hazardous job tasks in each department, those employees are not eligible for supervisory or management positions.

What equal protection test applies to TEAB's policy of not promoting visually-impaired employees?

(A)  Strict scrutiny.

(B)  Intermediate scrutiny.

(C)  Rational basis review.

(D)  Undue burden test.

210.  The City of Thompsonville is a rural community with a population of about 4,000. The Thompsonville City Council recently passed an ordinance that applies to all commercial businesses in the city with the following signage:

> Flashing signs, signs with flashing or reflective disks, signs with flashing lights or lights of changing degrees of intensity or color, or signs with electronically scrolled messages (except government required signs and signs which give time and temperature information).

The ordinance bans all such signage that is visible in the direct or peripheral vision of a driver of a vehicle traveling on a public roadway. The ordinance's Statement of Purpose recites that the ban is meant to promote traffic safety by reducing driver distractions. During the City Council meeting, the City Attorney explained that studies done by the United States Department of Transportation show that signage with flashing, changing, or moving displays are associated with increased accidents on interstate highways.

What is the strongest argument that the city's ordinance is unconstitutional?

(A)  The ordinance regulates commercial speech that is neither false nor misleading.

(B)  The ordinance is not supported by a substantial government interest.

(C)  The ordinance does not directly advance the government's interest.

(D)  The ordinance is more extensive than necessary to achieve the government's interest.

211.  The State of Utep recently passed a law that reduced the speed limit on its state highways from 70 to 60 miles per hour. The state's highway department had just completed a ten-year study that showed overwhelmingly that traffic accidents and fatalities were lower on state highways with a 60 mile per hour speed limit.

Many of these state highways go to the Utep State border and connect to roadways in an adjacent state. Each of the states bordering Utep has a speed limit of 70 miles per hour on their state highways. A national trucking company filed a federal lawsuit claiming that the new Utep speed limit violates the Dormant Commerce Clause because it forces interstate traffic to slow down when it enters Utep.

The Utep speed limit is most likely:

(A) Unconstitutional because Utep has discriminated against out-of-state traffic for the benefit of in-state traffic.

(B) Unconstitutional because Utep's legitimate interest in traffic safety does not clearly exceed the speed limit's burden on interstate commerce.

(C) Constitutional because the speed limit's slight burden on interstate commerce does not clearly exceed Utep's legitimate interest in traffic safety.

(D) Constitutional because the safety of state highways is a purely local matter that may be regulated by the states as they please.

212. Consider the facts from Question 209. Would TEAB's policy of not promoting visually-impaired employees survive scrutiny under traditional rational basis review?

ANSWER (two paragraphs):

213. Will the Court apply heightened rational basis review to TEAB's policy of not promoting visually-impaired employees?

ANSWER (two paragraphs):

214. Arkabama State University is a public, residential university serving 10,000 students. A student's tuition depends on whether she is deemed "in-state" or "out-of-state." Tuition for in-state students is $2,500 per year, and tuition for out-of-state students is $10,000 per year. An "in-state student" is defined as "any person whose legal address has been within Arkabama for twelve consecutive months." A person's "legal address," in turn, is defined as "the address for which at least three of the following applies: (1) it is where the person regularly receives mail, (2) it is listed on her driver's license, (3) it is listed on her most recent tax return, or (4) it is listed on a current voter registration." A student's status as of the first day of an academic year establishes her tuition for that entire year. If a student changes her status prior to the beginning of the next academic year, the change will be reflected in her tuition rate for that year.

The state's asserted purpose for the tuition differential is to equalize the burden of higher education between residents and non-residents. State residents shoulder the tax burden that heavily subsidizes Arkabama State University and non-residents do not. The tuition differential merely reflects this difference, asking out-of-state students to bear their fair share of the cost of a university education.

Does the university's higher out-of-state tuition violate the Article IV Privileges and Immunities Clause?

ANSWER:

215. Consider the naval blockade of North Korea described in Question 46. Assume that, rather than attempting to impeach the President, Congress invokes its authority under the War Powers Resolution. The War Powers Resolution, 50 U.S.C. § 1541 *et seq.*, requires that, if the President should commit American armed forces without congressional approval, these forces must be withdrawn after 60 days unless Congress declares war or approves an extension of time.

Would the War Powers Resolution survive constitutional scrutiny in the appropriate case?

ANSWER:

# ANSWERS

1.  **Answer (B) is the correct answer**. In *Marbury v. Madison*, 5 U.S. (1 Cranch) 137 (1803), Chief Justice Marshall wrote: "It is emphatically the province and duty of the judicial department to say what the law is." *Id.* at 177. To decide cases and controversies, federal courts must necessarily interpret and apply the United States Constitution. And when the Constitution and a federal statute are in conflict, the federal court must follow the Constitution. Otherwise, Congress and the President could ignore the Constitution without fear of judicial check. Denying the power of judicial review would defeat the point of having a written Constitution, which was to enumerate and limit government power.

    Marshall offered three other defenses of judicial review. First, federal judges take an oath to uphold the Constitution, and they would break their oath if they applied a statute that violated the Constitution. Second, Article III grants federal courts subject matter jurisdiction over *all* cases arising under the Constitution. This implies that federal courts have the power to hear and decide such cases, which entails interpreting the Constitution. And third, Article VI declares the Constitution to be the supreme law of the land, along with all federal laws made "pursuant thereto." To decide whether a federal law is entitled to supremacy, federal courts must determine whether that law is made "pursuant" to the Constitution, which entails interpreting the Constitution.

    The standard criticism of *Marbury* is that none of the above arguments requires federal courts to apply *the judge's* interpretation of the Constitution in deciding cases. By passing and signing a law, Congress and the President implicitly assert their conclusion that the law is constitutional. Why should courts not simply apply this constitutional understanding in deciding federal cases? While this jurisprudential question is fodder for continuing law school discussions, it is, as they say, purely academic. *Marbury* has established the power of judicial review, and no current member of the federal government has even suggested overturning that holding. The main ground of debate today is the proper breadth of judicial review, as well as the proper method of constitutional interpretation.

    **Answer (A) is incorrect** because *Marbury* specifically rejected this argument. According to Marshall, whether federal courts may review an executive decision depends on whether the decision is a matter of discretion or duty. When the President is granted *discretion* to act, such as when executive branch officials represent the nation in foreign affairs, *id.* at 166, federal judges ought not second guess executive branch officials. But when the President is under a *duty* to act, federal courts may enforce the duty. This duty-discretion distinction foreshadowed the political question doctrine, which bars judicial review of matters the Constitution textually commits to Congress or the

President. See Questions 14 through 16. Also, this part of *Marbury* is technically dicta, as the Court dismissed the case for lack of subject matter jurisdiction. Regardless, nothing in *Marbury* suggests that Presidential action is immune from judicial review.

**Answer (C) is incorrect** because the Court reached precisely the opposite holding. The Court read the Article III, Section 2 grant of original jurisdiction as exclusive. That is, the Supreme Court has original jurisdiction over only the types of cases listed in Article III, Section 2, and Congress cannot add to that list by statute. Because the writ of mandamus does not appear on that list, the Supreme Court could not exercise original jurisdiction over Marbury's case. **Answer (C) is incorrect** because it states the opposite conclusion.

**Answer (D) cannot be the correct answer** because only answer (B) is correct.

2.   **Answer (D) is the correct answer**. In *Martin v. Hunter's Lessee*, 14 U.S. 304 (1816), the Supreme Court of Virginia held that the United States Supreme Court had no appellate jurisdiction to review state court cases that interpreted the United States Constitution. The Supreme Court rejected this argument. The Court found the constitutional issue to be easy, as Article III grants federal courts jurisdiction over "*all* cases arising under the Constitution." If federal courts could not review state court decisions interpreting the Constitution, then federal courts could not hear all arising under cases, in clear violation of Article III. Justice Story noted the horrible consequences of allowing each state to interpret the Constitution for itself — the Constitution could mean something different depending on where a person lived. And as a matter of principle, the Constitution elevates "We the People of the United States" to ultimate sovereign over all American government, including the states. By exercising that sovereignty in ratifying the Constitution, "the People" bound the states to the Constitution, including the Article III grant of federal jurisdiction.

**Answers (A) and (B) are incorrect** because they misstate *Martin*'s holding. **Answer (A) is incorrect** because the case came to the Supreme Court on appellate jurisdiction, not original jurisdiction. Further, after *Marbury* it is highly doubtful that the Supreme Court would have had original jurisdiction over such a claim. Recall that *Marbury* limited the Supreme Court's original jurisdiction to those matters listed in Article III, Section 2, and *Martin* would not fit within any of the listed categories.

**Answer (B) is incorrect** because the Supreme Court did not interpret the Virginia State constitution. In addition, the Supreme Court has held that federal courts are bound by a state court's interpretation of that state's domestic law. *See Republican Party of Minnesota v. White*, 536 U.S. 765, 809 (2002).

**Answer (C) is incorrect** for two reasons. First, a federal statute granted the Supreme Court appellate jurisdiction to hear the case, so there was no need to rely on inherent power. Second, it is unclear whether federal courts have any inherent jurisdiction in the absence of a federal statute. The Court has stated many times that federal court jurisdiction is strictly limited to that granted by Congress, strongly suggesting Courts have no inherent power to hear cases.

3.  **Answer (A) is the correct answer.** In *Cooper v. Aaron*, 358 U.S. 1 (1958), the Court confronted Arkansas' repeated refusal to implement the desegregation mandated by *Brown v. Board of Education*, 347 U.S. 483 (1954). Specifically, the Court addressed the claim of the state's "Governor and Legislature that they are not bound by our holding in the *Brown* case." *Id.* at 17. The Court explained why Arkansas officials were wrong as a matter of constitutional text and precedent:

> Article VI of the Constitution makes the Constitution the "Supreme Law of the Land." In 1803, Chief Justice Marshall, speaking for a unanimous Court, referring to the Constitution as "the fundamental and paramount law of the nation," declared in the notable case of *Marbury v. Madison*, that "It is emphatically the province and duty of the judicial department to say what the law is." This decision declared the basic principle that the federal judiciary is supreme in the exposition of the law of the Constitution, and that principle has ever since been respected by this Court and the Country as a permanent and indispensable feature of our constitutional system. It follows that the interpretation of the Fourteenth Amendment enunciated by this Court in the Brown case is the supreme law of the land, and Art. VI of the Constitution makes it of binding effect on the states "any Thing in the Constitution or Laws of any State to the Contrary notwithstanding." Every state legislator and executive and judicial officer is solemnly committed by oath taken pursuant to Art. VI, ¶3 "to support this Constitution." Chief Justice Taney, speaking for a unanimous Court in 1859, said that this requirement reflected the framers "anxiety to preserve it [the Constitution] in full force, in all its powers, and to guard against resistance to or evasion of its authority, on the part of a State."

*Id.* at 18 (citations omitted). **Answer (A) is correct** because it sets forth this constitutional duty of state officials. *Id.* ("No State legislator or executive or judicial officer can war against the Constitution without violating his undertaking to support it.")

**Answer (B) is incorrect** because *Cooper* did not involve a case where the Arkansas State courts were being forced to hear a federal issue. Rather, the case came up through the United States District Court for the Eastern District of Arkansas and the Court of Appeals for the Eighth Circuit.

**Answer (C) is incorrect** because *Cooper* did not deal with parallel state proceedings with which the federal litigation might have interfered.

**Answer (D) is incorrect** because *Cooper* required the Court to interpret and apply the federal Constitution against an unwilling state. While it is true that federal courts must accept a state's definitive interpretation of its own law, *see Republican Party of Minnesota v. White*, 536 U.S. 765, 809 (2002), no issue of state law was raised in *Cooper*.

Note that the opinion in *Cooper* was jointly authored by the *entire Court*! The opinion begins:

> Opinion of the Court by The Chief Justice, Mr. Justice Black, Mr. Justice Frankfurter, Mr. Justice Douglas, Mr. Justice Burton, Mr. Justice Clark, Mr. Justice Harlan, Mr. Justice Brennan, and Mr. Justice Whittaker.

At this crucial moment in American history, each Justice took full responsibility for every word in the case, leaving no doubt that such obstruction had no sympathizers within the Court's chambers.

4. This question asks you to analyze whether the plaintiff has constitutional standing to bring the lawsuit in federal court. Article III grants federal courts jurisdiction over "cases" and "controversies," and the Court has interpreted these words to limit federal courts to deciding cases traditionally and historically associated with the judicial role. For example, federal courts may not issue advisory opinions that answer a hypothetical legal question, apart from a real controversy between actual parties. The justiciability material addresses other doctrines that limit when parties can litigate in federal court. The first doctrine is standing, which ensures that the parties to a case actually have something at stake in the litigation. For a plaintiff to have standing to sue in federal court, the plaintiff must show three things: (1) injury-in-fact, (2) that the defendant caused the plaintiff's injury, and (3) that a judicial remedy will redress the plaintiff's injury. *See Lujan.* The following questions apply and explain this test.

**Answer (C) is the best answer** because it is unclear whether a judicial decision striking down the lottery program would redress the plaintiff's injury. Because the plaintiff's injury is denial of entry into the United States, a judicial decision would have to result in his entry if it was to redress his injury. Yet, if the lottery is struck down, the plaintiff is not ensured entry. We know that he is not entitled to refugee status. Thus, his only option for legal entry would be to sail from Cuba to Florida. If he survives the voyage, he would be allowed to stay. But, whether the plaintiff would ever make and survive the voyage is highly speculative. The voyage itself is risky, and invalidation of the lottery program may cause Cuba to once again actively discourage such migration. Further, a judicial decision striking down the lottery program will not make a successful voyage any more likely. Thus, redressibility is lacking. And because lack of redressibility negates standing, **answer (D) is not the best answer.**

**Answer (A) is incorrect** because the plaintiff suffered a concrete injury when he was denied entry into the United States. **Answer (B) is incorrect** because it was the United States' decision, through the lottery program, that denied the plaintiff entry and caused his injury.

5. **Answer (B) is the best answer.**

Again, we must review the three elements of standing. First, FAIR has alleged concrete injury. Specifically, they allege harm to their children's education (by overcrowding of schools), to the community's health and safety (by decreased access to medical services and police protection), and their financial well-being (by decreased employment). Thus, **answer (A) is incorrect.**

Second, causation probably fails under the Supreme Court's decision in *Allen v. Wright*, 468 U.S. 737 (1984). In *Allen*, parents of African-American children challenged the IRS' failure to deny tax-exempt status to private schools that discriminated based on race. The plaintiffs' alleged injury was that the IRS' failure reduced their children's opportunity to obtain a desegregated education. While reduced opportunity for a desegregated education was a concrete injury, it was too speculative whether the IRS' action caused that injury. The injury relied on too many contingencies, such as whether there were private, racially discriminatory schools in the plaintiffs' communities, and whether withdrawal of tax-exempt status would open those schools to the plaintiffs' children. The Court concluded that the "links in the chain of causation between the challenged Government conduct and the asserted injury are far too weak for the chain as a whole to sustain . . . standing."

FAIR faces the same standing problem, as it relies on several speculative assertions. First, whether any of the harms occur depends on the number of Cuban nationals who seek entry under the lottery. Second, even assuming the maximum number of Cuban nationals obtain entry, their effect on education, employment, and police and medical services is speculative. For example, will localities shift resources to those areas, thus keeping the services constant? Will the newly-admitted Cuban nationals spend sufficient money in their new communities to support greater education, employment, and police and medical services? The answers to these questions depend on the actions of many actors who are not parties to FAIR's lawsuit. As in *Allen*, the causal chain is likely too attenuated. Thus, **answer (B) is the best answer**.

6. The Society has likely alleged sufficient injury. Harm to the aesthetic beauty and recreational use of a river is the type of injury that may support standing. *Sierra Club v. Morton*, 405 U.S. 727 (1972). Also, as required in *Lujan v. Defenders of Wildlife*, 504 U.S. 555 (1992), the Society alleges that its members actually do, and will continue to, use the Humongous Muddy River, and thus that they will suffer harm. A similar standing injury was upheld in *Friends of the Earth, Inc. v. Laidlaw Environmental Services (TOC), Inc.*, 528 U.S. 167 (2000). The wrinkle is that the injury may be considered "conjectural or hypothetical," and not actual or imminent, because the dam project still must pass through many procedural hurdles over several years. But *Lujan* anticipated this point, explaining that a "person who has been accorded a procedural right to protect his concrete interests can assert that right without meeting all the normal standards for redressability and immediacy." The Court then gave the specific example of a landowner challenging the government's failure to obtain an EIS for a dam project on adjacent land. Federal statutes may create the right to certain procedural protections *before* the government takes actions that affect its citizens. Failing to follow prescribed procedures violates these rights, inflicting a type of injury that, by itself, supports standing.

7. For both causation and redressability, the government may argue that it is entirely speculative whether preparation of an EIS will actually change the government's ultimate decision. If an EIS would not do so, the failure to prepare an EIS did not cause plaintiff's

injury, and an order requiring an EIS would not redress that injury. *See Florida Audubon Society v. Bentsen*, 94 F.3d 658 (D.C. Cir. 1996). On the other hand, the plaintiff can argue that its injury is not construction of the dam *per se*, but the *uninformed decision* whether to construct a dam that would result absent an EIS. Thus, the failure to prepare an EIS causes plaintiff's injury, and an order requiring an EIS would redress that injury. *See Committee to Save the Rio Hondo v. Lucero*, 102 F.3d 445 (10th Cir. 1996). Again, *Lujan*'s dicta on procedural rights supports that view.

8. **Note**: For those interested in reading more on this subject, this question is loosely based on a federal lawsuit filed in the Eastern District of Michigan. The District Court held that the plaintiffs, including a lawyer, had standing to challenge the terrorist surveillance program, *American Civil Liberties Union v. National Security Agency*, 438 F. Supp. 2d 754, 782 (E.D. Mich. 2006), and the Sixth Circuit reversed. *American Civil Liberties Union v. National Security Agency*, 493 F.3d 644 (6th Cir. 2007).

**Answer (A) is incorrect** because George has alleged an actual injury — the loss of clients — that harms him in the practice of his profession and causes him monetary harm. *See Meese v. Keene*, 481 U.S. 465 (1987).

**Answer (B) is incorrect** because George's harm is not generalized in the way that defeats standing. The Court has held that a plaintiff's injury is actual and concrete even if shared by many other people. An injury is generalized only if the plaintiff cannot differentiate herself from other citizens generally. Here, George is different — he plies a trade that causes him to communicate with those people most sensitive to the government's surveillance. Unlike other citizens, the program allegedly costs him clients and so money. George's injury may be shared by others in a similar situation, but it is not generalized.

**Answer (C) is incorrect** because it applies the wrong test. The nexus requirement applies only when a taxpayer is suing to challenge a legislative appropriation of funds as violating the Establishment Clause of the First Amendment. Because George is not relying on such taxpayer standing, the nexus requirement does not apply. *See Duke Power Co. v. Carolina Envt'l Study Group, Inc.*, 438 U.S. 59 (1978).

**Answer (D) is the best answer**. The Supreme Court has held that standing fails if it is speculative that either the government's challenged action caused the plaintiff's alleged harm, or that a judicial remedy will redress that harm. Here, there is a strong argument that George's claims of causation and redress are speculative. On the given facts, it is not clear why George is losing his international clients, or if enjoining the surveillance program will cause those clients to return. First, consider causation. This case is similar to *Allen v. Wright*, 468 U.S. 737 (1984), where the plaintiffs challenged the IRS' allegedly lax enforcement of a federal statute barring tax exempt status for private schools that discriminate based on race. The plaintiffs were parents of black children who attended public schools. The Court held that the plaintiffs' alleged injury of attending racially segregated public schools was a sufficient injury in fact. Causation, however, posed a problem. The parents argued that the following chain of causation connected the IRS' lax enforcement to their alleged injury of segregated public schools:

1.  the IRS under-enforced the statutory bar on tax exempt status,

2.  tax exempt status left racially discriminatory private schools with more money,

3.  the racially discriminatory private schools became more attractive to applicants, either by reducing tuition or spending money to improve the educational program,

4.  more parents of white children switched their children from public schools to the racially segregated private schools, and

5.  the public schools were less racially diverse.

The Court held that causation was speculative because the plaintiff had not alleged facts showing that this chain of causation was in fact true. The main problem is that the causation argument relied on the actions of two sets of third parties — that is, actors who were not parties to the litigation. Specifically, causation depended on the actions of the private schools and the parents of white school children. Because it was entirely speculative how either group behaved in response to the IRS's decisions, the Court held there was no causation. *See also Simon v. Eastern Kentucky Welfare Rights Organization*, 426 U.S. 26 (1976) (standing denied where it was speculative whether tax exempt status affected hospital's decision whether to provide care for the indigent).

Here, causation faces the same charge of speculativeness. George's causation argument relies on the behavior of third parties who are not part of the litigation — his clients and potential clients. George has not alleged any facts tending to show that the government's surveillance program likely caused his injury. Perhaps clients turned away due to a business downturn or dissatisfaction with George's work. As in *Allen*, George's standing claim is vulnerable to the charge that it rests on speculation.

Redress is also speculative, as a court order ending the program might not cause the clients to return. The clients may have retained other counsel, or may still fear other unannounced intelligence programs. This is similar to *Linda R.S. v. Richard D.*, 410 U.S. 614 (1973), where the Court also found redress speculative. There, a mother challenged the constitutionality of a state policy to not enforce child support orders regarding children born out of wedlock. Redress was speculative because even if the state changed its policy, and brought an enforcement proceeding, it was speculative whether the delinquent father would have the means or willingness to pay. The Court noted that redress will often be speculative when it relies on the behavior of third parties who are not before the court. The same is true here. George's clients are not parties to the lawsuit and so a court cannot order them to retain George. Instead, redress hinges on what the client's will do in response to a court order *issued to the federal government*. On the facts, it is speculative how George's former clients would react to such an order.

Because of the strong arguments regarding speculative nature of causation and redress, as well as the weakness of the arguments underlying the other answer choices, **(D) is the best answer**.

9. **Answer (D) is the best answer**. The other answer choices are incorrect because they rest on a misunderstanding of the nature of the plaintiff's injury. The Supreme Court has held that the standing injury for an Equal Protection Clause claim is denial of the *opportunity* to compete on a race-neutral basis. For example, in *City of Richmond v. J.A. Croson Co.*, 488 U.S. 469 (1989), a private contractor sued to challenge a city law that set aside a percentage of public sub-contracts for minority contractors. The private contractor's injury was *not* loss of an actual contract, but rather loss of the *opportunity to compete* for a contract on a race-neutral basis. To show causation, the private contractor did *not* have to show that the policy caused it to lose a sub-contract. Rather, being forced to compete under racially discriminatory criteria was itself an injury, and simply enacting a racial set-aside causes that injury. Further, enjoining the set-aside would redress the injury by allowing contractors to compete on a race-neutral basis. *See also Allen v. Wright*, 468 U.S. 737 (1984) (stigmatic injury that will support standing is limited to those who were subjected to discriminatory treatment).

**Answer (A) is incorrect** because it states the incorrect causation analysis for Equal Protection standing. The injury was the denial of an *opportunity to compete* for high school selection on a race-neutral basis, not denial of *admission* to a specific high school. The District's assignment plan considers race and so causes an Equal Protection injury. The Court so held in *Parents Involved in Community Schools v. Seattle School Dist. No. 1*, 127 S. Ct. 2738 (2007). Similarly, an order enjoining the District's use of race will redress that injury by allowing assignment on a race-neutral basis. For this reason, **Answer (B) is incorrect**.

**Answer (C) is incorrect** because it incorrectly describes the injury as denial of assignment to a specific school. As just discussed, application of racial criteria — standing alone — is the Equal Protection injury.

10. Under *Flast v. Cohen*, 392 U.S. 83 (1968), taxpayer status, standing alone, confers Article III standing to challenge government action only when the taxpayer can make two showings: (1) "the taxpayer must establish a logical link between that status and the type of legislative enactment attacked," and (2) "the taxpayer must establish a nexus between that status and the precise nature of the constitutional infringement alleged." *Id.* at 102–03. The taxpayer in *Flast* met this test: first, the challenged government action was a federal statute enacted under Congress' taxing and spending power, *see* Art. I, § 8, and second, the plaintiff alleged a violation of the Establishment Clause, which was intended as a limit on Congress' power to spend tax money in aid of religion. *Hein v. Freedom From Religion Foundation, Inc.*, 127 S. Ct. 2553 (2007), raised the question whether the President's allocation of general executive funds, which Congress had not mandated for any specific use, also satisfied the first *Flast* nexus. The Court held "no":

> In short, this case falls outside the "narrow exception" that *Flast* "created to the general rule against taxpayer standing established. . . ." Because the expenditures that respondents challenge were not expressly authorized or mandated by any specific congressional enactment, respondents' lawsuit is not

directed at an exercise of congressional power, and thus lacks the requisite "logical nexus" between taxpayer status "and the type of legislative enactment attacked."

*Id.* at 2568 (citations omitted).

11. **Answer (B) is the best answer** based on the facts. From what we know, there is no reason to believe that Dr. Jones will not regain her license. She is only required to attend three months of continuing medical education (which her affidavit tells us she has already begun), and then she may re-apply. Further, reinstatement is *mandatory* if the Board finds that she has attended the courses. For these reasons, it would be likely that Dr. Jones would be reinstated and thus the statute does not threaten to injure her.

**Answer (A) is not the best answer** because it does not consider the possibility that Dr. Jones will regain her license. Intervening events moot a case when "it can be said with assurance that there is no reasonable expectation that the alleged [injury] will recur, [and] interim . . . events have completely and irrevocably eradicated the effects of the alleged [injury]." *County of Los Angeles v. Davis*, 440 U.S. 625 (1979). In *Davis*, minority job applicants sued the county over an allegedly discriminatory civil service exam used in hiring. After the suit was filed, the county stopped using the challenged exam and instituted minority recruiting quotas. Because the county had completely eradicated the challenged behavior and showed no signs of going back, the case was moot. Here, conversely, the threatened injury will recur upon Dr. Jones' completion of the required continuing medical education courses. And, the evidence shows that she is likely to do so, as her affidavit states that she is currently in attendance. Thus, Dr. Jones' suspension likely does not moot her lawsuit. *See also Friends of the Earth, Inc. v. Laidlaw Environmental Services (TOC), Inc.*, 528 U.S. 167, 189 (2000) (case challenging defendant's pollution was not moot because defendant still had a permit allowing discharge of pollutants, even though defendant had closed and sold plant that had discharged the alleged excessive pollution).

**Answer (C) is not the best answer** because it ignores the factors discussed in the preceding paragraph. It is true that state law places the reinstatement decision in the Board's sole, unreviewable discretion. That discretion only extends to the decision whether Dr. Jones satisfies the stated criteria: whether she attended the required continuing education courses. Once this condition is shown, Dr. Jones *must* be reinstated. To argue that it is entirely speculative whether Dr. Jones will ever be reinstated asks a court to assume that the Board will ignore its responsibilities under state law. Federal courts will not do so.

**Answer (D) is incorrect** because there is nothing inherent in Dr. Jones' case that would systematically prevent judicial review. To meet that exception to mootness, (1) the challenged conduct must be "too short to be fully litigated prior to its cessation or expiration"; and (2) the parties must reasonably expect that "the same controversy will recur involving the same complaining party." *Murphy v. Hunt*, 455 U.S. 478 (1982).

Unlike the abortion context, there is nothing in Dr. Jones' circumstances that necessarily limits the time during which she is threatened with injury. For example, a pregnant woman has less than six months (and likely less, by the time she learns she is pregnant) within which to exercise her right to an abortion. *Roe v. Wade*, 410 U.S. 113 (1973). The abortion provider, however, will normally be continuously in the business of providing abortion services, and thus will have ample time to litigate her rights. Further, once Dr. Jones is reinstated, she should also have ample time to litigate her rights.

12.  **Answer (C) is the best answer**. The Court has held that the defendant's voluntary cessation of the challenged conduct does not moot a case unless it is absolutely certain that the defendant will not resume the challenged conduct. *See Friends of the Earth, Inc. v. Laidlaw Environmental Services (TOC), Inc.*, 528 U.S. 167, 189 (2000). In *Parents Involved in Community Schools v. Seattle School Dist. No. 1*, 127 S. Ct. 2738, 2751 (2007), the Supreme Court held that a school district's voluntary suspension of its racial student assignment plan did not moot the litigation. That holding dictates the same result here. Because the case is not moot, **Answer (A) is incorrect**.

**Answer (B) is incorrect** for the reasons discussed above in the answer to Question 9. The Equal Protection injury is denial of an opportunity to compete on a race-neutral basis, which is precisely what the District's policy does.

**Answer (D) is incorrect** because the facts do not fit this exception to the mootness rule. For a case to be capable of repetition yet evading review, a litigant must show two things: (1) the challenged conduct must be "too short to be fully litigated prior to its cessation or expiration"; and (2) the parties must reasonably expect that "the same controversy will recur involving the same complaining party." *Murphy v. Hunt*, 455 U.S. 478 (1982). For example, in *Roe v. Wade*, 410 U.S. 113 (1973), the Court held that a pregnant woman's abortion challenge met this test because, first, "the normal 266-day human gestation period is so short that the pregnancy will come to term before the usual appellate process is complete," and second, that "[p]regnancy often comes more than once to the same woman." Neither factor fits this case. First, as all of the students are entering their freshman year of high school, the parents have at least three years before their children are assigned for the final time during their senior year. Second, the students on whose behalf the case is brought will go through the District's high school only once. After graduation, there will be no recurrence of the situation that led to the litigation. In addition, the fact that the case might be capable of repetition yet evade review does not speak to the District's reason for seeking dismissal — suspension of the student assignment plan. For all of these reasons, **Answer (C) is better than Answer (D)**.

13. Ripeness has two main requirements: (1) the issues involved are suitable for judicial resolution, and (2) withholding judicial review will cause the plaintiff undue hardship. Consider each requirement in turn. First, the issue in Dr. Jones' lawsuit — the constitutionality of an abortion regulation — is a legal question repeatedly heard by federal courts. Indeed, the Supreme Court has explained that a purely legal question of this nature will satisfy the first element. *Abbott Labs. v. Gardner*, 387 U.S. 136 (1967). Second, while the statute has yet to be enforced against Dr. Jones, she faces undue hardship from possible enforcement of the statute. Dr. Jones' main business is providing abortion services. If she continues her work, she must either forgo income by ceasing post-first trimester abortions, or face substantial civil liability under the Act by performing such abortions. Further, it is inevitable that a law creating liability for post-first trimester abortions will be enforced against providers of such abortions. The economic incentive to litigate — wrongful death damages — is both powerful and clear. For that reason, enforcement is sufficiently imminent. The lawsuit should be ripe for judicial consideration.

14. Yes, because the *Baker v. Carr*, 369 U.S. 186 (1962), factors point in that direction. First, as the Constitution does not specifically define or limit the Senate's treaty role, the decision how to advise the President is textually committed to the Senate. In this respect, the present case is unlike *Powell v. McCormack*, 395 U.S. 486 (1969), where the Court found no political question. There, the question was *whether* Congress possessed a specific power — the power to exclude a member based on a criterion other than the qualifications listed in the Constitution. This issue of allocation of power was not a political question. Here, however, it is clear that the Senate has the power in question. The issue is *how* that power is best exercised. The Constitution's silence on this issue implicitly delegates that decision to the Senate.

Second, there is no easily discoverable judicial standard for deciding what form such "advice" should take. *See Nixon v. United States*, 506 U.S. 224 (1993), (the judiciary has no real standards to decide whether the Senate's use of a committee to take evidence in impeachment proceedings satisfied the Constitution's requirement that the Senate "try" all impeachments). Third, any judicial attempt to decide such a question would require policy judgments better suited to the political branches. For example, whether floor debate or confidential conversations best serves the "advice" function would depend on the political circumstances of a given treaty. Federal judges are not well situated to answer such questions. Fourth, any attempt to force such a definition on the Senate would show disrespect for the procedural decision of a coordinate branch — the Senate. Fifth, because the United States' credibility in foreign affairs rests to some extent on the finality of presidential and Senate action on international agreements, the judiciary would unduly disrupt such agreements with *ex post* review.

15. **Answer (C) is the best answer**. This case is similar to *Nixon v. United States*, 506 U.S. 224 (1993), where the Court addressed a constitutional challenge to the Senate process for impeaching a federal judge. There, the Senate chose to hold the impeachment trial before a committee of Senators who would report the trial record and their recommendations to the full Senate. The judge complained that the word "try" in Article I, section 3 meant that the Senate must conduct a judicial-type trial. Further, a judicial-type trial requires that all decision makers be present for the taking of the evidence. Consequently, the Senate's committee procedure violated the Constitution.

The Court dismissed the case as raising a political question for two reasons relevant to this question. First, the Constitution's text committed the decision to another branch by granting the Senate the "*sole* power to try all impeachments." This exclusive grant of authority entailed the power to determine what procedures to use at trial. Second, the impeachment decision was one that demanded finality. Recall that impeachment also applies to the President. If impeachment were justiciable, the identity of the nation's chief executive could be in doubt for months, or even years. Finality would be needed to allow the nation to get on with its affairs.

In this question, similar considerations weigh in favor of finding a political question. First, like the Senate's trial clause, the text of the House's impeachment clause appears to commit the issue to that chamber: "the sole power of impeachment." Article I, Section 2. As in *Nixon v. United States*, the word "sole" denotes an exclusive power over the subject, which would include the power to set procedures.

Second, there would seem to be a similar need for finality when impeaching the Vice President. For example, the Vice President is first in the line of succession to the presidency, so any doubt about the Vice President's status would also cast doubt on the line of succession. Given the importance of the President in domestic and foreign affairs, certainty in the line of succession is imperative. Because litigation over House impeachment procedures could create a long period of uncertainty, the lawsuit should be dismissed as a political question.

The above discussion shows that *both* textual commitment and finality support dismissal as a political question. **Answer (C) is the correct answer** because it includes both of these arguments. **Answers (A) and (B) are incorrect** because they select only one of the above arguments, and **Answer (D) is incorrect** because it selects neither argument.

16.  In *Vieth v. Jubelirer*, 541 U.S. 267 (2004), Pennsylvania voters challenged what they claimed was an unconstitutional political gerrymander of the state's congressional districts. A political gerrymander is " '[t]he practice of dividing a geographical area into electoral districts, often of highly irregular shape, to give one political party an unfair advantage by diluting the opposition's voting strength.' " *Id.* at 1773 n.1 (quoting *Black's Law Dictionary 696 (7th ed. 1999)). On the merits, a majority of the Court (in separate opinions) agreed on two important points. First, states may consider "political classifications" when drawing congressional districts, but second, the state may not apply those considerations "in an invidious manner or in a way unrelated to any legitimate legislative objective." Id. at 1793 (Kennedy, J., concurring in the judgment). A four-justice plurality, however, concluded that political gerrymandering claims always pose a political question because courts have no judicially enforceable standard for determining when a state makes improper use of political considerations. Id. at 1776–92 (Scalia, J., announcing the judgment of the Court). Justice Kennedy, providing a fifth vote on non-justiciability, concluded that these litigants had not proffered a judicially manageable standard for deciding political gerrymandering claims, and thus the case should be dismissed. Id. at 1796–97 (Kennedy, J., concurring in the judgment). But Justice Kennedy left open the possibility that future litigants might identify such standards, and thus he thought it unwise to categorically condemn all political gerrymandering claims as non-justiciable political questions. Id. at 1793–96 (Kennedy, J., concurring in the judgment). The Court re-affirmed this approach, with Justice Kennedy again in the middle, in League of United Latin American Citizens v. Perry, 126 S. Ct. 2594 (2006).*

The voters' only hope is to argue that their proposed standard provides the type of rule Justice Kennedy is waiting for. The voters have proposed a rule under which a political gerrymander violates the Constitution when a state's sole motive is to completely disenfranchise the voters of a political party. As Justice Kennedy rejected almost the same test offered by the litigants in *Perry*, it is unlikely that a majority of justices would find the case to be justiciable. The only difference from *Perry* is that the Illanoy Legislature attempted to completely disenfranchise a political party. Perhaps such an extreme, unmixed motive would provide the standard Justice Kennedy seeks.

17. **Answer (C) is the best answer** because FCG never requested (and thus the Commission never rejected) a special-use permit to operate a church in the existing building on the property. FCG had only requested a permit to construct additional buildings on the property, and the Commission rejected this request because of the burden the *additional structures* would impose on the local infrastructure. FCG never requested, and the Commission never ruled on, a special-use permit for the *existing structures*. Judicial review should wait until the Commission denies such a permit. FCG's claim is not ripe.

FCG can overcome the ripeness objection if it can show that postponing judicial review would cause undue hardship. This is likely not the case, however, because FCG should have known before it bought the property that (1) the land was zoned agricultural and thus a special use permit was needed to operate a church and school, and (2) granting such a permit is within the Board's discretion. By purchasing anyway, FCG voluntarily assumed the risk that it might never gain permission for its preferred use. And, it was FCG's decision to omit use of the existing structures from its first application for a special-use permit, necessitating a second application. Thus, any hardship imposed by delaying judicial review should not be undue.

**Answer (A) is incorrect** because FCG meets all three of the standing requirements: injury, causation, and redressability. FCG is injured because it cannot make a desired use of its land: operation of a church. This injury is traceable to the Commission, as FCG needs a special-use permit to operate a church on its land, and the Commission is the only body that can grant that permit. Finally, the preliminary injunction would redress FCG's injury, as it would direct the Commission to issue the special-use permit needed to operate a church.

**Answer (B) is incorrect** because the case involves a live controversy. FCG still wishes to operate a church on its property; Middle County law still requires FCG to obtain a special-use permit to do so; and the Commission has not yet granted a special-use permit.

**Answer (D) is incorrect** because the Eleventh Amendment does not protect municipalities, such as cities and counties, from suit in federal court. *See Mt. Healthy City School District Board of Education v. Doyle*, 429 U.S. 274 (1977). Eleventh Amendment immunity does attach if the state has cooperated in or controlled the challenged municipal action. *See Pennhurst State School & Hospital v. Halderman*, 465 U.S. 89 (1984) (state provided all funding for challenged municipal program). Here, however, we have no indication that the state did so with regard to the county's land use decisions.

18. **Answer (C) is the best answer.**

**Answer (A) is incorrect** because Mr. Diaz' lawsuit satisfies all three elements of standing: injury, causation, and redressability. First, the Department's inaction on the 2008 license request kept Mr. Diaz from attending the Book Fair, which prevented him from conducting part of his business. Thus, the Department caused Mr. Diaz a concrete injury by interfering with his ability to earn a living. Second, this injury is directly traceable to the Department's failure to grant the license. Third, a writ of mandamus ordering the Department to issue the license would redress Mr. Diaz' injury, as it would allow him to travel to the Book fair to conduct his business. Of course, *at the time the motion was filed*, the 2008 Book Fair had already taken place and the court could no longer issue an order redressing Mr. Diaz' injury. But, standing is determined based on the facts as they exist *at the time the lawsuit is filed*. As discussed below, post-filing changes are relevant to the issue of mootness.

Ripeness has two main requirements: (1) the issues involved are suitable for judicial resolution, and (2) withholding judicial review will cause the plaintiff undue hardship. Here, the issue is a legal question (*i.e.*, the propriety of the Department's inaction), and federal courts regularly decide such issues. Further, withholding judicial review will impose an undue hardship, as the Department's inaction on his 2008 license application interferes with his ability to earn a living. Thus, Mr. Diaz' claim is ripe, and **Answer (B) is not the best answer**.

**Answer (C) is the best answer** because the passage of time has made the 2008 license application a moot issue. Mr. Diaz has requested only a writ of mandamus, which is an order that the Department issue the license. The 2008 license covers travel dates that have already passed. Thus, a writ of mandamus ordering the issuance of the 2008 travel license would have no effect — the claim is moot.

Mr. Diaz' case does not likely fit the mootness exception for claims capable of repetition yet evading review. Such claims must meet two requirements: (1) the challenged conduct must be "too short to be fully litigated prior to its cessation or expiration"; and (2) the parties must reasonably expect that "the same controversy will recur involving the same complaining party." *Murphy v. Hunt*, 455 U.S. 478 (1982). For example, in *Roe v. Wade*, 410 U.S. 113 (1973), the Court held that a pregnant woman's abortion challenge met this test because, first, "the normal 266-day human gestation period is so short that the pregnancy will come to term before the usual appellate process is complete," and second, that "[p]regnancy often comes more than once to the same woman." The same cannot be said for Mr. Diaz' lawsuit. Unlike a pregnant woman, Mr. Diaz is not boxed into a narrow time frame. The dates of the Book Fair are set years in advance, as Mr. Diaz currently has applications pending for travel through 2012. Further, the applicable federal law does not limit how far in advance he may apply for a license. So, if he applies early enough, there should be time to obtain a writ of mandamus prior to the time he needs to travel.

**Answer (D) is incorrect** because Eleventh Amendment immunity protects only *state* governments from suit in federal court. Here, Mr. Diaz has sued an agency of the *federal* government.

19. Mr. Diaz' suit regarding his 2008 application may now satisfy the mootness exception for cases capable of repetition yet evading review. Again, the two elements are: (1) the challenged conduct must be "too short to be fully litigated prior to its cessation or expiration"; and (2) the parties must reasonably expect that "the same controversy will recur involving the same complaining party." *Murphy v. Hunt*, 455 U.S. 478 (1982). Recall that a pregnant woman's abortion challenge meets the first element because the 266-day human gestation period is far too short to allow for trial and appellate review. *Roe v. Wade*, 410 U.S. 113 (1973). Under the license application scheme described above, Mr. Diaz would have (at most) 365 days for his lawsuit to make it through the system. In reality, however, the time would be shorter, as he would not necessarily file his application precisely one year ahead of time, and he would not file a lawsuit until the Department had unreasonably delayed its decision. As in *Roe*, the time window is likely too short to allow full litigation of the controversy.

Second, Mr. Diaz might reasonably expect a repeat of the Department's delay in approving his license application. Mr. Diaz' regular business involves importing books and other materials, and he regularly attends book fairs as part of this business. Further, he has regularly attended the Cuban International Book Fair since 2000, and his license applications for Book Fairs through 2012 (though premature) show his intent to continue to do so. Thus, Mr. Diaz might reasonably expect repetition of this controversy with the Department.

20. **Answer (B) is the best answer.**

While it is clear that Mr. Diaz' suit should be dismissed, it is a very close question whether the proper grounds should be ripeness or lack of standing. Indeed, the question illustrates the potential overlap between the two doctrines. Let us start by considering the elements of standing: injury, causation, and redressability. First, the Department's undue delay on Mr. Diaz' license requests will keep him from attending the 2008 Book Fair, which will prevent him from conducting part of his business. This is a concrete injury. But, it is not clear that this injury is either actual or imminent. Mr. Diaz' license applications for 2010–12 are premature and thus there is no pending decision due from the Department. Until Mr. Diaz makes timely applications, there can be no undue delay. Further, the Department recently granted Mr. Diaz' license application for 2009, illustrating that it is speculative, at best, whether Mr. Diaz is threatened with imminent injury. This is a strong argument against standing and thus for Answer (A).

**Answer (B) is also a credible answer** because his lawsuit is tantamount to a pre-enforcement legal challenge, which is the typical case raising a ripeness issue. For example, a pre-enforcement challenge might involve an abortion provider who sues to enjoin enforcement of a criminal abortion law prior to taking any action that might violate the law. Here, Mr. Diaz' claims regarding the 2010–12 license applications are akin to a pre-enforcement challenge because those applications are premature — they may not be acted upon by the Department, and Mr. Diaz currently faces no threat of adverse decision or undue delay. He wishes to obtain a judicial ruling without awaiting the threat of such a decision or delay.

Ripeness has two elements: (1) the issues involved are suitable for judicial resolution, and (2) withholding judicial review will cause the plaintiff undue hardship. Mr. Diaz likely does not meet the second element. Simply put, he does not face identifiable hardship if his lawsuit is postponed until he makes a timely application. Waiting to file suit will not keep him from doing his business in the interim. Further, as the Department has already granted Mr. Diaz's 2009 license request, it appears that the Department is considering his applications in a timely and reasonable manner. There is no reason to believe that a timely application for 2010–12 is likely receive different treatment. Because delaying judicial review will not cause undue hardship, the new claims are not ripe for judicial review.

So, we have strong arguments against both standing and ripeness. Indeed, students who chose **either answer (A) or (B) have made correct legal analyses**. The basis for the authors preferring answer (B) is that ripeness is the more typical basis for denying pre-enforcement judicial review. Yet, even the Supreme Court has decided such cases on standing grounds. So, on an exam, we would likely give equal credit to students who chose answer (A) or (B).

**Answer (C) is incorrect** because the events that would allegedly cause the plaintiff's injury have yet to occur. There is still the possibility that judicial action could correct that injury. But, as discussed in the preceding paragraph, Mr. Diaz must wait until the appropriate time to file the lawsuit.

**Answer (D) is incorrect** because Eleventh Amendment immunity protects only *state* governments from private lawsuits in federal court. Here, Mr. Diaz has sued an agency of the *federal* government.

21. **Answer (B) is the best answer.**

We can quickly eliminate answer (D). The text of the Eleventh Amendment, as well as its application by the Supreme Court, is limited to suits against *states*. Here, the plaintiffs are suing the *federal* government. Thus, the Eleventh Amendment does not bar the suit, and **answer (D) is incorrect**.

Ripeness can also be easily ruled out. The ripeness test applies to lawsuits brought before the challenged law has been enforced or implemented. Here, the challenged law — Congress' declaration — is already being implemented against the plaintiffs, as their division has received deployment orders. Because the plaintiffs' lawsuit is not premature, **answer (C) is incorrect**.

Standing should also be satisfied. Recall that standing has three requirements: (1) injury-in-fact, (2) causation, and (3) redressibility. First, the plaintiffs face a concrete injury of serious physical harm or death, and the injury is imminent, as the plaintiffs currently face deployment. Second, the plaintiffs' injury is caused by the defendant's conduct, as we are told that their imminent deployment is pursuant to the congressional declaration challenged by the lawsuit. Third, a court order that the declaration is void and enjoining deployment would redress the plaintiffs' injury. Of course, one might speculate that Congress and the President might ignore a court order. But in performing a standing analysis, courts assume that the relevant parties will abide by its ruling. Because the plaintiffs likely have standing, **Answer (A) is not the best answer**.

Political question is the strongest grounds for opposing the plaintiffs' lawsuit. Recall that *Baker v. Carr*, 369 U.S. 186 (1962), established that an issue is a political question if any one of six factors is "inextricable from the case at bar." *Id*. at 217. This is likely so for several of the factors. First, the Constitution textually commits the question of war declarations to the political branches. Congress is given the sole power to declare war, with no textual limitation on the form or substance of such a declaration. And once declared, war is waged by the President. Further, Congress is charged with raising and maintaining the military. The Constitution envisions no direct role in the war process for the federal courts.

Second, the Constitution gives no "judicially discoverable or manageable standards" for judging the sufficiency of a congressional declaration of war. The Constitution simply says: "The Congress shall have Power . . . To declare war. . . ." The mere word "declare" holds no clues as to the form or content of the declaration, and the judiciary would have no principled basis for deciding that issue. Instead, as prohibited by the third factor, such a decision would require a policy decision not suited to the judiciary. And as prohibited by the fourth factor, a decision voiding the declaration would show disrespect for Congress, which made the declaration, and the President, who is deploying troops in reliance on it.

The fifth and sixth factors also weigh against judicial review. Declarations of war and deployment of troops are matters that require "unquestioning adherence to a political decision already made." Troops of foreign allies, as well as United States troops already overseas, rely on military pronouncements from Congress and the President when making decisions. If the threat of judicial intervention causes them to question that reliance, lives could be lost. Moreover, judicial second-guessing would erode Congress' and the President's credibility with our allies, embarrassing them on the world stage.

In sum, the *Baker* factors weigh heavily in favor of finding a political question. Thus, **answer (B) is the best answer**.

22. **Answer (B) is the best answer**. Just as with a lawsuit against a state itself, the Eleventh Amendment bars a private lawsuit against a state official that seeks payment of retrospective money damages. Otherwise, a private plaintiff could circumvent the Eleventh Amendment by simply naming a different party. Such artful pleading should not defeat the underlying policy of preventing a private plaintiff from forcing a state to pay money from its treasury. **Answer (C) is incorrect** because it states the incorrect rule for this case.

**Answer (A) is incorrect** because it states the wrong rule. Answer (A) addresses lawsuits that name the *state* as a party, whereas this question lists the state *official* as a party.

**Answer (D) is incorrect** because the Act was not passed under a grant of congressional power that abrogates state sovereign immunity. To date, the Court has held that Congress may abrogate state sovereign immunity only when acting pursuant to its power to enforce the Fourteenth Amendment, *see Fitzpatrick v. Bitzer*, 427 U.S. 445 (1976), and the Bankruptcy Clause. *See Central Virginia Community College v. Katz*, 546 U.S. 356 (2006). Further, in *Seminole Tribe of Fla. v. Florida*, 517 U.S. 44 (1996), the Court specifically held that Congress' Commerce Clause power does *not* abrogate state immunity. Because Congress invoked the Commerce Clause in passing the Act, the Act does not abrogate Garyland's sovereign immunity.

23. **Answer (A) is the best answer.** In *Ex parte Young*, 209 U.S. 123 (1908), the Court recognized a narrow exception to state sovereign immunity under the Eleventh Amendment: a private plaintiff may sue a state official for an equitable order directing prospective compliance with the law. This rule applies even if the order would require the state official to make prospective payments from the state treasury. Here, Patterson is seeking just such an order. Specifically, he seeks an order directing the state Treasurer to comply with the federal adoption leave requirement, including payment of salary during the week of paid leave. This lawsuit fits the *Ex parte Young* exception.

**Answer (D) is incorrect** because it does not recognize the *Ex parte Young* exception.

**Answer (B) is incorrect** because, as discussed in the answer to the preceding question, the Act does not abrogate state sovereign immunity.

**Answer (C) is incorrect** because it states the wrong rule. Answer (C) addresses lawsuits that name the *state* as a party, whereas this question lists the state *official* as a party.

24.  **Answer (D) is the best answer** because it accurately reflects a central principle of the separation of powers doctrine. This doctrine does not require an airtight separation between the branches of the federal government. It acknowledges that all branches might be involved in the process of governing in any particular area. For example, the President appoints members of the Supreme Court, but only with the advice and consent of the Senate. The President is Commander-in-Chief, but only Congress has the power to declare war and raise and support the army and navy. Therefore, even though under these facts the President is given significant power to build post offices and allocate money, this does not necessarily lead to the conclusion that the USPMA is unconstitutional. The argument could be made that the President's powers under this law are simply part of his duties to execute the laws of the United States. This is not to say the law is constitutional. A court may consider this law as going too far toward aggrandizing Presidential power and too far toward congressional abdication of its authority, especially considering the power given the President to change budget allocations. However, answer (D) still is the best choice because it acknowledges that airtight separation is not required under the separation of powers doctrine.

**Answer (A) is incorrect** because it is too limited in its conception of the separation of powers doctrine. Although looking at the text of the Constitution is a part of any separation of powers analysis, such an analysis usually goes beyond the text of the Constitution to determine if one branch of the federal government is usurping another branch's power or aggrandizing its own power. Answer (A) is incorrect because it assumes that the power Congress is given in the Constitution to create post offices would end the separation of powers analysis.

**Answer (B) is incorrect** because it assumes that the President has no authority over the creation of new post offices except in times of national emergency. The relationship between Congress's power to legislate and the President's power to enforce or implement the laws passed by Congress is complex. The blending of legislative and executive powers in order to create and implement national legislation is not limited only to those occasions when there is a national emergency.

**Answer (C) is incorrect** because it is based on two false assumptions. First, it assumes that if a law is passed by Congress and signed by the President is does not violate separation of powers principles. This is incorrect. In *INS v. Chadha*, 462 U.S. 919 (1983), for example, the Supreme Court struck down legislation on separation of power grounds that had been passed by Congress and signed by the President. The doctrine of separation of powers does not permit one branch to acquiesce in its own diminishment. One branch cannot consent to its extinction or reduced importance in our constitutional scheme.

The concept of separation of powers was woven into the Constitution so that each branch of federal government would serve to keep in check the powers of the other branches in order to avoid a concentration of power that threatens freedom and representative government. Therefore, legislation passed and signed according to constitutional procedure may still violate the concept of separation of powers.

Second, this answer assumes that efficiency necessarily justifies an encroachment by one branch on the power of another branch. While efficiency is a consideration in deciding some separation of powers cases, it alone can never justify an encroachment that affects the core function of a branch of the federal government. The checks and balances of the Constitution and the concept of separation of powers were not devised for purposes of efficiency but to protect freedom.

25. **Answer (C) is the best answer** because it does not preclude the possibility of blended or shared power between the branches of the federal government, as discussed in the preceding question. The Constitution is written in broad terms and explicit grants of power usually have not been interpreted to preclude other branches of government from participating in that area. Therefore, while Congress is given power to regulate commerce, this does not preclude the President from acting to foster commerce or control it under duly created laws. The Department of Commerce, in fact, is a part of the executive branch and is very involved in regulating commerce. Answer (C) does not mean that a court could not hold the USPMA to violate the concept of separation of powers. This answer only reflects upon the fact that the power given to Congress to establish post offices does not preclude Congress from giving authority to the President to help govern in this area.

**Answer (A) is incorrect** for the reasons stated in analyzing the previous question. A duly enacted statute may violate the separation of powers doctrine if it violates the checks and balances woven into the federal system to prevent one branch from gathering excessive power.

**Answer (B) is incorrect** because it reduces the complex analysis required under the separation of powers doctrine to an efficiency test. The USPMA is a complex statute that gives authority to the President to create post offices when that power is textually committed to the Congress. It might be argued that the USPMA is nevertheless constitutional because it recognizes the need for executive flexibility to handle the modern communications realities, and that Congress acted to make the government able to respond to this modern revolution. On the other hand, it could be argued that Congress cannot cede its authority to create new post offices to the President without any Congressional oversight. The citizens of the United States are entitled to have their elected legislative representatives decide how best to use their money or at least have greater oversight than is provided for by this statute. This last point is particularly important under these facts because the President also is given the power to reallocate budget appropriations. This is not to say that the law will be declared unconstitutional. Indeed, the question is constructed so that it is difficult to decide what a court would do if the law were challenged on separation of power grounds. Rather, Answer (B) is incorrect because it does not acknowledge the complex nature of the separation of powers doctrine.

**Answer (D) is incorrect** because in *Clinton v. City of New York,* 524 U.S. 417 (1998), the Supreme Court held that the line-item veto legislation was unconstitutional.

26.  **Answer (B) is the best answer.** The most significant issue from this fact pattern is whether the Congress can delegate to the President the authority to change budget allocations from one department to another. The argument against such a delegation is that it changes the budget statute passed by Congress without a vote by the Congress authorizing this change. A similar argument prevailed in *Clinton v. City of New York,* 524 U.S. 417 (1998), in which the Supreme Court declared the line-item veto unconstitutional. The Court stated that by exercising such a veto over a particular budget line, the President was changing an act of Congress, and this was not permitted even when Congress authorized it. Moreover, such control over budget allocations could violate the concept of separation of power by giving the President not only authority over how to implement the USPMA but also authority over how to fund these changes. This may aggrandize Presidential power beyond what was intended by the Constitution. On the other hand, Presidents have often impounded or delayed spending appropriations, and Congress has even given the President impoundment authority in various statutes. The point is that the USPMA's giving the President control over budget allocations after the budget has been passed by Congress may result in the statute being declared unconstitutional as causing too great an increase the President's power, violating the concept of separation of powers. This makes Answer (B) the best answer even though authority exists that might be used to justify this power as within the President's executive prerogatives.

**Answer (A) is incorrect** because it suggests that the separation of powers doctrine is found in the text of the Constitution. The separation of powers doctrine is a term of art referring to the structure of the Constitution that distributes the power of the federal government between the three branches of government and requires each branch to maintain its power in order to serve as a check and balance against another branch acquiring excessive power.

**Answer (C) is incorrect** because it makes too categorical a disclaimer of the President's power under Article II. Article II, Section 1 states that "The executive power shall be vested in a President of the United States of America." The extent of the President's executive power that flows from this language is the subject of much debate. Answer (C) does not acknowledge this debate or the absence of any clear test to decide when the President is acting within his constitutional powers under Article II and when he has transgressed.

In the question at hand, Congress has agreed to the scheme, so it is unlikely that Congress will react negatively to the President enforcing this law. However, the issue is whether

Article II provides support for the President having authority to create post offices and rearrange budget allocations as provided in the statute. Simply put, the issue is whether the executive authority created by Article II encompasses such action. Many Supreme Court cases have defined the executive authority very broadly, and thus it may well include the functions described in this question. See *Whitman v. American Trucking Associations,* 531 U.S. 457 (2001), and *Loving v. United States*, 517 U.S. 748 (1996).

**Answer (D) is incorrect** because the Department of Commerce and the Department of the Interior have no independent power apart from the President. These departments are part of the executive branch of government, which the President controls. Because all power within these departments is within the President's power, no usurpation has occurred.

27. In *Morrison v. Olson*, 487 U.S. 654 (1988), the Supreme Court considered whether the independent counsel statute violated the principle of separation of powers. The Court took what is called a "functional approach" in analyzing this question. It looked at whether the statute's limitation on the President's executive prerogatives "impeded the President's ability to perform his constitutional duty" and whether loss of some prosecutorial power was so central to the functioning of the executive branch as to require that the statute be declared unconstitutional for how it affected the ability of the President to perform his duties. The Court used this same functional approach in *Cheney v. United States District Court for the District of Columbia,* 542 U.S. 367 (2004), to decide whether the Vice President of the United States had to comply with a district court civil discovery order. The Vice President argued that this judicial order threatened "substantial intrusions on the process by which those in closest operational proximity to the President advise the President." The Supreme Court remanded the case to the court of appeals to inquire whether the district court's discovery order "constituted an unwarranted impairment of another branch in the performance of its constitutional duties."

If the Court continues on this path of using a functional approach to deciding separation of power questions, then it increases the chances of the USPMA legislation surviving a constitutional challenge. If the *Morrison* test is used, then the question will be whether the President's ability to create post offices and change budget allocations impedes Congress's ability to perform its function and whether these activities are so central to Congress's functioning that they cannot be shared with the President. Creation of new post offices under the USPMA is likely to pass this functional analysis. The budget allocation issue is a closer question because it could be argued that control over the purse is at the core of Congress's power. However, no matter the final decision, a functional approach allows more blending and sharing of power between the branches of government because it sees only matters that threaten central or core functions as violating separation of powers.

Please note that the Supreme Court has not always used the functional approach. At times the Court has been quite rigid in following the text of the Constitution in declaring certain innovative statutes unconstitutional because of separation of power considerations. *See INS v. Chadha*, 462 U.S. 919 (1983). This often is referred to as a "formalist" approach. If the Court were to use the formalist approach in this fact pattern, then it is likely that the statute would violate separation of power principles particularly in giving the President the power to change budget allocations.

28.  **Answer (A) is the best answer.** The non-delegation doctrine states that Congress cannot delegate its legislative authority to administrative agencies. To do so would violate the Constitution, which gives legislative authority only to Congress. It is obvious, however, that governing in an increasingly complex world requires Congress to authorize administrative agencies to promulgate standards under the laws Congress passes. Congress simply does not have the time or the expertise to legislate on the micro-level as often is required. The questions then are, when has Congress delegated its legislative function in violation of the Constitution, and when has it simply enabled agencies to promulgate rules and standards to implement legislative?

Courts have exhibited great deference in this area and have repeatedly sustained legislation against claims that Congress has given agencies excessively broad powers to set standards. The test is whether Congress has provided an intelligible principle guiding the exercise of the delegated power. So for example, in *Whitman v. American Trucking Associations*, 531 U.S. 457 (2001), the Supreme Court upheld Congress' giving the Environmental Protection Agency authority "to establish uniform national standards [for air pollutants] at a level that is requisite to protect public health." The Court found this to be a sufficiently intelligible principle, given by Congress to the EPA; thus, the statute was not in violation of the non-delegation doctrine. Considering this decision and others showing similar deference, it is likely that the standard given to the Postal Service for determining when to create new post offices would be held to provide an intelligible principle, and thus (A) is the best answer.

**Answer (B) is incorrect** because Congress cannot delegate its legislative prerogatives. The Constitution gives legislative power only to Congress and, under our system of checks and balances, Congress cannot legislate away its power. Therefore, Answer (B) is incorrect because it fails to recognize this point. While it is true that courts have shown great deference to Congress's delegation decisions, as discussed in analyzing Answer (A), this deference should not be misconstrued as allowing Congress to decide, without limit, what powers it can delegate.

**Answer (C) is incorrect** for the same reasons discussed in analyzing Answer (A). The Courts have shown great deference to Congressional delegation decisions, and several cases have upheld delegations as broad in terms as the one in this hypothetical.

**Answer (D) is incorrect** for two reasons. First, it is not clear that the USPMA violates the principles of separation of powers, discussed in Questions 24 to 27 above. Second, the non-delegation doctrine and the principle of separation of powers are not necessarily interchangeable. While the principle of separation of powers requires that Congress not delegate its legislative authority, a statute can violate separation of powers limits without necessarily violating the non-delegation doctrine. For example, in this hypothetical, the USPMA could be found to violate the principle of separation of powers because of the power it gives the President to transfer money from one agency to another. But the statute could also be found not to violate the non-delegation doctrine. Answer (D), therefore, is incorrect because it fails to acknowledge that separation of powers is broader than the non-delegation doctrine.

29. **Answer (D) is the best answer.** In *INS v. Chadha,* 462 U.S. 919 (1983), the Court was faced with a statute that delegated power to the Attorney General of the United States to suspend the deportation of individuals who were deportable. Prior to passing this law, Congress itself would act on requests from individuals to suspend their deportation. Thus, Congress was attempting to extricate itself from this duty by giving it to the Attorney General. However, in order to maintain some oversight in this area, the statute also permitted either house of Congress to veto a decision by the Attorney General to suspend deportation. This is called a legislative veto. The Supreme Court found this one-house legislative veto unconstitutional because it violated the requirements of bicameralism (acts of Congress must be passed by both the House of Representatives and the Senate) and the Presentment Clause (all acts of Congress have to be presented to the President for Presidential approval or veto). The Court considered the legislative veto to be the equivalent of legislation and thus unconstitutional for its failure to abide by the rules of bicameralism and presentment.

By looking only at the text of the Constitution in reaching its decision, the Supreme Court used a formalistic mode of analysis. Essentially, this means that the Court did not consider whether the legislative veto functionally upset the balance of power between the branches of government so as to violate the principle of separation of powers. As made clear in Justice White's dissent in *Chadha,* Congress had frequently added a legislative veto to its laws in order to maintain some oversight authority in its relationship with administrative agencies. Therefore, to Justice White the question was whether this tool employed by Congress to control administrative agencies so upset the checks and balances of the federal system as to be unconstitutional. Justice White used a functional approach to analyzing the separation of powers question raised by the legislative veto. But the Court did not accept this mode of analysis and opted, instead, for a close reading of Constitutional text, declaring the legislative veto unconstitutional for its failure to follow bicameralism and the presentment requirement.

**Answer (A) is incorrect** because *Chada* did not consider whether a legislative veto interfered with core functions of the executive branch or impeded the branch's ability to carry out its constitutional responsibilities. Rather, the Court used a formalistic approach, discussed above in analyzing Answer (B). However, it is important to note that the Court has often used a functional approach in its separation of powers cases. For example, in *Morrison v. Olson,* 487 U.S. 654 (1988), decided after *Chadha,* the Court looked to whether the statute in question compromised a core or central function in deciding if the principle of separation of powers was violated. Therefore, even though the Court was highly formalistic in its analysis in *Chadha,* you should not assume that it will use this approach in every case that contains a separation of powers issue.

**Answer (B) is incorrect** because legislation passed and signed according to constitutional principles may still violate the concept of separation of powers. See the discussion of this concept in the answer to Question 24. Separation of powers analysis looks to whether an action by one branch concentrates too much power in that branch, and this analysis does not end simply because the challenged action was duly enacted.

**Answer (C) is incorrect** because the Court's prior pronouncements on the legislative veto were not based on the non-delegation doctrine. Therefore, it is not as likely that the Court would use that principle to declare unconstitutional the legislative veto in this hypothetical. It is interesting to note, however, the relationship between the non-delegation doctrine and the legislative veto. As discussed in Question 28 above, courts have been extremely deferential in upholding legislation that delegates significant authority to administrative agencies. In attempting to maintain some oversight in these areas, Congress passed a number of statutes that used the legislative veto to control agency action. The legislative veto was an attempt to balance the ever-increasing power of the administrative agencies with a check in the form of the legislative veto. Being deprived of the legislative veto, Congress lost one of the tools previously at its disposal to ensure its delegation to administrative agencies did not go too far.

30.   **Answer (A) is the best answer.** In a number of cases, the Supreme Court has made clear that Congress is not permitted to delegate executive power to itself or its agents. Agents are defined to include individuals appointed by Congress to boards and commissions in the executive branch. The Commission created in this question is clearly within the executive branch because it is under the control of the President. In *Buckley v. Valeo,* 424 U.S. 1 (1976), the Court held that it was unconstitutional for Congress to appoint members to the Federal Election Commission. The Court stated that Article II, Section 2 of the Constitution vests the appointment power of inferior officers, such as those on this SLA Commission, in "the President alone, to the Courts of Law, or in the Heads of Departments." Congress does not appear in this list. Moreover, because this is an executive agency, Congress would be taking for itself executive powers in making these appointments. In *Bowsher v. Synar,* 478 U.S. 714 (U.S. 1986), the Court rejected a statute that gave the comptroller general power to implement the Balanced Budget and Emergency Deficit Control Act of 1985. The comptroller general is part of the legislative branch, and it was unconstitutional for the legislative branch to give itself or its agent executive power to implement legislation.

**Answer (B) is incorrect** because, as stated in Answer (A) above, the Constitution specifically gives the power of appointment of inferior executive branch officers to the President.

**Answer (C) is incorrect** for the same reasons discussed in the analysis of Answer (A). The Constitution does not give Congress appointment power over executive branch personnel, and the Supreme Court has held that congressional control over those who enforce or administer laws violates separation of powers principles. Separation of powers principles are not satisfied simply because one branch is sharing power with another branch. Further, the executive branch's apparent agreement to share the appointment power here does not end the inquiry. The Court has explained that Congress and the President cannot waive separation of powers limits on their own powers. This is because the very purpose of separation of powers is to check abuse of federal power, and thereby protect citizens from tyranny. So, regardless of any agreement among the branches, the question remains whether one branch has reached beyond its authority and thereby taken too much power. This aggrandizement of power threatens the checks and balances that were created to keep one branch from acquiring so much power as to threaten the constitutional structure.

**Answer (D) is incorrect** because courts do not always defer to the other branches of government when national security matters are involved. In several important cases, the Court has declared unconstitutional government actions defended on national security grounds. *See Youngstown Sheet & Tube,* 343 U.S. 579 (1952). In other cases, the Court has not accepted a national security rationale as sufficient to justify ignoring constitutional guarantees. *See Hamdi v. Rumsfeld,* 542 U.S. 507 (2004).

31. **Answer (C) is the best answer**, but only because the other three answers are so clearly wrong. Article II creates the executive branch of the federal government, and it is short and simple. It vests the executive power of the federal government in the office of President. But it does not tell us what is covered within the parameters of that executive power. In addition to the powers listed in Article II, the President has inherent powers. An understanding of the Court's approach to inherent presidential power begins with an understanding of the various opinions in *Youngstown Sheet & Tube*, 343 U.S. 579 (1952). The question before the Court in *Youngstown Sheet & Tube* was whether the President could justify his seizure of an entire industry based on his inherent executive powers. President Truman justified this seizure on grounds of national defense and the effect a steel strike would have on the Korean War.

By a vote of 6-3, the Supreme Court declared the President's action unconstitutional because it violated separation of powers principles. But the reasoning of each Justice in the majority was different. Justice Black viewed the President's power as limited to what is expressly given in the Constitution or by statute. Because no statute authorized the President to seize the mills and because no express provision of the Constitution provided such authority, Justice Black found the actions unconstitutional. To Justice Black, the Constitution gave the President no inherent executive authority.

Most of the majority did not agree with Justice Black's view that the President has no inherent executive authority. Several of the Justices looked at the actions of Congress in passing the Taft-Hartley Act and concluded that Congress had explicitly rejected the remedy of seizure of striking industries in times of national emergency. Therefore, Justices Frankfurter, Jackson, Burton, and Clark agreed that the President acted beyond his authority. Yet, each of these Justices recognized inherent executive authority that could, under the appropriate facts, include seizure of an industry to protect the nation.

When we combine these concurring opinions with the dissenting opinions, we should conclude that the Supreme Court has recognized the President's inherent executive authority under the Constitution. The constitutionality of his use of this inherent power depends on the facts. In this question the facts do not lead to a clear answer and require us to look closely at Justice Jackson's concurring opinion in *Youngstown Sheet & Tube*. This concurring opinion carefully describes the different possibilities in the relationship between the President and Congress that lead to different levels of inherent executive authority. To Justice Jackson, the President is most justified when acting pursuant to an express or implied authorization from Congress, and he is the least justified when acting in contravention to an express or implied statement of the will of Congress.

However, Justice Jackson also recognized a middle ground where Congress has not acted to grant or deny executive authority. In this area, Justice Jackson determined it was impossible to formulate any prescribed rules. Determining whether the President acted beyond his inherent powers in this middle ground would depend on whether the President's actions violated the separation of powers.

In this question the Court would consider whether beginning to build the fence was an emergency. This seems somewhat doubtful since completion of the fence will take time, which argues against this being an imminent threat. In that case, the Court might conclude that the President's inherent power does not cover such a drastic measure, and that the President has violated separation of powers principles. On the other hand, the facts presented to the Court may indicate that starting construction is sufficiently important to national security to justify the President in beginning the process, a process that Congress can stop at any time either through legislation or ceasing funding for the project. In any event, this question poses a situation in Justice Jackson's middle category: the President's action is neither authorized nor forbidden by Congress. The Court's decision will be based on the facts and not on any prescribed rules. Answer (C) is best because it is the only answer that adopts this flexible approach.

**Answer (A) is incorrect** because Article II does not specifically state that the President has authority to take action to protect the nation. Article II is a broad statement of executive authority with few specifics. The President's authority to protect the nation is based on inherent or implied power not a specific grant of power in Article II.

**Answer (B) is incorrect** because the President does not have to wait for Congress to pass a law before he may act to protect the nation. *See The Prize Cases*, 67 U.S. 635 (1863). Conditions may require immediate action, and even if Congress is debating a matter, the President may be justified in taking action to avert a threat. This is part of his inherent power. Nevertheless, under these facts, the on-going congressional debate of the electrified fence may persuade the Court that the President has exceeded his inherent power in taking action while this is happening. This is particularly true since Congress is considering weighty policy issues involving this matter. In Justice Jackson's middle category, the Court will examine all the surrounding facts to determine if the President is justified by his inherent power to take this action.

**Answer (D) is incorrect** because it does not correctly apply the reasoning found in Chief Justice Vinson's dissenting opinion. In his dissenting opinion, Chief Justice Vinson implied that the President has extensive inherent authority under the Constitution, and his actions to protect the nation were constitutional under this authority, without reference to authorization by Congress. If the reasoning in the dissenting opinion were followed in deciding the question, it is likely the President's actions would be upheld as constitutional.

32. In *Clinton v. City of New York*, 524 U.S. 417 (1998), the Supreme Court closely scrutinized the text of the Constitution and decided the case on a narrow reading of

whether the President's line-item veto authority violated the requirements in Article I, Section 7 for passing amendments to legislation. The Court in *Clinton v. City of New York* did not consider whether the President has any inherent authority under Article II to use a line-item veto. Indeed, the Court refused to consider separation of powers concepts in deciding the case. If the Court's approach in *Youngstown Sheet & Tube v. Sawyer,* 343 U.S. 579 (1952), had been followed in the line-item veto case, the Court would have decided whether the President's inherent executive powers justified the use of the line-item veto, especially in view of Congress authorizing the line-item veto. Given the number of Justices in *Youngstown Sheet & Tube* who agreed that the President had inherent executive authority and the number of Justices in that case who considered congressional authorization of Presidential action important in deciding the limits of Presidential power, it might well be that the Court would have upheld the constitutionality of the line-item veto if it had used the approach found in *Youngstown Sheet & Tube.*

33.   **Answer (B) is the best answer.** The Constitution clearly gives the President the appointment power over all federal officers. Article II, Section 2 states that the President: "shall nominate, and by and with the Advice and Consent of the Senate, shall appoint Ambassadors, other public Ministers and Consuls, Judges of the Supreme Court, and all others Officers of the United States, whose Appointments are not herein otherwise provided for. . .but the Congress may vest the Appointment of such inferior Officers, as they think proper, in the President alone, to the Courts of Law, or in the Heads of Departments." Therefore, if the only issue is whether the President may appoint members of this commission, then the appointment process used in this statute is constitutional.

The more interesting constitutional question is whether these commissioners are inferior officers so that Congress may vest some of the appointment power in the courts of law. If they are inferior officers, then Congress has power to decide who appoints them. If they are not inferior officers, then the President must appoint them. See the language of Article II, Section 2 quoted above. The Supreme Court has held that Congress has the ability to determine who is an inferior officer. *Ex parte Siebold*, 100 U.S. (10 Otto) 371 (1879). Commissioners of agencies have uniformly been considered inferior officers. *See, e.g., Rice v. Ames*, 180 U.S. 371 (1901). Further, the Court has looked at the power of the federal officer as compared to an executive branch cabinet secretary to decide whether an officer is inferior or not. For example, the Court considered an independent prosecutor to be inferior to the Attorney General in *Morrison v. Olson*, 487 U.S. 654 (1988), because the independent prosecutor had much less authority, was appointed for a set period of time, and was given specific instructions as to jurisdiction. Considering this precedent, the commissioners appointed in the question are likely to be seen as inferior officers. Therefore, Congress is not limited to vesting their appointment in the President.

**Answer (A) is incorrect** because the Constitution does not require that appointments be for any specific term of years, except that Article III judges are appointed for life terms.

**Answer (C) is incorrect** because the Constitution does not require that a specific removal procedure or any removal procedure be stated in legislation. Some legislation does mandate a certain removal procedure; some legislation does not. But Congress is not required in its legislation to provide for a removal procedure.

**Answer (D) is incorrect** because the Constitution allows the appointment power of inferior officers to be vested in the judiciary as discussed above. The Supreme Court has upheld the constitutionality of vesting this appointment power in the courts in *Morrison v. Olson*, 487 U.S. 654 (1988). However, as the Court stated in *Morrison*, the judiciary cannot retain any supervisory power once the appointment is made, as that would have separation of powers implications. Under the facts of the question, the judiciary does not retain supervisory powers; thus, the appointment of three members of the commission by the courts is likely constitutional. One caveat is in order. Because the statute is silent on the procedure for removal, this could be interpreted as giving both the President and the judiciary power to dismiss a commissioner. If so, then the statute may violate the separation of powers as the judiciary would be supervising an agency whose decisions the judiciary will be reviewing. Thus, the courts would have both executive and judicial authority in violation of separation of powers principles.

34. **Answer (C) is the best answer** because it takes into account the Supreme Court's holding in *Weiner v. United States*, 357 U.S. 349 (1958). In *Weiner,* the Supreme Court considered whether the President could remove a member of the War Claims Commission. The job of the War Claims Commission was to award claims based on merit and not on political influence. The statute creating the commission contained no specific removal provision. Therefore, the President argued that his power as head of the executive branch allowed him to fire the commissioner. The Supreme Court disagreed, stating that the President does not have absolute power to remove members of an agency that is to operate free from executive branch interference. In our hypothetical, the statute clearly states that the purpose of the Commission is to guard against political influence in border security matters. See Question 30. **Answer (C) is the best answer** because the President arguably violated separation of powers principles by firing the commissioners, thereby ignoring the statutorily mandated independence.

Obviously, the removal power case law does not clearly define when Congress can curtail the President's removal authority. The Supreme Court has held that the President, as head of the executive branch, may remove any member of the executive branch. *Myers v. United States*, 272 U.S. 52 (1926). However, the Court also has held that this inherent removal power does not extend to independent agencies created by Congress, which follows from the fact that such agencies are created to be independent of executive branch control. *Humphrey's Executor v. United States*, 295 U.S. 602 (1935). Many have argued that the Constitution creates a single executive. Therefore, allowing Congress to create independent agencies whose members are not subject to the President's removal power violates the separation of powers. The Court has not agreed with this position. See Answer (B) below. But then, the Court's decisions on removal authority are not entirely consistent or models of clarity. In this area we can say with some certainty that: 1) the President has power, almost without limitation, to remove members of the executive branch; 2) this power is only limited when the Court perceives a need for independence in an executive branch member—such as the independent prosecutor in *Morrison v. Olsen*, 487 U.S. 654 (1988) — or the need for independence in a commission or board — as in *Weiner*. But even then Congress cannot eliminate all executive removal power. See discussion of *Morrison* in Answer (D) below.

**Answer (A) is incorrect** because this Commission is not an independent agency. In Question 30 you are told that the Commission is under the President's control. Independent federal agencies are not under Presidential control. They are created by Congress and do not answer to the President. The power of Congress to create independent agencies, which are not part of the executive branch, has been upheld by the Supreme Court. *Humphrey's Executor v. United States*, 295 U.S. 602 (1935).

However, the facts in this question make it clear that this commission is not an independent agency since it is controlled by the President.

**Answer (B) is incorrect** for two reasons. First, nothing in the facts indicates that this commission engages in quasi-legislative and quasi-judicial tasks. Such tasks are often performed by independent agencies such as the Federal Trade Commission, which, for example, conducts administrative hearings and issues orders associated with these hearings. But it should be noted that deciding whether a board or commission engages in quasi-legislative and quasi-judicial tasks is not always an easy process. The analysis involved in this decision is part of the jurisprudence of Administrative Law. For Constitutional Law purposes, the distinction is important because generally the President has almost absolute authority to remove members of the executive branch, but does not have this broad removal authority over members of an independent agency. See Answer (C) above. Second, this answer is incorrect because if the Commission did engage in quasi-legislative and quasi-judicial tasks, then it likely would not be part of the executive branch as typically executive powers are not seen as including legislative and judicial prerogatives.

**Answer (D) is incorrect** because it fails to take into account the reasoning of the Court in *Morrison v. Olson*, 487 U.S. 654 (1988) by suggesting that the President is precluded from making such a claim. In *Morrison*, the Supreme Court considered the constitutionality of a statute that limited the power of the attorney general to remove an independent counsel only for cause. The Court looked at whether this removal limitation was "of such a nature that [it] impede[s] the President's ability to perform his constitutional duty." (Remember that the attorney general is a member of the President's cabinet, and thus a limitation on the attorney general is equivalent to a limitation on the President.) The Court noted that the statute did not absolutely stop the President from removing the independent counsel since the counsel could be removed for cause. An absolute ban on the President's removal power would likely have been held unconstitutional. The *Morrison* Court concluded that the limitations on removal in that case did not impede the President's ability to do his job, and thus were constitutional. But nothing in *Morrison* precludes the President from making the claim, in another case, that restricting his ability to remove a member of the executive branch unconstitutionally intrudes on his power. The answer is incorrect in stating that the President cannot even make this claim.

35. *Bowsher v. Synar,* 478 U.S. 714 (1986), involved the Balanced Budget and Emergency Deficit Control Act of 1985, which authorized the Comptroller General of the United States to report, and make recommendations on budget reductions, to the President in an effort to control the federal deficit. This Act was challenged on grounds that it imposed executive functions on the Comptroller General, who was not a member of the executive branch. The Court agreed that the Act was unconstitutional in its giving executive duties to the Comptroller General. The power of Congress to remove the Comptroller General was an important factor in the Court's conclusion that the Constitution was violated. The Court noted that by reserving "for itself the power of

removal of an officer charged with the execution of the laws," Congress gained control over executive functions forbidden to it by the Constitution. Thus, the Act was unconstitutional because it gave executive power to an officer who could be removed by Congress. In this decision, the Court took a formalistic approach to resolving the separation of powers issue, as contrasted to the functional approach advocated by Justice White in his dissent.

36. **Answer (A) is the best answer.** Although it is not a great choice, Answer (A) at least recognizes that, in answering the question, one has to consider the concept of executive privilege. The other answers do not consider how executive privilege affects the answer, and so are less correct than Answer (A). Answer (A) is not a great answer because it fails to address the nuances of executive privilege, such as whether it applies with more force to civil matters than it does to criminal inquiries. But, at least it recognizes the central role this privilege will play in deciding whether the President has to comply with the Freedom of Information Act request.

What is executive privilege? It is a privilege considered fully by the Supreme Court for the first time in *United States v. Nixon*, 418 U.S. 683 (1974), the case addressing whether President Nixon had to comply with a criminal subpoena for information related to the Watergate burglary. Presidents have claimed the privilege throughout American history, asserting that it was a necessary part of their ability to function as the nation's chief executive. Presidents have argued the evident need to protect the confidentiality of communications to the President. Without such protection, the President would not be able to receive candid advice and disturbing information. In *United States v. Nixon*, the Supreme Court acknowledged the existence of this executive privilege as it applied to confidential communications by and to the President. Therefore, any request to a President for evidence of communications to him, as in this question, would trigger an analysis of whether the communications were protected by executive privilege.

**Answer (B) is incorrect** because it fails to recognize the possibility that the President may have to produce this information even when separation of powers principles are considered. In *United States v. Nixon,* the Court recognized that a claim of executive privilege was "inextricably rooted in the separation of powers." However, the Court rejected the idea that the separation of powers foreclosed further analysis of whether the privilege absolutely protected the President. The *Nixon* Court found the privilege to be only "presumptive," which allowed a balancing analysis that weighed other considerations — such as the need for evidence in a criminal case — against separation of powers principles to decide whether the privilege would protect the President from having to produce the evidence. From this, it is clear that Answer (B) is incorrect because it fails to acknowledge that the President is not absolutely protected by separation of powers principles from having to produce confidential communications.

**Answer (C) is incorrect** because it does not acknowledge that adhering to the requirements of a statute, such as the Freedom of Information Act, does not resolve constitutional issues involved in forcing the President to surrender evidence of confidential communications. Filing a procedurally proper request is only the first step in the legal analysis. The next steps are to decide whether executive privilege arguably protects this information and whether the facts of the case and the need for the information outweigh the President's need to protect confidential communications.

**Answer (D) is incorrect** because it does not address the protections available to the President under the concept of executive privilege.

37.    **Answer (C) is the best answer** because it closely follows the Court's holding in *United States v. Nixon.* After balancing the competing interests presented by the facts in the case, the Supreme Court concluded that the best method to protect both the President's need for confidentiality and the public's need for the fair administration of criminal justice was to grant the President a presumptive privilege and then require the prosecutor to establish that the materials were "essential to the justice of the [pending criminal] case." This places the burden on the prosecutor to overcome the presumptive executive privilege granted the President before the prosecution can have access to the subpoenaed information. Unless the prosecutor can carry this burden, the subpoena should be quashed.

**Answer (A) is incorrect** because it assumes that the President is absolutely protected by the separation of powers from having to comply with a grand jury subpoena. This absolute position was rejected by the Supreme Court in *United States v. Nixon*, 418 U.S. 683 (1974), when the Court ruled that President Nixon's claim of executive privilege did not foreclose the possibility that he would have to comply with a criminal subpoena. Therefore, Answer (A) is incorrect because it assumes the subpoena would be quashed by the President's steadfast reliance on the separation of powers without more.

**Answer (B) is incorrect**, but it is a close call. To understand why this is true, it is important to understand the basis of the Court's decision in *United States v. Nixon*. In that case, the President did not argue that the subpoenaed material involved national security matters. Indeed, President Nixon made only a general claim of the need to protect confidentiality. The Supreme Court, in analyzing the President's general claim of confidentiality, made clear that its decision might be different if the President had made a more specific declaration that the subpoenaed materials involved military or diplomatic secrets. So *United States v. Nixon* does not answer whether the President's simple assertion of national security would be enough by itself to require a court to rule in the President's favor and deny access to the information.

One other part of the *United States v. Nixon* decision leads to the conclusion that Answer (B) is incorrect. In that case, the Court went to great lengths to discuss the powerful concepts of due process of law and the need for the fair administration of criminal justice. The Court made clear the importance it gives to these concepts with its decision to force the President to comply with a criminal subpoena in order to protect these ideals. Considering the weight and importance of these concepts, it seems reasonable to assume that the President cannot avoid a grand jury subpoena in a criminal matter by merely asserting that the communications involve national security. The courts will likely want some further showing — an affidavit or a more detailed explanation — of the effect on national security. It is not clear how much more the courts would require, and it seems unlikely that an *in camera* inspection would necessarily be ordered because even that might compromise national security. Nevertheless, given the great weight *United States v. Nixon* placed on protecting the fair administration of criminal justice, it is likely the President will have to do something more than just claim national security to be successful in quashing the subpoena.

**Answer (D) is incorrect** because the Court stated clearly in *United States v. Nixon* that a claim of executive privilege was not absolute even though President Nixon argued that this privilege was absolute under the separation of powers.

38.   **Answer (A) is the best answer** because it most accurately reflects the Supreme Court's reasoning in *Cheney v. United States District Court for the District of Columbia*, 542 U.S. 367 (2004). There, the Court was asked whether the Vice President must comply with a civil discovery order. The Vice President argued that separation of powers principles protected him from complying with the civil discovery order. Further, the Vice President argued that he did not have to assert a claim of executive privilege before a court could consider his separation of powers contentions.

The Court agreed that the executive branch may rely on separation of powers principles to resist a civil discovery order without first claiming executive privilege. The Court explained that executive privilege and separation of powers are not identical concepts, and that the President's ability to resist judicial process does not necessarily depend on a valid claim of executive privilege. The President may also resist compliance if discovery would impede his ability to perform his constitutional duties, which duties include the need to receive advice and recommendations untainted by fear of public disclosure. Therefore, **Answer (A) is clearly correct** and **Answer (C) is clearly incorrect.**

Prior to *Cheney*, the last significant Supreme Court pronouncement on executive privilege came in *United States v. Nixon*, 418 U.S. 683 (1974). *Cheney* also is important because it sheds new light on the constitutional parameters of executive privilege. How, then, does *Cheney* inform our understanding of executive privilege?

First, we can expect greater judicial protection of Presidential prerogatives in civil cases than in criminal proceedings. *Nixon* involved a criminal proceeding, and the importance of "every man's evidence" to the criminal justice system. According to *Cheney*, the need for information in a civil case is not as urgent or significant, and thus does not have the same "constitutional dimensions." Therefore, the President's decision to resist civil discovery creates less tension between the executive's need to protect confidentiality and the judiciary's need for evidence.

Second, the information sought from the President in the *Nixon* case was indispensable to the prosecution. If the Court had allowed President Nixon to resist the subpoena, the President's prerogatives would have thwarted a criminal prosecution, seriously eroding the judiciary's role in the constitutional scheme. Conversely, *Cheney* did not present facts of the same magnitude. Considering the tenuous nature of the underlying civil lawsuit, denial of the discovery request — or even loss of the case — would not impair the constitutional role of either Congress or the courts. After *Cheney*, we can expect greater judicial protection of Presidential prerogatives when the information sought is deemed non-essential to the core functions of a co-equal branch of the federal government.

Third, the subpoenas in *Nixon* were narrow in scope, and the prosecutor had made an initial showing that the requested material was necessary for the case. In contrast, the civil discovery requests in *Cheney* were sweeping, and the plaintiffs made no showing that the information sought from the Vice President was vital. While the lower court categorically refused to consider the Vice President's separation of powers argument until the Vice President first asserted executive privilege, the Supreme Court made clear that the executive branch need neither invoke executive privilege nor make particularized objections before its separation of powers claim will be heard. "*Nixon* does not require the executive branch to bear the onus of critiquing the unacceptable discovery requests line by line." After *Cheney*, we can expect courts to require those seeking civil discovery of private communications from the President to make an initial showing of significant need for the information before the executive branch must assert executive privilege or defend against production on separation of powers grounds.

**Answer (B) is incorrect** because a person may have to comply with a subpoena even if not a party to the federal lawsuit. See the Federal Rules of Civil Procedure pertaining to civil discovery.

**Answer (C) is incorrect** for the reasons stated in **Answer (A)**.

**Answer (D) is incorrect** because *Cheney* treated the discovery subpoena to the Vice President as meriting the same separation of powers scrutiny as would a subpoena request to the President. The core question is whether the essential functioning of a branch of government is impaired — here, the executive branch's need to obtain advice and recommendations without fear of public disclosure. The *Cheney* Court's separation of powers analysis was not limited to the technical question of whether the President or Vice President participated in the communication. Rather, the Court used a broader, more flexible approach that focused on whether disclosing the communication would impair the quality of advice and recommendations received by the executive.

39. *Marbury v. Madison*, 5 U.S. (1 Cranch) 137 (1803), did not address the question of whether the Supreme Court was the only branch of the federal government with the final authority to decide what is constitutional. The decision in *Marbury* was focused primarily on justifying the power of the Court to engage in any judicial review of the actions of the other two branches. Because the Constitution was silent on the issue of the Supreme Court's review of the other co-equal branches of government, Chief Justice

Marshall wanted to use the *Marbury* case to establish that principle. The Court in *United States v. Nixon*, 418 U.S. 683 (1974), however, went further and rejected President Nixon's argument that, as a co-equal branch of the federal government, the President was as able to determine the constitutionality of executive privilege just as well as the Court. While the *Nixon* Court cited *Marbury* as authority for its decision on this issue, the reasoning of *Marbury* is not authority for the proposition that the Court is the final arbiter of what is constitutional vis-à-vis conflicting decisions on constitutionality made by either the Congress or the President. Over time our nation has adopted the position that the Supreme Court has the final say even in constitutional disputes with one of the co-equal branches. But *Marbury* never went that far.

40. **Answer (B) is the best answer.** It is well established that the President is absolutely immune from a suit for money damages for conduct in office. This applies to sitting, as well as past, Presidents. *See Nixon v. Fitzgerald*, 457 U.S. 731 (1982).

**Answer (A) is incorrect** because it does not pertain to the facts given in the question. The facts are insufficient to decide if the President was a proper defendant under the Federal Rules of Civil Procedure. Because the answer gives an unequivocal answer that the case will be dismissed, it is obviously wrong. You do not have enough information to conclude that such a dismissal would occur.

**Answer (C) is incorrect** for the reasons stated in the discussion of Answer (B). The President does have absolute immunity from a suit for money damages, even if the suit alleges intentional wrongs. Absolute means exactly that: absolute — no matter what the allegations.

**Answer (D) is incorrect** because it assumes that a statute will prevail over the Supreme Court's decision that the President has absolute immunity in these cases. The statute will not prevail for a variety of reasons. First, nothing in the facts indicates that the whistle blower statute is specifically directed at the President. It is more likely that it is a general statute, and thus has little force behind it to justify using it against the President. Second, the Supreme Court's decision in *Nixon v. Fitzgerald* was based on separation of powers principles. The Court decided that case based on the President's unique role in our system of government. Given this unique role, the President must be free of worry about possible lawsuits related to his official duties. Clearly, the Supreme Court's reasoning in *Nixon v. Fitzgerald* was based on the separation of powers and the recognition of the constitutional structure that affords the President this distinct role. Thus the Supreme Court's decision is grounded in its interpretation of the Constitution. The Constitution takes precedence over a statute, providing another reason why Answer (D) is incorrect.

41. In *Mississippi v. Johnson*, 71 U.S. (4 Wall.) 475 (1866), the Supreme Court held that it did not have jurisdiction to enjoin the President. However, from the time of that decision until now, we have seen a great judicial willingness to permit suits for injunctions to go forward against government officials. The question then is whether this modern judicial willingness will affect today's Court in deciding whether to adhere to its 1866 decision in *Mississippi v. Johnson*. Arguably, the Court would adhere to this precedent and would require the dismissal of a civil lawsuit against a President even if limited to only injunctive relief. The same arguments made in *Nixon v.*

*Fitzgerald*, 457 U.S. 731 (1982), likely would prevail based on the need for the President to be free to make decisions without fear of legal consequences given his unique role in our constitutional structure. Can a sitting President be indicted and criminally prosecuted while in office? We have no definitive answer to this question. It was debated in 1974, when a grand jury was considering indicting President Nixon. It was debated in 1998, when President Clinton's possible perjury offense was discussed. But it has never been resolved. Many argue that the sole remedy for Presidential criminal behavior is impeachment and removal from office. Others dispute this and rely on the concept that no person is above the law, including the President.

42.   **The Answer (D) is the best answer.** This is the precise holding of the Court in *Clinton v. Jones*, and it meshes well with the discussion below in analyzing Answer (C). The Court held that separation of powers does not require the staying of *all* private actions against a sitting President for his or her actions before becoming President, but it did not foreclose a different result in a different case.

      **Answer (A) is incorrect** because the Supreme Court refused to give President Clinton temporary immunity while President even though he requested such immunity.

      **Answer (B) is incorrect** because the Supreme Court rejected this argument tendered by President Clinton as a justification for the temporary immunity he was seeking.

      **Answer (C) is incorrect** because the Supreme Court noted that separation of powers principles should be considered in evaluating the burden placed on a President when sued for unofficial behavior before becoming President. The Court stated that it had "no dispute with the initial premise" of President Clinton's separation of powers argument. *Clinton v. Jones,* 520 U.S. 681 (1997). However, it rejected the argument that allowing the lawsuit to proceed against the President would violate separation of powers. Thus, it did not reject completely the "possible application" of such separation of powers principles, making Answer (C) incorrect.

43. **Answer (D) is the best answer.** The Supreme Court has consistently held that the President has greater inherent power in matters of foreign policy than in the domestic arena. For example, in *United States v. Curtiss-Wright Export Corp.*, 299 U.S. 304 (1936), the Court agreed that the President could proclaim arms sales to foreign countries illegal. The Court held that the realities of foreign affairs require that the President speak for the country and be accorded greater inherent power to do so. The Supreme Court followed this course in *Dames & Moore v. Regan*, 453 U.S. 654 (1981), in which the Court upheld the President's authority to nullify attachments and liens on Iranian assets and to suspend legal claims against Iran as part of an agreement resolving a foreign policy dispute between the United States and Iran.

    **Answer (A) is incorrect** because it ignores the fact that the Department of Commerce is part of the executive branch. Therefore, authority given to it is equivalent to authority given the President. Because the President has inherent power in matters of foreign policy, his power is extended to the Department of Commerce.

    **Answer (B) is incorrect** because the non-delegation doctrine is unlikely to apply in this case. That doctrine prohibits Congress from delegating its constitutional powers to another branch of government. In this question, the President also has inherent power in the foreign policy field. Thus, Congress is not delegating powers that only it has under the Constitution, and thus is not violating the non-delegation doctrine. *See United States v. Curtiss-Wright Export Corp.,* 299 U.S. 304 (1936). Moreover, Congress arguably has given the Department of Commerce sufficiently intelligible principles to follow—national security and protecting the economy— to satisfy the non-delegation doctrine.

    **Answer (C) is incorrect** because it is too limited in explaining the basis for the President's inherent power in the foreign policy field. While part of this inherent power flows from his position as Commander-in-Chief, it also flows from the President's unique position as the paramount voice representing the foreign policy interests of the United States.

44. The answer is probably "yes," the President may unilaterally rescind a treaty. In *Goldwater v. Carter*, 444 U.S. 996 (1979), Senator Barry Goldwater sued President Carter because the President had rescinded a treaty with Taiwan as part of the United States formal recognition of the People's Republic of China. Senator Goldwater argued that the Senate must approve a treaty rescission just as it must approve a treaty. The Supreme Court dismissed the case on grounds of non-justiciability. The plurality of the

Court declared this to be a political question. Justice Powell concluded that the case was not ripe until the Senate acted to disapprove the rescission. In any event, it is likely that if Presidential action to rescind a treaty were challenged, it would be dismissed on justiciability grounds. Therefore, the President may act to unilaterally rescind a treaty unless the Supreme Court changes its decision in *Goldwater v. Carter*, agrees to review such a rescission, and declares it unconstitutional — which does not appear likely to happen.

45. **Answer (B) is the best answer.** Presidents have used executive agreements to achieve important foreign policy results for decades. For example, President Roosevelt, through the famous Lend-Lease Program, authorized by executive agreement the lending of naval vessels to Great Britain prior to the United States' direct involvement in World War II. The United States diplomatically recognized the Soviet Union by way of an executive agreement. *See United States v. Pink*, 315 U.S. 203 (1942). And, the President compromised legal claims of US citizens against Iran through an executive agreement. *See Dames & Moore v. Regan*, 453 U.S. 654 (1981). This is not to say that a President could not go too far in using executive agreements so that he is seen as usurping legislative power by avoiding presenting a matter for ratification as a treaty. In this question, it could be argued that the President is trying to change national environmental policy through the "back door" by making it part of a foreign policy initiative. The Court could look behind this, decide it gives too much power to the President (in violation of the separation of powers) and declare it unconstitutional. This is particularly true in this question since the ozone emission issue is already handled in a duly enacted federal law. But for now, the Supreme Court has permitted the President to use executive agreements to accomplish important foreign policy goals, even when those goals also involve domestic matters, such as compromising legal claims as in *Dames & Moore*.

**Answer (A) is incorrect** because an executive agreement cannot take control over a duly enacted federal law. Executive agreements are not considered the legal equivalent of a federal statute. However, a treaty—as contrasted to an executive agreement— is considered the legal equivalent of a statute. Therefore, if this matter had been handled by a treaty ratified by the Senate, the treaty would take precedence over the federal statute on ozone emissions since the treaty came later in time. Conversely, a federal statute that comes later in time takes precedence over an earlier treaty.

**Answer (C) is incorrect** because the Supreme Court, on several occasions, has upheld the President's power to act through executive agreements even if the President could have chosen to submit the matter to the Senate in the form of a treaty. *See Dames & Moore v. Regan*, 453 U.S. 654 (1981). Further, the Supreme Court has never declared such agreements to violate separation of powers principles because the President did not send the matter to the Senate in the form of a treaty. *See United States v. Pink*, 315 U.S. 203 (1942), and *United States v. Belmont*, 301 U.S. 324 (1937).

**Answer (D) is incorrect** because separation of powers principles do not limit the President's foreign policy power and prerogatives to crisis situations. Although a foreign policy crisis may increase the President's power to act in the foreign policy arena, a crisis need not exist for the President to act.

46.  **Answer (B) is the best answer.** Time and again federal courts have dismissed, as involving non-justiciable political questions, various challenges to the President's authority to take military action. Dozens of cases involving the Vietnam War were dismissed on this ground, *see, e.g., Holtzman v. Schlesinger,* 484 F.2d 1307 (2d Cir. 1973), *cert. denied,* 416 U.S. 936 (1974), as were challenges to President Reagan's military actions in El Salvador, *see, e.g., Crockett v. Reagan,* 720 F.2d 1355 (D.C. Cir. 1983), *cert. denied,* 467 U.S. 1251 (1984), and President Bush's actions in the First Persian Gulf War, *see, e.g., Ange v. Bush,* 752 F. Supp. 509 (D.D.C. 1990).

**Answer (A) is incorrect** because it attempts to resolve a complex constitutional question by referring to only one factor in the analysis — namely that the Constitution makes the President Commander-in-Chief. However, the Constitution also gives the Congress the power to declare war and to appropriate money for the funding of military action. Thus, the President and the Congress both have constitutional authority over military matters. Answer (A) is incorrect because it does not take into account this complex arrangement.

**Answer (C) is incorrect** because this answer is too broad. There is no absolute prohibition against the federal courts reviewing cases that involve foreign policy matters as this answer suggests. While the federal courts grant much inherent authority to the President in the foreign policy field, the Constitution does not ban the courts from reviewing certain foreign policy decisions. For example, in *Dames & Moore v. Regan,* 453 U.S. 654 (1981), the Court did consider the merits of the case, and upheld the President's power to settle legal claims by way of an executive agreement.

**Answer (D) is incorrect** because it has never been decided whether the President must obtain a war declaration from Congress before proceeding with an act of war. As stated in the analysis to Answer (A), the Constitution gives authority to both the President and Congress in handling military matters. While the Constitution states that Congress shall declare war, it does not say that the President cannot act militarily without such a war declaration. Whenever the federal courts have faced this question, they have dismissed the cases as being non-justiciable on political question grounds. Because of this history, we cannot say that the President's actions in this question would be declared unconstitutional, and Answer (D), therefore, is incorrect.

47.  **Answer (C) is the best answer** because it best takes account of the Court's decision in *Hamdi v. Rumsfeld,* 542 U.S. 507 (2004). That case decided whether a United States citizen captured in Afghanistan, and held as an enemy combatant at a United States military base, could ask the courts to issue a the writ of habeas corpus to review the

government's decision to detain him. The Secretary of Defense, a member of the executive branch, argued that respect for separation of powers precluded Hamdi from having an evidentiary hearing on the facts leading to his detention. Considering the military context of this detention, the Secretary argued that the federal courts should be restricted "to investigating only whether legal authorization exists for the broader detention scheme." According to the Secretary, during times of military conflict, separation of powers principles preclude courts from ordering a hearing to decide whether an individual was correctly detained by the executive branch. Such deference would show proper respect to the executive branch's authority over military and national security affairs.

The Supreme Court rejected this argument because it would unduly aggrandize executive branch power. Specifically, the Secretary's argument infringed on the necessary constitutional role of the judicial branch in evaluating a citizen's claim to liberty. Even if the detention involves military and national security matters, separation of powers principles require some judicial role when individual liberties are at stake.

Applying *Hamdi* to this question, we see that the President cannot deny the citizen-detainee a hearing on the validity of his detention. Obviously, this outcome raises many questions. Should it apply equally to foreign nationals? The Court did not definitively address this. In 2007, the Supreme Court granted review in a case that may answer this question. See *Boumediene v. Bush,* 127 S. Ct. 3078 (2007) *(granting certiorari).* Is such a hearing required on the battlefield? The plurality in *Hamdi* said no. Are detainees designated as enemy combatants entitled to the same due process procedures as other, run-of-the-mill prisoners? The plurality in *Hamdi* said no. The process that is due enemy combatants according to *Hamdi* is discussed below at Question 142.

**Answer (A) is incorrect** for the reasons stated above. The Court has made it clear that the President's inherent power to protect and defend the United States does not negate judicial power to decide cases involving individual liberty. Indeed, the Court in *Hamdi* cited *Youngstown Sheet & Tube,* 343 U.S. 579 (1952), for the proposition that "a State of war is not a blank check for the President when it comes to the rights of the Nation's citizens."

**Answer (B) is incorrect** because all Supreme Court decisions since the attacks on September 11, 2001, and the subsequent start of the War on Terrorism, have rejected the President's claim of broad executive power to stop terrorist activity. These cases include *Rasul v. Bush,* 542 U.S. 466 (2004) (involving the right of a non-citizen held at Guantanamo Bay to have his habeas corpus petition heard by a federal court); *Hamdi v. Rumsfeld,* 542 U.S. 507 (2004) (involving the President's decision to deny a hearing to imprisoned enemy combatants); *Hamdan v. Rumsfeld,* 126 S. Ct. 2749 (2006) (involving the President's order to try non-citizen enemy combatants by military tribunal). Many have hotly debated this topic. Some have argued that a crisis such as persistent terrorism against the United States and its citizens should be sufficient to allow the President flexibility in discovering and handling terrorists. Others have noted that nothing in the Constitution or its founding debates provides for any exceptions to constitutional requirements in times of crisis or emergency. Often the constitutions of other nations do provide specifically for emergency exceptions to certain provisions. Nevertheless, given current Supreme Court precedent, **Answer (B) is incorrect**.

**Answer (D) is incorrect** because the Court has acknowledged in almost all of its decisions that the President has inherent powers not found in the text of Article II. For a discussion of the President's inherent powers, see the answer to Question 31.

48. Both *Hamdi v. Rumsfeld,* 542 U.S. 507 (2004) and *Hamdan v. Rumsfeld,* 126 S. Ct. 2749 (2006), reinforce the Supreme Court's position in prior separation of powers cases such as *Youngstown Sheet & Tube,* 343 U.S. 579 (1952) and *Dames & Moore v. Regan,* 453 U.S. 654 (1981). *Youngstown* and *Dames & Moore* noted that while the President has broad inherent powers, presidential power has serious limitations. See Question 31 for a discussion of *Youngstown* and Question 43 for a discussion of *Dames & Moore.* Both *Hamdi* and *Hamdan* apply this concept of limited presidential power even when the President argues that the nation is at war, and that his decisions to protect the nation should stand without judicial oversight.

In *Hamdi*, the Court made clear that the President's inherent powers do not alter the constitutional balance that requires judicial review when the President imprisons a citizen, even an alleged enemy combatant captured on the battlefield. See the discussion of *Hamdi* in Question 47.

In *Hamdan,* the Court applied the blended power approach used in *Youngstown Sheet & Tube,* 343 U.S. 579 (1952), to strike down President Bush's executive order establishing military commissions. Both by treaty (the Geneva Convention) and statute (the Uniform Code of Military Justice), Congress had established that military commissions must adhere to certain procedural safeguards. Because President Bush's executive order did not apply those procedures for the Guantanamo Bay military commissions, the executive branch was acting at odds with a specifically stated position of the legislative branch, which is when the President's inherent power is at its lowest ebb, according to Justice Jackson's concurring opinion in *Youngstown*. In such cases, the executive can prevail only if the subject is one committed to the President's sole authority. Here, the power to constitute military commissions "can derive only from the powers granted *jointly* to the President and Congress in time of war." Because the President's sole powers did not include the unilateral creation of military tribunals, the executive order had to yield to the specific commands of Congress. Justice Kennedy's opinion concurring in part explains how this analysis is consistent with Justice Jackson's three-tiered framework in *Youngstown*.

49. **Answer (D) is the best answer** because it is most likely that the Supreme Court would dismiss any lawsuit seeking constitutional review of articles of impeachment on grounds that the lawsuit involves a political question. This is what the Supreme Court did in *Nixon v. United States*, 506 U.S. 224 (1993), which involved the impeachment of a federal judge named Walter L. Nixon (it did not involve President Nixon). Judge Nixon complained of the Senate procedures used in his impeachment trial. The Supreme Court dismissed the suit on political question grounds, as would likely happen here.

Nevertheless, questions exist as to the impeachment process. For example, what does the term "high Crimes and Misdemeanors" connote? Remember that the President can be removed from office under the Constitution only upon conviction of "Treason, Bribery, or other high Crimes and Misdemeanors." Article I, Section 2. During the impeachment proceedings of both Andrew Johnson and Bill Clinton, questions were raised about the meaning of this phrase. Some take the position that it means whatever Congress decides it means. Others contend that it only encompasses violations of criminal law. In another area, some have wondered whether the Supreme Court would allow impeachment or conviction of a President by use of questionable procedures, such a coin-toss to decide the issue.

In any event, because all the answers to the question have the Supreme Court deciding the merits of the lawsuit, all answers are incorrect. The most likely result is that the Supreme Court would dismiss any lawsuit that raised the constitutionality of these articles of impeachments as involving a political question and thus non-justiciable.

50. **Answer (D) is the best answer.** In *United States v. Lopez*, 514 U.S. 549 (1995), the Supreme Court explained that three categories of laws come within Congress' Commerce Clause power: (1) laws regulating the channels of interstate commerce; (2) laws regulating instrumentalities or people that travel or work in the channels of interstate commerce, and (3) laws regulating an economic or commercial activity (or a non-economic activity that is an essential part of a larger economic activity) that has a substantial aggregate effect on interstate commerce. The Safe Skies Act falls within *Lopez*' second category: laws that regulate instrumentalities of interstate commerce. *Lopez* explained that "instrumentalities" of interstate commerce include people or things that travel or operate in the channels of interstate commerce. The Court cited *Heart of Atlanta Motel, Inc. v. United States*, 379 U.S. 241 (1964), as an example of a case dealing with the instrumentalities of interstate commerce. In *Heart of Atlanta Motel*, Congress had proscribed racial discrimination in public accommodations, such as motels. National roadways are channels of interstate commerce, and the motels located along these roadways are instrumentalities that serve these channels. Thus, the law regulated instrumentalities of interstate commerce.

The same is true of the federal law described in this question. The nation's airplane routes are channels of interstate commerce, and the airplanes and airline employees traveling in those routes are instrumentalities and people within the channels. By criminalizing the assault or battery of a pilot or flight attendant, or the murder of a pilot, the Act validly regulates the activities of people traveling in the channels of interstate commerce.

**Answer (A) is incorrect** because it is incomplete. Answer (A) focuses only on the third category. (Application of the third category is discussed further below in the discussion of Answer (C).) Even if a federal law does not come within the third category, it is still constitutional if it comes within one of the other two categories. Answer (A) is incorrect because it mistakenly assumes that a federal law is unconstitutional because it fails to come within one of the three *Lopez* categories without taking into consideration the other two categories.

**Answer (C) is not the best answer** because it incorrectly applies the third *Lopez* category. That category only applies to laws where the *regulated conduct* itself is a commercial or economic activity, or is part of a larger commercial or economic activity that Congress is regulating. For example, in *Heart of Atlanta Motel*, the regulated activity was the commercial enterprise of *operating a hotel*. And in *Katzenbach v. McClung*, 379 U.S. 294 (1964), the regulated activity was *operating a restaurant* — Ollie's Barbecue. Conversely, in *Lopez*, the regulated activity was *gun possession in a school zone*, and in *United States v. Morrison*, 529 U.S. 598 (2000), it was *gender-motivated* *violence.* In *Lopez*, the United States argued that nearby operation of a school was a necessary circumstance of the crime, and that operating a school was an economic activity. But, *Lopez* explained that the third category is not so broad; it focuses on *the regulated activity itself*, and not the activity's surrounding circumstances.

In 2005, the Court decided a Commerce Clause case that clarified analysis under the third *Lopez* category. *Gonzales v. Raich*, 545 U.S. 1 (2005), held that Congress had the power to criminalize private cultivation, possession, and use of state-approved medical marijuana as part of its larger regulation of the drug trade. Because the conduct at issue involved neither the channels nor instrumentalities of interstate commerce, the question was whether Congress could sweep non-economic activity — individual cultivation, possession, and use of medical marijuana — within the scope of its regulation of a larger economic activity — the interstate market for drugs.

The specific law at issue in *Raich* was the Comprehensive Drug Abuse Prevention and Control Act, which the Court described as "a comprehensive regime to combat the international and interstate traffic in illicit drugs." *Id.* at 12. Further, the Act's purpose was "to conquer drug abuse and to control the legitimate and illegitimate traffic in controlled substances. Congress was particularly concerned with the need to prevent the diversion of drugs from legitimate to illicit channels." *Id.* To achieve these purposes, the Act divides drugs into five categories, with each category having "a distinct set of controls regarding the manufacture, distribution, and use of the substances listed therein." *Id.* at 14. The Act placed marijuana in a category for which manufacture, distribution, or possession of the drugs (except for a federal research study) is a crime.

The *Raich* Court began its analysis by noting the similar facts of *Wickard v. Filburn*, 317 U.S. 111 (1942). *Wickard* involved a federal agricultural price control law that prohibited a farmer from cultivating wheat beyond the farmer's allotted quota, even if the excess was used solely for the farmer's own consumption. The *Filburn* Court upheld application of the law to a farmer's personal consumption, holding that Congress may consider the aggregate effect of all who might engage in the regulated behavior:

> That [a single farmer's] own contribution to the demand for wheat may be trivial by itself is not enough to remove him from the scope of federal regulation where, as here, his contribution, taken together with that of many others similarly situated, is far from trivial.

*Id.* at 127–28. While one farmer growing a little extra wheat for personal use will not substantially affect national demand, the aggregate effect of all farmers who do so may be substantial. So, in regulating interstate commerce, Congress may consider the aggregate effect of individual conduct.

The analogy between *Wickard* and *Raich* is rather straightforward. Though a single individual cultivating and using medical marijuana will not have much (if any) effect on the interstate drug trade, such behavior aggregated across the entire nation could have a substantial effect. Congress could conclude that widespread availability of medical marijuana poses an unacceptable danger that such legal marijuana will be diverted to illegal uses or channels, making it more difficult to police illegal uses. Thus, in both *Wickard* and *Raich*, "the regulation is within Congress' commerce power because production of the commodity meant for home consumption, be it wheat or marijuana, has a substantial effect on supply and demand in the national market for that commodity." *Raich*, 545 U.S. at 19.

Those challenging the drug law in *Raich* responded to the *Wickard* analogy with their own analogies to *Lopez* and *Morrison*. Specifically, they argued that personal cultivation and use of marijuana was a non-economic activity outside Congress' regulatory reach, just as were bare possession of a gun in a school zone (in *Lopez*) and gender-motivated violence (in *Morrison*). The Court disagreed, distinguishing *Lopez* and *Morrison* in one important respect — in both cases, the challenged federal law regulated *only* non-economic activity. In *Lopez*, the statute forbade gun possession simpliciter, and not as part of a larger regulation of schools or gun trafficking. And in *Morrison*, the statute imposed liability for gender-motivated violence, and did not undertake a larger regulation of working conditions or the like. The Act challenged in *Raich* was different because it criminalized personal cultivation, possession, and use of marijuana in order to regulate a *larger economic activity* — the illegal drug trade. The Act "is a statute that regulates the production, distribution, and consumption of commodities for which there is an established, and lucrative, interstate market." *Id.* at 25–26. Conversely, the law challenged in *Lopez* criminalized gun possession standing alone, and not as "an essential part of a large regulation of economic activity, in which the regulatory scheme could be undercut unless the intrastate activity were regulated." *Lopez*, 514 U.S. at 561. Thus, *Raich* and *Lopez* can be distinguished based on the regulatory scope of laws at issue.

Last, the challengers in *Raich* argued the Act did not contain sufficient congressional findings that regulation of personal cultivation and use of medical marijuana was necessary to effective regulation of the interstate drug trade. The Court, however, held that Congress need only have "rationally concluded" that regulation of intrastate activity was necessary to success of the larger economic regulation. The Court found that it was not only "plausible," but "readily apparent" that intrastate cultivation and use of medical marijuana posed a threat to federal regulation of interstate marijuana trade. Doctors could impermissibly prescribe medical marijuana for recreational use, patients could continue marijuana use beyond their medical need, or illegal drug traffickers or users could try to disguise their contraband as medical marijuana. Congress could (but need not) rationally conclude that effective regulation of the interstate drug trade required regulation of these intrastate activities.

*Raich* clarifies the distinction between, on the one hand, laws that simply target intrastate non-economic activity (which are outside Congress' Commerce Clause power), and on the other hand, laws that target intrastate non-economic activity to more effectively regulate a larger interstate economic activity (which is within Congress' power). The Safe Skies Act described in this question is a free-standing prohibition of assault, battery, and murder unconnected to a regulation of a larger economic activity. This makes the Act more like the law struck down in *Morrison* than the law upheld in *Raich*.

*Raich* indicates that the answer to this question could change if Congress had simply inserted the assault, battery, and murder prohibitions into a larger federal air travel regulation instead of enacting a free-standing prohibition. This possibility led the dissenters in *Raich* to criticize the majority for applying a mere statutory drafting rule that Congress can easily satisfy by couching any regulation of intrastate non-economic activity as part of a larger federal regulation of interstate economic activity. *Raich*, 545 U.S. at 43 ("[T]he Court announces a rule that gives Congress a perverse incentive to legislate broadly pursuant to the Commerce Clause — nestling questionable assertions of its authority into comprehensive regulatory schemes — rather than with precision."). Time will tell whether the Court will read *Raich* to allow Congress such leeway.

In sum, the third *Lopez* category does not support the Safe Skies Act. Under *Lopez*, the regulated conduct is *violence against airline personnel*, and the purchase of an airplane ticket is simply a surrounding circumstance of that activity. So, while purchasing an airplane ticket is an economic activity, it is not an element of the regulated activity and thus does not satisfy the third *Lopez* category. And under *Raich*, there is no larger economic activity addressed by the regulatory scheme. The facts do not suggest that the statute is part of a larger regulation of the airline industry. Rather, the statute is a free-standing regulation of a non-commercial, non-economic activity — violent crime.

**Answer (B) is incorrect** because it overstates its point. *Morrison* held that violent crime (there, gender-motivated violence), standing alone, is the type of non-economic activity that Congress cannot regulate under the Commerce Clause, and thus is left to the states. *Morrison* emphasized, however, that the violent crime in that case was completely unrelated to either a commercial enterprise or interstate commerce. Here, as explained above, the proscribed violence is tied to employees working in the channels of interstate commerce, which distinguishes this case from *Morrison*. So, **answer (B) is incorrect** because it states that *all* violent crime, regardless of its connection to interstate commerce, lies beyond Congress' Commerce Clause power.

51.  **Answer (D) is the best answer.**

**Answer (A) is incorrect** because hospitals are not likely instrumentalities of interstate commerce. Instrumentalities are things or buildings that operate in and promote the flow of people and goods through the channels of interstate commerce. For example, tractor-trailers, airplanes, and cruise ships all carry people and goods through the channels of interstate commerce. Similarly, the gas stations, airports, seaports, hotels, and restaurants that serve these vehicles (and their passengers) are instrumentalities within the channels. *See Heart of Atlanta Motel, Inc. v. United States*, 379 U.S. 241 (1964). While a hospital may incidentally serve people who travel in interstate commerce, its primary function is not to facilitate such commerce.

**Answer (C) is incorrect** because *Wickard v. Filburn*, 317 U.S. 111 (1942), held that one must look at the *aggregate* effect on interstate commerce of all instances of the regulated activity. As discussed in the answer to the preceding question, *Wickard* dealt with a single farmer who grew wheat for his own use. While the wheat consumed by that one farmer had a *de minimis* effect on interstate commerce, the aggregate effect of all farmers who did so would be substantial.

The closer question is whether the Act regulates a commercial or economic activity. In *Lopez* and *Morrison*, the Court focused quite narrowly on the specific conduct set forth in the statute. In *Lopez*, the specific conduct was possession of a firearm while in a school zone; in *Morrison*, the specific conduct was gender-motivated violence. In neither case did the specific conduct involve an economic exchange or transaction. On that view, the Act does not involve an economic activity because the conduct proscribed — altering a newborn's identification — does not involve an economic exchange or transaction.

*Raich* may muddy the waters some on what counts as economic activity. There, the Court could be read to find that personal cultivation and consumption of medical marijuana was an economic activity. The Court quoted the following dictionary definition of "economics": "the production, distribution, and consumption of commodities." *Id.* at 25–26. Under this definition, the personal consumption of even home-grown marijuana is arguably economic. If correct, this reading of *Raich* could dramatically expand the universe of economic activities entitled to aggregation under *Wickard*.

In context, however, *Raich*'s definition of "economics" is not so broad. The definition was quoted in a portion of the opinion that characterized the *entire market* regulated by the Controlled Substances Act — the interstate market for drugs, both legal and illegal. The interstate drug market is "economic" because it involves "the production, distribution, *and* consumption" of drugs. *Id.* (emphasis added). Indeed, the Court described the regulated activity as an "established, and lucrative, interstate market." *Id.* By contrast, the Infant Protection and Baby Switching Prevention Act regulates a non-economic act (the altering of a newborn's identification record) standing alone, and not as part of a larger interstate economic activity. Indeed, there is no part of altering the newborn's identification that can be described as production, distribution, or consumption of a good or service. The simple act of altering the record is the offense. Thus, **(D) is the best answer**.

Answer (B) appeals to the holding in *Raich* that Congress may regulate non-economic activities in limited circumstances. As discussed in the answer to the preceding question, *Raich* held that Congress may regulate an intrastate non-economic activity when doing do is essential to regulation of a *larger economic activity*. Answer (B) correctly notes that provision of maternity and delivery room services is an economic activity, and suggests that the Act is part of the larger regulation of such services. Here, however, the Act is more like *Lopez* than *Raich*. In *Lopez*, the challenged statute focused solely on gun possession and did not reach into a larger economic activity, such as gun trafficking. Similarly, the Act focuses narrowly on altering the identification of newborns, leaving untouched any aspect of the economic activity of providing maternity and delivery services. Thus, **answer (B) is not the best answer**.

The Senate Report is a major difference from *Lopez*, where the Court had no congressional findings to aid its analysis. The Court will consider congressional findings to determine whether the regulated activity has a connection to interstate commerce that is not apparent to the "naked eye." But, as *Morrison* showed, the mere existence of such congressional findings will not end the Court's analysis. The findings must not rely on too attenuated a chain of logic to link the regulated activity to interstate commerce. For example, in *Morrison*, Congress' chain of reasoning tried to link gender-motivated violence to interstate commerce through the affects such violence have on worker productivity and consumer spending. The Court rejected this argument because so many activities affect either worker productivity or consumer spending habits that the argument could be used to link almost any activity to interstate commerce. This would give Congress virtually unlimited power, obliterating the Framers' intended distinction between matters that are national (and thus regulated by Congress) and matters that are local (and thus regulated by the states).

The Senate Report described above suffers the same flaw as the congressional findings in *Morrison*. The Report identifies three economic activities affected by child birth: "the parent's spending habits, investment strategies, and even career plans." As in *Morrison*, there is a virtually limitless array of activities that affect spending, investment, and career plans. For example, education and family law, two subjects *Lopez* and *Morrison* described as traditionally regulated by the states, have a substantial impact on these types of decisions. Thus, accepting the Report's reasoning would lead to limitless congressional power, a consequence against which the Court has steadfastly protected. This is yet another reason the Court should find the Act fails the substantial effects test.

52. **Answer (C) is the correct answer.** This question asks you to apply *Gonzales v. Raich*, 545 U.S. 1 (2005), to determine whether Congress can regulate a non-economic activity that does not involve the channels or instrumentalities of interstate commerce. As explained in the answer to Question 50, *Raich* held that the Commerce Clause reaches regulation of an intrastate, non-economic activity when Congress has a rational basis for concluding that such regulation is necessary to the successful regulation of a larger interstate economic activity. In *Raich*, Congress could regulate the personal cultivation and consumption of medical marijuana because Congress had a rational basis for concluding that such regulation was necessary to effective regulation of the interstate drug trade. Specifically, failure to control medical marijuana might allow diversion of such drugs to illegal uses, which would undermine the effectiveness of the comprehensive federal drug control laws.

Here, Congress has set forth a rational basis for regulating an intrastate, non-economic activity. Ronald's personal creation and possession of child pornography is likely not an economic activity, as Ronald never purchased or sold the images. The law that criminalizes his private possession, however, is part of a comprehensive regulation of a larger economic activity — the interstate market in child pornography. Further, Congress has articulated a rational basis (similar to that in *Raich)* for including the non-economic activity in its larger regulation: Personally created and possessed images could be diverted into the interstate child pornography market, thereby undermining the federal regulation of that market. Thus, **Answer (C) is the best answer**.

53.   According to *United States v. Lopez*, 514 U.S. 549 (1995), and *United States v. Morrison*, 529 U.S. 598 (2000), Congress may regulate activity that substantially affects interstate commerce if that activity is commercial or economic, or is part of a larger regulation of commercial or economic activity. Under PRFA, the regulated activity is state operation of prison facilities. Whether this activity is commercial or economic can be argued both ways. One the one hand, some states contract with private companies to run their prisons, and the Supreme Court has held that these private companies are not necessarily state actors when they do so. Thus, prison operation has become an area of private profit making. On the other hand, the same can be said for other government functions that are also provided by private actors. For example, both *Lopez* and *Morrison* noted that education is a traditional state function that likely lies beyond Congress' power. Yet, there is a long history of private schools providing educational services. Further, operating a prison is an integral part of the criminal justice system, and *Lopez* and *Morrison* point to the criminal law as a traditional state domain. So, while there is some support for viewing prison operation as a commercial or economic activity, the strongest indications from *Lopez* and *Morrison* are that the Court would not do so. And, if the activity is neither commercial nor economic, *Morrison* states that the Court has never allowed Congress to aggregate the effects of that activity to find a substantial effect on interstate commerce. And while *Gonzales v. Raich*, 545 U.S. 1 (2005), allows aggregation of a non-economic activity when regulation of that activity is essential to regulation of a larger economic activity, PRFA does not present such a case.

54.   PRFA is also doubtful on the other factors discussed in *Lopez* and *Morrison*. First, there is no jurisdictional element that ties individual instances of the regulated conduct to interstate commerce. PRFA applies to all prison regulations, regardless of their individual connection to interstate commerce. Second, any connection between the regulated activity and interstate commerce is likely attenuated at best. Prison regulations that substantially burden religious exercise might affect proper rehabilitation of prisoners, which might affect the prisoners' productivity when later re-entering society, which might then affect interstate commerce. But, this is the same type of speculative chain of inferences that the Court rejected in *Lopez* and *Morrison*. Third, PRFA has no congressional findings that illuminate a connection to interstate commerce that is unapparent to the naked eye.

55.   **Answer (B) is the correct answer.** First, note that the case is in the third *Lopez* category because the Act regulates neither the channels nor the instrumentalities of interstate commerce. Under the third category, Congress may rely on aggregate effects on

interstate commerce only if the regulated activity is either an economic enterprise or essential to the regulation of a larger economic activity. Here, the regulated activity is an employee's paid and unpaid leave. This means that that the Act applies *only* in the context of an existing employment relationship, which is an economic activity. So, Congress may aggregate the effects of that activity under *Wickard*. Further, *Raich* tells us that Congress need only have a rational basis for concluding that the regulated activity will have the required effect on interstate commerce. Here, while a single employee taking leave for adoption related activities (or being denied such leave) might have a minimal affect on interstate commerce, Congress could rationally conclude that the aggregate affect of all employees who seek such leave is substantial. This aggregation analysis is consistent with *Heart of Atlanta Motel* and *Katzenbach v. McClung*, where the Court allowed aggregation of the economic activities of operating a hotel and a restaurant, respectively.

**Answer (A) is incorrect** because it states a condition on Congress' power under the Spending Clause, not the Commerce Clause. For a discussion of Congress' Spending Clause power, see the answers to Questions 58 through 62.

**Answer (C) is incorrect** because it ignores the economic nature of the regulated conduct. In *Lopez* and *Morrison*, when the regulated conduct was non-economic, the Court pointed out that Congress was regulating in an area traditionally controlled by the states. In *Lopez*, gun possession in a school zone touched on the traditional state concern with education, and in *Morrison*, gender-motivated violence touched on the traditional state concern with violent crime. But each case was careful to note the non-economic nature of the regulated conduct removed it from Congress' reach under the Commerce Clause. Here, as discussed above, the regulated conduct is economic — terms of employment — and not a non-economic activity, such as adoption or family law, that is a traditional state concern.

**Answer (D) is incorrect** because it also ignores the fact that the regulated activity is economic. *Lopez* and *Morrison* applied these factors to non-economic activities. In both cases, because the regulated activity was non-economic, the government had to rely on an attenuated chain of reasoning to tie the activity to interstate commerce. In *Lopez*, the government argued that gun possession in a school zone affected learning, which in turn affected worker productivity. And in *Morrison*, the government argued that gender-motivated violence affected employee health, which in turn affected worker productivity. The Court rejected both arguments as effectively erasing any limits on Congress' Commerce Clause power. Because almost any non-economic activity has an arguable effect on worker productivity, accepting this argument would effectively give Congress unlimited power, which is directly contrary to the original understanding that Congress has limited and enumerated powers. Here, however, Congress need not rely on attenuated logic to link the regulated activity to interstate commerce because, unlike in *Lopez* and *Morrison*, the regulated activity is itself an economic activity — the terms of employment. So while the facts of the question note a potential link between adoption and worker productivity, that arguable link is not the Act's only tie to interstate commerce.

56. **Answer (B) is the correct answer.** Note again that the case is in the third *Lopez* category because the Act regulates neither the channels nor the instrumentalities of interstate commerce. The regulated activity is smoking in or near a child-related facility. While a child-related facility might happen to be located near a channel of interstate commerce, such as an airport or an interstate highway, that is not necessarily so. Consequently, the Act does not regulate either the channels of interstate commerce or the instrumentalities or people in those channels.

Under the third *Lopez* category, Congress may rely on aggregate effects on interstate commerce only if the regulated activity is either commercial or essential to the regulation of a larger economic activity. Here, neither is the case. First, the regulated activity is simply smoking in a designated location, which does not entail the production, purchase, or sale of a commodity or service. This is like *Lopez*, where the statute regulated the non-economic activity of gun possession when done in a specific location (*i.e.*, a school zone). Second, the facts tell us that the Act is a stand alone provision, meaning that it is not part of a comprehensive federal regulation of a larger economic activity. Thus, Congress cannot rely on *Raich*, where regulation of the possession of medical marijuana was upheld as necessary to the larger federal drug regulation.

**Answer (A) is incorrect** because it overstates its point. Congress may regulate an intrastate non-economic activity when doing so is necessary to successful regulation of a larger economic activity. This was the holding in *Raich*.

**Answer (C) is incorrect** because it is inconsistent with *Lopez* and *Morrison*. As discussed above in the answer to Question 51, the Court has held that congressional findings will not support regulation of an intrastate non-economic activity when those findings are based on an attenuated connection to interstate commerce. In both cases, Congress had found that the regulated activity (gun possession in *Lopez*, and gender-motivated violence in *Morrison*) had an effect on worker productivity. The Court rejected the findings because almost any non-economic activity (*e.g.*, divorce, raising children, hours of sleep, form of recreation, reading habits) could arguably affect worker productivity, which would give Congress the power to regulate almost every corner of American life. Here, Congress makes a similar argument in support of the Act — smoking near children affects their health, which in turn affects their future productivity in the workforce. *Lopez* and *Morrison* bar this argument.

**Answer (D) is not the best answer** because the Court has not allowed aggregation of the effects on interstate commerce for a non-economic activity that is not tied to successful regulation of a larger economic activity.

57.   **Answer (C) is correct and Answer (B) is incorrect** because the condition is not rationally related to the purpose for which the federal highway funds have been allocated. *South Dakota v. Dole*, 483 U.S. 203 (1987), is a good example of the rational relationship the Court requires. *Dole* involved a federal law that conditioned state receipt of highway funds on state adoption of a drinking age of twenty-one. The Court reasoned that federal highway funds allocated to maintain and repair interstate roadways were intended to promote safe interstate travel. A lower drinking age was rationally related to the same purpose, as it would deter underage drinking, which was logically related to reducing underage drunk driving. Of course, the fit between a twenty-one year-old drinking age and road safety was rather loose: not all teenagers who drink get behind the wheel of a car, and not all drunk drivers are under twenty-one. But the Court did not require a precise relationship between the condition and the funds' purpose. Instead, Congress only need show a logical relationship, regardless of over-or under-inclusiveness.

In our question, even such a loose logical relationship is missing. Assuming that the federal funds are allocated to promote safe travel, there is no plausible basis for concluding that abortions are related to safe travel. One could argue that women seeking an abortion often travel great distances to do so, and that such increased travel increases the risk of automobile accidents. Consequently, prohibiting certain abortions will decrease travel and thus decrease accident risks. But even assuming this is factually correct, the argument cannot prevail because it effectively abolishes the rational relationship requirement. Virtually any activity could arguably affect people's travel habits and thus road safety. There must be something about the regulated activity itself that is logically related to highway safety. Alcohol consumption is logically related to poor driving; having an abortion is not.

**Answer (A) is incorrect** because it is incomplete. It is true that the Fourteenth Amendment does not independently bar the condition. The condition requires states to prohibit all post-viability abortions, except those needed to protect the life or health of the mother. *Planned Parenthood v. Casey*, 505 U.S. 833 (1992), allows states to pass such abortion regulations. But a conditional spending law must still be rationally related to the purpose for which the federal funds have been regulated, and Answer (A) does not address that additional limit.

**Answer (D) is incorrect** because it is irrelevant to the Court's conditional spending test. Congress may spend federal funds for any purpose that promotes the general welfare, and not only those activities that fall within an enumerated power. Thus, constructing federal highways need not fall within an enumerated federal power, such as the Commerce Clause, for the appropriation to be constitutional. (Of course, constructing and maintaining interstate highways would be a valid Commerce Clause measure aimed at a channel of interstate commerce.) As repair and maintenance of federal highways promotes the general welfare (enabling safer interstate travel), the appropriation is constitutional. But even if the appropriation is constitutional, the *condition* on that appropriation is not constitutional unless it is rationally related to the funds' purpose. **Answer (C) is correct** because that rational relationship does not exist.

58. This conditional spending scheme likely satisfies the four-part test in *South Dakota v. Dole*, 483 U.S. 203 (1987). First, the condition must be stated unambiguously, which it is here — states must enact a version of the Act, or they lose 10% of their federal law enforcement funds. Second, the condition must serve the general welfare. Preventing misidentification of newborns, as well as the pain, suffering, and cost caused by such acts, are in the public welfare just as public highway safety was in *Dole*. Both protect the well-being of the citizenry. Also, because the Court accords Congress great deference on this question, the condition should easily satisfy this element. Third, the condition must be reasonably related to the purpose for which the federal funds have been allocated. *Dole* illustrates that the Court will define the funds' purpose quite broadly. There, the Court defined the purpose of highway funds as safe interstate travel, rather than a narrow focus on construction or maintenance of highways. Here, the purpose of federal law enforcement funds could be broadly defined as protection of public peace and safety. By destroying or altering a newborn's identification, one is effectively stealing that child from the parents, which would be a breach of the public peace. So, under the loose analysis allowed by *Dole*, the condition that states enact the Act should be reasonably related to the purpose of law enforcement funds. Fourth, the condition must not cause the states to violate an independent constitutional bar. Here, there is no provision of the Constitution that would prevent a state from punishing baby switching. Thus, there is no independent constitutional bar.

59. Even if a law passes the four-part test *South Dakota v. Dole*, 483 U.S. 203 (1987), as the above-described statute has, the Court will still ask whether Congress is coercing the states to act, as opposed to merely encouraging them to do so. In *Dole*, the condition was mere encouragement because the state lost only a small percentage (5%) of one type of federal funds. The same is true here. While the state will lose a higher percentage (10%) of funds, it will still receive the overwhelming majority of those funds (90%) even if it rejects the condition. Further, the condition applies only to a narrow class of funds, leaving all other federal funds (such as education, Medicare, Medicaid, etc.) unaffected. Given their relatively small amount, the state should be able to accommodate loss of these federal funds either by an incremental increase in tax revenue or reallocation of state spending. As in *Dole*, there is no coercion.

60. **Answer (D) is the best answer.** Again, consider the *South Dakota v. Dole*, 483 U.S. 203 (1987), four part test for legislation that conditions a state's receipt of federal funds: (1) the condition must serve the general welfare, (2) the condition must be unambiguous, (3) the condition must be reasonably related to the purpose for which the federal funds were appropriated, and (4) the condition must not require the states to take action that

violates an independent constitutional bar. Because the above statute meets these four requirements, **Answer (D) is the best answer**.

First, the general welfare requirement is quite easy to meet, as the Court gives substantial deference to Congress' judgment. Here, PRFA protects the free exercise of religion. Specifically, Congress may have concluded that allowing religious exercise promotes rehabilitation, which furthers one goal of incarceration. The Court would not second-guess such a congressional finding. Thus, **Answer (A) is incorrect**.

Second, the condition is unambiguous. States are posed a clear choice: enact PRFA or lose 4% of federal prison funding.

In applying the third element, *Dole* teaches that the Court defines quite broadly the interest that lies behind federal funds. For example, *Dole* involved federal funds appropriated for construction and maintenance of state roadways, conditioned on states enacting a minimum drinking age of twenty-one. How broadly one defines the purpose of the funds may determine whether the condition is reasonably related. If the purpose of the funds was stated as proper construction and maintenance of state roadways, it is hard to see how a general drinking age bears on those specific tasks. But if one states the purpose more generally as promoting *safe interstate travel*, as the Court did in *Dole*, a relationship exists. By getting states to set a uniform drinking age, Congress eliminated an incentive for young drivers to travel from a higher-drinking-age state to a lower-drinking-age state in pursuit of legal alcohol, which should reduce drunk driving. By broadly defining the purpose behind federal funds, *Dole* makes it more likely that a condition will be reasonably related to that purpose. Following *Dole*, the Court would not define the purpose of the federal funds as simply construction, maintenance, or operation of prisons. Rather, the Court would likely state a broader purpose, such as promoting prisons that effectively punish and rehabilitate inmates. Having states enact PRFA is reasonably related to this purpose. As stated above, Congress could rationally conclude that protecting prisoners' religious exercise promotes rehabilitation. Thus, **Answer (B) is incorrect.**

Fourth, the condition does not ask states to violate an independent constitutional bar. While Justice Stevens has argued that laws like PRFA violate the Establishment Clause because they give religious exercise special treatment, the Court has never accepted this argument, and there is no other provision in the Constitution that would bar state enactment of PRFA. Thus, **Answer (C) is incorrect**.

61. **Answer (B) is the best answer** because Congress has significantly increased the amount of federal funds withheld. In *Dole*, the Court explained that a law that meets the four Spending Clause requirements may still be unconstitutional if it *coerces* the states into legislating. *Dole* did not involve coercion because only 5% of the available funds were being withheld. It was unlikely that withholding such funds, which amounted to only about $200,000 annually, would put the states in a difficult position. States could easily make up such a shortfall or delay planned projects due to decreased funding. A condition

that would withhold 100% of prison funds would impose greater pressure on states for two reasons. First, it is a much larger percentage of money, and thus would likely put a larger hole in a state budget that relies on federal support of its prison system. Second, closing this hole would be more difficult than in *Dole*. On the one hand, the state could raise taxes, which would bring political retribution against state officials. On the other hand, there could be cutbacks in prison funding, which might lead to early release of offenders (another politically unpalatable decision). State officials may be put in an untenable position. Thus, while the 5% sanction in *Dole* was relatively mild, the 100% sanction here may be severe enough to constitute impermissible compulsion.

**Answer (A) is incorrect** because it improperly states the third element of the test from *South Dakota v. Dole*, 483 U.S. 203 (1987). That element asks whether the *condition* is reasonably related to the purpose of the federal funds, not whether the *amount of funds withheld* is reasonably related to the purpose.

**Answers (C) and (D) are incorrect** because they both misstate the applicable law. First, *Dole* rejected the proposition in Answer (C) that Congress may not use its Spending Power to indirectly enact a law (by encouraging the states to do so) that Congress could not enact directly. For example, in *Dole*, the Court explained that even if Congress could not enact a national drinking age, it could still use federal funds to encourage the states to do so. (*Dole* never decided whether the Twenty-First Amendment bars Congress from enacting a national drinking age.) Second, in *Garcia v. San Antonio Metro. Transit Auth.*, 469 U.S. 528 (1985), the Court rejected the proposition that Congress cannot use its enumerated powers to regulate traditional state functions.

62.   **Answer (D) is the correct answer** because the Spending Clause and the Necessary and Proper Clause allow Congress to enact laws that are rationally related to safeguarding federal funds. (**Answer (A) is incorrect** because it applies the "narrowly tailored" test, which is the wrong means-end standard.) The rational relationship test allows government wide discretion, requiring a relatively loose means-end fit. The Supreme Court's decision in *Sabri v. United States*, 541 U.S. 600 (2004), illustrates the breadth of this federal power. There, Congress criminalized bribery of any state or local official whose employer received more than $10,000 of federal funds, regardless of whether the bribe involved misuse of federal funds. The Court was unconcerned that the bribe did not directly involve federal funds, explaining that indirect involvement is enough: "Money is fungible, [and] bribed officials are untrustworthy stewards of federal funds. . . . Liquidity is not a financial term for nothing; money can be drained off here because a federal grant is pouring in there." *Id.* at 606. When criminal conduct is afoot within a government agency that handles federal funds, those funds are at risk. Federal funds may enable the crime by propping up the agency while the graft continues, or the funds may be the next target of the wrongdoers' scheme. In either case, punishing the first sign of bribery is rationally related to safeguarding federal funds from corrupt public officials.

The same analysis applies to the Anti-Embezzlement Act. When embezzlement of non-federal funds occurs, federal funds may either enable the embezzlement or be the embezzler's next target. Punishing all who embezzle from receiving federal funds is rationally related to protecting against theft. **Answer (B) is incorrect** because the rational relationship test does not require a direct nexus between the crime and the federal funds.

**Answer (C) is incorrect** because the Act does not improperly coerce state or local governments. While Congress may not use its Spending Clause power to coerce *government policy* decisions, the Act only criminalizes *individual abuse* of public office. What the *Sabri* Court said about the federal anti-bribery statute applies equally to the Act's embezzlement prohibition: The challenged federal law "bring[s] federal power to bear directly on individuals who convert public spending into unearned private gain, not a means for bringing federal economic might to bear on a state's own choices of public policy." *Id.* at 608.

63.    **Answer (A) is the best answer**. Section 5 of the Fourteenth Amendment grants Congress the power to "enforce the provisions of this Article." This text raises two questions for any statute purportedly enacted under its authority: First, is the statute tied to a provision of the Fourteenth Amendment? Second, does the statute "enforce" that provision? Here, RFEA meets both criteria. First, RFEA is tied to the Free Exercise Clause of the First Amendment, which is incorporated against the states through the Due Process Clause of the Fourteenth Amendment.

Second, RFEA is a proper enforcement measure because it is only remedial, providing equitable and legal redress for violations of existing constitutional standards. In *City of Boerne v. Flores*, 521 U.S. 507 (1997), the Court explained that section 5 of the Fourteenth Amendment empowers Congress to enact legislation that both remedies and prevents violations of that Amendment. Such legislation, however, must enforce the Supreme Court's prevailing interpretation of the Fourteenth Amendment. Congress cannot re-interpret the Fourteenth Amendment under the guise of providing a remedy or preventing future violations. RFEA is a straightforward remedial statute that satisfies *City of Boerne*. The statute merely provides redress for constitutional violations defined by "existing case law" — that is, the Constitution and the Supreme Court's prevailing interpretation. RFEA simply takes Supreme Court precedent as it finds it.

**Answer (B) is incorrect** because RFEA is a remedial, not a preventative, statute. **Answer (C) is incorrect** because RFEA *is* a proper remedial statute, and **Answer (D) is incorrect** because RFEA does not re-interpret the underlying substantive law of the Free Exercise Clause.

64.    **Answer (C) is the correct answer** because PRFA is neither appropriate remedial nor preventative legislation. This statute is similar to the Religious Freedom Restoration Act (RFRA), which the Court held exceeded Congress' power to enforce the Fourteenth Amendment. *City of Boerne v. Flores*, 521 U.S. 507 (1997). *Boerne* explained that section 5 of the Fourteenth Amendment empowers Congress to enact legislation that both remedies and prevents violations of that Amendment. In enacting such legislation, however, Congress is bound by the Supreme Court's prevailing interpretations of the Fourteenth Amendment. Thus, Congress may remedy or prevent violations of the Fourteenth Amendment *as interpreted by the Supreme Court*. Congress cannot re-interpret the Fourteenth Amendment.

As with RFRA, PRFA is a congressional attempt to enforce the Free Exercise Clause, which is incorporated against the states through the Due Process Clause of the Fourteenth

Amendment. In *Employment Division v. Smith*, 494 U.S. 872 (1990), the Supreme Court held that laws that target religious conduct receive strict scrutiny, which means that the government must show that the challenged law is narrowly tailored to a compelling government interest. When laws do not target religious conduct, then the Court applies rational basis review. In *Boerne*, the Court made clear that Congress must follow the holding in *Smith* when legislating to enforce the Free Exercise Clause.

**Answer (A) is incorrect** because PRFA is not appropriate remedial legislation. Remedial legislation would simply provide a remedy — such as damages — for a constitutional violation. PRFA does not do so; rather, it provides for invalidation of state laws. Further, PRFA sweeps far beyond any conduct that would violate *Smith*'s interpretation of the Free Exercise Clause. While *Smith* would uphold virtually all laws that do not target religious conduct, PRFA would subject all such laws to the strictest constitutional test. PRFA is not directed at simple Free Exercise Clause violations.

**Answer (B) is incorrect** because PRFA is not appropriate preventative legislation. The Court has explained that preventative legislation must be both congruent and proportional to a violation of the Fourteenth Amendment. As discussed in the preceding paragraph, PRFA applies to conduct that lies far outside *Smith*'s interpretation of the Free Exercise Clause. This lack of proportionality means that PRFA is not adequately drawn to prevent violations of that Clause.

**Answer (D) is incorrect** because it states a legal proposition rejected in *Garcia v. San Antonio Metro. Transit Auth.*, 469 U.S. 528 (1985). *Garcia* held that, so long as a law falls within an enumerated power, Congress may regulate even traditional state functions.

65. **Answer (C) is the correct answer.** In *United States v. Morrison*, 529 U.S. 598 (2000), the Supreme Court held that Congress did not have power to enact the Violence Against Women Act (VAWA) under either the Commerce Clause or Section 5 of the Fourteenth Amendment. The question here is whether some other power supports Congress' attempt to reenact VAWA under the above circumstances. We can quickly dispose of Answer (D) because there is no reason to believe that the foreign Commerce Clause supports VAWA any better than the domestic Commerce Clause. Both clauses allow Congress to regulate "commerce," and *Morrison* held that VAWA did not involve commerce or economic activity of any kind. Further, VAWA does not involve any exchange or activity with other nations. Thus, reenactment of VAWA cannot stand on the foreign Commerce Clause, and **Answer (D) is incorrect**.

That leaves us with the Treaty Clause of Article II, Section 2. The question is whether, in implementing a validly concluded treaty, Congress may enact a law that it otherwise lacks the power to enact under Article I. The Court addressed this question in *Missouri v. Holland*, 252 U.S. 416 (1920), where Congress, pursuant to a treaty, prohibited the killing or capture of certain migratory birds. Missouri challenged the law, arguing that no provision of Article I granted Congress power to regulate migratory birds. The Supreme Court rejected this argument, explaining that the Constitution does not limit Congress to its enumerated powers when implementing a treaty. (Consequently, **Answers (A) and (B) are incorrect**.) Rather, under the Necessary and Proper Clause, Congress may enact all laws necessary to execution of a valid treaty. (The Court has later suggested that Congress may not use this power to enact laws that would violate a specific constitutional prohibition, such as a provision of the Bill of Rights. *See Reid v. Covert*, 354 U.S. 1 (1957).) Thus, **Answer (C) is correct**.

66. In *Missouri v. Holland*, 252 U.S. 416 (1920), discussed in the answer to the preceding question, the Court held that Congress, in implementing a treaty, could pass legislation it did not have power to pass under Article I. This question goes one step further, asking whether Congress can use its power to implement treaties to enact legislation barred by a provision of the Constitution or an amendment. Under the Supreme Court's decision in *Planned Parenthood of Southeastern Pennsylvania v. Casey*, 505 U.S. 833 (1994), a law barring all abortions except those necessary to save the mother's life would be unconstitutional under the Due Process Clauses of the Fifth and Fourteenth Amendments. A plurality of the Court addressed this question in *Reid v. Covert*, 354 U.S. 1 (1957), explaining that the Treaty Clause was not a sufficiently broad grant of power to ignore the Constitution's specific limitations. So, while the Treaty Clause allows Congress to legislate beyond its Article I powers in implementing a treaty, it does not allow Congress to ignore specific limitations on federal power set forth in the

Constitution or its amendments. Because the statute described above violates the Fifth Amendment's Due Process Clause, it would be unconstitutional under the *Reid* plurality's reasoning.

67. **Answer (D) is the correct answer for the reasons explained below.**

Congress has power to pass laws in aid of any declared war effort. This question addresses the scope of that acknowledged power. **Answers (A) and (B) are incorrect** because they state two possible limits on that power: first, Congress can regulate only within the theater of war, and second, Congress' war powers exist only for the duration of hostilities. The Court's decision in *Woods v. Cloyd W. Miller Co.*, 333 U.S. 138 (1948), illustrates that neither limit restricts Congress' war power. *Woods* involved a federal law regulating domestic rents during World War II. The law applied even after President Harry Truman declared an end to hostilities. The war caused shocks to both the supply and demand sides of the rental market. Supply slackened during the war as building materials were diverted from residential projects to military use. Post-war demand spiked as soldiers returned from service. The resulting shortage of rental units caused sharp increases in rental prices. Acting under its war powers, Congress legislated to ease the economic transition from wartime to peacetime.

As with the Act, the rent control statute in *Woods* regulated both outside the theater of war and after the end of hostilities, and the Court upheld Congress' power to do so. First, no one questioned Congress' power to regulate outside the theater of war. This made abundant sense because a myriad of domestic activities — from the allocation of labor and raw materials, to consumption of food and other goods — affect the country's ability to effectively wage war. Second, the Court upheld the extension of Congress' war powers beyond the end of hostilities. Again, abundant sense supported the Court's judgment. The ripple effects of war do not end with the official cessation of fighting. A period of transition normally follows in which the nation redirects its efforts from fighting war to ordinary productive activities. Or, war might raise the specter of lingering threats to the public peace. Just as Congress has power to gear up for and wage war, it should have power to wind down from and address the continuing repercussions of war.

Of course, one objection to an expansive definition of Congress' war power is that it might swallow all other powers. In *Woods*, the Court acknowledged that "the effects of war under modern conditions may be felt in the economy for years and years, and that if the war power can be used in days of peace to treat all the wounds which war inflicts on our society, it may not only swallow up all other powers of Congress but largely obliterate the Ninth and Tenth Amendments as well." The rent control statute did not implicate that concern, however, because the problem it addressed — the housing shortage — "was a direct and immediate" result of the war. The same can be said for the Act at issue in this question. Congress feared that United States military action against a specific nation heightened the risk of a biological attack on American citizens. The Act merely ensures adequate measures for responding to such a retaliatory attack. For these reasons, **Answer (D) is the best answer**.

**Answer (C) is a red herring**. When Congress invokes its war powers, it need not show that the regulated activity substantially affects interstate commerce.

68. **Answer (B) is the best answer.** The essential question here is whether Congress can use its Taxing Clause power to indirectly regulate an activity that it cannot directly regulate. Recall that *United States v. Lopez*, 514 U.S. 549 (1995), held that Congress cannot use its Commerce Clause power to regulate possession of guns in a school zone. The tax described tries to reach a similar result through the Taxing Clause. Of course, the problem is that every tax has at least an incidental regulatory effect. A general sales tax has the incremental effect of reducing consumption of the goods taxed by raising their cost, and an income tax has the incremental effect of discouraging additional work hours by reducing the economic benefit derived from that incremental work. Such an effect is unavoidable. Thus, the Supreme Court has tried to distinguish between taxes that are penalties (which are primarily disguised attempts to regulate) and those that are true taxes (which are primarily revenue measures). So, the question here is whether the Act imposes a penalty or a true tax.

Before analyzing the Act under the Taxing Clause, we should dispose of two red herring answers. **Answer (D) does not state the correct legal test**. Congress may impose a true tax on an activity that it could not otherwise regulate. For example, in *United States v. Kahriger*, 345 U.S. 22 (1953), Congress taxed intrastate gambling operations. At that time, the Court had held that such operations were beyond Congress' Commerce Clause power. But, because the tax was a true tax and not a penalty, the statute was a valid exercise of Congress' Taxing Clause power.

**Answer (A) is also inapposite.** The Supreme Court has held that Congress may not commandeer states into making state law. This requirement is discussed under the topic "Federalism Limits on Federal Power." But, the Act does no such thing, as it applies only to private conduct. Indeed, the Court's anti-commandeering cases specifically say that Congress is supposed to regulate individual conduct, and not coerce the states to do so.

The next question is whether the Act imposes a penalty or a true tax. *Kahriger* suggests that the Court has become quite deferential in deciding this question. There, Congress taxed intrastate gambling, an activity which the Court had previously held Congress could not regulate directly. (The Court later expanded its interpretation of Congress' Commerce Clause power.) So, social and legislative history were pretty clear that Congress was trying to regulate indirectly what it could not regulate directly. Yet, the Court ignored this context, examining only the face of the statute. As long as the statute does not contain provisions "extraneous to any tax need," it will be upheld as a true tax.

Here, as in *Kahriger*, the Act's context strongly suggests that Congress had a regulatory motive. And, *Kahriger* teaches that such evidence of legislative motive is irrelevant. Unlike *Kahriger*, however, the Act contains a provision extraneous to any tax need. Specifically, the Act applies the tax only to activities in states that do not criminalize possession of gun in a school zone. There is no tax-based reason for this limitation. Rather, the only conceivable reason is regulatory — a tax intended to discourage gun possession in a school zone is only needed in states that have no criminal prohibition. This is similar to *Bailey v. Drexel Furniture Co.*, 259 U.S. 20 (1922), where Congress taxed only those goods of employers who violated a detailed set of child labor restrictions. (The Court had previously held that Congress could not regulate use of child labor; that holding has since been overturned.) There, the Court held that the statute's detailed labor restrictions revealed that the tax was primarily regulatory. For these reasons, **Answer (B) is a better answer than Answer (C).**

69.  **Answer (A) is the best answer.** We can quickly eliminate **Answer (D) as incorrect**, because it states the legal proposition rejected in *Garcia v. San Antonio Metropolitan Transit Authority v. Garcia*, 469 U.S. 528 (1985). There, the Court held that the state's main protection against generally applicable federal legislation was the safeguards inherent in the federal political process. This was true regardless of whether federal law regulated a traditional government function.

Since *Garcia*, the Court has recognized two main Tenth Amendment limits on federal power: Congress may neither commandeer state legislatures into making law, nor commandeer state executive or law enforcement officials into enforcing or implementing federal law. In *Reno v. Condon*, 528 U.S. 141 (2000), the Court explained the important distinction between commandeering and taking actions to comply with a generally applicable federal law. For example, commandeering occurred in *New York v. United States*, 505 U.S. 144 (1992), and *Printz v. United States*, 521 U.S. 898 (1997). In *New York v. United States*, Congress coerced state legislatures to exercise their legislative power to enact a radioactive waste disposal law specified by Congress. In *Printz*, Congress coerced local law enforcement officials into enforcing a federal gun law against private individuals. In each case, federal law directed state officials to exercise their sovereign power to regulate or enforce law against private citizens. This is what the Court's anti-commandeering rule forbids.

Conversely, *Condon* involved a generally applicable federal law that regulated public and private actors alike. Specifically, the Driver's Privacy Protection Act (DPPA) imposed restrictions on the handling and use of information obtained on driver's license applications. Of course, state and local government officials would have to take actions (expending public time and money) to comply with this federal law, such as creating policies and training employees to ensure proper handling of driver's license information. But, these actions would be taken to ensure state compliance with federal law, not to regulate or enforce the federal law against private citizens. The Court explained the difference as follows:

> [T]he DPPA does not require the states in their sovereign capacity to regulate their own citizens. The DPPA regulates the states as the owners of data bases [containing driver's license information]. It does not require the [State] Legislature to enact any laws or regulations, and it does not require State officials to assist in the enforcement of federal statutes regulating private individuals. We accordingly conclude that the DPPA is consistent with the constitutional principles enunciated in *New York* and *Printz*.

*Condon*, 528 U.S. at 151.

Here, the Act is on the *Condon* side of the commandeering line. State legislatures are not being directed to regulate their citizens, and state law enforcement officials are not being directed to enforce federal law against those same persons. Admittedly, states will have to take actions and expend resources to comply with the Act's reporting provisions. But, as in *Condon*, a state's own compliance with a generally applicable federal law is *not* commandeering. Because the Act does not commandeer the states, **Answers (B) and (C) are incorrect**. This leaves **(A) as the best answer**.

70.   **Answer (D) is the correct answer.** As discussed in the answer to the preceding question, the Supreme Court addressed this type of question in *Condon v. Reno*, 528 U.S. 141 (2000), where a federal statute regulated disclosure of private information found in driver's license records. Recall that the state argued that such a law effectively commandeered state officials because compliance with the federal law would require both the state legislature and other state officials to take actions they would not otherwise take. The Court rejected this argument, noting that the federal law commandeers only if it directs either the state legislature or other state officials to exercise their sovereign power over private actors. Here, the state will need to take some actions to comply with the act. None of these actions, however, entail sovereign action against private citizens. Thus, the Act does not commandeer the states, and **Answers (A) and (B) are incorrect**.

The *Condon* Court noted that its decision in *Garcia v. San Antonio Metropolitan Transit Auth.*, 469 U.S. 528 (1985), held that Congress may regulate states on the same terms as it does private actors. (*Garcia* allowed Congress to extend the federal minimum wage requirement to state employees.) Thus, **Answer (C) is incorrect, leaving Answer (D) as the correct answer**.

71.   This question asks whether Congress is impermissibly commandeering states into making law. *New York v. United States*, 505 U.S. 144 (1992), held that Congress cannot coerce states into making law by forcing them to enact one of two laws (neither of which Congress could have directed states to enact standing alone). Specifically, Congress instructed the states to either enact a federally-prescribed regulation of low-level radioactive waste or accept liability for all such waste within the state's borders (including privately held waste). The Court held that Congress could not pose the states either choice standing alone, and thus could not force states to choose between the two. First, Congress could not simply force states to enact a specific code into law. That would be commandeering, plain and simple. Second, Congress could not force states to take liability for privately-held waste. Doing so would effectively force states to enact a subsidy of privately-held waste. Again, forcing states to pass such a law was naked commandeering. Because Congress could direct states to enact neither option standing alone, it could not force states to choose between the forbidden options.

The federal Act in this question forces the same choice on the states. On the one hand, forcing states to enact the Act is simple commandeering. On the other hand, forcing states to accept liability for private conduct (here, baby switching) effectively forces states to enact a state subsidy for the private behavior. Again, forcing states to enact a subsidy is commandeering. As in *New York v. United States*, Congress cannot put states to this choice.

72. This is no longer commandeering. Instead, this is an exercise of Congress' Spending Clause power, which permits Congress to place conditions on a state's receipt of federal funds. The condition satisfies the four criteria for conditional spending, which are considered in more detail in Questions 58 to 62. (As a review, you should consider why the condition satisfies the test.) The closer question is whether the statute impermissibly coerces states into enacting the statute. In *South Dakota v. Dole*, 483 U.S. 203 (1985), the Court held that conditioning receipt of $200,000 in federal highway funds did not coerce the state. One billion dollars of Medicaid funds, however, is a much different choice. If such funds are withheld, states would have to either dramatically raise taxes to make up the shortfall or drastically curtail medical services for the poor. Either choice would put states in a politically untenable position. Thus, while technically not commandeering, this choice likely crosses the line into impermissible coercion of state law making.

73. This law is similar to the access provision upheld in *New York v. United States*, 505 U.S. 144 (1992). There, Congress gave states a choice between regulating the disposal of in-state low-level radioactive waste or being subject to a federal statute that denied non-complying states access to disposal sites in other states. The Court held that this law gave states a straightforward, permissible choice between adopting federal regulation and having state law preempted by federal law. Here, states are given the same choice: enact state legislation protecting identification of newborns or have state law preempted by the Act. Federalism principles do not bar this exercise of federal power.

74. **Answer (C) is the best answer.** The physician discipline provision is a clear case of commandeering the state legislature. Congress has directed the states to make a law, consistent with federal guidelines, that regulates the state's citizens. Specifically, Congress has directed states to enact federally-prescribed disciplinary procedures that apply to physicians licensed to practice by the states.

**Answer (D) is not the best answer** because the physician discipline provision does not direct any specific state law enforcement official to enforce the procedures against state citizens. (Perhaps another provision of the Act does so.)

**Answer (A) is incorrect** because it inaccurately characterizes the physician discipline provision. Unlike the Driver's Privacy Protection Act reviewed in *Reno v. Condon*, 528 U.S. 141 (2000), the physician discipline provision does not merely ask the state to comply with the generally applicable provisions of federal law. Rather, the provision directs states to exercise their sovereign legislative power to regulate their citizens consistent with a federal mandate. **Answer (B) is incorrect** for a similar reason. While Congress may apply a generally applicable federal law to a state's traditional functions, it may not commandeer a state to act. The physician discipline provision impermissibly does the latter.

75. **Answer (B) is the best answer.** The due diligence provision is a clear case of commandeering state executive or law enforcement officials. *Printz v. United States*, 521 U.S. 898 (1997), illustrates the point well. There, Congress directed local law enforcement officials to perform federal firearm background checks. Officials who violated the law were subject to a fine and imprisonment. The Court struck down the law, holding that Congress cannot commandeer state and local law enforcement into service of the federal government. Here, Congress has put state officials to the same basic choice: state physician licensing officials must perform a federally-mandated database check on all physicians or face a federal sanction.

**Answer (A) is not the best answer** because the physician discipline provision does not direct the state legislature to make any laws regulating the state's citizens. Congress has regulated for itself, prescribing the rules for the background checks. The constitutional problem is that Congress then commandeered state officials into enforcing those rules against their citizens.

**Answer (C) is incorrect** because it inaccurately characterizes the physician discipline provision. The due diligence provision does not merely ask the state to itself comply with the generally applicable provisions of federal law. Rather, the provision directs state officials to exercise their sovereign law enforcement power consistent with a federal mandate. **Answer (D) is incorrect** for a similar reason. While Congress may apply a generally applicable federal law to a state's traditional functions, it may not commandeer state officials to enforce the federal scheme. The due diligence provision impermissibly does the latter.

76. **Answer (A) is the best answer.** Congress is giving the states a choice between enacting the physician discipline provisions of the Integrity in Physician Discipline Act and forfeiting their Medicaid funds. As the Court explained in *New York v. United States*, 505 U.S. 144 (1992), this choice is basically an exercise of Congress' Spending Clause power to condition state receipt of federal funds. The Court further explained that at some point conditional spending might become so coercive as to constitute commandeering. In other words, a deprivation of federal funds may be so severe that it coerces states into making law, which is commandeering. So, the question here is whether placing a condition on receipt of Medicaid funds is coercive.

Comparison to *South Dakota v. Dole*, 483 U.S. 203 (1985) is helpful in analyzing the question of coercion. In *Dole*, South Dakota faced the loss of about $200,000 in federal highway funds. (The Court's decision in *New York v. United States* does not indicate how much funds states forfeited for noncompliance.) A state could easily make up this shortfall by a small revenue increase or reallocation of existing funds. Further, if the funds cannot be replaced immediately, services essential to public safety and health would not cease. The opposite seems true with Medicaid funds. One billion dollars is larger than some states' entire budgets. It is hard to understand how a state could absorb such a shortfall, either by increasing tax revenue or cutting budgets. Further, eliminating the Medicaid program would jeopardize the health and welfare of the state's poor. As compared to the highway funds in *Dole*, withholding Medicaid funds imposes a far more severe sanction. If we take seriously *Dole's* promise that funding conditions may become coercive, this would seem to be the extreme case. Indeed, one court of appeals has suggested that conditioning receipt of Medicaid funds would be coercive. *See West Virginia v. Department of Health and Human Services*, 289 F.3d 281 (4th Cir. 2002). Thus, while a close question, we believe that **Answer (A) is a better answer than Answer (C)**.

**Answer (B) is not the best answer** because the Act does not direct any state law enforcement official to enforce its terms against state citizens.

**Answer (D) is not the best answer** because Congress has not enacted any federal rules that displace state rules. Rather, Congress is coercing states to enact the relevant rules.

77. **Answer (D) is the best answer.** The choice described in this question is similar to the access provision upheld in *New York v. United States*, 505 U.S. 144 (1992). There, Congress had put states to the following choice: follow federal direction on disposal of low-level radioactive waste or federal law will deny access to waste disposal sites in other states. The second choice — denial of access — was simply federal preempting of state law. Congress was allowed to give states a choice between adopting a federal regulatory scheme and preempting state law. That is precisely the choice states face here. States must either adopt federal regulations of physician discipline, or a federal scheme of physician discipline will displace existing state regulations. Thus, **Answer (D) is the correct answer**. And, because Congress is not coercing or commandeering the states, **Answers (A), (B), and (C) are incorrect**.

78. The Eleventh Amendment provides:

> The judicial power of the United States shall not be construed to extend to any suit in law or equity, commenced or prosecuted against one of the United States by citizens of another State, or by citizens or subjects of any foreign State.

On its face, the Amendment seems to apply only to diversity suits against states. In *Seminole Tribe of Florida v. Florida*, 517 U.S. 44 (1996), however, the Court held that the Amendment also applies to federal question cases seeking money damages against states. Mr. Peterson's lawsuit is such a case, as he is suing the State of Texana for liability created by a federal statute. Thus, Mr. Peterson's case comes within the reach of the State's Eleventh Amendment immunity from private suit in federal court.

The next question is whether the Act's liability provision validly abrogates Texana's Eleventh Amendment immunity. The Court has held that Congress may abrogate this immunity only when it (1) unequivocally does so by statute, and (2) acts pursuant to an enumerated power that supports abrogation. Here, the Act satisfies the first requirement, but not the second. First, the Act clearly abrogates State Eleventh Amendment immunity, as it creates a form of liability — injury caused by breaching the due diligence obligation — that applies *only* against the states. Second, however, in enacting the Act, Congress did not rely on an enumerated power that can support abrogation. In *Seminole Tribe* and its progeny, the Court has held that most of Congress' Article I powers, including the Commerce and Patent Clauses, do not abrogate the States' Eleventh Amendment immunity. *See Seminole Tribe*, 517 U.S. at 63–73 (Indian Commerce Clause); *Florida Prepaid Postsecondary Educ. Expense Bd. v. College Savs. Bank*, 527 U.S. 627 (1999) (Patent Clause); *Kimel v. Florida Bd. of Regents*, 528 U.S. 62 (2000) (Interstate Commerce Clause). Indeed, only Congress' power to enforce the Fourteenth Amendment has been recognized to do so. *Fitzpatrick v. Bitzer*, 427 U.S. 445 (1976). Because Congress was acting under its Commerce Clause power, the Act cannot abrogate State Eleventh Amendment immunity, and Mr. Peterson's federal court lawsuit is barred.

**Note:** What if Mr. Peterson's federal court lawsuit is dismissed, and he refiles the suit in Texana State court? The state should argue that it would ordinarily be immune from such a lawsuit in its own courts, and that the Eleventh Amendment bars Congress from abrogating a state's immunity in its own courts.

79. The answer is both yes and no. First, consider the opening words of the Eleventh Amendment: "*The judicial power of the United States* shall not be construed to extend to any suit. . . ." By its terms, the Amendment applies only to lawsuits in federal court. In *Alden v. Maine*, 527 U.S. 706 (1999), however, the Court explained that the Eleventh Amendment stands for a larger principle of state sovereignty that extends beyond the words of its text. One aspect of that larger sovereignty is a state's immunity from suits in its own courts. As with the states' immunity in federal courts, Congress cannot abrogate this immunity unless it both (1) does so unequivocally and (2) acts under a power that supports abrogation. As discussed in the answer to the preceding question, this Act passes the first requirement but not the second. Thus, background constitutional principles of state sovereignty, of which the Eleventh Amendment is emblematic, bar Mr. Peterson's suit in Texana State court.

80. **Answer (B) is the correct answer**. In *Garcia v. San Antonio Metropolitan Transit Authority v. Garcia*, 469 U.S. 528 (1985), the Court held that Congress may regulate state employees under a general statute that covers both private and public employees. There, Congress had extended the federal minimum wage and maximum hours law to certain state employees. Here, Congress has done something similar — the Act includes state employees within a federal law that regulates adoption leave, which is an aspect of the employment relationship. Thus, the Act would be constitutional under *Garcia*.

**Answer (A) is incorrect** because it invokes the General Welfare Clause of Article I, Section 8, Clause 1. The Court has not interpreted that Clause as a grant of power to Congress. Rather, as discussed in the answers to Questions 58 to 62, general welfare has been interpreted as a limitation on Congress' power to attach conditions to the receipt of federal funds.

**Answer (C) is incorrect** because the Act does not commandeer the states. The Act requires the state to take action regarding its own employees, and does not require states to exercise lawmaking power over private actors, such as employees of private companies. This is the crucial distinction recognized by *Condon v. Reno*, 528 U.S. 141 (2000), where federal law regulated the handling of drivers license information maintained by public and private entities. *Condon* conceded that the state would have to take steps, including drafting rules and regulations, to comply with the federal drivers license law. But such in-house lawmaking is not commandeering. Commandeering only occurs when the federal government directs or coerces the state to make laws that regulate private actors. Because the Act does not force the state to do so, it does not commandeer.

**Answer (D) is incorrect** because it invokes the legal rule from *National League of Cities v. Usury*, 426 U.S. 833 (1976), which was overruled by *Garcia*.

81. **Answer (D) is the correct answer**. The choice posed by this question is a form of the conditional spending discussed earlier in the answers to Questions 58 to 62. Recall that states faced a similar choice in the case *South Dakota v. Dole*, 483 U.S. 203 (1987), where receipt of 5% of federal highway funds was conditioned on the state enacting a drinking age of 21 years or older. As in *Dole*, the conditional spending in this question should be constitutional. First, the condition — enact a law that provides adoption-related employment leave — promotes the General Welfare, as the Court has always treated protection and promotion of the family as a valid government interest. Second, the condition is unambiguous — the state is faced with a clear choice of two options. Third, the condition is related to the federal funds. The condition relates to adoption, and the funds support the foster care system and adoption services. Fourth, there is no independent constitutional bar to the state fulfilling the condition. A state law granting adoption-related leave would not offend a separate part of the Constitution. In addition to meeting the four *Dole* elements, the choice does not effectively coerce the state to make law. As in *Dole*, the Act imposes a modest incentive by placing the condition on only 5% of the funds.

**Answer (A) is incorrect** because *New York v. United States*, 505 U.S. 144 (1992), held that a non-coercive act of conditional spending is not commandeering.

**Answer (B) is incorrect** for two reasons. First, Answer (B) hints at the argument made in *United States v. Lopez*, 514 U.S. 549 (1995), that Congress does not have power to regulate matters traditionally regulated by the states. As discussed in the answer to Question 55, however, the terms of employment, such as paid and unpaid employee leave, is certainly an economic activity within Congress' power under the Commerce Clause. Second, *Dole* held that Congress can use conditional spending to encourage states to adopt laws that Congress itself might not have power to enact. So, even if Congress lacked power to regulate adoption, it could use its Spending Clause power to encourage states to do so. And this second reason also explains why **Answer (C)**, while a correct statement of the law, **is not the best answer**.

82. **Answer (A) is the correct answer**. The Act now poses the same choice as the unconstitutional provision of the federal statute in *New York v. United States*, 505 U.S.

144 (1992). Recall that one part of the Low Level Radioactive Waste Act gave states a choice between, on the one hand, enacting a federally-prescribed radioactive waste disposal scheme, and on the other hand, taking title to the radioactive waste within the state. Here, the Act poses a similar choice — enact the federal adoption regulation, or assume liability for expenses. As in *New York v. United States*, this choice coerces the states and so is an unconstitutional act of commandeering.

**Answer (B) is incorrect** because Congress does have power under the Commerce Clause to regulate the *subject* at issue: terms of employment leave. The Act is unconstitutional because of the *manner* in which Congress chose to regulate that subject — commandeering. **Answer (C) is incorrect** because it does not recognize this limitation on Congress' power to regulate subjects within the Commerce Clause power.

**Answer (D) is incorrect** because it invokes the legal rule from *National League of Cities v. Usury*, 426 U.S. 833 (1976), which was overruled by *Garcia*.

83.  **Answer (A) is the best answer.** The first issue in a Dormant Commerce Clause question is whether the state law discriminates between in-state and out-of-state commerce. On the one hand, if the law discriminates, it is *per se* invalid, with one minor exception. On the other hand, if the law treats in-state and out-of-state commerce evenhandedly, then one must balance the state's interest against the law's burden on interstate commerce.

Here, it is a close call whether the law discriminates. On the one hand, it does not distinguish between firms based on their residence (i.e., state of incorporation or principal place of business). For example, a New York corporation can sell automobiles in Arkabama if it has a physical location in Arkabama and obtains the appropriate license. On the other hand, Arkabama has limited the retail sale of automobiles to those physically present within the state. Firms with no in-state presence are absolutely excluded from making retail sales to Arkabama consumers.

The Court addressed an analogous situation in *C&A Carbone, Inc. v. Town of Clarkstown*, 511 U.S. 383 (1994). There, a city ordinance required all local solid waste be processed at a designated facility within the city. A local waste collection firm challenged the ordinance because the firm wished to ship its waste to an out-of-town processor. The Court held that the ordinance discriminated between local and interstate commerce by excluding out-of-state firms from a local market. Local firms that either generated or collected waste had a demand for processing services. The ordinance awarded local demand to local processors, denying out-of-state processors the ability to compete for that demand. The Court struck down similar local-processing require-ments in *Dean Milk Co. v. City of Madison*, 340 U.S. 349 (1951) (invalidating an ordinance requiring local processing of milk sold within the city).

The Arkabama law at issue here has the same effect. Arkabama consumers demand retail services for the sale of automobiles; the statute directs that only in-state firms may serve that demand. Out-of-state firms, such as Cars.com, are excluded from serving that same demand. Because the statute is discriminatory, the balancing test used for evenhanded laws does not apply. Thus, neither **Answer (C) nor (D) is the best** because each relies on the evenhanded balancing test.

Discriminatory state laws are invalid unless the state has a reason to discriminate against out-of-state commerce other than its origin. For example, in *Maine v. Taylor*, 477 U.S. 131 (1986), the state had prohibited the importation of baitfish. The state claimed that introduction of imported baitfish into the state's waters would harm the state's ecosystem. At trial, the lower court found that: (1) out-of-state baitfish possess parasites not found in the state's native fish, (2) shipments of out-of-state baitfish may contain other non-native fish to the state's waters that may upset the ecosystem, and (3) there was no feasible method to screen out-of-state baitfish for parasites or non-native fish. Based on these findings, the Court upheld the import ban because (1) the out-of-state commerce (*i.e.*, the baitfish) posed a unique threat to the state's interests, and (2) banning importation was the only feasible means to protect the state's interest.

The question for the Arkabama law is whether out-of-state automobile retailers pose a unique threat to the state's interests. The Arkabama legislature seeks to prevent fraud in automobile sales. Certainly, prevention of fraud is a significant state interest. But, it is not clear that out-of-state retailers pose a special risk of fraud. The law's preamble claims that a special fraud risk exists when retail sales do not take place face-to-face. But, the statute does *not* require all retail sales to take place face-to-face. An in-state retailer could make a long-distance sale to a customer in another city, with negotiation and sale taking place by phone, fax, or e-mail. If long-distance sales pose a unique risk of fraud, that risk is not confined to out-of-state retailers. For this reason, Arkabama does not have an acceptable reason to discriminate against out-of-state commerce. Thus, **Answer (A) is the best answer.**

84. **Answer (C) is the best answer.** The first question is whether the tolling provision discriminates between in-state and out-of-state commerce, as different tests apply to discriminatory and evenhanded state laws. This law is evenhanded because it applies to *all civil litigants* regardless of their residence or citizenship. For example, the statute applies the same to a Texana defendant who leaves the state as it does to a New York defendant who does the same. For this reason, the Texana statute is different from the tolling provision examined in *Bendix Autolite Corp. v. Midwesco Enters., Inc.*, 486 U.S. 888 (1988), where the state law tolled the applicable statute of limitations for organizations located outside the state that had not designated an agent for service of process. In *Bendix*, the Court explained that the law discriminated because it treated differently in-state and out-of-state businesses. The Texana statute does not make such a distinction. Thus, **Answer (A) is incorrect**.

Because the law is evenhanded, the Supreme Court applies a balancing test in deciding whether the law is constitutional. The test balances the state interest behind the challenged law against the law's burden on interstate commerce. *See Kassel v. Consolidated Freightways Corp.*, 450 U.S. 662 (1981). If the burden on interstate commerce outweighs the state's interest, the statute is unconstitutional. Because an evenhanded state law may violate the Dormant Commerce Clause, **Answer (B) is incorrect**.

Here, the state has little, if any, present interest served by the statute. When first enacted, the statute surely served the interest of preventing a potential civil defendant from avoiding liability by evading personal jurisdiction during the statute of limitations. But, since the law was passed, the Supreme Court has held that states may exercise personal jurisdiction over defendants who are physically outside the state at the time of service.

*International Shoe Co. v. Washington*, 326 U.S. 310 (1945). (The Court made the same observation in *Bendix*, where it dealt with non-resident corporations that could be reached under the state's long-arm jurisdiction.) Thus, tolling the statute of limitations solely because the defendant has left the state is no longer necessary to ensure full compensation of state residents.

Conversely, the Texana tolling provision significantly burdens interstate commerce by increasing the cost of interstate travel. If a person commits an act to which the Texana tolling provision might apply, the person must continually decide whether traveling outside the state is worth the cost of extending the applicable statute of limitations. For example, assume that a Texana resident is in a car accident and is unsure whether the other driver will sue. And, because Texana was the place of the accident, the state would have specific personal jurisdiction over any lawsuit arising out of the accident. Shortly after the accident, the resident receives a job offer that would require relocation to another state. Accepting the job would effectively extend the statute of limitations indefinitely, leaving the resident forever subject to suit in Texana. This would defeat one of the very purposes of the statute of limitations — ensuring a sense of repose and the ability to plan one's affairs without perpetual threat of suit. By nullifying this protection on account of interstate travel, the Texana tolling provision substantially burdens interstate commerce.

In sum, the Texana tolling provision no longer serves a state interest, yet it imposes a substantial burden on interstate travel. This should be enough for the statute to fail the balancing test. Thus, **Answer (C) is better than Answer (D)**.

85. **Answer (C) is the best answer**.

As long ago as *Dean Milk Co. v. City of Madison*, 340 U.S. 349 (1951), the Supreme Court held that the Dormant Commerce Clause applies to local and municipal laws. Thus, **Answer (A) is incorrect**.

Ordinarily, the next step would be to perform a Dormant Commerce Clause analysis, beginning with the question whether the ordinance discriminates between in-state and out-of-state commerce. That analysis is unnecessary, however, because the ordinance fits within the market participant exception. Under that exception, a state may contract on any terms it wishes when participating within a market, even terms that discriminate against out-of-staters, without violating the Dormant Commerce Clause. For example, in *Reeves, Inc. v. Stake*, 447 U.S. 429 (1980), South Dakota required all cement produced at state-run plants be sold to in-state customers. While such discrimination against out-of-state customers would ordinarily violate the Dormant Commerce Clause, South Dakota could do so when it participated in the private market for sale of cement. Thus, if Jibbs County is participating in the private labor market, it may favor local residents.

The Supreme Court recognized an important limit on the market participant exception in *South-Central Timber Development, Inc. v. Wunnicke*, 467 U.S. 82 (1984). There, the Court held that the exception does not apply to contract terms that reach beyond the market exchange between the government and its contracting partner. For example, *Wunnicke* involved the contracts Alaska used to sell its timber. The contracts required that purchasers process the timber in-state. The Court held that the market participant exception applies to *only the market in which the state actually participates*. While Alaska participated in the market for *sale* of timber, its contract imposed restrictions in the separate, downstream market for *processing* that timber. Thus, the exception did not apply, and the processing requirement was invalid.

In the present case, one could argue that Jibbs County has imposed a downstream restraint. The county participates only in the market for general contracting services, but it imposes a restraint that affects the separate, downstream market for the contractor's employees. While appealing, this logic has been rejected in the case of *White v. Massachusetts Council of Construction Employers, Inc.*, 460 U.S. 204 (1983). There, as here, a municipality had imposed a residence preference on its general contractors. In holding that the city was protected by the market participant doctrine, the Court explained that both the general contractor and its employees were effectively "working for the city." Consequently, the city was treated as a participant in the market for hiring the contractors' employees. Similarly, the county should be treated as a participant in the market for its contractor's employees. Consequently, the county's preference is not a downstream restraint, and thus **Answer (D) is incorrect**. Further, as a market participant, the city's preference for local residents is shielded from Dormant Commerce Clause scrutiny. Thus, **Answer (B) is incorrect**.

86.  **Answer (D) is the best answer**. Minnesota's mulch ban discriminates against out-of-state commerce, and so the per se rule of unconstitutionality applies. Recall that under the per se rule, a state law is invalid unless the state has a reason to discriminate against out-of-state commerce other than its origin. The Minnesota law is similar to the state law upheld in *Maine v. Taylor*, 477 U.S. 131 (1986). There, the Court upheld the state ban on imported baitfish because (1) the out-of-state commerce (*i.e.*, the baitfish) posed a unique threat to the state's interests, and (2) banning importation was the only feasible means to protect the state's interest. Here, the same can be said for the Minnesota mulch ban. First, the out-of-state commerce (*i.e.*, the mulch) poses a unique threat to the state's ecosystem because the termite has yet to invade the state. Second, banning mulch imports is necessary to protect the state's ecosystem because no method exists to feasibly screen mulch for the termite. Thus, Minnesota's mulch law fits within *Taylor*'s narrow allowance for discriminatory state laws.

**Answer (A) is incorrect** because it does not recognize the narrow exception to the per se rule adopted in *Taylor*.

**Answer (B) is incorrect** because it misstates the underlying law. The Court has repeatedly held that states have concurrent, albeit limited, power to regulate interstate commerce. Answer (B) incorrectly states that Congress' power over interstate commerce is exclusive.

**Answer (C) is incorrect** because it states the wrong legal rule. Regardless of whether a state regulates a local matter, the Dormant Commerce Clause restricts *how* the state regulates that subject. Even regarding purely local matters, a state cannot regulate in a manner that discriminates against out-of-state commerce or imposes an unjustified burden on interstate commerce. Answer (C) incorrectly ignores this limit on state power.

87.   **Answer (D) is the best answer because of the reasons explained below.**

As with the Dormant Commerce Clause, the Supreme Court has held that the Article IV Privileges and Immunities Clause applies to municipal and local laws. *See United Building and Construction Trades Council v. City of Camden*, 465 U.S. 208 (1984). Thus, **Answer (A) is incorrect**.

Answer (C) raises the question whether a state or local law is exempt from the Clause because the government is acting as a market participant. Recall that the Court applies such a market participant exception to the Dormant Commerce Clause. In *City of Camden*, however, the Court rejected the same exception under the Article IV Privileges and Immunities Clause. Thus, **Answer (C) is incorrect**. Instead, the Court applies a two-part test. First, the Court asks whether the state or local government has discriminated regarding a privilege or immunity of state citizens. If not, the law does not violate the Clause. Here, the county discriminates regarding the right to engage in a common calling (construction work), which the Court has held to be a privilege and immunity of state citizens. *See Hicklin v. Orbeck*, 437 U.S. 518 (1978) (right to jobs related to oil and gas pipeline regarded privilege or immunity of state citizens). For this reason, **Answer (B) is incorrect**.

One might argue that the ordinance does not actually discriminate against out-of-town employees, as it does not directly restrict a contractor's freedom to hire them. But, this argument ignores the Supreme Court cases that have struck down laws charging non-residents higher license fees. For example, in *Toomer v. Witsell*, 334 U.S. 385 (1948), the Court struck down a state law that imposed a much higher commercial shrimp boat licensing fee on non-residents ($2,500) than on state residents ($25.27). Jibbs County's ordinance discriminates in the same way, as it places a financial burden solely on non-resident employees. The $1,000 subsidy gives the contractor a powerful incentive to hire county residents. The subsidy would allow the contractor to either (1) offer the county resident a higher wage, or (2) keep the subsidy as additional profit. Thus, the ordinance discriminates by imposing an economic burden solely on non-resident employees, by either discouraging their hiring or giving them lower wages.

If, as here, the challenged law burdens a privilege or immunity of state citizens, the Court asks a second question: Is the discrimination justified? Discrimination is justified only if (1) the government has a "substantial reason" for treating out-of-staters differently, and (2) the challenged law bears a "substantial relationship" to that interest. In applying the second element, the Court has asked whether the government could have vindicated its "substantial reason" with a less discriminatory measure. Here, the county's reason for the hiring preference is to protect the local economy. Substantial unemployment has battered the local economy, choking off tax revenues and chasing middle class residents away. In *City of Camden*, the Court indicated that an effort aimed at local economic survival would constitute a "substantial reason."

The next question, however, is whether the ordinance's hiring preference was the least discriminatory measure that could achieve the county's end. *City of Camden* and *Hicklin* are relevant to this question. *Hicklin* struck down a state law imposing a resident hiring preference on firms working on oil and gas leases. The preference applied not only to general contractors and subcontractors paid by the state, but to all firms that provided supplies or services to those general contractors and subcontractors. Conversely, in *City of Camden*, the Court refused to strike down a local hiring preference limited to general contractors and subcontractors paid by the state. (The Court remanded the case for further fact-finding regarding the government's interest.) The Court explained that the *City of Camden* ordinance was much narrower than that in *Hicklin*, as it had no "ripple effects" extending beyond the general contractors and subcontractors with whom the government dealt directly.

The Jibbs County ordinance is more like the law in *City of Camden* because the county has limited its preference to only general contractors and subcontractors working on county projects. As in *City of Camden*, the Court would not strike down the county ordinance as invalid on its face. Instead, the Court would require a factual hearing where the county would have to prove both the existence of the economic exigencies that purportedly lie behind the ordinance, as well as whether the hiring preference ameliorates that problem. Thus, **Answer (D) is the best answer**.

88.   **Answer (C) is the best answer as explained below.**

Recall that a two-part test applies under the Article IV Privileges and Immunities Clause. First, has the state discriminated against non-residents regarding a privilege or immunity of state citizenship? If so, the state must show that: (a) it has a "substantial reason" for treating out-of-staters differently, and (b) the challenged law bears a "substantial relationship" to that interest. **Answer (A) is incorrect** because it applies the wrong standard of review.

Here, the question can be answered under the first step of the test. The Court has generally found only constitutional rights and the right to work in an occupation, profession, or trade to be privileges and immunities of state citizenship. Further, and of particular relevance to the New Island park fee, the Court held, in *Baldwin v. Montana Fish and Game Commission*, 436 U.S. 371 (1978), that the state could charge non-residents as much as twenty-five times more for an elk-hunting license than it charged residents. The Court concluded that elk hunting was "a recreation and a sport," and "not a means to the nonresident's livelihood." Therefore, hunting is not a privilege and immunity of state citizenship entitled to heightened protection. The same is true of the activities burdened by the New Island non-resident fee — snorkeling, row boating, and hiking. Thus, the fee is not subject to further scrutiny under the Article IV Privileges and Immunities Clause. (**Answer (D) is incorrect** because it assumes that the fee should be analyzed under part two of the test), making **Answer (C) correct**, and **Answer (B) incorrect**.

89.   There are three situations in which federal law preempts state law: (1) federal law expressly preempts state law, (2) state law conflicts with the terms or purpose of federal law, and (3) Congress has so completely regulated a field that no room remains for state regulation. We can quickly eliminate express preemption, as the Act contains no express preemption provision. Next, we can eliminate conflict between state law and the *terms* of federal law. Relevant state law neither requires something that SVAA prohibits, nor prohibits something that federal law requires. Stated simply, it is possible for a health care provider to comply with both state and federal law here. If state tort law requires written informed consent, nothing in the Act imposes a conflicting obligation. So, the question is whether the state tort action conflicts with the Act's purpose, or whether the Act so occupies the field that it leaves no room for state tort law.

For conflict preemption, the question is whether the Act's informed consent standard establishes a floor or a ceiling. Clearly, Congress wanted health care providers to obtain *at least* the informed consent required by the Act. But, was Congress opposed to imposition of *additional requirements* by states? The Court treats this question as one of congressional intent. *Geier v. American Honda Motor Co.*, 529 U.S. 861 (2000), illustrates the Court's analysis. In *Geier*, the Court addressed a state law product liability claim that a car was defectively manufactured because it did not have a driver's side airbag. A Department of Labor safety standard required car manufacturers to install some form of passive restraint, such as an airbag or automatic seatbelt, but did not specify which restraint a manufacturer must use. The Court found that the standard intentionally left manufacturers discretion to determine which restraint(s) offered the best balance of cost and safety for specific vehicle models. In short, Congress mandated flexibility as the best regulatory approach. The state product liability claim threatened to eliminate that flexibility by imposing tort liability unless the manufacturer chose a single restraint — airbags. Because the rigidity imposed by state tort law conflicted with flexibility intended by the Department's rule, the federal rule preempted state tort law. The same analysis could apply to the SVAA. The House Report states that Congress intended health care providers to determine the best manner in which to deliver information about the smallpox vaccine. Specifically, Congress was concerned that a one-size-fits-all disclosure procedure would undermine the flexibility needed to adapt to the chaos of mass vaccinations. A state tort claim seeking a rigid written consent requirement would eliminate the flexibility so prized by Congress. As in *Geier*, the rigid rule imposed by state tort liability conflicts with the federal purpose of maintaining flexibility. Therefore, the Act preempts the state product liability claim.

Field preemption is either inapplicable or irrelevant to this case, depending on how one defines the relevant field of regulation. On the one hand, if the field is vaccinations generally (or medical care generally), the field is still largely left open to the states. The Act confines itself to distribution and administration of a single vaccine — that for smallpox. States may still regulate administration of other approved vaccines, such as deciding which vaccines school children must have. On the other hand, if the field is narrowly defined as the regulation of smallpox vaccinations, then the analysis mirrors that regarding conflict of purpose in the preceding paragraph. Analysis of field preemption would add nothing.

90. In *McCulloch v. Maryland*, 17 U.S. 316 (4 Wheat.) (1819), the Supreme Court first recognized the doctrine of intergovernmental tax immunity. The Court held that Maryland could not tax the Bank of the United States because a state's taxing power extends only to those to whom it is politically accountable. When Maryland taxed the national bank, it effectively taxed the citizens of every other state in the nation. This violated the principle of no taxation without representation. More recently, the Court has interpreted *McCulloch*'s principle to mean that states may not impose a discriminatory tax on federal employees and instrumentalities. (As in *McCulloch*, states still may not tax the United States itself or "an agency or instrumentality so closely connected to the government that the two cannot realistically be viewed as separate entities." *United States v. New Mexico*, 455 U.S. 720 (1982).) For example, a state may tax *all* wages evenhandedly, including wages of federal employees. But, a state may not impose a higher tax on federal wages. *See Davis v. Michigan Department of Treasury*, 489 U.S. 803 (1989). Here, New Island's tax is constitutional because it is evenhanded, treating federal judges the same as all other in-state wage earners.

91. Yes. In *Davis v. Michigan Department of Treasury*, 489 U.S. 803 (1989), the Supreme Court held that it is not enough that a state tax federal employees on the same terms as most other in-state wage earners. A state must also apply the same tax treatment to federal employees that it applies to *its own employees*. In *Davis*, Michigan imposed a general tax on retirement benefits (including federal benefits), but exempted state employee retirement benefits from the tax. The Court held that such discrimination between federal and state employees (or retirees) — which New Island has done here — is unconstitutional.

92. **Answer (B) is the best answer.** Federal law preempts state law in three circumstances: (1) federal law expressly preempts state law, (2) state law conflicts with the terms or purpose of federal law, or (3) federal law so completely occupies a field of regulation that it leaves no room for state regulation. This case falls in the second category because state and federal law directly conflict with one another. It is impossible to comply with both ATELA and the New Arkansas wrongful death statute. On the one hand, ATELA says that DrugVac shall be immune from civil liability due to the use of its smallpox vaccine. On the other hand, the New Arkansas wrongful death statute says that DrugVac may be liable to the doctor's family due to the use of the smallpox vaccine. When state and federal law are incompatible, the Supremacy Clause provides that federal law trumps state law. U.S. Const. Art. VI, Cl. 2. Thus, ATELA preempts the New Arkansas wrongful death statute, and **Answer (B) is the best answer.**

We can **eliminate Answers (C) and (D)** because the New Arkansas wrongful death statute does not discriminate against out-of-staters. (Recall that the Article IV Privileges and Immunities Clause, discussed above, applies only to state laws that discriminate against out-of-staters.) Typical state wrongful death statutes simply provide a civil remedy for the families of those killed by another's wrongful conduct. The same remedy applies regardless of the victim's (or her family's) residence or citizenship. Thus, **Answers (C) and (D) are incorrect** because they both mistakenly assume that the New Arkansas wrongful death statute is discriminatory.

**Answer (A)** refers to the Dormant Commerce Clause test applied to evenhanded state laws. Because the New Arkansas wrongful death statute does not discriminate against out-of-state commerce, the evenhanded balancing test would apply. But, the wrongful death statute should easily survive the balancing test, as would most generic state tort laws. The state has a significant interest in compensating those harmed by the wrongful acts of another. In addition to retribution for and deterrence of wrongful acts, such compensation also prevents the victim's family from becoming a ward of the state. On the other side of the scale, there is little imposition on interstate commerce. As wrongful death actions are common throughout the United States, application of the New Arkansas statute should not discourage or make more costly DrugVac's interstate operations. Indeed, federalism tolerates nontrivial (and even substantial) variations among state tort laws.

93. **Answer (C) is the best answer**.

At the outset, we can easily dispose of Answers (A) and (B), both of which assume that New Arkansas is discriminating against out-of-state commerce. The sales tax, however, applies evenhandedly, imposing the same tax rate regardless of the vendor's location. Thus, **Answers (A) and (B) are incorrect**.

State taxation of interstate commerce is subject to scrutiny under both the Due Process Clause and the Commerce Clause. The Supreme Court described the analysis under each Clause in *Quill Corp. v. North Dakota ex rel. Heitkamp*, 504 U.S. 298 (1992). First, the due process analysis mirrors the Court's analysis in personal jurisdiction cases. The Court asks whether the entity taxed has directed sufficient activity at the taxing state that the entity taxed should reasonably expect to be subject to that state's taxing authority. In *Quill*, the Court held that the test was satisfied when an out-of-state "mail-order house . . . is engaged in continuous and widespread solicitation of business within a State." The same should be true here. By soliciting and fulfilling Internet orders from New Arkansas residents, BuyBooks.com has directed business activity at the state. Further, over $1 million in sales is a substantial amount. Thus, applying the sales tax to BuyBooks.com would not violate the Due Process Clause, and **Answer (D) is incorrect**.

The Commerce Clause portion of the analysis was established in *Complete Auto Transit, Inc. v. Brady*, 430 U.S. 274 (1977), which created a four-part test under which a state tax on interstate commerce is valid only if it:

> [1] is applied to an activity with a substantial nexus with the taxing state, [2] is fairly apportioned, [3] does not discriminate against interstate commerce, and [4] is fairly related to the services provided by the state.

*Brady*, 430 U.S. at 279. The *Quill* case is, again, instructive on how the test applies to the New Arkansas sales tax. In *Quill*, the Court held that an out-of-state firm has a "substantial nexus with the taxing state" only if the firm maintains a "physical presence" within that state, such as a "small sales force, plant, or office." Thus, a firm that only has mail-order or catalogue contact with the taxing state lacks a "substantial nexus" with that state. BuyBooks.com is in a similar position. It has no personnel, office, or property in the state. Also, its only contact with customers is through a long-distance medium — the Internet. Because BuyBooks.com lacks a substantial nexus with New Arkansas, the Commerce Clause bars imposition of the sales tax. Thus, **Answer (C) is the correct answer**.

94. **Answer (D) is the best answer.** The Thirteenth Amendment is unusual because it reaches private behavior, unlike most other constitutional provisions that limit only government action. However, because the Thirteenth Amendment forbids slavery and involuntary servitude, these behaviors are forbidden absolutely without regard to whether the violator is a public entity or a private individual.

**Answer (A) is incorrect.** It is important to understand that the Fourteenth Amendment, unlike the Thirteenth Amendment, only prohibits government behavior and does not apply to private behavior. *Civil Rights Cases,* 109 U.S. 3 (1883). This is where we get the term "state action." It means that a constitutional provision only applies to action taken by a government. Indeed, because the owner of the business was not the government, Jane Doe could not bring an action under the Fourteenth Amendment, because that Amendment requires a state actor.

**Answer (B) is incorrect** because the Thirteenth Amendment does not address receiving pay for work; rather, it prohibits slavery and involuntary servitude. Thus, a person who is not paid for work does not have a Thirteenth Amendment claim unless the failure to pay is part of a system of enslavement, as in this case.

**Answer (C) is incorrect** for the reasons previously stated. The Thirteenth Amendment reaches private behavior.

95. **Answer (B) is the best answer.** The law is clear that when government officials are acting in their official capacity their actions constitute state action even if their actions are illegal. This ensures that the state, in order to avoid liability, acts to make its officials behave legally and responsibly.

**Answer (A) is incorrect** because the result is the same even when government officials act outside their official duties. The test is not whether their behavior was within their duties, but whether they were acting while in their official capacity. So, for example, if these police officers were involved in a fight while off-duty and out of uniform, then they would not be acting in their official capacity, and their behavior would not be deemed state action.

**Answer (C) is incorrect** because, for state action purposes, the state is considered to include local governments. Don't become confused by the term "state action." It is not limited to action by the states, but rather applies to any government action, state, local, or federal.

**Answer (D) is incorrect** because physical violence directed at a person by a government or government official is considered to be a violation of personal liberty.

96.  Congress has enacted legislation under various provisions of the Constitution, such as the Commerce Clause and Section 5 of the Fourteenth Amendment, that prohibit by statute discrimination by private individuals. For example, the Civil Rights Act of 1964 prohibits discrimination by private employers and places of public accommodation (such as restaurants and hotels) on the basis of race, sex, etc. Such statutes reach private action even though the Fourteenth Amendment only prohibits state action. The important point is to distinguish between constitutional and statutory prohibitions.

97.  **Answer (B) is the best answer.** This hypothetical follows closely the facts in *Marsh v. Alabama*, 326 U.S. 501 (1946), in which a Jehovah's Witness was punished under the state's criminal trespass laws for distributing literature in a "company town." The company prohibited distribution of religious literature without its permission. The company claimed the right to stop such distribution on its private property. The *Marsh* Court rejected the argument that the company, as a private landowner, could restrict distribution of literature without violating the Constitution. The Court created what is called the "public function" rule in deciding when private activity will be considered public activity, and thus subject to same constitutional limitations imposed on government behavior. The Court looked at the facts — the company's ownership and operation of the entire town — including providing general access to stores and businesses. The Court concluded that because these businesses were built and operated primarily to benefit the public and because their function was primarily a public function, the private activity became a public activity regulated by the Constitution. As such, the Jehovah's Witness could not be prosecuted for trespass just as she could not be prosecuted for trespass on any typical city street. Given this holding, Answer (B) is correct because ABC Company is also running a town, the function of which is primarily public. ABC Company then would come under the "public function" rule and would have to follow the Constitution.

**Answer (A) is incorrect** for the reasons stated above.

**Answer (C) is incorrect** because, if this town were to be considered private property, then the activist would not have a First Amendment right to distribute the literature. The First Amendment only forbids limitations on freedom of speech when the government or some other public actor is doing the limiting. It does not prohibit a private owner from refusing access to his property to those who wish to use it for speech-making purposes.

**Answer (D) is incorrect** because the First Amendment has been held to apply to the states by way of the Due Process Clause of the Fourteenth Amendment under the Incorporation Doctrine.

98.  **Answer (A) is the best answer.** This hypothetical closely follows the facts in *Jackson v. Metropolitan Edison Co.*, 419 U.S. 345 (1974). In that case the Supreme Court found that a private utility company did not violate procedural due process by failing to give notice and hearing to a customer whose service was terminated for nonpayment. The *Jackson* Court limited the "public function" rule to when a private entity exercises powers *traditionally exclusively reserved to the State.* The Court then reasoned that,

because it is not uncommon for private companies to provide utilities, such a service was not traditionally exclusively reserved to the states, and so the company's private function was not converted into a public function. Therefore, constitutional limitations on government behavior, such as procedural due process, did not apply to this private utility company. Under this holding then, Answer (A) is correct. Also, please note that this answer focuses only on whether the Fourteenth Amendment would impose on the private company some notice and hearing requirement. This is not to say, however, that private utility companies do not have to obey statutory law that may require such notice and hearing before terminating utility services.

**Answer (B) is incorrect** for the reasons stated above. Given the "traditionally exclusively" test, ABC's operation of the electric company is not a public function.

**Answer (C) is incorrect** because the Fourteenth Amendment does not, in and of itself, apply to private behavior.

**Answer (D) is incorrect** because it is too broad. For example, if the state operated this electric company, then the state would have to follow the dictates of procedural due process in handling its business. This might mean that the state would have to offer those who did not pay their bill some type of notice and hearing under the Fourteenth Amendment that a private company would not have to offer.

99.   First, *Hudgens* came after the Court's decision in *Jackson v. Metropolitan Edison Co.*, in which the Court stated that a private function only becomes a public function when the private entity is exercising powers that are traditionally exclusively reserved to the state. Because operating a shopping center or a business is not a function traditionally exclusively reserved to the state, a privately-owned shopping center is not constrained by the Constitution and can control who has access to its property. Second, *Marsh* is distinguishable under its facts. *Marsh* involved the classic "company town" in which *all aspects of the town* were owned by the company. In essence, the company was operating as a city, and the operation of cities is traditionally exclusively a public function. For these reasons it is possible to reconcile *Hudgens* and *Marsh.* However, note that a strong argument could be made that modern shopping malls, with their amusement areas and indoor parks, are analogous to town squares. The more closely analogous, the stronger the argument that such malls are similar to the company town in *Marsh,* are performing a public function, and should have to abide by the same constitutional requirements as the state.

100.  **Answer (C) is the best answer.** The Court has held, on several occasions, that private schools do not perform a public function because education is not traditionally exclusively a public endeavor; and, as such under the *Jackson v. Metropolitan Edison Co.* test, private school actions are not considered to be state action. Even when a private school receives almost all its funding from the government, the Court has held that the private school still is not performing a public function, and thus is not subject to constitutional requirements imposed on governments. *See Rendell-Baker v. Kohn,* 457 U.S. 830 (1982).

**Answers (A) and (B) are incorrect** for the reasons stated above.

**Answer (D) is incorrect** because nothing in constitutional law endorses this position, and the answer is much too broad to be accurate. For example, public school teachers do not lose their free speech rights. They continue to be protected by the Constitution. It may well be that a particular school district or a state education agency may impose contractual terms on public school teachers to limit their ability to advocate in the classroom. By agreeing to sign such a contract, the teachers are bound by the terms. However, this is not the scenario found in Answer (D). Answer (D) just says teachers are not protected by the Constitution — which is clearly wrong.

101. **Answer (B) is the best answer.** This question asks you to consider the Court's holding in *Shelley v. Kraemer,* 334 U.S. 1 (1948), in which the Court was faced with racially restrictive covenants that were enforced by courts in Missouri and Michigan. This judicial enforcement stopped the sale of property to African-Americans despite the willingness of the sellers to transfer their property in disregard of the restrictive covenant. Therefore, the parties would have consummated the transaction except for the enforcement of the racially-restrictive covenants by the judicial system. The Supreme Court held that this judicial enforcement of a racially-restrictive contract amounted to state action. Therefore, this enforcement caused the state to discriminate on the basis of race, which is forbidden by the Fourteenth Amendment. Answer (B) is the closest to the Court's holding in *Shelley* because the covenant in question could be viewed as one that discriminates arbitrarily without a legitimate purpose against Spanish speakers in violation of the Fourteenth Amendment's Equal Protection Clause.

*Shelley* was significant because it converted the judicial enforcement of a private contract into state action. After the *Shelley* decision, many questioned the breadth of the opinion and whether it forced all private behavior to comply with the Constitution before a private party could seek judicial relief. The Court has never gone this far and has seldom relied on *Shelley,* but neither has it repudiated the holding. For example, the Court did not extend *Shelley* when a state prosecuted for trespass individuals who "sat-in" at a restaurant that refused to serve blacks. *Bell v. Maryland,* 378 U.S. 226 (1964). The Court avoided the issue of whether to extend *Shelley* in this context, although some members of the Court thought the extension was logical. The logic was that without the state's prosecution for trespass, the individuals would have no fear of entering the restaurant. Therefore, it was the state's legal actions that were helping the private restaurant continue its discrimination.

One difference noted by commentators between *Shelley* and *Bell* focuses on the willingness of the sellers in *Shelley* to go forward with the sale. In contrast in *Bell,* the owner of the restaurant was not willing to serve blacks. Therefore, it is argued that judicial enforcement of private matters only rises to the level of state action when the judicial enforcement blocks the agreement of the parties. While this is an interesting analysis, the Court has not adopted this distinction, and *Shelley* remains good law.

The Court's decisions in the state action area are often difficult to reconcile. In some measure this is a function of the decisions being so fact-bound on the question of whether the state's involvement with private activity rises to a level sufficient to convert the private activity to public action.

**Answer (A) is incorrect.** Given the holding in *Shelley*, judicial enforcement of a private contract may be seen as state action sufficient to trigger application of the Fourteenth Amendment to prevent a denial of equal protection.

**Answer (C) is incorrect** because it was not the state court but the restrictive covenant that limited Ruth Adams's contract rights. The issue was not whether the covenant restricted her contract rights — it did — but whether enforcement created state action that fostered arbitrary discrimination.

**Answer (D) is incorrect** because it limits the application of *Shelley* to racially-restrictive covenants without any support in the case law for such a limitation. Some scholars have suggested that *Shelley* should be limited to fact patterns that deal with judicial enforcement of racial discrimination. The Court, however, has never said this. Indeed, in *Lugar v. Edmonson Oil Co.*, 457 U.S. 922 (1982), the Court found state action because a court issued a prejudgment attachment writ, and in *Edmonson v. Leesville Concrete Co.*, 500 U.S. 614 (1991), the Court found state action when private parties based peremptory challenges on racial discrimination.

102. **Answer (C) is the best answer, although it is a close call between Answer (B) and Answer (C).** The question focuses on whether a relationship between a state actor and a private party is sufficiently interdependent, or symbiotic, so that the private party's action is considered to be that of the state. Here the facts suggest an interdependent relationship between WasteAway and New Jersey, making it unlikely a court would grant a motion to dismiss.

Certain facts, similar to those in *Burton v. Wilmington Parking Authority,* 365 U.S. 715 (1961), indicate a symbiotic relationship here. In *Wilmington Parking Authority*, the City of Wilmington, Delaware operated a building that leased space to a private restaurant that would not serve African-Americans. The Court found sufficient entanglement between the city and the restaurant to convert the private, discriminatory behavior into state action. As in *Wilmington Parking Authority,* the state's behavior in this question resembles that of a private individual. It has not contracted with WasteAway to perform traditional government functions. Rather, it wants to protect itself from being assessed more penalties. Further, the benefits to the state arguably parallel those in *Wilmington Parking Authority*, where the state had financially profited by its relationship with the restaurant. One the other hand, the state's benefit here is not as directly tied to financial profit as in *Wilmington Parking Authority.*

Yet, conflicting authority makes answering this question difficult. In *Rendell-Baker v. Kohn*, 457 U.S. 830 (1982), the Court suggested that the acts of private contractors working under a government contract do not become public acts, even when a private contractor does nothing but government contract work. This suggestion in *Rendell-Baker* is difficult to reconcile with the Court's *Wilmington Parking Authority* decision. Because *Rendell-Baker* deals with private schools, which traditionally receive government contracts, and because the Court only suggested, but did not hold, in *Rendell-Baker* that private contractors would not be converted to public actors, *Wilmington* is the best authority to answer this particular question. Thus, **Answer (C) is the best answer,** especially at the preliminary motion to dismiss stage of the litigation.

**Answer (A) is incorrect** because private actors may be obligated to comply with the Fourteenth Amendment if the private actor is considered either to be performing a public function or to have such an interdependent relationship with the state that its behavior is considered state action. For example, private companies that operate prisons must follow constitutional limitations imposed on states.

**Answer (B) is incorrect** for the reasons stated in Answer (C).

**Answer (D) is incorrect** because both Answer (A) and Answer (B) are incorrect. What happens if we decide that Answer (B) is the best answer, given the conflicting authority making this call between Answer (B) and Answer (C) difficult, as discussed above? Answer (D) would still be incorrect because it also relies on Answer (A), which is clearly wrong.

103. **Answer (D) is the best answer.** This answer follows the Court's holding in *Moose Lodge No. 107 v. Irvis*, 407 U.S. 163 (1972). In that case the lodge received a state liquor license, and from this the plaintiffs argued a sufficient relationship between the Lodge and the state to convert the lodge's private racial discrimination into state action. The Court disagreed and held that the mere fact that the state regulates or licenses a business activity does not change the private action into state action.

**Answer (A) is incorrect** for the reasons stated above.

**Answer (B) is incorrect**. The collection of sales tax does not place the state in a symbiotic relationship with the club. If it did, then every private business that collects and pays sales tax would be converted into a state actor. Further, if the relationship was not sufficiently interdependent in *Moose Lodge* to convert private action to state action, then it is certainly not sufficient under the facts here.

**Answer (C) is incorrect** because it misses the point of the question. It is true that private clubs are permitted to discriminate, but this question has added facts, such as state licensing, that may convert the private activity to public activity under *Wilmington Parking Authority*. Therefore, Answer (C) is incorrect because it fails to analyze the significance of the club's relationship with the state.

104. It is unlikely that the relationship between the state and the hospice would convert the hospice's private activity into government activity. In *Blum v. Yaretsky*, 457 U.S. 991 (1982), the Supreme Court held, under almost identical facts, that a privately-owned nursing home receiving Medicaid payments from the state and regulated by the state was nevertheless a private actor, and its behavior did not become state action as a result of its connection to the state.

Can *Blum* and *Wilmington Parking Authority* be reconciled? Yes, if we consider the nature of the state's activities in each case. In *Wilmington Parking Authority*, the business arrangement between the state and the restaurant mirrored private business arrangements. The state was acting as an entrepreneur, leasing out space to a restaurant that discriminated on the basis of race. The state could have made it a contractual requirement that the restaurant not discriminate. It did not, and yet it continued to reap profit from its relationship with the restaurant. In *Blum*, however, the state was acting in accordance with usual governmental duties — regulating nursing homes and making payments for care. Its behavior was not unusual or beyond what government normally does. Perhaps, then, we can see the holding in *Wilmington Parking Authority* as limited in application to when the state's relationship with the private actor is unusual or beyond typical government dealings. In any event, it is safe to say that state action decisions are fact-bound and, at times, difficult to reconcile.

105. **Answer (C) is the best answer.** Understanding substantive due process begins with understanding the concept of fundamental rights. As free people, United States citizens have much liberty. We are free to work, live and associate usually without any restrictions. Yet, government also has power to regulate our behavior using what we call "police powers." So, for example, while a citizen has the liberty to own a home, the government may enact zoning laws that bar homeowners from conducting certain businesses out of their homes.

When fundamental rights are involved, the government is more restricted in how it may regulate. Specifically, the government may regulate a fundamental right only if it has a compelling reason to do so, and the regulatory means chosen are necessary (or narrowly tailored) to achieve the government's objective. Also the government bears the burden of proof on both requirements. This is called strict scrutiny review. The Supreme Court has never articulated a test for determining when a reason is compelling, but it seems to envision a government purpose that is vital as opposed to only important. Similarly, the Court has not created a formula for when the means are necessary, but the government is required to show that it could not achieve its goal through other less restrictive means.

When a fundamental right is not involved, the challenged regulation need only serve a legitimate government interest, and the means selected only need be rationally related to achieving that interest. Further, the citizen challenging the regulation bears the burden of showing that the law is neither legitimate nor rational. This is called rational basis or rationality review. Obviously, then, different legal outcomes are likely to flow from whether a right is classified as fundamental or not.

The Supreme Court has held that almost all the rights protected by the Bill of Rights are fundamental. See the answers to Questions 107 and 108 for a discussion of which Bill of Rights have been deemed fundamental. These are called enumerated rights. The Supreme Court has ruled in various cases that other rights are fundamental. These are called *unenumerated* fundamental rights because they are not specifically listed in the Bill of Rights. For example, the Court has held that the right to marry is a fundamental right even though it is not enumerated in the Bill of Rights. *See Loving v. Virginia,* 388 U.S. 1 (1967).

The Court struggles when asked to decide whether an unenumerated right is fundamental because such a ruling will restrict substantially the government's power to regulate, and is likely thwarting the will of the majority. The most controversial modern example

289

is the right of a woman to terminate a pregnancy. The Court's decision in *Roe v. Wade,* 410 U.S. 113 (1973), making pregnancy termination a fundamental right, prevented almost all state regulation of abortions. Not surprisingly, then, the Court infrequently declares an unenumerated right to be fundamental.

Your study will provide you with several cases in which the Supreme Court has decided that an unenumerated right is fundamental, but the right to education is not one of these. *San Antonio Independent School District v. Rodriguez,* 411 U.S. 1 (1973). Therefore, **Answer (C) is the best answer** because it clearly says that the right to an education is not a fundamental right. For the same reasons, **Answer (A) is incorrect.** Note, however, that **Answer (A)** does give the correct test—the strict scrutiny test—for analyzing any government regulation of a fundamental right.

**Answer (B) is incorrect** because, once again, reliance on the continued existence of a government entitlement program is not a fundamental right.

**Answer (D) is incorrect** because these students likely do have standing. According to the facts, they were injured by the change in this program, their injury was caused by the change in the program, and their injury would be redressed if Texas is forced to reinstate the prior financial assistance program.

106.  **Answer (D) is the best answer,** although the possibility always exists that the compelling facts presented in this question may result in a different answer some day. This is because the Court has held that the Due Process Clauses of the Fourteenth and Fifth Amendments have substance, and this substance contains both enumerated rights found in the Bill of Rights and unenumerated rights that the Court determines to be fundamental. Since it is within the power of the Court to declare a right fundamental, the Court might some day decide that a person has a fundamental right to gain access to experimental medical treatment if the person's life is at stake, and the person gives a fully informed consent. However, as of today, the Court has not held that an individual has a fundamental right to receive a drug, even in an attempt to save the individual's life.

**Answer (A) is incorrect** because it provides only a general answer that is not attentive to the facts of the question. The right to life is fundamental, without a doubt. But the issue is whether the government is violating her fundamental right by deciding to withhold this drug from Sarah. If the government is violating a fundamental right, then any government decision not to provide the necessities of life — such as food, shelter and medical care — to all citizens also could be viewed as threatening to life. The Court has refused to require the government to take action to provide for such needs. In *DeShaney v. Winnebago County Department of Social Services,* 489 U.S. 189 (1989), the Court stated that "our cases have recognized that the Due Process Clauses generally confer no affirmative right to government aid, even where such aid may be necessary to secure life, liberty, or property interests of which the government itself may not deprive the individuals." This answer, therefore, is incorrect because it assumes that the threat to Sarah's life, caused by her disease and not the government, requires the government to make the drug available to her.

**Answer (A) also is incorrect** because it applies the Fourteenth Amendment to the federal government. Recall that the Due Process Clause of the Fourteenth Amendment protects against state interference, and the Due Process Clause of the Fifth Amendment protects against federal government interference. **Answer (B) is incorrect** for the same reason.

**Answer (C) is incorrect** because the Supreme Court has not found the right to receive medical care to be a fundamental right under these facts. The Court has held that the government has a duty to provide essential services only in extraordinary circumstances, such as when a person is in custody. *Youngberg v. Romero,* 457 U.S. 307 (1982). Although even in these situations, the government has considerable discretion in determining how it will provide the services.

107. **Answer (B) is the best answer**, because the Due Process Clause of the Fourteenth Amendment has never been held to incorporate within its protections the Seventh Amendment guarantee of a civil jury trial. This means that the Seventh Amendment has never been applied to the states, and thus a state may devise a procedure that does not provide for a civil jury trial without violating the Fourteenth Amendment Due Process Clause.

This leads, however, to the larger question as to why the Due Process Clause of the Fourteenth Amendment has any substantive content at all. How has it come to pass that the Due Process Clause has been used to apply any of the Bill of Rights to the states, and why is the Due Process Clause of the Fourteenth Amendment not limited to procedural matters as suggested by the term "due process"?

Essentially this began in 1908 with the Court's decision in *Twining v. New Jersey*, 211 U.S. 78 (1908), in which the Court stated it "is possible that some of the personal rights safeguarded by the first eight Amendments against national action may also be safeguarded against state action, because a denial of them would be a denial of due process of law . . .If this is so, it is not because those rights are enumerated in the first eight Amendments, but because they are of such a nature that they are included in the conception of due process of law."

From this the Court in a series of later decisions has incorporated most of the first eight amendments, the core of the Bill of Rights, into the Due Process Clause of the Fourteenth Amendment, thus making most of the Bill of Rights apply to the states and placing the same limits on the state governments as the Bill of Rights places on the federal government. What parts of the Bill of Rights have *not* yet been incorporated into the Fourteenth Amendment's Due Process Clause? The Second Amendment "right to bear arms," the Third Amendment right to not have soldiers quartered in one's home, the Fifth Amendment right to a grand jury indictment, the Seventh Amendment right to a civil jury trial, and the Eighth Amendment prohibition of excessive fines have, thus far, not been extended against the states.

This selective incorporation of some of the Bill of Rights leads to the question of why not incorporate into the Due Process Clause *all* of the Bill of Rights? Several Supreme Court justices have advocated just this position, which is called "total incorporation." Other justices have favored what has been termed "selective incorporation," arguing that due process in the Fourteenth Amendment embodies the concepts of fundamental fairness and ordered liberty and may embrace rights other than those contained in the

Bill of Rights. The justices favoring selective incorporation have argued that, while many of the first eight amendments contain provisions that reflect the concepts of fundamental fairness and ordered liberty, the Bill of Rights and the Due Process Clause of the Fourteenth Amendment are not equivalent, and, therefore, total incorporation is conceptually inaccurate. That said, selective incorporation acknowledges the existence of fundamental rights in addition to those listed in the Bill of Rights.

**Answer (A) is incorrect** because the Seventh Amendment guarantee of a civil jury trial has never been incorporated into the Fourteenth Amendment Due Process Clause, and thus a state does not violate the Fourteenth Amendment by failing to provide for a civil jury in medical malpractice cases.

**Answer (C) is incorrect** because the legislation at issue is state legislation. The Seventh Amendment only applies to the federal government. *See, Barron v. Mayor & City Council of Baltimore*, 32 U.S. (7 Pet.) 243 (1833). The Bill of Rights never applies to the states unless the provision has been incorporated first into the Fourteenth Amendment Due Process Clause.

**Answer (D) is incorrect** because, once again, the Fifth Amendment's Due Process Clause, does not apply to the states. It only applies to the federal government.

108. These justices have argued that the history surrounding the adoption of the Fourteenth Amendment supports the position that the drafters of the amendment intended to make the entire Bill of Rights applicable to the states. Some historical analysis does support this position, but not all. Further, these justices have argued that total incorporation provides better control over excessive judicial discretion. It limits the fundamental rights that could be read into the Due Process Clause of the Fourteenth Amendment to only those listed in the first eight amendments of the Constitution. Selective incorporation, on the other hand, gives license to judges "to roam at will the limitless area of their own beliefs" to determine what is a fundamental right protected by the Fourteenth Amendment. *Adamson v. California,* 332 U.S. 46, 71-72 (1947) (Black, J., dissenting.)

109.    **Answer (A) is the best answer** primarily due to the date given in the hypothetical.
        Prior to 1937, many Supreme Court decisions struck down legislation on the basis of
        a doctrine known as economic substantive due process. This doctrine held that freedom
        of contract is protected as a liberty and property right under the Due Process Clause
        of the Fourteenth Amendment and that an individual's freedom to enter into contracts
        of his own choosing could not be regulated by the government without a legitimate
        government purpose. Further, the Court rejected as illegitimate most government
        attempts to redress inequities in wealth or bargaining position. The Court's adherence
        to this doctrine of economic substantive due process is identified with the case of
        *Lochner v. New York*, 198 U.S. 45 (1905), and this era in the Court's history is often
        referred to as the "*Lochner* era." During this time the Court declared as unconstitutional
        approximately 200 state laws that attempted to regulate such matters as minimum hours,
        *Lochner*, minimum wages, *Adkins v. Children's Hospital,* 261 U.S. 525 (1923),
        unionization, *Adair v. United States*, 208 U.S. 161 (1908), and price regulations,
        *Williams v. Standard Oil Co,* 278 U.S. 235 (1929).

        However, the *Lochner*-era Court was not always consistent and at times decided that
        legislation interfering with economic freedom was nevertheless constitutional. For
        example, three years after *Lochner,* the Court upheld an Oregon law that mandated
        maximum working hours for women. *Muller v. Oregon,* 208 U.S. 412 (1908). The *Muller*
        Court found this to be a legitimate government regulation due to "women's physical
        structure and the performance of maternal functions." Given the difficulty in reconciling
        all the *Lochner*-era Court's decisions, it is difficult to say without qualification that the
        Court would have declared the Nebraska legislation in the hypothetical to be unconstitu-
        tional under the Due Process Clause of the Fourteenth Amendment. Yet, Answer (A)
        is the most correct because, during this time, the Court was more likely to strike down
        such economic legislation as violating liberty and contract rights than it was to uphold
        such legislation. For the same reasons, **Answer (B) is incorrect**.

        It is important to understand the Court's jurisprudential basis for finding substantive
        content in the Due Process Clause during the *Lochner* era. The underlying issue at play
        in the doctrine of economic substantive due process is whether rights other than those
        specifically mentioned and protected by the Constitution — called unenumerated rights
        — are of such magnitude that they are protected because they are encompassed within
        the Constitution's concepts of liberty and property without being specifically listed in
        the Constitution.

        Early in its history, the Supreme Court suggested that the Constitution protected natural
        rights. For example, in *Calder v. Bull,* 3 U.S. (3 Dall.) 386 (1798), Justice Chase claimed

that the "great first principles of the social compact" could not be abrogated by legislative authority. In that same case, Justice Iredell disagreed that the Court could strike down a duly-enacted law because the Court judged it to be against natural justice. This debate between Justices Chase and Iredell has been replayed in every generation since. In the *Lochner* era, the Court was firmly on the side of finding substantive content within the phrase "due process of law." By doing this, the Court held that due process not only required procedural fairness but also prohibited government from regulating in certain areas involving the "natural" freedom to contract and hold property. As stated by the Supreme Court in *Allgeyer v. Louisiana,* 165 U.S. 578 (1897): "The liberty mentioned in the [Fourteenth] amendment. . .[is] deemed to embrace the right of [a] citizen to be free in the enjoyment of all his faculties, to be free to use them in all lawful ways; to live and work where he will; . . .and for that purpose to enter into all contracts which may be proper, necessary, and essential to his carrying out to a successful completion the purposes above mentioned." From this reasoning, the Court found that the liberty protected by the Due Process Clause of the Fourteenth Amendment included the liberty to contract, even though "liberty to contract" is not specifically named in the Constitution as a right protected by that document.

**Answer (C) is incorrect** because it is too vague a claim against the state. The alleged harm is not tied to any particular provision of the Constitution. The Supreme Court has always rejected attempts to have the Constitution protect the general public against economic inequities occasioned by the normal functioning of business and government. *See, e.g., San Antonio Independent School Dist. v. Rodriguez*, 411 U.S. 1 (1973).

**Answer (D) is incorrect** because the Privileges and Immunities Clause of the Fourteenth Amendment has been interpreted so narrowly as to be inapplicable to this hypothetical.

110. **Answer (B) is the best answer** because it reflects the dramatic change in the doctrine of economic substantive due process that occurred after 1937. From 1937 to date, the Court has never declared such economic regulation to violate the Due Process Clause of the Fourteenth Amendment. Therefore, the same legislation that was likely to be seen as unconstitutional during the *Lochner* era will pass constitutional muster today.

The historical background for this change in constitutional jurisprudence is as follows. The Great Depression placed enormous pressure on governments to respond to the economic despair of the populace. Franklin Roosevelt came into office and within his first 100 days was successful in having Congress pass a number of laws that regulated the economy and could be viewed as infringing on the liberty of contract protection associated with the *Lochner* era. Indeed, in a series of cases the Supreme Court struck down much of this New Deal legislation as beyond Congress's power under the Commerce Clause. The reaction to the Court's decisions in these cases was intense. President Roosevelt proposed his infamous court-packing plan as an attempt to place on the bench justices who would support the government's ability to regulate economic activity. Although President Roosevelt's court-packing plan failed, the firestorm over the Court's jurisprudence in the both the Commerce Clause area and in economic due process cases eventually led to a change in the Court's position on these issues.

For example, in 1934, the Court upheld New York's price control on milk. *Nebbia v. New York*, 291 U.S. 502 (1934). In 1937, it upheld a state minimum wage law for women. *West Coast Hotel Co. v. Parrish*, 300 U.S. 379 (1937). In both cases the Court made clear that economic regulation would be reviewed only: (1) to see if the purpose of the legislation was legitimate and not arbitrary, and (2) if the means to accomplish the purpose were rationally related to the purpose.

Therefore, in the post-*Lochner* era, Answer (B) is correct because bolstering the economic position of wheat farmers is a legitimate state objective, especially for a state like Nebraska that no doubt needs a healthy wheat sector for its economy. Moreover, the means chosen to achieve this purpose are rationally related to that purpose. In modern terms, this standard of review is called rationality review.

You may be concerned that the legislation in this question violates the Commerce Clause since it could affect interstate commerce. This may be true, and you are referred to the discussion above on the Commerce Clause. But the terms of this question make it clear that the subject you are being asked to consider is the substantive component of the Due Process Clause and not other constitutional issues. Therefore, you should choose the best answer given the parameters of the question.

**Answer (A) is incorrect** for the reasons stated above.

**Answers (C) and (D) are incorrect** for the same reasons given in analyzing the preceding question.

111. Given the modern Court's exceedingly deferential standard of review for economic legislation and the willingness of the Court to find post-hoc justifications for such legislation, it is unlikely that a due process attack on this New York legislation will succeed. This is true even though the purpose of helping small business seems to have not materialized given the data on the size of the businesses able to obtain a license. The Court may find that the legislature was within its power to adopt such a law for the purpose stated even if the law did not achieve its aim. The legislature can be unwise or wasteful without fearing that the Court will dismantle its legislative scheme. *See Williamson v. Lee Optical of Okla., Inc.*, 348 U.S. 483 (1955).

Some have expressed displeasure with the extreme deference shown in the modern Court's review of economic legislation and have suggested that the Court could engage in rationality review with more of a bite — especially when it appears that the legislation is nothing more than an exertion of raw political power in order to obtain one-sided legislation. While this discussion is interesting and may bear fruit some day, at present the Court has staunchly held to its position that the Due Process Clause of the Fourteenth Amendment does not allow the Court to engage in anything other than rationality review of such legislation. The Court has steadfastly refused to engage in any heightened scrutiny of economic legislation.

112.    From early on, the Court has engaged in debate as to whether rights protected by the Constitution are only those specifically listed in the Constitution, such as freedom of speech, or whether other rights that flow from natural law or from our concept of ordered liberty also are protected by the Constitution even if not specifically named therein. In *Twining*, the Court discussed whether the first eight amendments were incorporated into the Due Process Clause of the Fourteenth Amendment. The *Twining* Court held that, if they are incorporated, it is not because they are enumerated, but "because they are of such a nature that they are included in the conception of due process of law." Thus in addressing the incorporation idea, the Court initially took the position that rights were incorporated into the Fourteenth Amendment because of the nature of the rights rather than because they were enumerated. This, in essence, was saying that the Due Process Clause had content that limited not only the procedure a government offered but also the laws a government could pass.

Once the idea was planted that due process had a content that included important individual rights not enumerated in the Constitution, then it became possible for the Court to consider what other rights were included in the concept of due process. Eventually, this led the Court to decide that liberty to contract was included within the concept of due process and that this right could not be abrogated by state laws.

113.  **Answer (D) is the best answer** because it combines the reasoning of the majority of
the Court in its decision in *Griswold v. Connecticut*, 381 U.S. 479 (1965). To understand
the several opinions in *Griswold*, one has to understand the context in which the case
arose. Since 1937, the Court had repudiated the concept of substantive due process
championed during the *Lochner* era. The Court stated clearly that it no longer sat as
a super-legislature invalidating laws. During this time, the Court held true to this
jurisprudential position and affirmed laws that seemed unwise or intended only to benefit
special interests. Therefore, when faced with this Connecticut law, with its serious
invasion of marital privacy, the Court was faced with a difficult choice: uphold the law
with its serious disregard for individual liberty or revitalize the repudiated doctrine of
substantive due process.

One of those most critical of the Court's use of substantive due process was Justice
William O. Douglas. Therefore, it is interesting that he wrote the opinion for the Court
in *Griswold* declaring the Connecticut law unconstitutional. In order to avoid accepting
again the idea that the Due Process Clause had substantive content, Douglas did not
base his decision on that clause. Rather, he found that various provisions of the Bill
of Rights created a penumbra of a zone of privacy that protected citizens from
government intrusion. His opinion found that marital privacy was within this zone of
privacy that comes from the penumbra emanating from the Bill of Rights. Therefore,
Douglas was able to reject the Connecticut statute without violating his prior repudiation
of substantive due process.

Other members of the Court's majority were not adverse to concluding the Due Process
Clause had substantive content and that the Due Process Clause protected fundamental
rights from government intrusion. Three members of the Court, Chief Justice Warren,
Justice Goldberg, and Justice Brennan, accepted Justice Douglas' reasoning and also
accepted the idea that certain unenumerated fundamental rights were protected by the
Due Process Clause of the Fourteenth Amendment. Therefore, it is correct to say that
both Answer (A) and Answer (B) reflect fully the reasoning of the Court in its decision
in *Griswold* and that either Answer (A) or Answer (B) standing alone would not be
as accurate a statement of the Court's reasoning. Moreover, Justice Douglas' penumbra
doctrine has subsequently fallen by the wayside, making it even more important to
understand the other basis for the *Griswold* decision, which has become the dominant
position in the law of substantive due process.

**Answer (C) is not correct** because the Court declared the Connecticut statute to be
unconstitutional. Answer (C) also is incorrect because it suggests that the Court used
rationality review in reaching its decision, which it did not.

114.  **Answer (D) is the best answer**, because only a year after the Court decided *Griswold v. Connecticut*, 381 U.S. 479 (1965), it would be acceptable to argue that its holding only affected the state's power to interfere with marital privacy. Since the couple in the hypothetical is unmarried, the best argument is to contend that *Griswold* does not apply to this couple given their marital status.

The Court and scholars continue to struggle with the question of how to define the right to privacy created in *Griswold*. Indeed, later cases, such as *Eisenstadt v. Baird*, 405 U.S. 438 (1972), *Roe v. Wade*, 410 U.S. 113 (1973); *Moore v. City of East Cleveland*, 431 U.S. 494 (1977); *Troxel v. Granville*, 530 U.S. 57 (2000); and *Lawrence v. Texas*, 539 U.S. 558 (2003), suggest that the privacy right acknowledged in *Griswold* was more than a right to marital privacy. Nevertheless and despite how the holding in *Griswold* has been used as a springboard to expand on this right to privacy, the essential holding in *Griswold* was limited to the right to marital privacy. All justices who voted to strike down this Connecticut law focused on the ways the law invaded the right to marital privacy. While the justices did refer to a general "right of privacy," the description of this right was one of marital privacy

**Answer (A) is incorrect** because not all of the parties are different. In *Griswold* the State of Connecticut was one party as it is in this question. Therefore, the Court's decision in *Griswold* is binding on the state. Moreover, the effect of Supreme Court decisions is not so limited. Obviously, a Supreme Court case is very similar to other law suits in binding only the specific parties to the suit. Nevertheless, as with other appellate decisions, the holding of a particular Supreme Court case will serve as precedent involving other parties. When the Court said in *Griswold* that the Connecticut law was unconstitutional, its holding would be powerful precedent even if all parties were different.

**Answer (B) is incorrect** because the holding and reasoning in *Griswold* are much broader than provided in this answer. The Court held the Connecticut law was unconstitutional because it violated marital privacy. True, the citizens challenging the law in *Griswold* were those who assisted others in obtaining contraceptive devices, but this does not affect the sweep of the *Griswold* decision. *Griswold* held the law violated the Constitution because of how it affected those who wanted to use contraceptives as well as those who assisted them. Again, it is important to understand that the effect of a Supreme Court decision interpreting the Constitution goes beyond the parties and their narrow claims. It reaches a law that regulates individual behavior in the same or similar way.

**Answer (C) is incorrect** because the legislative repeal of a statute does not affect its validity once it has been declared unconstitutional by the Supreme Court. The fact that the statute was not repealed by the legislature is not important: it cannot be applied against married couples after *Griswold* even if it has not been repealed. However, you must look closely at a decision to see whether the statute was declared unconstitutional on its face or as applied. If it is declared unconstitutional on its face, a rare occurrence, then it is unconstitutional for all purposes. But if it is declared unconstitutional as applied, then it is only invalid as applied to facts similar to those in the case. *Griswold* was an "as applied" decision because it looked at the Connecticut law as it applied to married couples and those who would assist them in obtaining contraceptives. It looked at no other applications of the statute, and the statute was not limited to married couples. Therefore, Connecticut did not have to repeal the statute after the *Griswold* decision because the Court had not said the statute could not be used in situations different than in *Griswold*. This answer is incorrect, however, because it assumes that *Griswold* has no effect on the outcome of any new case simply because the statute is on the books and not repealed.

115. **Answer (B) is the best answer**. This answer is problematic, but it is the best choice. Why is it problematic? The contours of the privacy right protected by *Roe v. Wade*, 410 U.S. 113 (1973), continue to be debated. The fundamental right acknowledged by the holding in *Roe* is actually fairly narrow. According to the Court, a woman has a fundamental right to terminate a pregnancy. Therefore, it can be argued the right to procreate or not procreate is broader than the right acknowledged in *Roe*—to terminate a pregnancy — and that *Roe* does not protect against other government regulation of procreation. Obviously, a right to terminate a pregnancy has implications for procreation and is bound up with the notion that the government should not be able to tell us when and when not to procreate. **Answer (B)** is the best answer because it acknowledges this link between *Roe* and the fundamental right to procreate.

Additionally, even if *Roe* did not specifically acknowledge a fundamental right to procreate, the Supreme Court has done so in *Skinner v. Oklahoma*, 316 U.S. 535 (1942). While the Court in *Skinner* did not specifically overrule older precedent that allowed involuntary sterilization, *Buck v. Bell*, 274 U.S. 200 (1927), the best analysis is that *Skinner* does make the right to procreate a fundamental right.

The answer to the question is phrased to include the Fifth Amendment as well as the Fourteenth Amendment because the government action is federal, not state. Remember that the Fourteenth Amendment applies to state government action, and that the Fifth Amendment Due Process Clause restricts the federal government in many of the same ways. Therefore, the Fifth Amendment prohibits the federal government from violating unenumerated fundamental rights in the same way the Fourteenth Amendment restricts state government.

**Answer (A) is incorrect** because it does not accurately reflect the fundamental right acknowledged in *Roe*. Obviously, a strong argument could be made after *Roe*, and indeed even after *Griswold v. Connecticut*, 381 U.S. 479 (1965), that the right of privacy includes the right to personal autonomy — or, as some have phrased it, the right to be left alone by the government. And, language in the Court's decision in *Lawrence v. Texas*, 539 U.S. 558 (2003), strongly reinforces this argument. Nevertheless, this answer is incorrect because the Court has never recognized a fundamental right to personal autonomy.

**Answer (C) is incorrect** because the Court has never recognized a fundamental right to pursue research under the Due Process Clause for any reason. One could argue that some of the broad language in *Meyer v. Nebraska,* 262 U.S. 390 (1923) created a fundamental right to conduct research, but the Court has never converted this sweeping language into a holding making the right to do research fundamental. It also might be argued that freedom to conduct research is connected to freedom of speech and thus protected by the First Amendment. First Amendment jurisprudence does not prohibit the government from imposing limits on scientific research for public safety, health and moral reasons. For example, scientific research on humans is generally not permitted for moral reasons.

**Answer (D) is incorrect** because the Court has never recognized such a broad fundamental right to be free from government decisions.

116.   In addition to saying that a woman has a right to terminate a pregnancy, *Roe* also held that a state has an important interest in protecting potential life, and that this state interest becomes compelling at the point the fetus can survive outside the woman. At the time *Roe* was decided, fetal viability was placed at the beginning of the third trimester of pregnancy. Therefore, during the third trimester the state's interest in fetal life is compelling, and the state can ban abortions. Prior to fetal viability, the state's interest in the potential life of the fetus is not sufficiently compelling to allow it to ban abortions.

Note that the Court uses different tests to review government activity depending on the nature of the right affected by the state regulation. So if the affected right is held to be a fundamental right, the Court examines whether the state regulation has a compelling purpose and whether it is narrowly tailored to accomplish that purpose. If the right is not fundamental, then the Court uses the rationality test that requires only that the purpose be legitimate and the means employed to achieve the purpose be rational. (See discussion below in the answer to Question 122 on whether *Lawrence v. Texas,* 539 U.S. 558 (2003), has changed the parameters of rational basis review.)

117.   **Answer (B) is the best answer.** The joint opinion in *Planned Parenthood v. Casey,* 505 U.S. 833 (1992), signed by Justices O'Connor, Kennedy, and Souter is remarkable for two reasons. First, it reaffirmed the holding in *Roe v. Wade,* 410 U.S. 113 (1973), that a woman has a constitutionally protected liberty interest in being allowed to terminate a pregnancy prior to fetal viability. This holding was not expected since some of the five Justices who voted to reaffirm this *Roe* holding, notably Justices Kennedy and O'Connor, had indicated in earlier decisions that they might vote to reverse *Roe.*

Second, this decision is remarkable because it creates a new test by which to evaluate whether state regulations directed at the abortion decision are unconstitutional. While *Casey* affirmed a woman's constitutionally-protected right to terminate a pregnancy, it discarded the test used in *Roe* to evaluate state abortion regulations. According to *Roe,* a state had to have a compelling reason for any abortion regulation. *Casey,* however, created a weaker test, the undue burden test, to evaluate a state abortion regulation.

While this new test permits more state regulation, *Casey* reaffirmed the holding in *Roe* that prior to fetal viability a woman has a constitutional right to terminate a pregnancy. Answer (B) accurately reflects the Court's decision in *Casey* because it acknowledges that state regulations of abortion will be evaluated under the undue burden standard.

**Answer (A) is incorrect** because the Court did affirm that a woman has a constitutionally protected liberty interest in being able to terminate a pregnancy. Many commentators, and indeed some of the dissenters in *Casey*, make much of the fact that the joint opinion did not term this to be a fundamental right, but it is clear from the joint opinion that *Casey* reaffirmed that a woman's right to terminate a pregnancy prior to fetal viability is protected by the Constitution.

**Answer (C) is incorrect** because it is incomplete. It does not contain the exceptions for a woman's life or health. Both *Roe* and *Casey* make clear that a state's prohibition of abortions after fetal viability must contain exceptions to protect a woman's life and health. The maternal health exception may be in some doubt after the Court's decision in *Gonzales v. Carhart*, 127 S. Ct. 1610 (2007).

**Answer (D) is incorrect** because *Casey* rejected *Roe's* trimester approach altogether. The joint opinion in *Casey* makes a simple division between when the fetus is viable and when it is not. Prior to viability, a state may regulate abortions so long as the regulations pass the undue burden test. After viability, the state may ban abortions so long as a woman may obtain an abortion to protect her life or health.

118. **Answer (C) is the best answer** because it recognizes the undue burden test as the controlling test for reviewing pre-viability abortion regulations. To see this, one must understand why undue burden came to be the controlling test even though only three justices in *Planned Parenthood v. Casey*, 505 U.S. 833 (1992), adopted that test.

First, in evaluating the various opinions in *Casey*, lower courts divided the Court into three groups. The first group included Justices O'Connor, Kennedy, and Souter, who created a new test for state abortion regulations: the undue burden test. This test is more permissive toward state regulation of abortion than the "compelling interest" standard used in *Roe v. Wade*, 410 U.S. 113 (1973). Therefore, more state regulation is likely to be upheld using this test. The second group included Justices Rehnquist, White, Scalia, and Thomas, who favored returning abortion to the category of a non-fundamental right, enabling courts to use the rationality test in reviewing abortion regulations. If the rationality test were used, it is difficult to conceive an abortion regulation that would not pass constitutional scrutiny. The third group included Justice Blackmun, and probably Justice Stevens, who wanted to retain *Roe's* compelling interest test in reviewing such regulations. This test would uphold fewer pre-viability abortion regulations than either of the other two tests.

Second, the lower courts asked which of the three tests would garner a Supreme Court majority in a given case. On the one hand, if a judge wants to uphold an abortion regulation, she cannot use the rationality test alone, because only four justices supported that test in *Casey*. In addition, she must make sure the law passes the undue burden test because, if it does, then the law will also satisfy those justices who apply the less stringent rationality test. On the other hand, if the judge wants to declare an abortion regulation unconstitutional, she cannot use the compelling interest test alone, because only two justices supported that test in *Casey*. She must also make sure that the justices applying the undue burden test would find the law unconstitutional, which would yield a five-vote majority for overturning the law. Because the undue burden test is pivotal no matter which way a lower federal court rules, it has become the prevailing test in analyzing the constitutionality of abortion regulations.

**Answer (A) is incorrect** because only two justices in *Casey* favored retaining the compelling interest test used in *Roe*. If a lower court were to use the compelling interest test, it would increase its chances of making an erroneous decision, as discussed in connection with Answer (C).

**Answer (B) is incorrect** for the reasons stated in the discussion of Answer (C).

**Answer (D) is incorrect** because only four justices in *Casey* favored rationality review of abortion regulations. If a lower court were to use rationality review, it would increase its chances of making an erroneous decision, as discussed in connection with Answer (C).

119. **Answer (A) is the best answer.** The Court's decision in *Gonzales v. Carhart*, 127 S. Ct. 1610 (2007), was the first time the Court has upheld an abortion regulation that did not provide an exception for the woman's health. Because of this, you may have chosen Answer (B) as the best answer. However, a close reading of *Gonzales* makes it clear that the Court was not saying that any abortion regulation that excludes a health exception will be upheld. To understand this, we must first understand the *Gonzales* decision.

The federal statute at issue in *Gonzales* made it a crime for a doctor to use a procedure called intact dilation and evacuation. Intact dilation and evacuation is a variation on other forms of the dilation and evacuation procedures used in second trimester abortions. This statute provided an exception for the life of the mother but not for the health of the mother. In upholding the constitutionality of this statute, the Court substantially departed from its prior abortion decisions that appeared to mandate that all abortion regulations include exceptions for maternal health. *See Stenberg v. Carhart*, 530 U.S. 914 (2000); *Planned Parenthood v. Casey*, 505 U.S. 833 (1992). Moreover, the *Gonzales* Court upheld the statute despite medical expert testimony in the trial court stating that the banned procedure would sometimes be necessary to protect a woman's health. The Court noted that other experts who testified at the trial disagreed with this conclusion. This mixed expert medical testimony forced the Court to address the question whether an exception for maternal health was constitutionally required when medical uncertainty exists. The Court held the maternal health exception was not constitutionally required even in the face of medical uncertainty when a statute is attacked on its face, rather than as applied, and when there exists "the availability of other abortion procedures that are considered to be safe alternatives."

Therefore, the *Gonzales* decision must be viewed within the narrow parameters of the case. The decision is limited to a specific procedure that is available to a doctor performing a second trimester abortion. The challenged statute banned one procedure —intact dilation and evacuation — and medical experts concluded that safe alternatives existed to the banned procedure. Given these parameters of the *Gonzales* decision, it is not correct to say that the Court would uphold all legislation that omitted an exception for the woman's health. Regulations that ban or require other procedures must rest on expert medical testimony that whatever is banned or required will not threaten a woman's health. Therefore, **Answer (B) is incorrect** as abortion jurisprudence now stands.

This is not to say that the *Gonzales* decision is insignificant. The Court emphasized repeatedly that government "has a legitimate and substantial interest in preserving and promoting fetal life." This emphasis makes clear that the Court is inclined to support abortion regulations, and that making abortions more expensive or difficult to obtain does not create an undue burden. Moreover, the expert opinions in *Gonzales* were mixed, with the weight of medical opinion on the side of providing a health exception. However, the Court held that a maternal health exception is not constitutionally required even in the face of medical uncertainty. Prior to *Gonzales,* it was assumed that medical uncertainty would require the legislation to contain a maternal health exception. That assumption no longer appears to apply. After this decision the legislative body may add a regulation that some medical experts conclude poses a risk to a woman's health in certain circumstances without providing a health exception.

**Answer (B) is incorrect** for the reasons stated above.

**Answer (C) is incorrect** because the Court in *Planned Parenthood v. Casey*, 505 U.S. 833 (1992), upheld the constitutionality of a 24-hour waiting period. However, the statute at issue in *Casey* did contain an exception for the woman's health as well as her life.

**Answer (D) is incorrect** because *Gonzales* and *Casey* permit a state to pass regulations that promote the state's substantial interest in fetal life. This may include favoring birth over abortion and attempting to persuade a woman not to have an abortion, provided such regulations do not place an undue burden on a woman's right to terminate a pregnancy. Therefore, the sonogram requirement will not be unconstitutional simply because women do not request it. It will unconstitutional only if it places an undue burden on the woman's right. This question does not address if the sonogram requirement will increase the cost of an abortion or whether the state will pay the additional cost. Depending on how expensive this is and who pays for it, this additional cost may result in a finding of undue burden. However, because this answer does not ask you explore the "undue burden" aspects of this statute, Answer (D) is not correct.

120.   **Answer (C) is the best Answer.** Following *Griswold v. Connecticut,* 381 U.S. 479 (1965), the Court has issued a number of decisions that expand the liberty protected by the Due Process Clause to make it broader than the right to marital privacy. *Roe v. Wade,* 410 U.S. 113 (1973), expanded the right of privacy to include the right of a woman to terminate a pregnancy. While *Roe* did not hold directly that the right recognized in that case was a right to control one's procreation, in later decisions the Court has noted that the personal decisions related to procreation are protected by the Constitution. *See, e.g., Planned Parenthood v. Casey,* 505 U.S. 833 (1992). While the Supreme Court has not directly held in a due process case that control over one's procreation is a fundamental right, it has certainly stated this to be true in cases reviewed under the Equal Protection Clause. *See Skinner v. Oklahoma ex rel. Williamson,* 316 U.S. 535 (1942), and *Zablocki v. Redhail,* 434 U.S. 374 (1978). Therefore, given the holdings in *Roe* and *Casey* and the language in other cases on the fundamental right to procreate, it is very likely that the Court would strike down this population control law as a violation of the Due Process Clause of the Fourteenth Amendment, because it interferes with the fundamental right to procreate and because the state's reason for the law is not sufficiently compelling to justify this extreme intrusion. While a lack of potable water is dangerous to the health of the state's citizens, this possibility is in the future, is not certain, and is not necessitated by a lack of alternative means to protect the state's water supply. In order to regulate a fundamental right, a government must not only have a compelling reason, it must also tailor the means adopted to be the least intrusive on the fundamental right. Clearly, this legislation is not the least intrusive means available.

     **Answer (A) is incorrect.** Since *Griswold,* and continuing through *Roe, Casey, Washington v. Glucksberg,* 521 U.S. 702 (1997), and *Lawrence v. Texas,* 539 U.S. 558 (2003), the Court has recognized that the Due Process Clause of the Fourteenth Amendment has substantive content and is not just limited to issues of procedural fairness.

     **Answer (B) is incorrect.** When a fundamental right is being regulated — and as discussed above it is likely the right to procreate is a fundamental right — then the state must have a compelling justification. Rationality review will not suffice.

     **Answer (D) is incorrect,** but interesting. In *Griswold,* Justice Goldberg used the Ninth Amendment as part of his reasoning as to why the Connecticut contraceptive statute was unconstitutional. Justice Goldberg noted that the Ninth Amendment is not an independent source of rights protected by the Constitution, but that it offers support for the idea that more rights are protected by the Fourteenth Amendment than are listed in the Bill of Rights. After *Griswold,* lower federal courts have, on occasion, used the Ninth Amendment to justify the finding of a fundamental right. Indeed, the lower court that initially declared the Texas abortion statute unconstitutional in *Roe* did so by finding this fundamental right to be protected by the Ninth Amendment. The idea of the Ninth Amendment as a separate source of constitutionally-protected rights has not gained currency or a following. Today, the Court does not rely on it as a source of constitutional rights. Rather, if the Court is to find an unenumerated right to be fundamental, it will find this right in the Due Process Clause of the Fourteenth Amendment. Therefore, Answer (D) is incorrect because the Ninth Amendment is not an independent source of rights.

121. **Answers (B) and (D) are the best answers.** The key to answering this question is to notice that you are asked what the majority held. This requires an analysis of Justice O'Connor's concurring opinion since she was the fifth vote. Although the other four justices also concurred, they limited their concurrences in the judgment. Remember that when a justice states that a concurrence is only in the judgment, it means that the justice accepts the holding but not necessarily the reasoning. Justice O'Connor did not limit her opinion to concurring only in the judgment, and this signals basic agreement with the majority's opinion. Nevertheless, she decided that her position on this case needed to be explained, and therefore, we must decide how her explanation limits or explicates the majority opinion.

First, Justice O'Connor's opinion shows no disagreement with Answer B, which is part of the holding articulated by Chief Justice Rehnquist. Indeed, a fair reading of every opinion in this case supports this position and rejects a facial challenge to the constitutionality of the statute's ban on assisting suicide, whether or not a physician is the one doing the assisting. Therefore, **Answer (B) is clearly correct.**

Second, Justice O'Connor's concurring opinion indicates no disagreement with the constitutionality of applying this statute to the facts of this case. Under these facts the group members seeking the right to physician-assisted suicide were "competent, terminally ill adults who wish to hasten their death by obtaining medication prescribed by their doctors." The Court held, and Justice O'Connor voiced no opposition, that this group had no fundamental right to physician-assisted suicide. **This makes Answer (D) also correct.** Moreover, this also emphasizes that you should look carefully at whether a statute is challenged on its face (meaning that a litigant is seeking a declaration that the statute is unconstitutional no matter how it is applied), or whether it is being challenged as applied under the facts of the case, or whether it is challenged both on its face and as applied.

**Answer (A) is incorrect** because it changes the facts of the actual case decided and because it ignores the implication of Justice O'Connor's concurring opinion. The group seeking review were not terminally ill patients greatly suffering and in pain. Therefore, the Court's holding cannot be construed to cover this group. Moreover, Justice O'Connor took special care to explain in her opinion that the doctors in this case were allowed under state law to give suffering patients sufficient medication to alleviate the pain, even to the point of causing unconsciousness and hastening death. The availability of medication to terminally ill individuals experiencing great pain was important to Justice O'Connor and thus indicates some reluctance on her part to uphold the constitutionality of a state law that would bar physicians from administering such medication, even if it hastened death. We do not know what Justice O'Connor would do in such a case, but it is important to read her concurring opinion as leaving open the possibility that a person has a constitutionally-protected right to not suffer during the course of dying.

**Answer (C) is incorrect.** The majority never defined its holding as applying to the concept of "death with dignity." Its holding is limited to physician-assisted suicide in the case of terminally ill individuals. Some of the justices who concurred in the judgment defined the right being examined as having "death with dignity" implications. These concurring opinions certainly signal that several members of the Court may be willing in other cases to closely examine whether the state can infringe on how a person chooses to die. But for now, this opinion, as well as the concurring opinions, cannot be read as creating a fundamental right to "die with dignity."

122.   **Answer (D) is the best answer** because it recognizes that the Court's decision in *Lawrence v. Texas*, 539 U.S. 558 (2003), is rather narrow. The Court held only that "[t]he Texas statute furthers no legitimate state interest which can justify its intrusion into the personal and private life of an individual." While the Court's factual analysis made a number of pronouncements that may profoundly affect future due process jurisprudence, these pronouncements were not necessary to the case's holding. Answer (D) is the best answer because it recognizes the case's limited holding.

Nevertheless, it is important to ponder the dicta and statements of the *Lawrence* majority for insight into the future direction of substantive due process. First, *Lawrence* overruled *Bowers v. Hardwick*, 478 U.S. 186 (1986). Therefore, to the extent that *Bowers* permitted states to criminalize private, consensual homosexual conduct, it is no longer the law. Second, the *Lawrence* majority made it clear that liberty protected by the Constitution "presumes an autonomy of self that includes . . . certain intimate conduct." This strongly suggests that the Court now includes personal autonomy, and possibly sexual liberty as protected by the Due Process Clause. However, the *Lawrence* Court did not clearly mark the parameters of this autonomous liberty interest, and we will have to wait for further developments.

Third, *Lawrence* did not springboard from its pronouncement on personal autonomy to an explicit holding that private sexual conduct was a fundamental right. Rather, it simply held that Texas's intrusion into private conduct under the statute was *illegitimate*. In earlier cases, language describing a state's purpose as illegitimate has signaled rationality review. And it seems clear that the *Lawrence* majority reached its decision by using a form of rationality review and without declaring private sexual conduct a fundamental right. However, it is obvious that the nature of the rationality review used in *Lawrence* is more searching than the rationality review used by the Court when evaluating economic legislation. See the discussion on economic legislation above at Questions 110 and 111. Moreover, the rationality review used by the *Lawrence* majority is more searching than that used by the Court in reaching its decision in other cases where the liberty interest being examined is not deemed a fundamental right. Indeed, Justice Scalia's *Lawrence* dissent characterizes the Court as applying "an unheard-of form of rational-basis review that will have far-reaching implications beyond this case."

What can we glean from this aspect of the *Lawrence* decision? First, it may signal a new test in the substantive due process area-a test somewhere between rationality review and "compelling interest" review. This test would permit a more searching examination of the government's restriction on personal liberty but would not require a compelling government interest before allowing some regulation. Second, it may signal the first step toward the Court recognizing that some private, consensual sexual conduct is protected as a fundamental liberty interest. If sexual liberty is recognized as fundamental, this will have implications not only with regard to same-sex marriage but also for the regulation of private, consensual sexual behavior generally.

**Answer (A) is incorrect** because the Court did not "reject" extending the liberty protected by the Due Process Clause to consensual, private homosexual conduct. The word "reject" implies some type of active disapproval. The Court was silent on the issue of whether such conduct was protected as a fundamental liberty interest. See the discussion above in connection with Answer (D). While the Court did not recognize this fundamental right, neither did it explicitly reject such a right. Further, given the Court's tone and general statements on the importance of intimate associations to the human condition, a strong argument could be made that the Court came very close to declaring some consensual, private sexual conduct to be a fundamental right.

**Answer (B) is incorrect** for the reasons stated in connection with Answer (D) and Answer (A). The Court did not recognize consensual, private homosexual conduct to be a fundamental right.

**Answer (C) is incorrect** because again the term "reject" does not accurately capture the Court's position on this issue. The majority did not reject the idea that the Texas statute, which only prohibited homosexual sodomy but not heterosexual sodomy, violated equal protection of the laws. Rather, the *Lawrence* Court decided the case on broader due process grounds. Indeed, the majority stated clearly that a decision on equal protection grounds alone would not cure the ills caused by the Texas statute because "[i]f protected conduct is made criminal and the law which does so remains unexamined for its substantive validity, its stigma might remain even if it were not enforceable as drawn for equal protection reasons." Therefore, it is not accurate to say that *Lawrence* rejected the argument that the Texas statute violated equal protection of the laws.

123.  **Answer (A) is the best answer.** This question goes to the heart of the debate on how best to handle substantive due process. The Supreme Court's decisions imposing its concept of "liberty of contract" in the *Lochner* era placed in focus the danger of having nine unelected justices determine national economic and social policy. The backlash to *Roe v. Wade,* 410 U.S. 113 (1973), encouraged the Court to continue to be restrained in finding new fundamental rights. At the same time, cases such as *Griswold v. Connecticut,* 381 U.S. 479 (1965), and *Roe v. Wade* relied on historical support for prohibiting certain government behavior. As stated in *Planned Parenthood v. Casey*, 505 U.S. 833 (1992), "It is a promise of the Constitution that there is a realm of personal liberty which the government may not enter." Hence, even under a restrained approach, the present-day Supreme Court continues to agree that the Due Process Clause has substantive content that protects citizens from intrusive government action.

Given this struggle between fear of excessive judicial power and fear of governmental tyranny over individual liberties, the Supreme Court has attempted to balance itself between the two positions by creating a methodology that recognizes both sides of the debate. Most often, the Court has looked to history and tradition to support its decision that a right is fundamental. By looking at history and tradition, the Court has attempted to limit any impetus to impose its own values and world view on the country, while at the same time allowing it to protect certain liberties.

However, the Court has not always referred to tradition and history in making these decisions. This is clear in *Roe* and *Lawrence v. Texas*, 539 U.S. 558 (2003). It also is true in cases dealing with racial inequities. For example, in *Loving v. Virginia*, 388 U.S. 1 (1967), the Court struck down the Virginia miscegenation law even though history and tradition certainly supported Virginia banning interracial marriage. And, in the equal protection area, the Court has created somewhat heightened scrutiny for gender laws even though, again, history and tradition would support laws distinguishing between men and women. Therefore, we cannot say the Court *only* looks at tradition and history to determine whether a right is fundamental. Yet, Answer (A) is correct because in recent cases the Court has looked extensively at history and tradition in making this determination. *See Troxel v. Granville*, 530 U.S. 57 (2000); *Washington v. Glucksberg*, 521 U.S. 702 (1997); *Michael H. v. Gerald D.*, 491 U.S. 110 (1989); *Moore v. City of East Cleveland*, 431 U.S. 494 (1977).

What, then, is the difference between Answer (A) and Answer (C)? Answer (C) takes the "history and tradition" approach one step further. It requires the tradition to be described in its most specific form. The plurality part of the Court's decision in *Michael H. v. Gerald D.* highlights this approach. This case involved parental visitation rights for a father who sired a child out of wedlock. The mother was married to another man. To Justice Scalia, the case involved what rights were traditionally accorded to "adulterous natural fathers." Clearly, our tradition provides few rights to such individuals. To Justice Brennan, however, the right involved in the case was most fairly described as the right of a parent to have a relationship with his child. Justice Scalia objected to the description of the right in such general terms. Justice Scalia argued that the tradition must be viewed more specifically. Justice Kennedy and O'Connor, although joining in the decision, refused to endorse Justice Scalia's "most specific level of generality" methodology. Answer (C) adopts Justice Scalia's approach in *Michael H. v. Gerald D.*, an approach only adopted by a plurality in that case, and not adopted in other cases.

**Answer (B) is incorrect** because it ignores the Court's continued and significant reliance on history and tradition.

**Both Answers (C) and (D) are incorrect** because they reflect methodologies advanced by some members of the Court but not adopted by a majority of the Court. Answer (C) was the methodology articulated by Justice Scalia in *Michael H. v. Gerald D.* Answer (D) reflects the methodology suggested by Justice Souter in his concurring opinion in *Glucksberg*.

124.   The Takings Clause allows government to take private property if (1) the property is taken for "public use," and (2) the government pays "just compensation." U.S. Constitution, Amendment V. Here, we are told that the Town of Plainview will pay just compensation. So, the issue is whether the land has been taken for public use. This is arguably not so, as the Town took the property and then sold it to a *private* party. In *Hawaii Housing Authority v. Midkiff*, 465 U.S. 1097 (1984), the Court explained that government may do so as long as "the exercise of the eminent domain power is rationally related to a conceivable public purpose." *Id.* at 241. In *Midkiff*, the state used its eminent domain power to break a local land oligopoly. Concentration of private land ownership had "created artificial deterrents to the normal functioning of the state's residential land market and forced thousands of individual homeowners to lease, rather than buy, the land underneath their homes." *Id.* at 242. So, the state took land from large landholders and re-distributed it among a greater number of citizens. The Court affirmed this approach in *Kelo v. City of New London*, 545 U.S. 469 (2005), explaining that federal courts should defer to local judgments concerning whether a public purpose exists, as well as what scope of taking is required to serve that interest. *Id.* at 488-89. There, the Court upheld a taking that transferred property to a private developer as part of a development plan designed to remedy urban blight in the affected neighborhood. The Court held that "the comprehensive character of the plan" and "the thorough deliberation that preceded its adoption" both evidenced the city's public purpose.

       Here, Plainview has a conceivable public purpose for its taking: alleviating the traffic and law enforcement problems caused by inadequate parking at the Tatum Mall. Further, providing Big Box Realty with land for additional parking is rationally related to solving the parking problem. And Plainview's taking has additional indicia of public purpose identified in *Kelo*: careful study and deliberation showing that the plan was to solve a public problem, and not simply to benefit a private land owner. Thus, a court should uphold Plainview's action as a permissible taking for public use.

125.   **Answers (A), (C), and (D) are incorrect** because they inaccurately describe the Ordinance's effect. First, consider Answer (A), which correctly states the applicable rule of law. In *Lucas v. South Carolina Coastal Council*, 505 U.S. 1003 (1992), the Supreme Court held that a regulation is a per se taking if it permanently eliminates all economically beneficial use of land, making the land valueless. The Court explained that valueless means loss of 100% of value. If even five percent of the land's value remains after the regulation, *Lucas'* per se rule does not apply. *Id.* at 1019 n.8. Here, while the Ordinance has reduced Ronald's land to a mere eighth of its former value, he still has $10,000 worth of value remaining. The *Lucas* per se rule does not apply.

**Answer (C) is incorrect** because the Ordinance is not a development exaction. Exactions involve government decisions that condition approval of requested land development on some action by the landowner. For example, consider a landowner who applies for a permit to expand an existing structure on her property. An exaction would occur if the government conditioned approval of the permit on the landowner doing something with her land, such as creating a public bike path. *See Dolan v. City of Tigard*, 512 U.S. 374 (1994). The government would be using the permitting process to exact a bike path from the landowner. Here, there is no condition or exaction; the Ordinance simply orders Ronald to leave his land undeveloped.

**Answer (D) is incorrect** because the Ordinance is not forcing Ronald to endure a physical invasion of his land. In *Loretto v. Teleprompter Manhattan CATV Corp.*, 458 U.S. 419 (1982), the Court held that a city ordinance took private property when it forced apartment owners to endure physical invasion of their land for installation of cable equipment. Here, the Ordinance does not force anyone or anything onto Ronald's land. Rather, the Ordinance simply *allows* Ronald to invite people onto his land for hunting and fishing. Ronald retains the choice whether to do so.

**Answer (B) is correct** because it applies the general, default regulatory takings analysis. The Court has applied this analysis in a line of cases dating from *Penn Central Transp. Co. v. City of New York*, 438 U.S. 104 (1978). In practice, the analysis focuses on two main issues: first, is the challenged regulation substantially related to a legitimate government interest? and second, how severely does the regulation affect the property? The regulation is less likely to be a taking when the government's interest is strong and the effect on the property is mild, and vice versa.

*Penn Central* illustrates how the Court applies this test. There, New York City denied a developer the right to build in the airspace above Grand Central Terminal, which served primarily as a railway station. The city did so to preserve the landmark status of the Terminal. The Court held that the city's interest was strong while the imposition on the landowner was relatively light. Regarding the city's interest, the Court explained that "preserving structures and areas with special historic, architectural, or cultural significance is an entirely permissible government goal." *Id.* at 129. Doing so promotes the city's aesthetic beauty as well as its citizens' quality of life.

Regarding the impact on the landowner, the Court considered several factors. First, the landmark law did not interfere with the landowner's "primary expectation concerning the use of the parcel." *Id.* at 136. For several decades prior to purchase, the Terminal had been operated as a railway station, and the landmark law allowed continued use for that purpose. Thus, the landowner could still earn a " 'reasonable return' on its investment." *Id.* Second, the landmark law conferred an "average reciprocity of advantage" upon all landowners. While the Terminal's value might decrease due to restriction on its development, its value would also increase due to the preservation of landmarks throughout the remainder of the city. Third, while the city had rejected specific proposals for developing the Terminal, the city never stated it would prohibit all such proposals. Future development was possible if it preserved the Terminal's landmark character. Fourth, in exchange for not developing above the Terminal, the city granted the Terminal's owner transferable development rights. These rights allowed the Terminal's owner to develop other parcels within the city. Together, these factors minimized the landmark law's impact on the Terminal-owner's property.

Here, Ronald can make a strong case that the Ordinance impermissibly takes his property. First, his land's value has substantially decreased — it is now worth only one eighth it former price. Second, unlike in *Penn Central*, the Ordinance destroys Ronald's primary investment-backed expectation for the property. Dixon is being built out for residential use, and Ronald purchased his lot solely for such use. The Ordinance now eliminates that use, leaving Ronald with no realistic alternatives. Third, there is no average reciprocity of advantage. Residential owners in the area will reap the benefit of maintaining a bear habitat, keeping bears from menacing their homes. Ronald, however, will not receive any of this benefit as he cannot make residential use of his land. Indeed, the very intent of the Ordinance is that Ronald's land be used to benefit the rest of the Town. *See Armstrong v. United States*, 364 U.S. 40, 49 (1960) (Takings Clause is "designed to bar Government from forcing some people alone to bear public burdens which in all fairness and justice should be borne by the public as a whole"). Fourth, unlike *Penn Central*, where the landowner was given transferable development rights, the Town has not given Ronald any property right or other value in return for restricting his land. A court could find that this severe imposition on Ronald's property so outweighs the state's interest in public safety that the Ordinance takes his property.

126. While the Town's interest in public safety remains strong, the six-month moratorium interferes less with Ronald's property rights than did the permanent development ban. Six months is much less severe, more akin to the normal delay in applying for a building permit or a zoning variance than a regulation that takes property rights. *See First English Evangelical Lutheran Church v. County of Los Angeles*, 482 U.S. 304, (1987) (leaving aside the question of whether "normal delays" in obtaining government approval are compensable temporary taking). Further, Ronald's primary expectation for the land — building a residence — can still be realized, albeit after a short delay. Also, a moratorium offers an average reciprocity of advantage. The moratorium ensures adequate time for the Town to study the bear problem and reach an intelligent solution. Better government decisions benefit all Town residents. In sum, given the strong government interest and the greatly-reduced effects on Ronald's property rights, the Town's six-month moratorium should not be a taking. Of course, if the Town either extends the moratorium or makes the prohibition permanent, the analysis would change again, as the Town would increase the burden on Ronald's property rights.

127. **Answer (D) is the best answer**. The government owes just compensation for any taking of property, regardless of its duration. *First English Evangelical Lutheran Church v. County of Los Angeles*, 482 U.S. 304 (1987). Temporary appropriation of private property gives rise to just compensation measured by the value of the owner's lost use.

Here, Ronald would have a right to damages measured by any loss caused by the six-month delay in developing his property. Thus, **Answer (A) is incorrect**.

**Answers (B) and (C) are incorrect** because whether the land has any remaining economically viable use is irrelevant to whether compensation is owed. As long as the court finds a taking, just compensation is owed.

128. **Answer (A) is the best answer**. *Hodel v. Irving*, 481 U.S. 704 (1987), established that elimination of the right of inheritance constitutes a taking of private property. *Hodel* involved certain Indian lands that had become unproductive due to their ownership structure. Federal law severely limited Indians' rights to transfer the land, leaving inheritance of an undivided interest as the main form of conveyance. Over several generations, ownership of the land was divided among a greater and greater number of heirs. Eventually, so many people had an undivided ownership interest in certain parcels that productive use became impossible. To undo this mess, Congress passed a law that escheated these fractionated interests to the Indian tribe, depriving future heirs of their right to inherit these virtually valueless interests. Further, given the federal restrictions on *inter vivos* transfers, landowners had no feasible means to avoid the escheat statute. Because the right to devise and inherit property is essential to property ownership, any law that extinguished those rights took private property.

Here, the State of West Arifornia has done the same thing to the owners of each square foot. Neither will nor intestate succession will transfer ownership at death. Instead, the Town of Gorse becomes owner regardless of the owner's actions. Thus, as in *Hodel*, the state has taken private property.

**Answers (B) and (D) are incorrect** because the state's interest is irrelevant to the outcome. Regardless of the gravity of the state interest supporting the law, or the relationship of the escheat statute to that interest, destroying the right to devise or inherit property is a taking.

**Answer (C) is incorrect** because the property's value is not relevant to the question of whether the statute took private property. Elimination of the rights to devise and inherit is enough to find a taking.

129. **Answer (C) is the best answer**. Just compensation is measured by the amount of the property owner's net *loss*, and the District Court found that the one-square-foot parcels were valueless. It is true that the land will have positive value once ownership is consolidated in the Town's hands. But, the Supreme Court recently explained that just "compensation must be measured by [the property owner's] net losses rather than the value of the public's gain." *Brown v. Legal Found. of Wash.*, 538 U.S. 216, 237 (2003). Thus, "if [the property owner's] net loss was zero, the compensation that is due is also zero." *Id.* For this reason, **Answer (A) is incorrect**.

**Answer (B) is incorrect** because it is not relevant to the proper measure of just compensation. Rather, destruction of essential sticks in the bundle of property rights is relevant to whether government regulation is a taking.

**Answer (D) is incorrect** because the strict scrutiny test is not used to determine whether just compensation is due.

130. **Answer (C) is the best answer.** In *Loretto v. Teleprompter Manhattan CATV Corp.*, 458 U.S. 419 (1982), the Supreme Court held that the government takes private property when it forces a private land owner to suffer a forced physical invasion of her land by a third party. There, a New York City ordinance required apartment building owners to allow a private cable company to install cable wires and a small box necessary to provide cable service to the building's residents. Here, the Brainia Ordinance forces a similar invasion. Specifically, the Village requires access for officials from a private a college to install equipment necessary for wireless Internet access. As in *Loretto*, this forced physical invasion by a third party is a per se taking.

**Answers (A) and (B) are incorrect** because a forced physical invasion is a per se taking, regardless of the regulation's effect on either the property's value or the owner's expectations.

**Answer (D) is incorrect** because *Loretto* established a per se rule for physical invasions, making the invasion a taking regardless of the government's asserted purpose.

131. **Answer (C) is the best answer.** The Ordinance uses the permit approval process to exact a property interest — the right to enter the land and install equipment for wireless Internet access — from the permit applicant. The Supreme Court has held that such exactions are takings unless the condition is roughly proportional to some public concern created by the applicant's proposed land use. *Dolan v. City of Tigard*, 512 U.S. 374 (1994); *Nollan v. California Coastal Comm'n*, 483 U.S. 825 (1987). For example, if a proposed land development would increase flooding, the government could condition permit approval on actions mitigating that threat to public health and safety. Here, however, the Village can show no link between the condition and the proposed development. The Village only noted possible pedestrian concerns in its permit decision. There is no logical connection between the flow of pedestrians and wireless Internet access. Indeed, according to the Village, creating wireless Internet access will increase patronage of local businesses, which would further exacerbate pedestrian problems.

Because the condition is not roughly proportional, **Answer (D) is incorrect**.

**Answer (B) is incorrect** because it incorrectly states that rational basis review is the proper test. The *Dolan* Court specifically noted that "roughly proportional" requires a stronger means-end relationship than does rational basis review.

**Answer (A) is incorrect** because it mistakenly assumes that the condition would make the property valueless.

132. **Answer (A) is the correct answer** because a regulation takes private property when it makes the property valueless. *See Lucas v. South Carolina Coastal Council*, 505 U.S. 1003 (1992). **Answers (B) and (D) are incorrect** because post-regulation transfer of

the property does not extinguish the right to compensation. *See Palazzolo v. Rhode Island*, 533 U.S. 606 (2001). The consideration Kirk paid James presumably reflected the value of the unfiled claim for just compensation.

Answer (C) refers to an exception to *Lucas'* per se rule: "Where the State seeks to sustain regulation that deprives land of all economically beneficial use, we think it may resist compensation only if the logically antecedent inquiry into the nature of the owner's estate shows that the proscribed use interests were not part of his title to begin with." *Lucas*, 505 U.S. at 1027. Title to real property is held subject to background common law rules, such as the rules against private or public nuisances. Consequently, such rules do not take private property, even if they prohibit the only economically viable use of land. Similarly, statutes, administrative regulations, and other government decisions that merely duplicate the result under a common law rule will not be takings. Here, the city's environmental Ordinance does not parallel any common law restriction of land use. And, "[a] law does not become a background principle for subsequent owners by enactment itself." *Palazzolo*, 533 U.S. at 630. Thus, **Answer (C) is incorrect**.

133.  **Answer (D) is the best answer**. Generally, regulations that prohibit all economically viable use of land are a taking. *See Lucas v. South Carolina Coastal Council*, 505 U.S. 1003 (1992). However, as discussed in the answer to the preceding question, such a regulation is not a taking if it merely duplicates a background common law property rule. Here, the permit decision parallels the common law rule prohibiting public nuisances. Specifically, using land in a manner that would cause flooding would be a public nuisance. *See Lucas*, 505 U.S. at 1029. By denying WasteCo's permit request, the state regulators merely prevented conduct that the common law already prohibited. Thus, WasteCo has not suffered a taking.

**Answer (A) and (B) are incorrect** because they ignore the *Lucas* exception for regulations that parallel common law property rules.

**Answer (C) is incorrect** because it mistakenly applies the test for government exactions. This question does not involve an exaction because the government has simply denied WasteCo's permit request. An exaction would involve approval of WasteCo's request conditioned on WasteCo taking some action respecting its land.

134. **Answer (D) is the best Answer** because it most accurately summarizes the holding in *Home Building & Loan Association v. Blaisdell*, 290 U.S. 398 (1934). *Blaisdell* is a significant case in Contract Clause jurisprudence because it made clear that legitimate government action under the state's police power is not an unconstitutional impairment of existing contracts. The issue before the Court in *Blaisdell* involved a Minnesota law that created a moratorium on foreclosure of mortgages during the Great Depression. Obviously, this impaired existing mortgage contracts. Yet, the Court upheld the Minnesota law against a Contract Clause attack, stating that government had the power to protect the community in this way. Further, the Court held that a valid exercise of police power was permissible under the Contract Clause.

The question after *Blaisdell* was whether anything remained of the Contract Clause. Since 1934, the Supreme Court has only twice struck down state legislation as violating the Contract Clause. *See Allied Structural Steel Co. v. Spannaus,* 438 U.S. 234 (1978); *United States Trust Co. v. New Jersey*, 431 U.S. 1 (1977). In *Allied Structural Steel*, Justice Stewart declared, "the Contract Clause [is] not a dead letter." Yet, given the Court's great deference to state legislation when attacked under the Contract Clause, it is reasonable to question whether the Clause has much remaining vigor.

**Answer (A) is incorrect** because the *Blaisdell* Court strongly rejected original intent as a deciding principle in reaching its decision. Chief Justice Hughes, writing for the Court, stated: "If by the statement that what the Constitution meant at the time of its adoption it means today, it is intended to say that the great clauses of the Constitution must be confined to the interpretation which the framers, with the conditions and outlook of their time, would have placed upon them, the statement carries its own refutation." It is difficult to find a stronger rejection of original intent in any Supreme Court decision.

**Answer (B) is incorrect** because *Blaisdell* is one in a line of cases in which the Court backed away from its reliance on substantive economic due process to strike down economic legislation. Prior to decisions such as *Blaisdell*, the Court relied on the doctrine of substantive economic due process to strike down a host of state and federal statutes, holding that such legislation violated the freedom of contract under the due process clauses. During the zenith of economic substantive due process, the Court did not rely much on the Contract Clause because freedom of contract was well protected by its due process jurisprudence. Nevertheless, it was for *Blaisdell* to make clear that the Contract Clause was limited by a valid exercise of police power and that the Contract Clause would not be used, in the future, to block economic legislation.

**Answer (C) is incorrect** because it does not accurately state the holding in *Blaisdell*. The Court in *Blaisdell* did not rely on a "substantial impairment" test to trigger a Contract

317

Clause review of legislation. The "substantial impairment" test was developed much later by the Court in *Energy Reserves Group v. Kansas Power & Light*, 459 U.S. 400 (1983).

135.   **Answer (B) is the best answer** because it follows the test developed by the Supreme Court in *United States Trust Co. v. New Jersey*, 431 U.S. 1 (1977), for examining government behavior that impairs government contracts, as distinguished from government behavior that impairs private contracts. When government behavior affects contracts between private parties, the Court has displayed great deference to the choice by the state to regulate. However, when the contract impaired is between the government and a private party, the Court more closely scrutinizes such government behavior under the Contract Clause. In *United States Trust*, the Court declared that New Jersey had violated the Contract Clause by repealing a law that had prohibited the use of toll funds to subsidize railroad passenger service. This repeal had the effect of impairing the contract between bond holders and the state. The state had promised the bond holders that tolls would not be used to subsidize the railroad, which was feared to be a money-losing venture.

In reaching this decision, the Court articulated a more rigorous standard when reviewing government action that impairs government contracts, as contrasted to private contracts. Justice Blackmun stated:

> As with laws impairing the obligations of private contracts, an impairment [of State obligations] may be constitutional if it is reasonable and necessary to serve an important public purpose. In applying this standard, however, complete deference to a legislative assessment of reasonableness and necessity is not appropriate because the State's self-interest is at stake. [If] a State could reduce its financial obligations whenever it wanted to spend money for what it regarded as an important public purpose, the Contract Clause would provide no protection at all.

Further, the Court found that New Jersey had other alternatives to funding the railroad, and it rejected the idea that it was for the legislature alone to chose between alternatives. The Court held that a state was not completely free to consider all possible alternatives when it was impairing the rights of parties who had entered into contracts with the government, and "a State is not free to impose a drastic impairment when an evident and more moderate course would serve its purpose equally well."

Thus, the Court in *United States Trust* imposed two stricter requirements when government contracts are subject to scrutiny under the Contract Clause. First, the legislation impairing the contract must be necessary as well as reasonable, and second, the alternative chosen must be the one with a less drastic effect on the government contracts. The action by Nevahoma in this question does not meet this stricter standard of review, making Answer (B) the best choice.

**Answer (A) is incorrect** because it does not address the most important issues when considering the Contract Clause. When a party challenges a government law or regulation as violating the Contract Clause, the party almost always claims that the change in law altered the underlying assumptions held by the party prior to entering into the contract. So, saying that the Nevahoma law altered the bond holders' underlying assumptions is self-evident, but does not help answer whether this rises to the level of violating the Constitution. To answer that question when a government contract is involved, we have to consider: first, whether altering the assumption amounts to a substantial impairment; second, whether the impairment was a necessary and reasonable use of the police powers, and third, whether the means chosen were the least drastic impairment of the contract available.

**Answer (C) is incorrect** because it is untrue. The Contract Clause applies to government contracts.

**Answer (D) is incorrect** because it does not recognize the greater degree of scrutiny the Court uses in evaluating an alleged impairment of a government contract, as discussed above in connection with Answer (B).

136.  **Answer (C) is the best answer**. The Contract Clause only applies to existing contracts, not future contracts. *Ogden v. Saunders*, 25 U.S. (12 Wheat.) 213 (1827). The Clause was adopted to stop states from enacting laws that would help debtors avoid their contractual obligations in times of economic distress. The fear apparently was that a depressed economy would pressure state legislators to pass legislation that helped citizens avoid contractual obligations by changing the terms of these contracts. Hence, the Contract Clause forbids this sort of legislative tinkering with existing contracts.

**Answer (A) is incorrect** because states can be sued, even though sovereign. While there are limitations on when a state is subject to legal process, Answer (A) is incorrect because it asserts, without reservation, that states, being sovereign, can never be sued.

**Answer (B) is incorrect** because it ignores the substance of the claim made in the lawsuit. The suit involves a claim brought under the Contract Clause. The law suit does not raise a due process objection. The correct answer to this question has to address the precise claim brought, which is a Contract Clause claim.

Interestingly, if this lawsuit had been filed against the federal government, then a court would be correct to use due process to rule on the claim. The Contract Clause only places a limit on state governments; it does not apply to federal government actions. However, when faced with federal government behavior that impairs contracts, courts have considered whether the federal government violated due process principles in engaging in the alleged impairment. *See Pension Benefit Guaranty Corp. v. R.A. Gray & Co.*, 467 U.S. 717 (1984), (holding that due process principles are not equivalent to Contract Clause limitations on the states, and that the Court would review claims that federal behavior impaired contracts with the deference usually accorded in reviewing national economic legislation under due process principles).

**Answer (D) is incorrect** for the reasons stated in Answer (C).

137.   **Answer (A) is the best answer** because it is in line with almost all Supreme Court decisions determining whether legislation resulted in a "substantial impairment" of an existing contractual obligation. First, it is important to remember that under *Energy Reserves Group v. Kansas Power & Light*, 459 U.S. 400 (1983), an impairment has to be deemed "substantial" to trigger any further review of the statute under the Contract Clause. And the Supreme Court has not been often willing to find substantial impairment. For example, in *Energy Reserves Group*, the contract at issue permitted the contract price to match any governmentally fixed price. Kansas subsequently passed a law that prevented this matching of the contract price with the governmentally-fixed price. The Court held that the Kansas law was not a substantial impairment because Energy Reserves Group knew, at the time of contracting, that it was subject to both state and federal regulation and that the relevant market — natural gas — was highly regulated. Therefore, Energy Reserves Group's reasonable expectations were not substantially impaired. *See also General Motors v. Romein*, 503 U.S. 181 (1992). Considering these cases as well as the Court's tendency to find no substantial impairment, it seems unlikely that the lower court's ruling will be reversed.

**Answer (B) is incorrect** because it misapplies the *Energy Reserves Group* test. Under that test, the Court evaluates the government's purpose only after it decides whether the alleged contract impairment is "substantial." Further, the *Energy Reserves Group* test requires that the exercise of the police power be "significant and legitimate." Answer (B) incorrectly states the standard as whether the government's use of its police power is "valid."

**Answer (C) is incorrect** because the Court in *Energy Reserves Group* held that only a "substantial" impairment violates the Contract Clause.

**Answer (D) is incorrect** for the reasons stated in connection with Answer (A).

138. **Answer (C) is the best answer.** Your analysis should focus on whether Jane has a property interest in her job that is protected by procedural due process. It was not until *Goldberg v. Kelly,* 397 U.S. 254 (1970), that the Supreme Court discarded the rights-privileges distinction and held that receiving a government benefit could become a property interest, which required providing due process when the government attempted to alter or deny the continued enjoyment of that property interest. *Goldberg* has been used to find a property interest in continuing government employment. In subsequent cases the Court has limited *Goldberg* so that not every government program creates a constitutionally protected property interest for the beneficiary. Rather, a property interest is created only when the beneficiary of the government action is or becomes entitled to the benefit. Further, the Court has held that the Due Process Clause does not create property rights. Instead, the existence of an entitlement is determined by an independent source such as state law or the rules and understandings that state law creates. *See Board of Regents v. Roth,* 408 U.S. 564 (1972).

Whether Jane has an entitlement to her paralegal job will be determined by looking at state law, which means we have to examine the terms and conditions of her employment contract. The terms of the contract appear to have been agreed to orally. It is important that nothing was said to Jane about the consequences of failing the bar examination. Therefore, she was not disabused of any expectation she might have had about continuing in this position. This, combined with the past practices of the County Attorney's Office of allowing other law students similarly situated to continue as paralegals, strongly suggests that she was reasonable in concluding that her job would continue despite her bar examination results. If she was reasonable to so conclude, then she is entitled to that position — or, said differently, she has a property interest in her job. For these reasons Answer (C) is correct. Please note, however, that a trier of fact presented with all the facts associated with the practices of this office regarding similarly-situated paralegal employees may find that Jane's expectations were not reasonable, and she did not have a property interest. *See Perry v. Snidermann,* 408 U.S. 593 (1972).

**Answer (A) is incorrect** because it does not acknowledge the possible property interest Jane has in her continued employment.

**Answer (B) is incorrect** because it fails to acknowledge the Supreme Court's rejection of the old "rights-privilege" distinction, and it does not fully appreciate the significance of *Goldberg v. Kelly.*

**Answer (D) is incorrect** because precedent exists that does not require a pre-termination hearing under these facts. *See Arnett v. Kennedy,* 416 U.S. 134 (1974).

139.    **Answer (A) is the best answer.** The change in facts between this question and the one that preceded it make it much less likely that Jane has a property interest in her job. Here, Jane does not have the benefit of others in the past retaining their jobs after failing the bar examination. This, combined with the employment being at-will under the contract, strongly suggest that Jane had no entitlement to continue with her employment as a paralegal. Without such an entitlement, she has no property interest and can be dismissed at the employer's will.

**Answers (B) and (D) are incorrect** for similar reasons and involve the so-called "taking the bitter with the sweet" doctrine. Under this doctrine, the procedure due can be limited by the terms of the law creating the property interest. This means that a government employer could make dismissal without cause a term of the employment contract, and a court could not impose greater procedural due process since the employment contract by its terms limited the required procedure. This doctrine has been repudiated by the Supreme Court in *Cleveland Board of Education v. Loudermill,* 470 U.S. 532 (1985), in which the Court made it clear that once a property right is found to exist, then it is for the courts to decide what procedures are required under the Due Process Clause and that a court's decision on proper process cannot be limited by the terms of the contract. Therefore, Answer (B) is incorrect since it would allow the contract to limit the process Jane is due, and Answer (D) is incorrect because *Loudermill* has held otherwise. But, remember that the limited procedure provided by the contract will be used to decide if a property right exists at all.

**Answer (C) is incorrect** because nothing in the question indicates that the actual terms of her contract say anything about whether she has a property interest in her job.

140.    **Answer (C) is the best answer** because it most closely follows the Supreme Court's decisions in *DeShaney v. Winnebago County Department of Social Services,* 489 U.S. 189 (1989) and *Town of Castle Rock v. Gonzales,* 545 U.S. 748 (2005). These decisions stated the general principle that an individual does not have a property interest in government protection from private harm. As *DeShaney* explained, the Due Process Clause does not require "the State to protect the life, liberty, and property of its citizens against invasion by private actors. The Clause is phrased as a limitation on the State's power to act, not as a guarantee of certain minimal levels of safety and security."

Both *DeShaney* and *Gonzales* also noted that the government behavior in each case was inaction rather than action, and that inaction did not create a property interest. A property interest exists only when the government does something to create an entitlement as, for example, giving someone a job or other benefit as discussed in the answer to Question 138.

In this question nothing suggests that the individuals who died were entitled to any level of enforcement by Virginia of its environmental protection laws. Therefore, they did not have a property interest in this enforcement, making Answer (C) correct. Note that this answer does not preclude other possible causes of action under state law, which is beyond the scope of this question.

**Answer (A) is incorrect** because it does not respond to the facts of the question. While it is accurate to say the Due Process Clause protects life as well as liberty and property, the Clause only offers this protection if a *state* deprives an individual of life. The Clause does not protect against private behavior. The facts here state that the toxic discharge was done by a private company. Therefore, unless the plaintiffs can show they had a property interest in how Virginia enforced its environmental laws, the Due Process Clause's protection of life will not provide them relief.

**Answer (B) is incorrect** because it states only a general proposition without providing reference to a specific law or duty. Governments are expected to protect citizens, but that general statement does not translate into a specific legal cause of action against a state under these facts, as discussed in connection with Answer (C).

**Answer (D) is incorrect** because the political question doctrine applies almost invariably to the relationship between the three branches of the federal government, addressing whether the text of the Constitution and separation of powers principles commit to one branch certain duties and powers. This question has nothing to do with the relationship between the three branches of the federal government. A more interesting question, but not one raised here, is whether Virginia could claim sovereign immunity and ask dismissal of the suit based on that doctrine. That answer would depend on whether Virginia has waived it claim of sovereign immunity either by statute or for this case.

141. **Answer (D) is the best answer** because it best reflects the balancing test for such cases created by the Supreme Court in *Mathews v. Eldridge,* 424 U.S. 319 (1976). *Mathews* held that courts should examine three factors in deciding what procedure the Constitution requires: "First, the private interest that will be affected by the official action; second, the risk of an erroneous deprivation of such interest through the procedures used, and the probable value, if any, of additional or substitute procedural safeguards; and finally, the Government's interest, including the function involved and the fiscal and administrative burdens that the additional or substitute procedural requirement would entail."

Under this test, we can conclude: first, that Jane has an important interest in keeping her job; second, while there is some risk that an employer could be wrong in the reasons for dismissal, this risk is not significant considering the employment relationship will allow the employer a good opportunity to evaluate the employee; and, third, giving Jane a hearing prior to termination could add to the county's fiscal burden because she will remain on the payroll during this time and through any appeals. On balance, while Jane has an important interest in keeping her job, the small risk of an erroneous evaluation by her employer, coupled with the fiscal burden on her employer, weigh against requiring a pre-termination hearing under the *Mathews v. Eldridge* balancing test.

**Answer (A) is incorrect** for the same reasons discussed in the answer to Question 139. The decision as to whether procedures surrounding a taking of property are sufficient to satisfy the Due Process Clause is not governed by the procedures established in the contract. As the Court said in *Cleveland Board of Education v. Loudermill*, 470 U.S. 532 (1985), once a property right is established then the procedures that must be followed prior to taking away the property are decided by the courts and not by the procedures agreed to by the parties when they entered into the relationship that created the property right.

**Answer (B) is incorrect** because it is not supported by the facts as given or by the law. Nothing in the facts indicates that Jane and the county ever discussed what would happen if she failed the bar examination. Therefore, the facts do not support a conclusion of unfairness, especially because Jane could not satisfy the needs the county had for a lawyer. As such, the county is not unreasonable in dismissing her. More importantly, procedural due process is not equivalent to "fairness." Procedural due process is a much more sophisticated concept that balances the right infringed against the government's interest in fiscal and administrative burdens. This sophistication is not captured by the term "fair," which is not used in court opinions defining the parameters of procedural due process.

**Answer (C) is incorrect** because it suggests that a standardized list exists that, if followed, satisfies the constitutional requirements for procedural due process. This is not true. Each case is evaluated on its facts by a court in deciding whether, in those circumstances, a certain procedure is required. Answer (C) is also incorrect because it ignores precedent that seldom requires a hearing prior to dismissal, although some type of hearing may be required after dismissal.

142.   **Answer (B) is the best answer** because it relies on the Supreme Court's decision in *Hamdi v. Rumsfeld,* 542 U.S. 507 (2004). In *Hamdi,* the Court was asked to consider the constitutionality of detaining an American citizen as an enemy combatant without a hearing on the facts leading to his detention. Hamdi argued that he was denied his constitutional right to liberty and sought a writ of habeas corpus to challenge his detention as violating his right to due process. The government countered that more process would be unworkable and constitutionally intolerable given the facts of war surrounding Hamdi's capture and detention. The Court acknowledged the legitimate concerns voiced by both sides and balanced these competing interests under the doctrine articulated in *Mathews v. Eldridge,* 424 U.S. 319 (1976).

Following *Mathews,* the Court evaluated the significance of the individual liberty interest affected, the probable value of additional safeguards to prevent a mistake in the detention decision, and the burdens on the government of providing additional procedures. In evaluating these interests, the Court recognized that Hamdi had a serious liberty interest at stake and that the government's process for detaining enemy combatants was not likely to detect and correct errors. The Court also noted the government's significant interest in detaining those who pose a threat to the security of the United States as well as the substantial burden on the military during war time if Hamdi were accorded the process due a run-of-the-mill prisoner.

The Supreme Court concluded that a citizen-detainee seeking to challenge his detention must receive notice of the factual basis for his detention and must be given a fair opportunity to rebut the Government's factual assertions before a neutral decision-maker. However, the Court made clear that aside from these core elements of procedural due process, other procedures afforded a citizen-detainee "may be tailored to alleviate their uncommon potential to burden the executive at a time of ongoing military conflict." These "tailored" procedures could include the use of hearsay and presumptions in favor of the government. In other words, the government would not be forced to give the same procedural protections afforded most prisoners.

**Answer (A) is incorrect** for the reasons stated for Answer (B).

**Answer (C) is incorrect** because the Supreme Court in *Hamdi* refused to address directly whether the President has such power under Article II. The President argued that Article II gave him inherent power to protect the nation, which power includes his authority to detain individuals who the President found to constitute a threat to the nation's security. The Supreme Court sidestepped this argument by finding the prisoners in *Hamdi* were detained under authority of the AUMF, rather than under the President's inherent powers. Moreover, no other Supreme Court case has acknowledged Presidential power of this magnitude—namely the power to imprison a citizen based only on a Presidential finding and with no judicial oversight. But remember that several Supreme Court cases have acknowledged that the President does have broad inherent powers under Article II. The events following September 11 have raised many questions regarding the scope of this inherent power and the proper role of judicial oversight. The cases decided to date have favored judicial oversight and have not supported the President's assertions of broad inherent power to devise procedures for detaining suspected terrorists. But many cases are still working their way through the system, so we should expect to see more on this subject.

**Answer (D) is incorrect** because the Supreme Court has not ordered the cessation of detentions under the AUMF. Indeed, in *Hamdi*, the Court upheld the authority of the President to detain alleged terrorists under the provisions of the AUMF.

143.    The Supreme Court has held that the Due Process Clause is not implicated when the state is negligent. *See Daniels v. Williams,* 474 U.S. 327 (1986); *Davidson v. Cannon,* 474 U.S. 344 (1986). The Court reasoned in these cases that an unconstitutional deprivation of liberty, life, or property requires more intent and more abuse of power than exists in a negligence case. The Court has not yet decided whether other states of mind, such as recklessness or gross negligence, are sufficient to implicate the Due Process Clause. Lower courts have found deprivation based on recklessness but not on gross negligence.

It is interesting to note, however, that *Jones v. Flowers,* 126 S. Ct. 1708 (2006), seemed to move toward a recklessness standard, although the Court did not state this directly. There, the government sought to sell real property for failure to pay property taxes. The state sent notice by certified mail to the property owner's address, but the notice was returned unclaimed. Two years later, the state placed a notice of tax sale in the local newspaper. After the sale, the owner sued the state on the grounds that the tax sale took his property without due process of law. The Court held that the government is required to take further steps when it learns that prior notice has not reached the property owner.

> We do not think that a person who actually desired to inform a real property owner of an impending tax sale of a house he owns would do nothing when a certified letter sent to the owner is returned unclaimed. If the Commissioner prepared a stack of letters to mail to delinquent taxpayers, handed them to the postman, and then watched as the departing postman accidentally dropped the letters down a storm drain, one would certainly expect the Commissioner's office to prepare a new stack of letters and send them again. No one "desirous of actually informing" the owners would simply shrug his shoulders as the letters disappeared and say "I tried." Failure to follow up would be unreasonable, despite the fact that the letters were reasonably calculated to reach their intended recipients when delivered to the postman.

And the later newspaper notice was not enough: "Following up by publication was not constitutionally adequate under the circumstances presented here because, as we have explained, it was possible and practicable to give Jones more adequate warning of the impending tax sale."

144.   **Answer (A) is the best answer.** Parents have a liberty interest in the custody of their children. *Santosky v. Kramer,* 455 U.S. 745 (1982). Courts have held that parents' fundamental right to custody of their children is a liberty, not a property, interest. (Thank goodness!) The state's action in this question deprives parents of their children for a two-week period without a hearing or other procedure to make sure the reasons for the deprivation are valid. Thus, it provides no procedural protections against the two-week loss, depriving the parents of their liberty without due process of law. **This also makes Answer (C) incorrect.** The Due Process Clause covers deprivations of liberty and life as well as property.

**Answer (B) is incorrect** because no authority gives a child a liberty interest in his or her "best interest." It is unlikely, moreover, that such a right would be granted, as it would constitutionalize family law.

**Answer (D) is incorrect** under the test developed in *Mathews v. Eldridge*, 424 U.S. 319 (1976), discussed in the answer to Question 141. Under that balancing test, the parents' interest is especially strong, even when the deprivation is for a short period of time. Few parents would agree to have their children in the custody of strangers for two weeks. Further, under the *Mathews* test, the likelihood of mistakes is high. We don't know how "domestic abuse" is defined. We don't know how much proof is required to trigger this law. Would a phone call from a neighbor suffice? Moreover, since the government will have administrative and fiscal costs in using this law in any event, providing judicial review immediately has few additional costs. On balance then, the process does not appear to be sufficient under the *Mathews* test.

145. **Answer (D) is correct and Answer (C) is incorrect for the same reasons**. The Fourteenth Amendment to the Constitution was passed after the Civil War and contains within it several concepts important to understanding individual rights jurisprudence, including such concepts as due process and equal protection of law. It also contains the following language: "No State shall make or enforce any law which shall abridge the privileges or immunities of citizens of the United States." This is called the Privileges and Immunities Clause. Four years after the passage of the Fourteenth Amendment, the Supreme Court in the *Slaughter-House Cases,* 83 U.S. (16 Wall.) 36 (1873), interpreted the Privileges and Immunities Clause so narrowly and to include so little that the clause has never been used to apply the Bill of Rights to state action. Prior to the Supreme Court's *Slaughter-House* decision, it was fairly debatable whether the drafters of the Privileges and Immunities Clause intended for it to protect certain individual rights, including some of the rights protected by the Bill of Rights. However, after the *Slaughter-House* decision the debate ended, and the reach of the Privileges and Immunities Clause was drastically diminished. Therefore, even if the right to a civil jury trial as provided by the Seventh Amendment were to apply to states, it would not be by way of the Privileges and Immunities Clause. The Supreme Court's holding in the *Slaughter-House Cases* forecloses that result. Therefore, Answer (C) is incorrect and Answer (D) is correct because the Privileges and Immunities Clause is so narrowly interpreted that it does not protect a state citizen's right to a state civil jury trial. There is one possible caveat. In *Saenz v. Roe,* 526 U.S. 489 (1999), the Court used the Privileges and Immunities Clause to invalidate a California law that restricted a new resident's welfare benefits to the level provided by the state from which the resident moved. It remains to be seen whether *Saenz* signals a new trend to reinvigorate the Privileges and Immunities Clause.

**Answer (A) is incorrect** because the Bill of Rights applies only to the federal government and not to the states. *Barron v. Mayor & City Council of Baltimore,* 32 U.S. (7 Pet.) 243 (1833). *Barron* focused on the Fifth Amendment's takings clause, which prohibits the taking of private property for public use without just compensation. Barron complained that Baltimore's actions in diverting waterways ruined his wharf, and he was, therefore, entitled to compensation under the Fifth Amendment. The Supreme Court, in an opinion authored by Chief Justice John Marshall, rejected Barron's claim by holding that the Fifth Amendment did not apply to state or local government actions. It was limited to federal government behavior.

**Answer (B) is incorrect** because many of the rights set forth in the Bill of Rights are enforceable against the states by operation of the Fourteenth Amendment's Due Process

Clause. Interestingly, however, the Seventh Amendment, guaranteeing a right to a civil jury in cases with more than $20 in controversy, has not been held to apply to the states. Despite this, Answer (B) is incorrect because it states that "none of the Bill of Rights applies to the states." Just because one part of Answer (B) is correct — that the Seventh Amendment does not apply to the states — is not enough to make the entire answer correct.

146. Because the reimbursement limitation discriminates among state citizens based on their length of citizenship, this Act is covered by *Saenz v. Roe*, 526 U.S. 489 (1999). *Saenz* involved a California welfare law that calculated a person's benefits during the first year of state citizenship based on the amount the person would have received in the state they moved from. The Court noted that the challenged law discriminated among people who were *all conceded to be state citizens.*

The Court struck down the benefit law because neither of the state's justifications was sufficient. First, California argued that the differential welfare benefits would discourage people from moving to the state simply to receive increased welfare benefits. The Court held that deterring migration was an impermissible purpose because it penalized exercise of the constitutional right to travel. Second, California argued that the differential benefits saved the state money. The Court held that the benefit scheme was not properly related to this interest:

> Neither the duration of respondents' California residence, nor the identity of their prior states of residence, has any relevance to their need for benefits. Nor do those factors bear any relationship to the state's interest in making an equitable allocation of the funds to be distributed among its needy citizens.

*Id.* at 507. While saving money for the state treasury is a legitimate purpose, the state may not discriminate among its citizens in doing so, unless the basis for discrimination (in *Saenz*, duration of residence) is logically related to the subject of the discrimination (in *Saenz*, welfare benefits). *Id.* ("In short, the State's legitimate interest in saving money provides no justification for its decision to discriminate among equally eligible citizens.").

In this question, just as in *Saenz*, the State of Ventura discriminates among state citizens based on the duration of their residence. A woman who is a Ventura citizen receives reimbursement if she was a state resident for her entire pregnancy, while a woman who is *also a state citizen* is denied those benefits because her residence was less than her entire pregnancy. Under *Saenz*, neither of Ventura's purposes justify the law. First, the interest in discouraging migration to the state is an impermissible purpose. Second, Ventura's legitimate interest in saving money is not properly related to the reimbursement limitation. As in *Saenz*, duration of residence is not logically linked to either a woman's need for the reimbursement (which is linked to indigence) or Ventura's interest in equitable allocation of its health care funds.

147. The Supreme Court applies three general tests under the Equal Protection Clause, and each test corresponds to a different set of classifications. Racial and ethnic classifications are analyzed under a test known as "strict scrutiny"; classifications based on gender and legitimacy are analyzed under a test known as "intermediate scrutiny"; and all other classifications are analyzed under a test known as "rational basis review." The answer to Question 149 describes the elements of each test.

**Answer (B) is incorrect** because the gambling law has nothing to do with gender or legitimacy, and **Answer (D) is incorrect** because the law does not discriminate based on race or ethnicity. Thus, **Answer (A) is the best answer** because neither strict scrutiny nor intermediate scrutiny apply; and, therefore, this case falls within rational basis review.

The Court has applied heightened equal protection scrutiny when a fundamental or otherwise significant right is involved. For example, the Court has done so when analyzing discrimination involving the right to vote, *see Bush v. Gore*, 531 U.S. 98 (2000), as well as discrimination against the children of non-citizens regarding public education. *See Plyler v. Doe*, 457 U.S. 202 (1982). But those cases do not apply here. The Roark statute does not burden the right to vote or to attend public school, and the Court long ago rejected economic interests, such as one's occupation, as involving a fundamental right. *See West Coast Hotel Co. v. Parrish*, 300 U.S. 379 (1937). Thus, **Answer (C) is incorrect**.

148. **Answer (A) is the best answer** because neither strict scrutiny nor intermediate scrutiny apply; therefore, this case falls within rational basis review.

As discussed in the answer to the preceding question, strict scrutiny applies to laws that classify based on race or ethnicity, and intermediate scrutiny applies to laws that classify based on gender and legitimacy. The New City ordinance has nothing to do with gender or legitimacy (making **Answer (B) incorrect**), so the question is whether it has something to do with race or ethnicity. On its face, the ordinance does not single out any racial or ethnic group for different treatment. According to *Washington v. Davis*, 426 U.S. 229 (1976), however, a facially neutral law may still classify based on race or ethnicity if the law was *intended* to have a differential effect. As the Court stated, the law must have been enacted *because of*, *not despite*, its racially disparate impact. Here, the ordinance fails the *Davis* test for two reasons. First, there is no evidence that the ordinance disparately affects specific racial or ethnic groups. Second, while the City Council has expressed its displeasure with "those people" who drive New York City cabs, we have no basis to conclude that the reference is to a racial or ethnic group as opposed to simply cab drivers who do not tend to their appearance. As the person challenging the law has the burden of proof on the *Davis* test, intentional racial discrimination has not been shown and thus **Answer (D) is incorrect**.

**Answer (C) is incorrect** because, as discussed in the answer to the preceding question, the Court has not applied heightened Equal Protection scrutiny to laws that burden economic rights, such as the right to earn a livelihood in the trade of one's choice.

149.   **Answer (D) is the best answer.** As discussed above in the answer to the preceding two questions, the Court applies three general tests under the Equal Protection Clause: strict scrutiny, which is the test set forth in Answer (A); intermediate scrutiny, which is the test set forth in Answer (B); and rational basis review, which is the test set forth in Answer (D). The test in Answer (C) is the Court's characterization of the government interest required to survive the intermediate scrutiny test.

As discussed in the answer to the preceding question, there are two ways to determine the basis on which a statute classifies people. First, one can look on the face of a statute. On its face, the Arkabama Jury Integrity Act classifies based on whether English is one's first language. As neither race, ethnicity, nor gender is implicated, the face of the law provides no basis for strict or intermediate scrutiny.

Second, a facially neutral law will receive heightened scrutiny if it was *intended* to discriminate based on race, ethnicity, or gender. *Washington v. Davis*, 426 U.S. 229 (1976) (race); *Personnel Administrator of Mass. v. Feeney*, 442 U.S. 256 (1979) (gender). Under this test, it is not enough that the law disparately affects a group. Rather, the government must have acted *because of* such a disparate effect, and not merely *despite* that effect. Here, there is no reason to believe that the law disparately affects one gender or the other, so there is no basis for finding intentional gender discrimination. Thus, **Answers (B) and (C) are incorrect**. It is a closer case regarding race and ethnicity. On the one hand, people for whom English is a second language will be disproportionately dispersed into several racial and ethnic groups that are not native English speakers. On the other hand, members of those same racial and ethnic groups who speak English as their first language are not excluded. Without more evidence as to the genesis of and intent behind the Act, it would be very difficult to conclude that the law discriminates based on race or ethnicity. Thus, **Answer (D) is a better answer than Answer (A)**.

150.   *City of Cleburne v. Cleburne Living Center*, 473 U.S. 432 (1985), involved a city's denial of a permit to operate a group home for the mentally retarded. The Court noted that local law did not require such a permit for hospitals, nursing homes, or fraternities and sororities. The city offered several reasons for distinguishing group homes for the mentally retarded from these other facilities: the fear of neighboring landowners, threat of harassment by students attending a nearby high school, the proposed site was located in a flood plain, and liability concerns for such a group home. The Court claimed to apply rational basis review, which ordinarily requires *the party challenging the law* to

show either that the government had no legitimate interest, or that the challenged law is not rationally related to that interest. While the Court concluded that assuaging the fear of neighboring landowners was not a legitimate government interest, the remaining three purposes were sufficient. The Court, however, found that the city had not established a rational relationship between those purposes and denying a permit for the group home. For example, the Court held that the city had not explained why the risk of flooding posed a greater threat to group homes for the mentally retarded than to a nursing home or hospital. This unexplained under-inclusiveness was fatal to the city's action.

The Court's analysis in *Cleburne* differs from traditional rational basis review in two main respects. First, rational basis review ordinarily permits substantial over-and under-inclusiveness, because the government must be permitted flexibility in shaping laws that do not discriminate against a suspect class. *Cleburne,* however, faulted the city for the under-inclusiveness of its classification to the asserted purposes. Second, the government ordinarily bears no burden of proof under rational basis review. Instead, "those attacking the rationality of the legislative classification have the burden 'to negative every conceivable basis which might support it.' " *F.C.C. v. Beach Communications, Inc.*, 508 U.S. 307, 315 (1993). *Cleburne*, however, required the city to explain why it believed that a group home for the mentally retarded was relevantly different from other structures, such as a nursing home. *Cleburne*, then, arguably heightening rational basis review by increasing the government's burden in these two respects.

**Note**: Several of the following answers discuss the requirements of traditional rational basis review and the heightened form applied in *Cleburne*, and explain when the Court will apply one version of the test or the other.

151. The answer depends on whether the Court believes that the ordinance is a covert attempt to target an unpopular group. When this is so, the Court has applied more searching scrutiny than traditional, deferential rational basis review. *See Romer v. Evans*, 517 U.S. 620 (1996) (sexual orientation); *City of Cleburne v. Cleburne Living Center*, 473 U.S. 432 (1985) (mentally retarded); *United States Dept. of Agriculture v. Moreno*, 413 U.S. 528 (1973) (hippies). The timing of the ordinance (post-September 11), as well as the reference to "those people" who drive cabs, may suggest an attack on cab drivers of Middle Eastern descent or appearance. Other evidence of animus might include a statement of bias in the legislative record, *see City of Cleburne* and *Moreno*, or the Court's belief that a certain class has been subject to social animus. *See Romer*. If the Court concludes that such animus underlies the law, then it will strike down the law as it is quite over-and under-inclusive. For example, there are many evils that affect tourists' opinions of New City that the law does not reach, such as the dress of sidewalk vendors, as well as vendors at concessions in public venues, such as train and bus stations. Further, there are many items of apparel banned by the ordinance that would not portray New City in a bad light. For example, in certain ethnic garb, such as that Mr. Bahman seeks to wear, a driver would not appear disheveled or unkempt. If, however, the Court concludes that animus is not involved, it will likely uphold the law as a valid regulation of economic matters. *New York City Transit Authority v. Beazer*, 440 U.S. 568 (1979) (excluding methadone users from employment as a transit worker); *Williamson v. Lee Optical of Okla., Inc.*, 348 U.S. 483 (1955) (restricting certain lens work to licensed optometrists or ophthalmologists or those with a prescription from such a doctor); *Railway Express Agency v. New York*, 336 U.S. 106 (1949) (prohibiting advertising on motor vehicles except for advertisements for the vehicle owner's business).

152. **Answer (C) is the best answer** because the Court might more carefully scrutinize the relationship between Arkabama's interest and the Act's classification. By classifying based on whether English is one's first language, the law may be seen as targeting recent immigrants. To the extent that recent immigrants are seen as a politically unpopular or powerless group, the Court may bring a more skeptical eye to the question whether the classification is adequately tailored to the government's purpose. For example, there is no explanation why proven fluency in English, as evidenced by graduation from an American high school or college or by some other credible measure, would not achieve the government's goal. While the government does not bear this burden under traditional rational basis review, covertly heightened rational basis review (as some call it) can demand such greater justification for over-and under-inclusiveness. Thus, of all the objections stated above, **Answer (C) is the strongest argument against constitutionality**.

Before turning to discussion of rational basis review, we should dispose of two answers that incorrectly state the applicable law. First, **Answer (A) is incorrect** because it is another way of saying that the Act deserves strict scrutiny. Once it is determined that the Act deserves rational basis review, we have concluded that neither the facial nor intended basis of classification is race, ethnicity, or gender. As is discussed shortly, the Court may still consider whether the Act targets a politically unpopular group (as opposed to a discrete and insular minority) and thus apply a heightened form of rational basis review.

Second, **Answer (D) is incorrect** because it mistakenly assumes that rational basis review allows a litigant to challenge a law with evidence not considered by the legislature while drafting and debating the challenged law. In *Minnesota v. Clover Leaf Creamery Co.*, 449 U.S. 456 (1981), the Court rejected such evidence, considering only the information before the legislature at the time it acted. There, the state had banned the sale of milk in non-returnable plastic containers, but allowed such distribution in non-returnable paper containers. The government's asserted purpose was environmental cleanliness and conservation. The litigants challenging the law argued that the legislature's true purpose was to protect in-state paper companies from competition from out-of-state plastic container makers. In support of this argument, they offered evidence not considered by the state legislature tending to show that the state's law would actually *increase* harm to the environment. The Court rejected this argument, explaining: "Where there was evidence before the legislature reasonably supporting the classification, litigants may not procure invalidation of the legislation merely by tendering evidence in court that the legislature was mistaken." So, trial evidence cannot defeat the Arkabama legislature's reasonable judgment on the evidence before it when it passed the Act.

Under a traditional application of rational basis review, the Act is almost certainly constitutional. First, the government has a legitimate purpose: promoting the effectiveness and accuracy of jury decisions. If jurors cannot understand testimony, or if they are unwilling to accept the version of testimony offered by the state's official interpreter, jurors could make legal errors in fact determinations. Indeed, the accuracy of jury decisions is an interest of constitutional significance, protected by both the Due Process Clause and the Jury Clauses of the Fifth and Sixth Amendments. The state should have no problem defending the legitimacy of its interests.

Similarly, under traditional rational basis review, Arkabama should have no problem showing that its classification is rationally related to its legitimate purpose. Whether English is one's first language is relevant to one's ability to follow and comprehend testimony in English. The link is not wholly irrational, and that is all that is required by rational basis review. *See FCC v. Beach Communications, Inc.*, 508 U.S. 307 (1993) ("[A] legislative choice . . . may be based on rational speculation unsupported by evidence or empirical data.").

Of course, the classification is both over-and under-inclusive. The law is over-inclusive because some people for whom English is a second language understand English perfectly well. Conversely, the law is under-inclusive because some for whom English is their first language may still have difficulty comprehending testimony, whether due to poor education or other circumstances. But, under rational basis review, the Court has tolerated substantial over-and under-inclusiveness. For example, in *New York City Transit Authority v. Beazer*, 440 U.S. 568 (1979), the Court allowed the Transit Authority to exclude methadone users from employment as transit workers even though many within the class were just as safe as workers from the general population, and many outside the class (who were eligible for employment) were more unsafe workers. Substantial over-inclusiveness is allowed because requiring mathematical precision is often impractical. Substantial under-inclusiveness is allowed because the government is allowed to tackle one part of a larger problem at a time. *See Williamson v. Lee Optical of Okla., Inc*, 348 U.S. 483 (1955); *Railway Express Agency v. New York*, 336 U.S. 106 (1949).

As we have said, the preceding analysis tracks the Court's traditional application of rational basis review. Recently, however, the Court has shown a willingness to analyze more closely the relationship between purpose and classification when the state targets a politically unpopular group. For example, in *City of Cleburne v. Cleburne Living Center*, 473 U.S. 432 (1985), the Court carefully scrutinized the government's argument that denying a permit for a home for the mentally retarded was rationally related to concededly legitimate government interests. And, in *Romer v. Evans*, 517 U.S. 620 (1996), the Court was similarly skeptical of a Colorado constitutional amendment that prohibited state or local government from enacting or enforcing legal protections based on sexual orientation. In each case, the Court changed how it analyzed whether a rational relationship existed, not its analysis of whether the state's interest was legitimate. Thus, even if the Arkabama Act targets a politically unpopular group, that would not change the above analysis of Arkabama's legitimate purposes. **Answer (B) is not the best answer**.

153. **Answer (B) is the correct answer** because the Act is rationally related to the legitimate interest in protecting the integrity of sporting events from the corrupting influence of gambling.

**Answer (A) is incorrect** because it mistakenly states that a law is constitutional simply because it falls within the state's police power. In modern constitutional law, the term "police power" has become a label for a state or local regulation aimed at the public health, safety, or welfare. Even laws in this general category must survive rational basis review. Because Answer (A) suggests that laws within the police power are not subject to any additional scrutiny, that answer is incorrect.

**Answers (C) and (D) are incorrect** because the under-and over-inclusiveness identified are not fatal to the law's constitutionality. Rational basis review permits substantial under-and over-inclusiveness in government classifications because requiring a tighter fit would deprive the government of the flexibility it needs in formulating ordinary economic regulations. For example, government must have the flexibility to address a problem one step at a time, focusing first on the most acute part of the problem. Otherwise, government might lose time in addressing an urgent concern, or worse, fail to act at all. Here, the state may have concluded either that professional sporting events are different from other sporting events when it comes to gambling, or that gambling poses the most serious threat to the integrity of non-professional sporting events. Either conclusion is conceivable, which is enough to find a rational relationship. And since there is no indication that the Act either targets an unpopular group or rests on impermissible bias or prejudice, the heightened rational basis review applied in *Cleburne v. Cleburne Living Center*, 473 U.S. 432 (1985), does not apply here.

154. The answer to the preceding question should not change for two main reasons. First, the evidence described in this question merely shows that the law may be under-inclusive because it legalizes gambling in some sports where the threat of bribery remains. The Court has consistently held that such under-inclusiveness is tolerable in mere economic regulations. *See F.C.C. v. Beach Communications, Inc.*, 508 U.S. 307, 315 (1993). Second, the evidence challenges the state's factual basis for its distinction between professional and all other sporting events. The Court has explained that a state only need a conceivable basis for its distinction: "the absence of 'legislative facts' explaining the distinction '[o]n the record' has no significance in rational-basis analysis." *Id.* Further, rational basis review does not allow a party to challenge legislative fact finding with evidence from outside the legislative record. *See Minnesota v. Clover Leaf Creamery Co.*, 449 U.S. 456, 464 (1981). Thus, the additional evidence described in this question does not change the rational basis analysis described in the preceding answer.

155.    **Answer (D) is the best answer** because none of the first three answers is consistent with current precedent.

When the government discriminates based on gender, its action must survive intermediate scrutiny. Under this standard, the government must show that it was acting to serve an important interest, and that gender discrimination substantially furthers that important interest. Here, ASU likely meets the first requirement, as it has two important interests: (1) fielding a team that meets the physical demands of the sport, and (2) protecting the health and safety of female students. *See United States v. Virginia*, 518 U.S. 515 (1996) (Virginia Military Institute had an important interest in admitting only students who could withstand the physical rigors of its unique educational method); *Craig v. Boren*, 429 U.S. 190 (1976) (health and safety are important government interests). The next question is whether excluding women from the football team is a permissible means of achieving those ends.

The Court has upheld gender discrimination as a permissible regulatory means when men and women are inherently, physically different in some relevant respect. For example, the fact that women face pregnancy and men do not was sufficient to uphold a statute that punished only males for statutory rape. *See Michael M. v. Superior Court*, 450 U.S. 464 (1981) (plurality opinion). Also, because the biological facts of birth make identification of the natural mother easier than identification of the biological father, the Court has held that Congress may impose different paternity standards (for immigration purposes) on mothers and fathers of children born in the United States. *Nguyen v. INS*, 533 U.S. 53 (2001). ASU's football policy, however, differs from these cases in an important respect: The physical differences relied on by ASU are not inherent in gender. Surely, ASU can show that many (if not most) women cannot meet the physical requirements for participation in Division III football. But, *United States v. Virginia* held that government may not judge all women based on the average physical capabilities of women as a whole. If some women meet the unique physical requirements of a given task, they must be given an opportunity to participate. Thus, in *United States v. Virginia*, the Court held that the Virginia Military Institute (VMI) could not exclude qualified women from admission to their unique educational method. Similarly, ASU should allow qualified women to try out for the football team. Thus, **Answer (A) is incorrect.**

Once we acknowledge that qualified women may try out for the team, there does not seem to be any unique interest in protecting women. ASU has an interest in protecting *all* qualified students who try out for their sports teams, male or female. If qualified men can play safely, so can qualified women. Thus,   **Answer (B) is incorrect.**

Answer (C) is similar to an argument rejected in *United States v. Virginia*. There, VMI argued that the changes required to convert VMI into a co-ed campus, such as enhanced privacy and gender separation for certain purposes, would ruin essential elements of the VMI experience. The Court rejected this argument because it did not believe that the changes affected anything essential about a VMI education. As evidence, the Court cited the United States military's successful integration of women. Similarly, the Court would likely find that any changes needed to accommodate female students, such as separate locker rooms, do not affect essential aspects of the team sports experience, which would include practices, games, and off-field meetings and sessions. Thus, **Answer (C) is incorrect.**

156.	**Answer (B) or (C) is the best answer.** The threshold issue is what tier of equal protection scrutiny applies to this law. Because the state health benefits treat men and women differently, the law discriminates based on gender, and is subject to intermediate scrutiny. The only possible argument to the contrary would rely on *Geduldig v. Aiello*, 417 U.S. 484 (1974). In that case, a state's disability insurance excluded coverage for pregnancy and childbirth-related disabilities. The Court upheld the law, holding that the state policy was not gender discrimination, as the policy did not draw any line based on whether a recipient was male or female. The state simply determined that a single condition — pregnancy — should not be covered. The New Island policy is different in that it uses gender to separate those who do and do not receive a type of coverage. New Island has chosen to cover some birth control expenses, but designates which are covered by the gender of the recipient. Intermediate scrutiny applies.

Under intermediate scrutiny, the government must show that (1) the challenged law serves an important government purpose, and (2) the gender distinction is substantially related to that important purpose. *United States v. Virginia*, 518 U.S. 515 (1996). Additionally, in *Mississippi University for Women v. Hogan*, 458 U.S. 718 (1982) and *United States v. Virginia*, the Court explained that the government must have an "exceedingly persuasive justification" for using gender to classify. It is currently unclear what role the "exceedingly persuasive justification" language plays in equal protection analysis of gender classifications. One likely meaning is that any government purpose must be actual and not hypothetical, and that the Court will examine evidence and history to determine whether the government's asserted purpose was its actual purpose. *See United States v. Virginia* (history belied state's assertion that purpose of single-sex military school was to provide a diversity of educational opportunities within the state). A second possible meaning is that the Court will review more closely those gender classifications believed to reflect a gender stereotype. This reading would make sense of a passage in *Nguyen v. INS*, 533 U.S. 53 (2001), that accorded the "exceedingly persuasive justification" language no special significance, describing it as mere shorthand for intermediate scrutiny. *Nguyen* is distinguishable from both *Hogan* and *United States v. Virginia* in that the latter two cases involved gender stereotypes while *Nguyen* arguably did not. Thus, the "exceedingly persuasive justification" formulation may mean stronger scrutiny of gender classifications that raise the specter of gender stereotyping.

**Answer (D) is incorrect** because it mistakenly assumes that the existence of an important government interest is enough to survive intermediate scrutiny. As discussed in the preceding paragraph, however, intermediate scrutiny also requires that the important purpose be substantially related to gender.

New Island argues that its policy is to prevent unwanted pregnancies. This interest is analogous to the interest upheld in *Michael M. v. Superior Court*, 450 U.S. 464 (1981). In *Michael M.*, a state punished a male for having sex with a female (not his wife) who was under eighteen years old, but not vice versa. The state claimed that the law was meant to prevent illegitimate pregnancies, and the Court accepted this purpose as sufficient to justify gender discrimination. Here, the purpose is somewhat different, focusing on all unwanted pregnancies regardless of the parents' marital status. The state interests, however, are very similar. In both cases, the state has significant concern for whether the child will receive adequate care. Further, introducing an unwanted child into a relationship can cause instability and undue hardship for the prospective parents, and the parents or the child may ultimately end up being wards of the state. So, while a close question, New Island likely has an important interest in preventing unwanted pregnancies. Thus, **Answer (A) is not the best answer**.

The closer question here is whether New Island's discrimination between men and women regarding birth control is substantially related to its purpose of preventing unwanted pregnancies. The Court has found that real differences between men and women regarding pregnancy can justify gender discrimination. In *Michael M.*, the Court upheld a state law punishing only men for the crime of statutory rape. As noted above, the law was intended to prevent illegitimate pregnancies. The state argued that the physical burden of pregnancy provided women a natural disincentive from sexual intercourse that has no biological parallel in men. To equalize the incentives, then, the state needed to impose criminal punishment on men. The Court upheld this legislative rationale. In *Nguyen*, the INS presumed the birth mother's parenthood but required the purported father to prove paternity. The Court again accepted pregnancy as a legitimate distinguishing factor, because the facts of birth make the identity of the natural mother readily ascertainable. Paternity is not as easily shown.

Here, New Island is trying to make a similar argument. Women are the only gender who can become pregnant, and the physical and emotional burden of pregnancy provide women with a strong disincentive to unwanted pregnancies and thus a strong incentive to procure birth control measures. Men face no similar natural deterrent. Thus, to equalize the incentives between the genders, New Island needed to subsidize male use of birth control. This parallels the argument in *Michael M.*

In response, those challenging the law would argue that the New Island law really reflects stereotypes about which gender ought to bear primary responsibility for birth control decisions. Men are supposed to be the dominant partner in any heterosexual relationship, including decisions regarding sex and procreation. As the Court has held in *United States v. Virginia* and *Hogan*, state enforcement of gender stereotypes violates the Equal

Protection Clause. In *United States v. Virginia*, the stereotype was that women were not willing or able to enroll in military-style education. In *Hogan*, the stereotype was that the nursing profession was for women.

The argument is very close. On current precedent, the deciding factor will be whether a majority of the Court believes that the New Island policy is based on a gender stereotype. Strong arguments can be made on both sides, and the cases give us little, if any, basis on which to judge the question. Thus, we list **both Answer (B) and Answer (C) as the best answers**.

157.    **Answer (B) is the best answer.**

In *City of Richmond v. J.A. Croon Co.*, 488 U.S. 469 (1989), the Supreme Court held that even benign racial classifications are subject to strict scrutiny. Thus, **(A) is incorrect**. Under strict scrutiny, the government must show that its use of race (1) serves a compelling purpose, and (2) is narrowly tailored to that purpose. The Supreme Court has recognized very few compelling government interests: national security, *see Korematsu v. United States*; 323 U.S. 214 (1944), remedying systemic race discrimination in public education, *see Brown v. Board of Education,* 349 U.S. 294 (1955) ("*Brown II*"); remedying identified race discrimination in employment, *see Croson* and *Adarand Constructors, Inc. v. Pena*, 515 U.S. 200 (1995); and promoting diversity in higher education. *See Grutter v. Bollinger*, 539 U.S. 306 (2003); *Gratz v. Bollinger*, 539 U.S. 244 (2003).

On its face, the LAPD's promotion policy seems to serve the interest of remedying identified race discrimination in employment. But the Court in *Croson* and *Adarand* was careful to require the government to produce evidence that such discrimination had previously occurred — otherwise, the government has no interest to vindicate. Here, the LAPD offers three pieces of evidence, none of which survive scrutiny. First, the LAPD states that while 20% of city residents are African-American, only 4% of the patrol officers are African-American. The Court rejected a similar argument in *Croson*, where the city attempted to justify a construction hiring quota based on data that showed a smaller percentage of minorities in the local construction industry than in the city's population. The Court held that such evidence did not prove prior discrimination, because the government may not assume that racial groups will move into various trades in proportion to their percentage in the general population. Second, the city relies on data showing race discrimination in Atlanta, Houston, and Miami. The Court rejected similar evidence in *Croson*, where the city pointed to evidence of race discrimination in other cities. Without more, race discrimination in one city does not prove similar discrimination in another city. Third, the LAPD seeks to overcome educational disadvantages that African-American children suffered due to the city's previously racially-segregated public schools. Again, *Croson* rejected a similar argument. There, the Court explained that there is no way to know how many minorities would be in the construction industry absent prior discrimination in education. Such speculation does not give the government a compelling reason to use a race classification. The same argument applies here. The city has no way of knowing how many African-Americans would be patrol officers absent racially-segregated public schools.

The city has not identified any past discrimination in the hiring of patrol officers. Without past discrimination identified, the city's policy has nothing to remedy. The city has no compelling purpose behind its hiring policy. Therefore, **Answer (B) is correct.** (And, thus, **Answer (D) is incorrect**.) One might also argue that the hiring policy is not narrowly tailored because it is not in any way designed to meet prior race discrimination. But, the better reading of *Croson* is that the narrowly-tailored test need not be applied because there is no identified past discrimination against which to measure the policy's hiring target. Thus, while defensible, **Answer (C) is not the best answer**.

158.    This new purpose changes the analysis in an important respect, though it likely does not change the answer. First, it offers a possible compelling government purpose. The city points to public safety through more effective law enforcement. This interest may be akin to the public safety rationale accepted in *Korematsu*. Of course, *Korematsu* arguably involved a higher interest, as the internment sought to prevent sabotage of a national war effort. But, the police protect the public from the daily threat of domestic crime, and effective local law enforcement is essential to a community's continued prosperity. So, effective law enforcement is arguably a compelling government interest. But, even if effective law enforcement is a compelling government interest, there is no evidence that the LAPD's community policing plan, and its racial target, are narrowly tailored to achieving that purpose. The city would need strong evidence proving that the racial composition of the police force has a significant affect on the effectiveness of law enforcement. Further, the government would need to show that race-neutral means, such as better integrating non-minority officers into minority neighborhoods, do not advance the same goal. Without such evidence, which the LAPD has not offered, the hiring policy is not narrowly tailored to promoting public safety through more effective law enforcement.

159.    **Answer (B) is the best answer.**

**Answer (A) is a red herring.** The Court has held that even benign use of race is subject to strict scrutiny. *See Adarand Constructors, Inc. v. Pena*, 515 U.S. 200 (1995); *City of Richmond v. J.A. Croson Co.*, 488 U.S. 469 (1989). Further, the Supreme Court recently held that consideration of an applicant's race in college and law school admissions warrants strict scrutiny. *See Parents Involved in Community Schools v. Seattle School Dist. No. 1*, 127 S. Ct. 2738 (2007); *Grutter v. Bollinger*, 539 U.S. 306 (2003) (law school admissions process); *Gratz v. Bollinger*, 539 U.S. 244 (2003). Thus, the mere fact that a race classification is benign does not end the analysis.

Strict scrutiny requires that a race classification be narrowly tailored to serve a compelling government interest. **Answer (C) is incorrect** because it wrongly concludes that the Law School lacks a compelling interest. The Law School asserts an interest in the educational benefits of a diverse student body, and that racial diversity enhances those benefits. In *Grutter*, the Court explained that racial diversity may enrich classroom discussions, increase "cross-racial understanding," better prepare students for a diverse workplace, produce well-rounded citizens, and better prepare future leaders to govern a diverse nation. *Grutter*, 539 U.S. at 330. Further, a graduate school or college need not produce evidence that its admissions process actually seeks such benefits. Rather, "attaining a diverse student body is at the heart of [a college or graduate school's] proper institutional mission, and . . . 'good faith' on the part of a university is 'presumed' absent 'a showing to the contrary.'" *Id.* at 308. Thus, the Court will accept the Law School's assertion that it actually seeks to promote diversity (and its corresponding benefits), unless those challenging the admissions program prove that the Law School's motives lie elsewhere. Because the question provides no evidence of racial bias or favoritism, the Law School should be found to have a compelling purpose.

The more difficult question is whether the Orabama Law School's admissions process is narrowly tailored to achieve racial diversity. Specifically, is the Law School's practice of automatically awarding racial and ethnic minorities one point narrowly tailored to achieving a diverse student body? To answer this question, we must consider two recent Supreme Court decisions that reviewed race-conscious admissions practices at the University of Michigan's College of Literature, Science, and Arts (Michigan College) and Law School (Michigan Law School). *See Gratz*, 539 U.S. at 244 (reviewing College's admissions process); *Grutter*, 539 U.S. at 306 (reviewing Michigan's Law School admissions process). There, the Court held that Michigan Law School's admissions process was narrowly tailored to achieving diversity, but that Michigan College's process was not. Understanding the difference between the two admissions processes is the key to answering this question.

In *Grutter*, the Court explained that narrow tailoring requires a university to give each applicant individualized consideration, during which all applicants compete against one another for all available seats. The admissions process must consider "all the qualities valued by the university," and not just race. *Grutter*, 539 U.S. at 340. This is because diversity lies along many axes, such as a student's unique skills, experiences, or background. A college or university has a compelling interest in achieving diversity-at-large, with race as one factor among many. Thus, "a university's admissions program must remain flexible enough to ensure that each applicant is evaluated as an individual and not in a way that makes an applicant's race or ethnicity the defining feature of his or her application." *Id.* at 336-37. As a sensible bright line rule, the Court stated that a racial admissions quota can never constitute individualized consideration.

A good starting point is to determine whether Orabama Law School has established a racial quota, as such admissions programs are never narrowly tailored. A racial admissions quota has two traits. First, it establishes a fixed number of admissions seats for applicants of a designated race or ethnicity. Second, in applying for the fixed number of seats, members of the designated group are insulated from competition against other applicants. *Id.*. For example, a medical school admissions process imposed a racial quota when it set aside 16 out of 100 class seats for members of designated minority groups. *See Regents of Univ. of Cal. v. Bakke*, 438 U.S. 265 (1978). The set-aside established a fixed number, and minority applicants alone competed for these seats, insulated from consideration against non-minority applicants.

Here, the question is whether Orabama Law School's goal of admitting an "essential minimum" of minorities is a racial quota. Orabama's "essential minimum" is similar to the "critical mass" Michigan Law School sought to admit. Michigan Law School argued that it could not achieve the educational benefits of racial diversity unless racial and ethnic minorities felt comfortable participating in academic life. This comfort level, in turn, depended on whether a critical mass of minority students attended the law school. Michigan Law School defined critical mass as a desirable range of enrolled students, and this range served as a flexible admissions goal. In any given year, precisely where or whether minority admissions fell within this range depended on the make up of the Law School's overall applicant pool.

The Court concluded that Michigan Law School's critical mass concept shared neither hallmark of a racial quota. First, critical mass does not establish a fixed number of admissions seats. Rather, it establishes a flexible goal linked to the school's compelling interest in the educational benefits of racial diversity. Second, critical mass does not insulate minorities from competition against other applicants. Rather, race is considered as a plus factor that may be overcome by the diversity contributions of other applicants. Here, the Orabama Law School has done the same thing. The "essential minimum" policy neither establishes a fixed number of seats nor insulates minority applicants from competition in the general applicant pool.

While it does not impose a racial quota, the question remains whether Orabama Law School gives applicants sufficient individualized consideration. This question is a close call, as Orabama's admissions process shares features of the Michigan Law School admissions process upheld in *Grutter* as well as the Michigan College admissions process struck down in *Gratz*. Consider each in turn.

First, consider the Michigan College admissions process. The college calculated a "selection index," which consisted of a maximum of 150 points. Academic factors accounted for up to 110 points of the index, with the remaining points awarded for so-called "soft variables." The Court described some of the soft variables: "Michigan residents, for example, receive 10 points, and children of alumni receive 4. Counselors may assign an outstanding essay up to 3 points and may award up to 5 points for an applicant's personal achievement, leadership, or public service." *See Gratz*, 539 U.S. at 278. Further, *all* racial minorities received 20 additional points, regardless of how their admissions file compared to the remaining applicants. This racial bonus "ensure[d] that the diversity contributions of applicants cannot be individually assessed." *Id.* at 279 (O'Connor, J., concurring). Further, the "bulk of admissions decisions are executed based on selection index score," with only a very few applicants getting more individualized review. *Id.* at 280. This "nonindividualized, mechanical" process was not narrowly tailored because it made race the deciding factor for many applicants. *Id.* ("race [was] a decisive factor for virtually every minimally qualified underrepresented minority applicant.").

The Orabama Law School admissions process shares some aspects of the Michigan College process. Like Michigan College, Orabama's one-point racial or ethnic bonus is awarded automatically, regardless of other aspects of an applicant's admissions file.

This smacks of the "nonindividualized, mechanical" process frowned on by the Court. Unlike Michigan College, the bonus is not so large as to be insurmountable by non-minority applicants. In the Michigan College process, a Michigan resident with an outstanding essay and exceptional leadership potential only musters eighteen points, still two points shy of the minority bonus. Conversely, the Orabama process awards only one point for minority status, which may be easily matched or overcome by other soft variables considered by the Committee.

Now consider the Michigan Law School process. As described above, the Law School considered all applicants against one another, while pursuing the background goal of admitting a critical mass of minority students. The Court explained why this process accorded sufficient individualized consideration:

> [T]he Law School engages in highly individualized, holistic review of each applicant's file, giving serious consideration to all the ways an applicant might contribute to a diverse educational environment. The Law School affords this individualized consideration to applicants of all races. There is no policy, either *de jure* or *de facto*, or automatic acceptance or rejection based on any single "soft" variable. Unlike the [Michigan College] program . . ., the Law School awards no mechanical, pre-determined diversity "bonuses" based on race or ethnicity.

*Grutter*, 539 U.S. at 309. Like the Michigan Law School, Orabama does not bestow "automatic acceptance or rejection based on any single 'soft' variable." Unlike Michigan Law School, Orabama gives a "mechanical, pre-determined diversity" bonus of one point "based on race or ethnicity."

Whether Answer (B) or Answer (D) is the best answer depends on whether Orabama Law School's admissions process is more like the permissible Michigan Law School process or the impermissible Michigan College process. While this is a close question, we give the nod to upholding the Orabama Law School admission practice. The Court has clearly held that race may be a "plus" factor in admissions decisions, but not the deciding factor. Adding one point based on race acts as a plus, without overwhelming other aspects of diversity. Given how the Court defines the educational benefits of racial diversity, each minority applicant potentially furthers that interest simply because their presence on campus, standing alone, would contribute toward achieving a critical mass. That merits a small plus, which one point would seem to be. Whether a given minority applicant would further serve the goal of overall diversity will depend on the many other factors considered throughout the Orabama Law School admissions process. For example, an applicant lacking academic ability will not receive a high score from the three readers in the second step of the admissions process. Because one point would not overcome a low score, unqualified minority applicants will not be admitted due to the one-point bonus. Further, the one point awarded to racial or ethnic minorities is matched by the one-point bonuses awarded for *all* "additional criteria" considered in step three of the admissions process. Thus, no aspect of diversity is rated more highly than any other, and the ultimate admission decision will hinge on the totality of the applicant's file, not on any single bonus.

While Orabama Law School awards a "mechanical, predetermined" one-point bonus to racial and ethnic minorities, that point is likely no more than a permissible "plus" that leaves minorities to compete against the general applicant pool for all available seats. Because Orabama's one-point bonus is likely narrowly tailored, **Answer (B) is a better answer than Answer (D).**

160.  This question asks you to read closely and count noses in all of the opinions in *Parents Involved in Community Schools v. Seattle School Dist. No. 1*, 127 S. Ct. 2738 (2007). To see why **Answer (D) is correct**, we will review each of the other answer choices, and identify which of the justices voted to support each government interest.

The government interest set forth in **Answer (A)** received a majority of five votes: Justice Kennedy's concurring opinion endorsed this interest, as did Justice Breyer's dissenting opinion, which was joined by Justices Stevens, Souter, and Ginsberg. It is unclear whether Chief Justice Roberts' plurality opinion, joined by Justices Scalia, Thomas, and Alito, would extend *Grutter*-type diversity to elementary and high schools. The plurality opinion concluded that "[t]he present cases are not governed by Grutter" for two reasons: first, the Seattle and Louisville school districts did not seek broad, *Grutter*-type diversity, instead, focusing only on race; and second, *Grutter* relied on the unique context of higher education. *Id.* at 2754. The plurality did not explain whether the second distinction was sufficient, or if a true *Grutter*-type plan might be allowed in elementary and high schools. Regardless, Justice Kennedy and the four dissenters provide five votes in support of *Grutter*-type diversity in elementary and high schools.

The government interest set forth in **Answer (B)** was endorsed by all nine justices in *Parents Involved*: Local public schools have "the compelling interest of remedying the effects of past intentional discrimination." *Id.* at 2752.

Last, the government interest set forth in **Answer (C)** received a majority of five votes. Once again, Justice Kennedy's concurring opinion endorsed this interest, *id.* at 2791 ("To the extent the plurality opinion suggests the Constitution mandates that state and local school authorities must accept the status quo of racial isolation in schools, it is, in my view, profoundly mistaken."), as did Justice Breyer's dissenting opinion. Chief Justice Roberts' plurality opinion rejected remedying racial isolation as a compelling government interest. *Id.* at 2757 ("However closely related race-based assignments may be to achieving racial balance, that itself cannot be the goal, whether labeled "racial diversity" or anything else.").

In sum, **Answer (D) is correct** because at least five justices endorsed each of the government interests listed in Answers (A), (B), and (C).

161. **Answer (B) is the best answer.**

What equal protection standard of review applies to a law that classifies based on legitimacy? While the Court waffled on this question for a number of years, it finally settled on intermediate scrutiny in *Clark v. Jeter*, 486 U.S. 456 (1988). So, to be constitutional, the New Island ten-year statute of limitations must satisfy the same test as gender classifications: the statute must be substantially related to an important government interest. Because **Answers (A) and (C)** apply a different test — rational basis review — those answers **are incorrect**.

The first question under intermediate scrutiny is whether New Island has an important government purpose. This is likely so. According to the applicable legislative history, New Island imposed the statute of limitations to ensure accurate paternity determinations. In *Clark*, the Court accepted the same interest in reviewing a state law that set a six-year statute of limitations on support actions by children born out of wedlock. The first part of the test is satisfied.

*Clark* is also instructive on the second part of the intermediate scrutiny test: whether the statute is substantially related to the government's important purpose. In *Clark*, the Court found that a six-year statute of limitations was not so related. The Court began with the observation that blood tests allowed great accuracy in determining paternity, regardless of the age of the child. For example, even when *Clark* was decided in 1988, "sophisticated tests for genetic markers permit the exclusion of over 99% of those who might be accused of paternity, regardless of the age of the child." Today, with more sophisticated methods, paternity can be determined with virtual certainty. So, passage of time does not pose a significant obstacle to proof of paternity.

Further evidence against a substantial relationship can be found in the other New Island statutes of limitations set forth in the question. For example, children born to married parents have eighteen years to prove paternity for support purposes, and no limitations period applies to paternity suits either for inheritance or by the natural father. New Island offers no reason why paternity proof problems exist only in support suits by a child against an alleged father not married to the natural mother. Indeed, there is no conceivable basis for believing that the alleged father's marital status at the time of birth has any bearing on the quality of evidence of paternity. *Clark* reached the same conclusion regarding a state's six-year statute of limitations. Because the same result should apply to New Island's ten-year statute of limitations, **Answer (B) is a better answer than Answer (D).**

162.  **Answer (D) is the best answer.**

The first question is what level of equal protection scrutiny applies to the city's citizenship requirement. By classifying based on whether a person is a United States citizen, the ordinance discriminates against aliens legally residing in this country. The Supreme Court has held such state laws merit either rational basis review or strict scrutiny, depending on the matter involved. Rational basis review applies to state laws excluding resident aliens from governmental functions; strict scrutiny applies to all other state laws discriminating against resident aliens. *See Graham v. Richardson*, 403 U.S. 365 (1971) (strict scrutiny for state law denying resident aliens welfare benefits); *Foley v. Connelie*, 435 U.S. 291 (1978) (rational basis review for state law forbidding employment of resident aliens as state troopers). So, the question becomes whether operation and maintenance of public transportation equipment is a governmental function.

Before analyzing the question of governmental function, note that **Answers (A) and (C) are incomplete and thus incorrect**. Whether a resident alien has been excluded from a governmental function merely determines the proper standard of review. Whether the law is constitutional depends on whether the challenged law survives scrutiny under that standard of review. The conclusion that operation and maintenance of public transportation equipment is or is not a governmental function does not itself resolve the constitutionality of the city's ordinance.

The Court has explained that "governmental functions" are those government tasks that involve either policymaking or broad discretion. For example, state elected and appointed officials with substantial policymaking power (such as appointed judges and heads of state agencies) perform governmental functions. *See Sugarman v. Dougall*, 413 U.S. 634 (1973). state troopers and teachers have also been found to exercise sufficient discretion to perform government functions. *See Foley* (state troopers); *Ambach v. Norwick*, 441 U.S. 68 (1979) (elementary and secondary school teachers). State troopers exercise wide discretion and judgment in determining when and how to enforce the laws; teachers exercise similarly wide discretion and judgment in influencing the values and knowledge of the nation's future voters and government officials. Conversely, notaries public perform "essentially clerical and ministerial" tasks that are not governmental functions. *See Bernal v. Fainter*, 467 U.S. 216 (1984).

Here, operating and maintaining public transportation equipment is closer to the work of a notary public than that of a state trooper or teacher. The transportation employee is not given substantive discretion, such as the trooper's decision when to enforce the law and the teacher's decision what to teach. Rather, the transportation employee's decision seems more mechanical, dictated by considerations far removed from public policy concerns. For this reason, transportation employees do not likely perform governmental functions, and strict scrutiny applies to the city's job criterion. Thus, **Answer (B)**, which applies rational basis review, **is incorrect**.

The city's citizenship criteria would likely fail strict scrutiny. In *Dougall*, the Court held that a state's interest in undivided employee loyalty is not served by a citizenship requirement imposed on menial positions that do not perform governmental functions. The city is attempting to do the same thing. Thus, **Answer (D) is the best answer**.

163.  **Answer (B) is the best answer.** The Court would likely uphold the citizenship requirement under rational basis review. First, the Court has held that state and local governments have a legitimate interest in the undivided loyalty of their policymaking officials. Further, the city ordinance is rationally related to that interest because it applies the citizenship requirement *only* to those employees with policymaking authority. As with state troopers and school teachers, the citizenship requirement for these public board members should survive rational basis review

As in the preceding question, **Answers (A) and (C) are incorrect**. Whether a given job is a governmental function merely determines the proper equal protection standard of review and not the law's ultimate constitutionality.

Board members perform governmental functions. Recall that elected state and local officials ordinarily fall within this class of government employees. Further, the board is charged with policymaking discretion, a hallmark of a governmental function. Deferential rational basis review applies to the citizenship requirement for board members. Thus, **Answer (D) is incorrect** because it applies the strict scrutiny standard of review.

164.  **Answer (B) is the best answer.** As in the two preceding Questions, **Answers (A) and (C) may be dismissed at the outset**, although for a different reason. While the governmental function test is used in analyzing state and local discrimination against resident aliens, that test plays no role in analyzing federal laws that discriminate on that basis. Rather, the Supreme Court held in *Mathews v. Diaz*, 426 U.S. 67 (1976), that such federal laws generally receive rational basis review. The judiciary owes these federal laws such deferential review because the Constitution commits immigration and foreign affairs largely to the political branches. Further, a citizenship requirement is not "wholly irrational." Congress may use federal employment eligibility as a carrot to encourage resident aliens to apply for naturalization, or Congress may keep such eligibility as a bargaining chip for dealing with other nations. Either way, the citizenship requirement is rationally related to a legitimate congressional end. Thus, **Answer (B) is the best answer. Answer (D) is incorrect** because it applies strict scrutiny.

165. The registration process classifies students based on whether they and their parents are legally in the United States. Ordinarily, this classification merits simple rational basis review, and the classification would be easily upheld. But, this case warrants closer scrutiny because the Court has accorded undocumented children heightened review when access to education is involved. *Plyler v. Doe*, 457 U.S. 202 (1982), reviewed a state law that charged undocumented children tuition to attend public schools that other children attended free of charge. The Court heightened the review for three reasons. First, it was unfair to punish the children for a status (undocumented alien) that was not their fault but that of their parents. Second, as undocumented aliens whose parents could not vote, the children lacked any protection in the political process. Third, because education is essential to successful participation in American society, denying undocumented children that opportunity would impose a "lifetime hardship." Thus, while undocumented children are not a suspect class, and education is not a fundamental right, *see San Antonio Independent School District v. Rodriguez*, 411 U.S. 1 (1973), the combination warranted heightened scrutiny. As the Court later clarified, that heightened scrutiny is the intermediate scrutiny applied to gender and legitimacy classifications. *See Kadrmas v. Dickinson Public Schools*, 487 U.S. 450 (1988).

The question, then, is whether the registration process deserves the same heightened scrutiny applied in *Plyler*. On the one hand, we have the same classification (undocumented children) and the same right being denied (education). On the other hand, the denial is not nearly as severe as in *Plyler*. In *Plyler*, the undocumented children were denied *any* education, while all other children were given that valuable opportunity. Conversely, the educational opportunity provided during the summers must not be nearly as essential if the District offers it to only 1% of its students. Undocumented students are part of the vast majority of students — 99% of all students in the LAISD — who are deprived the summer education. By receiving the same treatment as the overwhelming majority of their classmates, the undocumented students are hardly condemned to a lifetime of hardship as compared to their documented colleagues. Thus, there is a strong basis for distinguishing *Plyler* and applying rational basis review.

166.   **Answer (A) is the correct answer.**

The key to this question is determining the appropriate equal protection standard of review for age classifications. In *Massachusetts Board of Retirement v. Murgia*, 427 U.S. 307 (1976), the Court applied rational basis review. Because **Answers (B) and (C) apply a different standard of review, they are incorrect**.

Under rational basis review, Arkabama's amendment to its motor vehicle code only need be rationally related to a legitimate state interest. Promoting traffic safety is clearly a legitimate state interest. *See Railway Express Agency v. New York*, 336 U.S. 106 (1949) (traffic safety promoted by law prohibiting advertising on certain motor vehicles). Further, the law need not be precisely tailored to the interest; it may be both over-and under-inclusive. For example, in *Murgia*, the Court upheld a state mandatory retirement age of 50 for police officers. While many officers over age 50 surely are still fit to serve, and many officers below that age are not, the classification need not be perfect. All rational basis review requires is that age not be an irrational basis for achieving the government's purpose. The *Murgia* Court held that age had a rational, albeit imperfect, connection to job performance. The same can be said for driving performance. Though many in their 80's can still drive safely and many below that age cannot, the 80-year-old cut off is not irrational. Thus, **Answer (A) is better than Answer (D).**

167.  **Answer (C) is the best answer**.

**Answer (A) is incorrect** because none of Mr. Mater's material is obscene. Under *Miller v. California*, 413 U.S. 15 (1973), material is obscene, and thus unprotected under the First Amendment, when a jury can answer "yes" to the following three questions:

> (a) whether "the average person, applying contemporary community standards" would find that the work, taken as a whole, appeals to the prurient interest; (b) whether the work depicts or describes, in a patently offensive way, sexual conduct specifically defined by the applicable state law; and (c) whether the work, taken as a whole, lacks serious literary, artistic, political, or scientific value.

*Id.* at 24. For First Amendment purposes, then, obscenity is limited to material of a sexual nature. Because nothing on Mr. Mater's web site or in his speeches concerns sexual matters, his speech will not be deemed obscene.

**Answer (B) is incorrect** because there is no First Amendment category of unprotected speech called "hate speech." Such speech will be unprotected when it either incites listeners to imminent lawlessness or constitutes fighting words. But the mere fact that speech is hateful does not rob it of First Amendment protection.

**Answer (D) is not the best answer** because neither Mr. Mater's web site nor his speeches meet the core requirements of fighting words. *Chaplinsky v. New Hampshire*, 315 U.S. 568 (1942), defined fighting words as "those that by their very utterance inflict injury or tend to incite an immediate breach of the peace." There, a protestor directed the epithet "You are a God damned racketeer" to a police officer during an arrest. The Court held that such a face-to-face insult constituted fighting words. Conversely, in *Cohen v. California*, 403 U.S. 15 (1971), the Supreme Court held that walking through a public courthouse wearing a jacket bearing the words "Fuck the Draft" was not fighting words. The Court explained its conclusion as follows:

> [Fighting words are] those personally abusive epithets which, when addressed to the ordinary citizen, are, as a matter of common knowledge, inherently likely to provoke violent reaction. While the four-letter word displayed by Cohen in relation to the draft is not uncommonly employed in a personally provocative fashion, in this instance it was clearly not "directed to the person of the hearer." No individual actually or likely to be present could reasonably have regarded the words on appellant's jacket as a direct personal insult.

*Id.* at 20. Here, as in *Cohen*, Mr. Mater was not directing any abusive statements to the lawyers themselves in a manner that would provoke an immediate response. The web site was more like Cohen's jacket, a display open to all onlookers, and the speech was delivered to his supporters, none of whom were likely to attack Mr. Mater in response. Thus, none of Mr. Mater's speech fits the definition of fighting words.

**Answer (C) is the best answer** because it is the best fit of all the types of unprotected speech. In *Brandenburg v. Ohio*, 395 U.S. 444 (1969), the Court established the modern standard for determining when speech advocating unlawful action loses its First Amendment protection. The main tension here is the potential for the slippery slope. On the one hand, the government has an interest in preventing a speaker from inciting a crowd to lawless action. On the other hand, free speech protects the abstract discussion of unlawful conduct, such as the necessity of violence in resisting a tyrannical government. Further, the heated rhetoric of one's political opponents could be mistaken, intentionally or inadvertently, for advocacy of lawlessness. To draw this line, *Brandenburg* required proximity between the speech and future unlawful action:

> [This Court's] decisions have fashioned the principle that the constitutional guarantees of free speech and free press do not permit a state to forbid or proscribe advocacy of the use of force or of law violation except where such advocacy is directed to inciting or producing imminent lawless action and is likely to incite or produce such action. "[T]he mere abstract teaching . . . of the moral propriety or even moral necessity for a resort to force and violence, is not the same as preparing a group for violent action and steeling it to such action." A statute which fails to draw this distinction impermissibly intrudes upon the freedoms guaranteed by the First and Fourteenth Amendments. It sweeps within its condemnation speech which our Constitution has immunized from governmental control.

*Id.* at 447-48 (citations omitted). The Court has never clarified either how imminent the lawless action must be (hours? days? weeks?), or how likely such action must be.

Here, it is a close call whether Mr. Mater's speech fits *Brandenburg*'s definition. One can easily understand his speech as advocating lawless action. First, his web site labels the lawyers as "traitors," which suggests the capital offense of treason. Second, his speech makes the following arguable call to action:

> When faced with a similar threat, our Founding Fathers took up arms. Lest we invite another 9/11, it is the responsibility of true Americans, like yourselves, to do whatever you can, by any means available, to stop this grave threat to our Nation's future.

And these words arguably instigated an imminent response — the murder of a lawyer identified on his web page the day after the speech. So while not a clear case, incitement of imminent lawlessness is the strongest government argument for punishing Mr. Mater's speech.

168.   **Answer (D) is the best answer**.

**Answers (A) and (B) are incorrect** for the reasons set forth in the answer to Question 167. **Answer (A) is incorrect** because obscenity deals with sexual material, and none of Rev. Sanders' speech concerned sexual matters. **Answer (B) is incorrect** because hate speech, standing alone, is not an unprotected class of speech.

**Answer (C) is not the best answer** because nothing in Rev. Sanders' speech seems calculated to incite his followers to imminent lawless action. Recall from the answer to the preceding question that *Brandenburg v. Ohio*, 395 U.S. 444 (1969), allows the government to punish speech that advocates imminent lawless action and is likely to produce such action. Rev. Sanders' speech does not fit this definition. None of his quoted words call his followers to lawless action. Further, the facts tell us that Rev. Sanders has conducted such protests around the country, but does not mention any prior acts of violence by his followers or listeners against mourners or others. Rev. Sanders' speech is likely protected under *Brandenburg*.

**Answer (D) is the best answer** because the category of fighting words is the closest fit to Rev. Sanders' speech. The answer to the preceding question explained that *Chaplinsky v. New Hampshire*, 315 U.S. 568 (1942), and *Cohen v. California*, 403 U.S. 15 (1971), defined "fighting words" as personal insults or epithets directed to a person in such a manner as to provoke an immediate violent reaction. Here, Rev. Sanders preaches within earshot of mourners, which is arguably similar to the face-to-face confrontation in *Chaplinsky*. Also, shouting at a nearby group of mourners is surely more targeted than was wearing a jacket in *Cohen*. Further, one of the slogans that Rev. Sanders shouts at mourners — "I'm glad your son is dead" — is the arguable equivalent of a personal insult. Indeed, one could conceive of a mourner being moved to violence by such words about a recently deceased loved one. So while Rev. Sanders' speech is not definitely fighting words, that category fits better than do the categories described in the other three answers.

## TOPIC 52:
## FREE SPEECH: OFFENSIVE SPEECH

### ANSWERS

169.  **Answer (D) is the correct answer.**

In identifying the proper standard of review, the first question is whether the government is regulating speech based on its content. Generally, the Court applies more stringent scrutiny to laws that target speech based on its content than laws that are content-neutral or that regulate only the time, place, or manner of speech. Here, the FCC rule is clearly content-based, as it defines the applicable class of speech with specific reference to what the speaker says — the speech must include patently offensive content that demeans women.

The next question is whether the speech singled out by the FCC's rule is "low value speech." If so, the speech receives reduced protection; if not, judicial review is more stringent. Low value speech includes: obscenity (defined as material that "taken as a whole, appeals to the prurient interest, is patently offensive in light of community standards, and lacks serious literary, artistic, political, or scientific value." *Ashcroft v. Free Speech Coalition*, 535 U.S. 234 (2002)); fighting words (words that "by their very utterance inflict injury or tend to incite an immediate breach of the peace," *Chaplinsky v. New Hampshire*, 315 U.S. 568 (1942)); and libel (defined differently for public and private figures, *see New York Times Co. v. Sullivan*, 376 U.S. 254 (1964)).

Here, the FCC rule targets speech discussing patently offensive matters dealing with sex. While this language sounds similar to the definition of obscenity, it is the accepted definition of a less offensive category known as "indecency." The Court has put indecent speech in a middle ground between low value speech (such as obscenity) and fully protected speech. (Thus, **Answer (A) is incorrect** because indecency is not treated as low value speech.) That middle ground was recognized in the case *FCC v. Pacifica Foundation*, 438 U.S. 726 (1978), where the FCC sanctioned a radio station for its daytime broadcast of an indecent monologue by comedian George Carlin. The Court did not establish a standard of review, instead stating that the protection to which indecent material is entitled will "not be the same in every context." In the context of a radio broadcast, government regulation of indecent material is more warranted for two reasons. First, radio listeners might be unwillingly confronted with indecent material without prior warning. People frequently scan the radio dial happening upon stations without easy means to know what lies where. Second, the medium is "uniquely accessible to children," and the government may properly shield children from indecency.

The Court later clarified the applicable standard of review, explaining that content-based restrictions aimed at indecent speech must survive strict scrutiny. That is, such restrictions must be narrowly tailored to a compelling government interest. *United States v. Playboy Entertainment Group, Inc.*, 529 U.S. 803 (2000). Further, a law is not narrowly tailored unless the government used "the least restrictive alternative" that would achieve its objective. For example, the *Playboy* Court reviewed a federal law that effectively banned sexually explicit indecent programming from cable television between the hours of 6 A.M. and 10 P.M. While the government had a compelling interest in doing so — protecting children from exposure to such material — it did not choose the least speech-restrictive regulatory alternative for achieving that interest. For example, the Court observed that cable television operators are able to block specific channels for specific homes. Thus, government could have protected children and imposed less burden on adult speech by allowing parents to block channels they do not want their children to see. Of course, in *Pacifica*, "station blocking" technology did not exist for radios, and thus a ban on daytime broadcasts was likely the least restrictive alternative.

Here, as in *Pacifica* and *Playboy*, the government restricts the broadcast of indecent material in the name of protecting children. Ordinarily, the next step of the analysis would be to apply strict scrutiny. However, the FCC rule runs afoul of another free speech doctrine, which prohibits viewpoint discrimination. The Court explained in *R.A.V. v. City of St. Paul*, 505 U.S. 377 (1992), that, regardless of the type of speech involved, government may not banish one viewpoint from the debate. So, in *R.A.V.*, a city could not punish only those fighting words that arouse anger based on race, leaving unrestricted those fighting words that express support for racial harmony. While the city could ban all fighting words, it could not remove that rhetorical arrow from the quiver of one side of the debate. Such viewpoint discrimination was unlawful without further scrutiny.

*R.A.V.*, however, does allow some content-based regulation within a class of low-value speech. The Court explained the scope of permitted regulation as follows: "When the basis for the content discrimination consists entirely of the very reason the entire class of speech at issue is proscribable, no significant danger of idea or viewpoint discrimination exists." *Id.* at 388. For example, obscene speech is considered of low value because it concerns prurient matters. Thus, government may treat types of obscene speech differently based on their degree of prurience. While content-based, such regulation is permissible. The Supreme Court recently applied the same analysis to a state law that banned cross-burning with the intent to intimidate. The Court explained:

> The First Amendment permits Virginia to outlaw cross burnings done with the intent to intimidate because burning a cross is a particularly virulent form of intimidation. Instead of prohibiting all intimidating messages, Virginia may choose to regulate this subset of intimidating messages in light of cross burning's long and pernicious history as a signal of impending violence. Thus, just as a state may regulate only that obscenity which is the most obscene due to its prurient content, so too may a state choose to prohibit only those forms of intimidation that are most likely to inspire fear of bodily harm.

*Virginia v. Black* 538 U.S. 343 (2003).

The FCC rule enforces a type of viewpoint discrimination prohibited by *R.A.V.* Indecent material is banned when it demeans women, but not when it expresses a different viewpoint on gender issues. Further, unlike *Virginia v. Black*, there is no claim that indecent material that expresses such a message is troublesome for the very reason that indecency receives lesser protection. Thus, the FCC rule is unconstitutional without further scrutiny, and **Answer (C) is the correct answer. Answers (B) and (D) are incorrect** because they assume that the constitutionality of the FCC rule depends on whether it satisfies strict scrutiny.

170.  As *United States v. Playboy Entertainment Group, Inc.*, 529 U.S. 803 (2000), held, laws that target indecent speech are content-based restrictions subject to strict scrutiny. The question is whether the twelve-hour indecency blackout period is narrowly tailored to serve a compelling government purpose. *FCC v. Pacifica Foundation*, 438 U.S. 726 (1978), and *Playboy* both recognize that government has a compelling interest in protecting children from exposure to indecent material. So, the key issue is whether the blackout period is narrowly tailored to that interest. Or, as the Court has explained, whether the government could have employed a less speech-restrictive means to achieve that same end.

Comparisons to *Pacifica* and *Playboy* are useful on the question of narrow tailoring. On the one hand, in *Pacifica*, a daytime ban was narrowly tailored because there was no effective way to notify radio listeners when and where indecent material was being broadcast. People flipping through a radio dial in the car might stumble upon indecent material. On the other hand, in *Playboy*, the ban was not narrowly tailored because technology allowed parents to protect their children by blocking cable channels they did not want their children to view. The main distinction is whether parents have an effective means of self-help in protecting their children from indecent material.

Broadcast television, which is the subject of the FCC rule described above, falls somewhere between radio and cable. On the one hand, parents cannot block broadcast television stations, leaving the possibility that children will discover indecent material while channel surfing. (In *Playboy*, the Court noted this difference between cable and broadcast media.) On the other hand, parents have ample warning, through television schedules and the like, as to when and where potentially indecent material will appear on television. The concerned parent can use that notice to monitor their child's television viewing. This is a close case. Given that broadcast television offers no practical technology to keep indecency out of their homes (and thus away from their children), the balance may tip in favor of the daytime ban. It further helps the government's case that the restriction applies only during hours when children are awake and might be viewing television.

171. **Answer (B) is the best answer.** This question asks whether a sentence-enhancement statute is an unconstitutional viewpoint discriminatory law. Recall that *R.A.V. v. City of St. Paul*, 505 U.S. 377 (1992), held that government cannot discriminatorily burden speech based on viewpoint, even if that speech is otherwise unprotected fighting words. So, while the government may ban all fighting words, it may not selectively ban fighting words that express a particular viewpoint, such as racial prejudice. The Michinois sentence enhancement arguably does so, as it punishes the motive — or viewpoint — that lies behind the act of violence. In *Wisconsin v. Mitchell*, 508 U.S. 476 (1993), however, the Court explained that a sentence enhancement for racially motivated crimes, while viewpoint discriminatory, was *not* a regulation of speech. The Court distinguished *R.A.V.* as follows: "[W]hereas the ordinance struck down in *R.A.V.* was explicitly directed at expression (i.e., 'speech' or 'messages'), the statute in this case is aimed at conduct unprotected by the First Amendment." Further, the forbidden motive for which the sentence is enhanced "is thought to inflict greater societal and individual harm."

Michinois has done the same as the state in *Mitchell*. First, the statute is "aimed at" violent crime, which is not protected activity under the First Amendment. Second, the forbidden motive used for sentence-enhancement is a particularly harmful one. As with racially-motivated violence, gender-motivated violence instills fear in a wider community, suggesting that all women are potential targets. For these reasons, **Answer (B) is the best answer.**

**Answers (A), (C), and (D) are incorrect** because they assume that the Michinois law is subject to strict scrutiny. Because the law does not target speech, it receives no First Amendment scrutiny.

172.  **Answer (A) is the best answer.**

When it comes to First Amendment scrutiny of campaign finance laws, the Supreme Court takes a two-track approach, distinguishing contributions from independent expenditures. In *Buckley v. Valeo*, 424 U.S. 1 (1976), the Supreme Court explained that campaign contribution limits warrant less judicial scrutiny because, first, such contributions are less communicative than other political speech, and second, individuals may still take direct actions to support their preferred candidate. The Court has since clarified that the First Amendment requires a contribution limitation to be "closely drawn" to a "sufficiently important interest." *Nixon v. Shrink Missouri Government PAC*, 528 U.S. 377 (2000). This test is less demanding than strict scrutiny. Thus, **Answer (B) is incorrect** because it mistakenly assumes that strict scrutiny is the proper standard of review; and **Answer (C) is incorrect** because it mistakenly assumes that restraints on political speech are unconstitutional without further scrutiny.

The Court's decision in *McConnell v. Federal Election Commission*, 540 U.S. 93 (2003), reaffirmed and applied the *Buckley v. Valeo*, 424 U.S. 1 (1976), approach to regulations of campaign finance. The heart of this approach is the distinction between campaign contributions and expenditures. On the one hand, contribution limits are constitutional so long as they are "closely drawn" to a "sufficiently important interest." *McConnell*, 540 U.S. at 136. Further, "the prevention of corruption or its appearance constitutes a sufficiently important interest to justify political contribution limits." *Id.* at 143. On the other hand, spending limits receive "closer scrutiny than limits on campaign contributions." *Id.* at 134.

Starting with *Buckley* and continuing through later cases, the Court has consistently held that preventing corruption or its appearance is a sufficiently important government interest. The question, then, is whether a $50 contribution limitation is closely drawn to this interest. In *Buckley,* the Court upheld a $1,000 (in 1976 dollars) contribution limit, and, in *Nixon,* the Court upheld a $1,075 (in 2000 dollars) contribution limit. Here, the limit is about twenty times less — only $50. The question is whether a drastically reduced limit is still closely drawn. In *Nixon*, the Court explained how it would decide this question:

> whether the contribution limitation was so radical in effect as to render political association ineffective, drive the sound of a candidate's voice below the level of notice, and render contributions pointless. Such being the test, the issue in later cases cannot be truncated to a narrow question about the power of the dollar, but must go to the power to mount a campaign with all the dollars likely to be forthcoming.

*Nixon*, 528 U.S. at 397. This is where opponents of the contribution limit should focus. On its face, there is a credible argument that the West Dakota limit is radical, as it potentially cuts a candidate's war chest to one-twentieth its prior size. Then again, we would need to know the size of the average campaign contribution. Both *Buckley* and *Nixon* acknowledged that most contributions are well below the federal $1,000 limit. While it is not clear that opponents of the law would prevail, this is their strongest legal attack of the choices given.

**Answer (D) is incorrect** because the limit does not discriminate based on the contributor's viewpoint. Supporters of all parties — and all points of view — are equally bound.

The Court's decision in *Randall v. Sorrell*, 126 S. Ct. 2479 (2006), confirms that **Answer (A) is the best answer**. In an opinion joined by Chief Justice Roberts and Justice Alito (and providing the narrowest grounds for the Court's decision), Justice Breyer explained why Vermont's $200 campaign contribution limit violated the First Amendment:

> As compared with the contribution limits upheld by the Court in the past, and with those in force in other states, [Vermont's] limits are sufficiently low as to generate suspicion that they are not closely drawn. The Act sets its limits per election cycle, which includes both a primary and a general election. Thus, in a gubernatorial race with both primary and final election contests, the Act's contribution limit amounts to $200 per election per candidate (with significantly lower limits for contributions to candidates for state Senate and House of Representatives. These limits apply both to contributions from individuals and to contributions from political parties, whether made in cash or in expenditures coordinated (or presumed to be coordinated) with the candidate.

> These limits are well below the limits this Court upheld in *Buckley*. Indeed, in terms of real dollars (*i.e.*, adjusting for inflation), the Act's $200 per election limit on individual contributions to a campaign for governor is slightly more than one-twentieth of the limit on contributions to campaigns for federal office before the Court in Buckley. Adjusted to reflect its value in 1976 (the year Buckley was decided), Vermont's contribution limit on campaigns for statewide office (including governor) amounts to $113.91 per 2-year election cycle, or roughly $57 per election, as compared to the $1,000 per election limit on individual contributions at issue in Buckley. (The adjusted value of [Vermont's] limit on contributions from political parties to candidates for statewide office, again $200 per candidate per election, is just over one one-hundredth of the comparable limit before the Court in Buckley, $5,000 per election.) Yet Vermont's gubernatorial district — the entire state — is no smaller than the House districts to which Buckley's limits applied. In 1976, the average congressional district contained a population of about 465,000. Indeed, Vermont's population is 621,000 — about one-third larger.

> Moreover, considered as a whole, Vermont's contribution limits are the lowest in the Nation. [Vermont] limits contributions to candidates for statewide office

(including governor) to $200 per candidate per election. We have found no state that imposes a lower per election limit. Indeed, we have found only seven states that impose limits on contributions to candidates for statewide office at or below $500 per election, more than twice [Vermont's] limit. We are aware of no state that imposes a limit on contributions from political parties to candidates for statewide office lower than [Vermont's] $200 per candidate per election limit. Similarly, we have found only three states that have limits on contributions to candidates for state legislature below [Vermont's] $150 and $100 per election limits. And we are aware of no state that has a lower limit on contributions from political parties to state legislative candidates. The comparable Vermont limit of roughly $200 per election, not adjusted for inflation, is less than one-sixth of Missouri's current inflation-adjusted limit ($1,275).

*Id.* at 2492–94. The same analysis would apply to West Dakota's lower limit of $50, which squares with **Answer (A)** — that the limit amount is not closely drawn to the government's interest. Rather, the limit is likely so low as to prevent some non-incumbents from running for office against well-known and financed incumbents. *Id.* at 2495 ("[T]he record suggests, though it does not conclusively prove, that Act 64's contribution limits will significantly restrict the amount of funding available for challengers to run competitive campaigns.").

173. Expenditure limitations receive higher judicial scrutiny than contribution limitations because they are considered a greater burden on a person's right to speak in favor of their preferred candidate. *Buckley v. Valeo*, 424 U.S. 1 (1976). The Court has consistently struck down such expenditure limits on individuals, *Buckley*, political action committees, *FEC v. National Conservative PAC*, 470 U.S. 480 (1985), and political parties, *Colorado Republican Federal Campaign Committee v. FEC*, 518 U.S. 604 (1996). In each case, the Court held that truly independent expenditures (i.e., expenditures not coordinated with the candidate or her campaign) do not pose a sufficient risk of corruption or its appearance to justify limits. In each of those cases, the Court struck down a contribution limit of the same size as in this case — $1,000. Therefore, West Dakota's independent expenditure limitation is unconstitutional.

174. **Answer (D) is the correct answer**. As noted above, *McConnell* applies two standards of review depending on the type of campaign regulation. Expenditure restrictions receive heightened scrutiny, while contribution restrictions receive a more lenient standard of review. So, the first question is which type of restriction does the Act impose?

One can argue both ways on how to characterize the soft-money prohibition. On the one hand, the Act could be viewed as an expenditure limitation because it prohibits state and local parties from *spending* certain types of money. On the other hand, the Act could be viewed as a contribution limitation because the spending limits are tied to *how the money was contributed*. *McConnell* placed the federal equivalent of the West Maine law on the contribution side of the fence:

[F]or purposes of determining the level of scrutiny, it is irrelevant that Congress chose . . . to regulate contributions on the demand rather than the supply side. The relevant inquiry is whether the mechanism adopted to implement the contribution limit, or to prevent circumvention of that limit, burdens speech in a way that a direct restriction on the contribution itself would not. That is not the case here.

*McConnell*, 540 U.S. at 138-39 (citations omitted). So, the Act's soft money ban need only survive the more lenient standard of review.

The first question under the more lenient standard of review is whether West Maine has a sufficiently important interest for the Act's restrictions. Since *Buckley*, preventing corruption and its appearance has been such an interest. In *McConnell*, the Court explained that this interest allows government "sufficient room to anticipate and respond to concerns about circumvention of regulations designed to protect the integrity of the political process." *Id.* at 137. The Bipartisan Campaign Reform Act of 2002 (BCRA), which *McConnell* reviewed, is an example of such a law. Congress strictly limited contributions to national political parties. Congress did so to prevent circumvention of earlier contribution limitations established by the 1974 law upheld in *Buckley*, which strictly limited contributions to candidates for federal office. To get around the 1974 limits, wealthy contributors would make large contributions to the candidate's political party, and the party would use the contributions to promote the candidate's campaign. So, wealthy donors were contributing to political parties hoping to purchase the same influence as would a direct contribution.

Of course, the link between contribution and corruption is more attenuated when the donor gives to a political party instead of the candidate. One the one hand, when the donor contributes directly to the candidate, the candidate is aware of the donation and its size, and the candidate may then feel beholden to the contributor. While such contributions do not equal corruption, *Buckley* held that they raise an appearance of corruption that Congress may target.

On the other hand, contributions to political parties require that we connect more dots between the contribution and its influence. First, the donor must contribute to the political party with the purpose of supporting a specific candidate. Second, the party must know of the donor's intent. Third, the party or the donor must let the candidate know of the donor's donation. Fourth, the candidate must verify that the donation has been made. Fifth, the candidate must feel beholden to the donor. A main question in *McConnell* was whether contributions to political parties posed a high enough risk of corruption or its appearance to constitute a sufficiently important interest for Congress to regulate. The Court concluded that Congress had produced sufficient evidence to show that contributions to political parties posed the same threat of corruption or appearance of corruption as do contributions directly to the candidate. *Id.* at 667 ("close affiliation [between candidates and national party committees] has . . . placed national parties in a position to sell access to federal officeholders in exchange for soft-money contributions").

The key to this question is knowing that the government bears the burden of proving that regulated campaign contributions pose a risk of corruption or its appearance. *McConnell* described the government's evidentiary burden as follows: " 'The quantum of empirical evidence needed to satisfy heightened judicial scrutiny of legislative judgments will vary up or down with the novelty or the plausibility of the justification raised.' " *McConnell*, 540 U.S. at 144. Specifically, the government will need more empirical evidence if a claimed threat is "novel" or "implausible," and less evidence if a claim aligns with "common sense." *Id.*

In *McConnell*, the Court explained that while there was intuitive appeal to Congress' claim of corruption, it was most persuaded by the voluminous legislative record Congress had produced. Congress had thoroughly documented how contributors used political parties to circumvent all prior attempts to limit campaign contributions: "The record in the present case is replete with . . . examples of national party committees peddling access to federal candidates and officeholders in exchange for large soft-money donations." *Id.* at 150. Further, Congress had amassed evidence that such access was not benign: "[L]obbyists, CEOs, and wealthy individuals alike all have candidly admitted donating substantial sums of soft money to national committees not on ideological grounds, but for the express purpose of securing influence over federal officials." *Id.* at 147. And evidence showed that federal officeholders themselves recognized that soft-money contributions bought influence. *Id.* On this record, the Court held: "It was not unwarranted for Congress to conclude that the selling of access gives rise to the appearance of corruption." *Id.* at 154.

Here, the Act is vulnerable because its legislative history contains *no findings* regarding corruption or its appearance in state or local elections. Indeed, the Legislature professed its ignorance on the issue, labeling the Act an "experiment" and directing the State Election Commission to report back about whether the Act was needed. The West Maine Legislature seemed prodded to action by federal campaign finance reform, taking a shoot-first-ask-questions-later approach to state and local elections. With no evidence that soft-money contributions are corrupting state and local elections, West Maine lacks a sufficiently important interest for the contribution limits. Because West Maine has not proven a sufficiently important interest, **Answer (D) is the correct answer. Answers (A) and (B) are incorrect** because they mistakenly assume that West Maine has proven a sufficiently important reason for banning soft money.

**Answer (C) is incorrect** because political parties are not constitutionally privileged to influence their candidates. If the government can prove that contributors are using parties to corrupt candidates, government may take steps to prevent such influence.

175. **Answer (B) is the best answer.**

Permit requirements are a classic prior restraint of speech. Any organization that wants to engage in expressive activity in the public forum of City Park must obtain prior approval. If the city refuses, the speech is barred from the public forum. Of course, the city has significant interests at stake in the permit case, including mediating among competing requests to use a public resource and protecting public safety and health when such use is requested. To this end, the city may regulate the time, place, and manner in which speakers use a public forum. But, in doing so, the city must not judge the content of the speaker's speech. So, the first question is whether the city's permit process is a content-based regulation. (**Answer (A) is incorrect** because it mistakenly assumes that the prior restraint imposed by a permit requirement is unconstitutional per se.)

On its face, the permit process is a time, place, and manner restriction, and not a content-based regulation, as it does not direct the Planning Manager's decision to the message or ideas of the permit applicant. However, in deciding whether a permit requirement is content-based, the Supreme Court has not limited itself to the face of the law:

> Where the licensing official enjoys unduly broad discretion in determining whether to grant or deny a permit, there is a risk that he will favor or disfavor speech based on its content. We have thus required that a time, place, and manner regulation contain adequate standards to guide the official's decision and render it subject to effective judicial review.

*Thomas v. Chicago Park District*, 534 U.S. 316 (2002). Thus, even a time, place, and manner restriction may be invalid if it creates an undue risk of content-based discrimination in its application. **Answer (C) is incorrect** because it assumes that a time, place, and manner restriction is valid without further review.

The next question is whether the permit process contains adequate standards to control the Planning Manager's discretion. Such standards may be found either in the law itself or in a clear pattern or practice in administering the permit process. For example, in *Forsyth County v. Nationalist Movement*, 505 U.S. 123 (1992), the Court reviewed a local ordinance that gave a local official discretion to set the permit fee "in order to meet the expense incident to the administration of the Ordinance and to the maintenance of public order in the matter licensed." The Court held that this provision gave the local official standardless discretion to set the permit fee, which he could use to discriminate among applicants based on the content of their speech. Further, the local official's practice had not shown a pattern or practice that limited his discretion.

The Los Arkansas permit standard is similarly standardless. The Planning Manager is told to consider the "public interest" without any guidance as to what specific factors he or she should consider or how he or she should weigh those factors. Because the Planning Manager has never explained prior decisions, we have no way to discern a pattern or practice that might limit discretion. Further, the vague "public interest" standard may invite consideration of a speaker's message. Is it in the public interest to allow speech opposed by an overwhelming majority of local citizens? That the ordinance even allows the Planning Manager to ask this question reveals the serious risk of content-based discrimination. As in *Forsyth County*, the permit requirement lacks adequate standards.

Because the permit process lacks adequate standards, it amounts to a prior restraint based on the content of the speech. Such restraints may only be upheld when stringent procedural safeguards are met:

> (1) any restraint prior to judicial review can be imposed only for a specified brief period during which the status quo must be maintained; (2) expeditious judicial review of that decision must be available; and (3) the censor must bear the burden of going to court to suppress the speech and must bear the burden of proof once in court.

*FW/PBS, Inc. v. City of Dallas*, 493 U.S. 215 (1990). Here, no such process is accorded. Not only is there no judicial review of a permit denial, there is no review of any kind. Thus, as stated in Answer (B), the permit process is unconstitutional because it delegates the Planning Manager standardless discretion without adequate procedural safeguards. **Answer (D) is incorrect** because it mistakenly assumes that the permit process would be constitutional if it survived strict scrutiny.

176.  The difference is that speakers may now obtain judicial review of a permit denial. The main question is whether review in the state's general civil courts meets the First Amendment requirement of stringent procedural safeguards for content-based prior restraints. In *City of Littleton Colorado v. Z.J. Gifts D-4, L.L.C.*, (2004), the Court rejected a facial challenge to such judicial review of decisions under a city adult-business licensing ordinance. The Court explained that ordinary judicial review was an adequate safeguard for this specific ordinance because "[w]here (as here . . .) the regulation simply conditions the operation of an adult business on compliance with *neutral and nondiscretionary criteria*, and does not seek to censor content, an adult business is not entitled to an unusually speedy judicial decision. . . ." *Id.* at 2226 (emphasis added). A court could easily and quickly review the city's application of the ordinance's "neutral and nondiscretionary criteria." Further, the state's rules of civil procedure, like the Federal Rules of Civil Procedure, "provide for a flexible system of review in which judges can reach a decision promptly in the ordinary case, while using their judicial power to prevent significant harm to First Amendment interests where circumstances require." *Id.* Thus, on its face, ordinary judicial review did not threaten undue delay of licensing decisions. Of course, a license applicant could still challenge a specific instance of judicial review if the court unreasonably delayed the proceedings.

The availability of ordinary judicial review should not change the constitutional fate of the City of Los Arkansas' permit process. Unlike the ordinance in *City of Littleton*, the Los Arkansas ordinance does not contain "neutral and nondiscretionary" criteria. In *City of Littleton*, the license criteria focused on objective factors, such as the age of the applicant or whether the applicant was authorized to do business in the state. Such factors are easy to judge — age and authority to do business can be objectively verified from public documents, leaving little room to manipulate the licensing process to covertly censor the applicant's speech. Conversely, the Los Arkansas ordinance leaves the Planning Manager wide discretion to deny a permit based on her subjective determination of the "public interest." This serious risk of censorship should distinguish the Los Arkansas permit process, making ordinary judicial review an inadequate procedural safeguard. Instead, the city (or the state) must likely establish special procedures that ensure "an unusually speedy judicial decision." *Id.*

177. **Answer (C) is the best answer.**

As in Question 175, the fee provision acts as a prior restraint of speech. Before gaining entrance to the public forum, the speaker must first pay the fee. The government has an interest in recouping costs associated with processing the permit request as well as special costs associated with the applicant's use of the public forum. The issue is whether the fee provision is content-based or lacks adequate standards. On its face, the fee provision does not refer to the content of any speech by the permit applicant. (**Answer (A) is incorrect** because it mistakenly assumes that the prior restraint imposed by a permit requirement is unconstitutional *per se*.)

The next issue is whether the ordinance provides adequate standards to guide the Planning Manager in setting the fee. On this question, it is helpful to compare *Forsyth County v. Nationalist Movement*, 505 U.S. 123 (1992), with *Thomas v. Chicago Park District*, 534 U.S. 316 (2002). In *Forsyth County*, the Court held that the ordinance lacked adequate standards because the local official's *only* guidance in setting a permit fee was to do so "in order to meet the expense incident to the administration of the Ordinance and to the maintenance of public order in the matter licensed." Conversely, in *Thomas*, the Court noted that the challenged ordinance provided objective criteria for reviewing permit applications. For example, the city could deny a permit if that application contained a false statement, the applicant had not paid the application fee, or the applicant's intended use posed an undue risk to public health or safety. The Court found these to be adequate standards.

Here, the question is whether the five fee-setting criteria establish adequate standards so that the Planning Manager is restrained from setting the fee in a discriminatory manner. While a close question, the criteria seem closer to those in *Thomas* than in *Forsyth County*. All five criteria appeal to objective factors. Criteria 1 and 2 set a specific fee based on an ascertainable number of attendees. Criteria 3 and 4 appeal to verifiable costs incurred by past uses of the City Park. And, criterion 5 establishes a specific police-to-crowd ratio. The Planning Manager must address all of these objective factors in his or her decision, which can then be reviewed by the board. Given that the criteria and decision are based on objective factors, the board can exercise meaningful review. All this strongly suggests that the five fee criteria establish adequate standards. Thus, **Answer (B) is not the best answer**.

Because it is a content-neutral time, place, and manner restriction, the fee requirement will be valid if it is narrowly tailored to serve a significant governmental interest, and leaves open ample alternatives for communication. The fee should survive this test. First, the city has a significant interest in seeing that those who use City Park bear their fair share of the costs of doing so. Second, the five criteria are aimed at tailoring the fee to only those costs caused by the applicant's proposed use. Third, applicants who cannot pay the fee have ample alternatives of communication. They may still hand out leaflets and engage in other similar speech activities. Or, they may gather at a private facility to engage in the same conduct. They are only kept from using a public space. Because the fee requirement likely passes this test, **Answer (C) is the correct answer**.

**Answer (D) is incorrect** because it mistakenly assumes that the ordinance's fee provision discriminates based on the viewpoint expressed by the permit applicant's speech.

178. **Answer (B) is the best answer.** First Amendment protection of private association applies only to groups "organized for specific expressive purposes." *New York State Club Association v. City of New York*, 487 U.S. 1 (1988). For example, the Boy Scouts engage in expressive association because their stated mission is to instill certain values in their members, and "[i]t seems indisputable that an association that seeks to transmit . . . a system of values engages in expressive activity." *Boy Scouts of America v. Dale*, 530 U.S. 640 (2000). Adesta Regional Golf Club is not organized to express any set of values, but rather to provide recreational and social opportunities for its members. In *New York State Club Association*, the Court held that the First Amendment does not protect the associational interests of such non-expressive organizations. **Answers (A), (C), and (D) are incorrect** because they mistakenly assume that New Island's anti-discrimination law is subject to First Amendment review of some kind.

179. **Answer (C) is the best answer.**

Once again, the threshold issue is the proper First Amendment standard of review. Advertising falls within a category known as commercial speech, which the Supreme Court has defined as any speech that does "no more than propose a commercial transaction." *See Virginia State Board of Pharmacy v. Virginia Citizens Consumer Council*, 425 U.S. 748 (1976). At one time, the Supreme Court considered such speech unprotected by the First Amendment. *See Valentine v. Chrestensen*, 316 U.S. 52 (1942). Today, however, the Court treats commercial speech as a special category, somewhere between fully protected speech and low value speech, with its own test. *Central Hudson Gas & Electric Corp. v. Public Service Commission*, 447 U.S. 557 (1980), sets forth the four-part commercial speech test:

First, the commercial speech must concern a lawful activity and not be misleading. If this is not so, the speech is treated as low value speech.

Second, the challenged government action must serve a substantial interest.

Third, the challenged action must directly advance the government's interest.

Fourth, the challenged action must not be more extensive than necessary to achieve the government's interest.

The Court has explained that the fourth step does *not* require that the challenged government action be the least speech-restrictive alternative. *See Board of Trustees of SUNY v. Fox*, 492 U.S. 469 (1989). There, the Court explained the fourth part of the test as follows:

What our decisions require is a " 'fit' between the legislature's ends and the means chosen to accomplish those ends," — a fit that is not necessarily perfect, but reasonable; that represents not necessarily the single best disposition but one whose scope is "in proportion to the interest served;" that employs not necessarily the least restrictive means but [a] means narrowly tailored to achieve the desired objective.

*Id.* at 480. Given this test, we may dismiss Answers (A) and (D). **Answer (A) is incorrect** because it mistakenly assumes that strict scrutiny applies. **Answer (D) is incorrect** because it mistakenly assumes that rational basis review applies.

The next step is to analyze whether the city's advertising ban passes the four-part *Central Hudson* test. First, nothing in the question suggests either that the sale of ephedra-containing supplements is illegal or that advertising of such supplements is misleading.

Thus, the city's ban does not regulate a form of low-value speech subject to minimal scrutiny; rather, the city's ban must survive the remainder of the *Central Hudson* Test.

Second, the city's ban must serve a substantial government interest. As explained above, the city is concerned about the safety and health of college and high school athletes involved in recreational and team sports. Whether due to lack of maturity or pressure to succeed, these athletes may make inappropriate use of ephedra-containing supplements and cause substantial harm to themselves. The Court has accepted a similar health and safety rationale regarding advertising of alcohol. *See Rubin v. Coors Brewing Co.*, 514 U.S. 476 (1995); *44 Liquormart, Inc. v. Rhode Island*, 517 U.S. 484 (1996).

Third, the city's ban must directly advance the government's substantial interest. This is a close question, as is illustrated by the Court's decisions in *Coors* and *44 Liquormart*. In *Coors*, federal law had banned listing alcohol content on beer labels to discourage beer companies from competing for customers based on their beer's higher alcohol content. The Court held that the label ban did not directly advance the government's interest because it still left beer companies free to tout alcohol content in their advertising: "The failure to prohibit the disclosure of alcohol content in advertising, which would seem to constitute a more influential weapon in any strength war than labels, makes no rational sense if the government's true aim is to suppress strength wars." Further, the label ban did not apply to wine and "hard" liquor, yet the government's concern for "strength wars" logically applied to such beverages. In sum, the Court concluded that the "irrationality of this unique and puzzling regulatory framework ensures that the labeling ban will fail to" advance the government's substantial purpose.

In *44 Liquormart*, the state prohibited all advertising of alcohol prices, except on in-store displays and signs. The ban was intended to raise the price of alcohol (by preventing price competition), thereby reducing alcohol sales, and promoting the state's interest in "temperance." Four justices questioned whether the advertising ban directly advances temperance. While "common sense supports the conclusion that" an advertising ban will lead to higher prices, and thus alcohol demand and consumption will be "somewhat lower," the state had not put on evidence that the resulting reduction in alcohol consumption would be sufficient to promote temperance. (The remaining concurring justices decided the case under the fourth part of the *Central Hudson* test, which we discuss next.) For these justices, common sense or intuitive logical appeal are not sufficient to show that a speech ban directly advances the government's substantial interest. Rather, it is a fact issue on which the government bears the evidentiary burden.

Here, there are strong arguments on both sides of the third prong of the *Central Hudson* test. First, consider the arguments against the city's advertising ban. Like *Coors*, the city allows other avenues of advertising to exist, such as print, broadcast, and other advertising *outside* of sporting events. This other advertising may influence young athletes to experiment with ephedra, thereby undermining the government's interest. Also, like *44 Liquormart*, the city has not offered any evidence that its targeted advertising ban will actually reduce ephedra use by high school and college athletes.

While some effect on ephedra use may be "common sense," whether the effect will be substantial enough to directly advance the government's interest has not been proven. *See also Lorillard Tobacco Co. v. Reilly*, 533 U.S. 525 (2001) (state tobacco advertising regulation was supported by substantial empirical evidence linking tobacco advertising to tobacco demand among minors).

Now consider the arguments in support of the city's advertising ban. Unlike *Coors*, the city's advertising ban targets advertisements posing a logically higher threat to the city's interest. The city is concerned about ephedra use by high school and college *athletes*, and the ban applies to advertising that targets *sporting events*. Such advertisements are more likely to reach athletes, and are more likely to make an implicit (if not overt) connection between ephedra and athletic performance. Thus, while in *Coors* the government's labeling ban seemed haphazard and arbitrary, the city's advertising ban seems rational and targeted. And, as to *44 Liquormart*, we must remember that only four justices concluded that the ban on price advertising did not directly advance the state's interest in temperance.

While reasonable arguments exist on both sides of part three of the *Central Hudson* test, part four — whether the city's regulation is more extensive than necessary — seems more straightforward. Again, consider *Coors* and *44 Liquormart*. In *Coors*, the Court concluded that the federal government had less speech-restrictive alternatives to prevent strength wars. For example, measures "such as directly limiting the alcohol content of beers, prohibiting marketing efforts emphasizing high alcohol strength (which is apparently the policy in some other Western nations) or limiting the labeling ban only to malt liquors" might prevent strength wars while banning less speech. The same was true in *44 Liquormart*, where alternate means such as "educational campaigns," limits on "[p]er capita purchases of alcohol," and a higher sales tax on alcohol were thought to promote temperance while prohibiting less speech.

The city's ban on ephedra advertising is similarly flawed. The city had many regulatory alternatives that prohibit less speech. For example, the city might ban purchase of ephedra-containing products by anyone 21 or under, levy a higher sales tax on such products, or institute a campaign to educate local high school and college athletes concerning ephedra's health effects. The existence of such alternatives proves that the city's ban is likely more extensive than necessary to achieve its substantial interest.

In the end, strong arguments support both Answer (B) and Answer (C). **We give the edge to Answer (C)**, however, because (as explained above) current case law more strongly supports that answer.

180. **All the answers are partially right and partially wrong.** This is true because history does not show agreement among the framers on the meaning of the Religion Clauses or on the proper relationship between church and state. Some of the framers wanted a strict separation; others envisioned a nation that would be welcoming to expressions of faith by government officials. A discussion of these differing historical views and how these views are used and debated even today is found in Justice Thomas' concurring opinion and Justice Souter's dissenting opinion in *Rosenberger v. Rector and Visitors of the University of Virginia,* 515 U.S. 819 (1995). Therefore, **Answer (A) and Answer (B)** each reflect the view of some of the framers, but neither answer is totally correct.

**Answer (C)** reflects the interpretation of history by Justice Scalia in his dissent in *McCreary County v. ACLU of Kentucky,* 545 U.S. 844 (2005). Justice Scalia noted the many times in history our government leaders, both state and federal, have prayed to one God. From this, he found it acceptable to permit government to acknowledge a single Creator. Once again, history is mixed on the religious views of the framers. Some were Christian and believed in a single Creator; others were Deists who did not acknowledge a single Creator. Therefore, **Answer (C)** and **Answer (D)** are both partially correct and partially incorrect.

181. **Answer (C) is the best answer** because the other three answers are incorrect. Further this answer makes sense from a non-legal, pragmatic viewpoint.

**Answers (A) and (B) are incorrect** because the Religion Clauses have been interpreted to allow the government to accommodate religious expression without requiring government to do so. Therefore, the Attorney General is permitted to require his wardens to accommodate religious expression without violating the Establishment Clause unless this accommodation favors religion over non-religion or favors a particular religion. The program in the preceding question would violate the Establishment Clause because it favors religion over non-religion by giving benefits to those who engage in religious practices. The Attorney General's order in this question does not favor any religion or religious practice, but rather ensures that obstacles are not placed in the way of religious expression. Therefore, **Answer (A) is incorrect.** But the Attorney General may also decide not to make this accommodation without violating the Free Exercise Clause, unless his decision is intended to harm a particular religious practice. As the facts do not indicate any desire to harm a particular religion or to punish those who do not practice religion, **Answer (B) is incorrect.**

This question is based, in part, on the Supreme Court's decision in *Cutter v. Wilkinson,* 544 U.S. 709 (2005), where it decided that the Religious Land Use and Institutionalized

Persons Act (RLUIPA) did not violate the Establishment Clause. That statute prohibits government from "impos[ing] a substantial burden on the religious exercise of a person residing in or confined to an institution" unless the burden passes strict scrutiny. state prison officials challenged this requirement as a non-neutral endorsement of religion that violated the Establishment Clause.

The Court in *Cutter* repeated its long-standing position that there is play in the joints between the Free Exercise Clause and the Establishment Clause. RLUIPA was squarely within the permissible play in these joints for three reasons. First, the statute "alleviates exceptional government-created burdens on private religious exercise." Commitment or confinement gives the government "a degree of control unparalleled in civilian society and severely disabling to private religious exercise." This counsels greater government latitude to accommodate the religious exercise of those in its care.

Second, RLUIPA's mandated accommodation did not unduly burden non-beneficiaries — here, the government prison system. The statute did "not override" the government's "other significant interests," allowing prison officials to implement practices and policies that restrict religious exercise if narrowly tailored to the government's compelling interest in the safe operation of its prisons and other institutions. In short, RLUIPA does not force states to sacrifice their legitimate interests to the free exercise rights of those in their custody. Third, "RLUIPA does not differentiate among bona fide faiths." Such denominational neutrality weighs in favor of constitutionality.

The lesson to be learned from *Cutter* and similar decisions is that government is not violating either the Free Exercise Clause or the Establishment Clause when it makes neutral decisions that do not favor or punish a particular religion or those who are not religious. But, when government attempts too much accommodation of a religious practice or particular religion, it risks violating the Establishment Clause. Conversely, when it attempts too much neutrality, it risks violating the Free Exercise Clause, as for example if government did not permit inmates to practice any religion at all.

**Answer (D) is incorrect** for the reasons already stated. It is highly unlikely that the Attorney General would be held to have violated the Free Exercise Clause by repealing the order, especially under these facts. Moreover, even without the possibility of additional violence in the prisons, it is unlikely that the Attorney General could not repeal the order. As stated above, government is not violating the Free Exercise Clause if it decides not to accommodate religion.

182. **Answer (B) is the correct answer.** This question asks whether a generally applicable law violates the Free Exercise Clause when it incidentally burdens religious practices. In *Employment Division v. Smith*, 494 U.S. 872 (1990), the Court answered this question in a case that considered a state law that punished the use of certain controlled substances, including peyote. It was undisputed that the sincere religious beliefs of some local Native Americans required sacramental use of peyote. The Court explained that generally applicable laws — such as the state's drug law — do not violate the Free Exercise Clause. This is true regardless of whether the challenged law burdens a core religious practice, because judges are ill-suited to the task of classifying religious practices. Thus, **Answer (C) is incorrect**.

The next question is whether the Town's alcohol ban is a generally applicable law. Of course, all laws target specific people or types of conduct and thus are not truly generally applicable. For example, even a 70-miles-per-hour speed limit targets those who drive faster than the limit to the exclusion of those who do not. In the Free Exercise context, however, "generally applicable" means that the challenged government action does not selectively burden only those whose conduct is religiously motivated. For example, in *Church of Lukumi Babalu Aye, Inc., v. City of Hialeah*, 508 U.S. 520 (1993), a series of city ordinances effectively prohibited the slaughter of animals only when done as part of a religious ceremony. While the city claimed that the ordinances were intended to promote public health and safety, the laws were grossly under-inclusive because they only applied to religious sacrifices, permitting other slaughtering that posed substantially the same or greater health concerns. Conversely, the drug law at issue in *Smith* was not so targeted. There, the prohibition on peyote use applied to *all users*, regardless of motivation.

Here, the Town alcohol ban does not selectively target religiously-motivated conduct. *All* alcohol purchases and consumption are targeted, regardless of motivation. Consequently, the ban is not under-inclusive, punishing religiously motivated conduct while excluding equally threatening secular conduct. Thus, the ban fits within *Smith*'s general rule that generally applicable laws do not violate the Free Exercise Clause.

The general rule announced in *Smith* has an important exception: a generally applicable law may be unconstitutional if it burdens a so-called "hybrid-right." By hybrid-right, the Court meant that the challenged law burdened conduct protected both by the Free Exercise Clause *and* some other constitutional right. For example, a parent's decision to send a child to private religious school implicates *both* the parents' Free Exercise rights as well as the parents' substantive due process right to control their child's education. *Smith* involved no such hybrid right. While sincere, religious use of peyote implicated Free Exercise rights, no other constitutional protection was at issue. The Town's ordinance does not likely fit the hybrid-right exception. Purchase and consumption of alcohol does not implicate a second constitutional right that would make this a hybrid-right case. All we have is the incidental burden on Free Exercise rights, which does not warrant heightened scrutiny. Thus, **Answer (D) is incorrect**.

**Answer (A) is incorrect** because it mistakenly assumes that strict scrutiny is the proper constitutional test.

183.   **Answer (D) is the correct answer.**

As discussed in the answer to Question 182, generally applicable laws do not violate the Free Exercise Clause. Thus, the first question here is whether the Town ordinance is generally applicable. Recall from the answer to Question 182 that a generally applicable law is one that does not selectively burden religiously-motivated conduct. Here, the law is like the one struck down in *Church of Lukumi Babalu Aye, Inc., v. City of Hialeah*, 508 U.S. 520 (1993). There, a series of city ordinances that banned animal slaughtering effectively applied only to ritual sacrifices performed by members of the Santeria religion. By selectively banning religiously-motivated slaughtering, the ordinances were not generally applicable. The same is true of the Town's ordinance. When all of the provisions are read together, the ordinance applies only to alcohol consumption that occurs on the premises of the Town's only Catholic Church. Further, if the Town's purpose is to protect public safety, the ordinance is grossly under-inclusive, as it ignores *all other alcohol consumption* within the Town. As in *Church of Lukumi Babalu Aye*, the Town selectively burdens religiously motivated conduct, and thus the ordinance is not a law of general applicability. Thus, **Answer (B) is incorrect**.

When challenged government conduct selectively burdens religiously-motivated conduct, the next question is whether the government's purpose was "to disapprove of a particular religion or of religion in general." *Church of Lukumi Babalu Aye*, 508 U.S. at 532. If so, strict scrutiny applies. The question whether the government was biased toward religion is closely connected to the issue whether the law is generally applicable. Indeed, the Court has said that "failure to satisfy one requirement is a likely indication that the other has not been satisfied." *Id.* at 531. For example, in *Church of Lukumi Babalu Aye*, the Court explained that the fact that the challenged ordinances targeted only religiously-motivated animal slaughter was powerful evidence that the city's purpose was to disapprove of religious animal sacrifice. The Court also pointed to evidence in the legislative record that citizens were morally opposed to religious animal sacrifice and wanted to ban such acts.

Here, the question is whether the Town's selective ban on alcohol consumption is neutral toward religion. As in *Church of Lukumi Babalu Aye*, the ban's selectivity strongly suggests that the Town is trying to show disapproval of sacramental use of alcohol. Unlike *Church of Lukumi Babalu Aye*, however, there are no specific statements indicating that the Town or its citizens are biased against either the Catholic religion or religion generally. Yet, the timing of the ordinance is somewhat suspicious, as it roughly coincides with the Church moving into Town. While perhaps not as clear as in *Church of Lukumi Babalu Aye*, the combination of selectivity and timing indicate that the Town ordinance is not neutral towards religion. Thus, the Town ordinance must survive strict scrutiny.

Under strict scrutiny, challenged government action must be narrowly tailored to a compelling government interest. Here, the government's interest is in protecting the public health and safety from the risks posed by drunk drivers. A similar interest was argued in *Church of Lukumi Babalu Aye*, where the city sought to protect public health from certain slaughtering of animals. There, the Court held that an otherwise compelling interest may not be compelling *under the circumstances* of the case. The Court explained: "Where government restricts only conduct protected by the First Amendment and fails to enact feasible measures to restrict other conduct producing substantial harm or alleged harm of the same sort, the interest given in justification of the restriction is not compelling." *Church of Lukumi Babalu Aye*, 508 U.S. at 546-47. The interest in public safety was not compelling because the city effectively prohibited only religious slaughter of animals, leaving unrestricted other slaughter that posed similar harm. Here, the same is true: the Town effectively restricts religious consumption of alcohol, leaving unrestricted other consumption that poses similar harm to public safety. Thus, the Town ordinance similarly fails to serve a compelling government purpose.

**Answer (A) is incorrect** because the ordinance does not survive strict scrutiny.

**Answer (C) is incorrect** because it mistakenly assumes that any law that burdens core religious practices is per se unconstitutional.

184. **Answer (A) is the best answer.** In *Locke v. Davey*, 540 U.S. 712 (2004), the Supreme Court looked at a similar set of facts. In *Davey*, the state provided funds to college students but prohibited students from using the funds to "pursue degrees that are 'devotional in nature or designed to induce religious faith.' " Because all conceded that the state could have included devotional studies within the program without violating the Establishment Clause, (citing *Zelman v. Simmons-Harris*, 536 U.S. 639 (2002), (upholding school voucher program that applied equally to secular and sectarian private schools)), the litigants argued that the religious exclusion must have been motivated by hostility to religion.

Recall that the Free Exercise Clause requires strict scrutiny for laws that selectively burden or disapprove of religiously-motivated conduct. The Court held that the funding exemption for devotional studies did not create such a burden or express such disapproval because it:

> imposes neither criminal nor civil sanctions of any type on religious service or rite. It does not deny to ministers the right to participate in the political affairs of the community. And it does not require students to choose between their religious beliefs and receiving a government benefit. . . .The state simply

pursued a policy that traces its roots to the Founding generation — "prohibition[] against using tax funds to support the ministry.

Further, the Court noted that the funding program allowed attendance at sectarian schools and the study of religion (as long as the degree was not in preparation for the ministry). According to the Court, the state had gone "a long way toward including religion in its benefits." Because the Court saw no "animus towards religion," it applied only weak scrutiny to the funding exclusion and easily upheld the law.

**Answer (B) is incorrect** because the Free Exercise Clause does not absolutely prohibit spending government money on sectarian education. First, it is typically the Establishment Clause, and not the Free Exercise Clause, that would be the source of the prohibition against the spending of government money on sectarian education. Therefore, because the answer refers to the wrong Religion Clause, it is incorrect. Second, in *Zelman v. Simmons-Harris*, 536 U.S. 639 (2002), the Court upheld the constitutionality of a government-funded school voucher program that was used by parents to send their children to religious schools. Therefore, the answer is incorrect because it fails to take into account the *Zelman* decision.

This is not to say that all aid to sectarian education would be constitutional. In cases of government aid to sectarian schools, the Court looks to whether the aid is given to all schools, both secular and religious. It also looks to whether the aid is given directly to the students rather than to the schools, and it considers whether the aid is actually used for religious instruction. When aid is given to all students, given directly to students and is not used for religious instruction, it typically will be constitutional. In cases where all three criteria are not met, the chances increase that the Court will see the aid as a violation of the Establishment Clause.

**Answer (C) is incorrect** for the reasons stated in Answer (A).

**Answer (D) is incorrect** for the reasons discussed in the answer to Question 182. The government may burden religious practice if the law is neutral and of general applicability.

185.    The Court did not overrule *Sherbert v. Verner*, 374 U.S. 398 (1963), in reaching its decision in *Employment Division, Dept. of Human Resources v. Smith*, 494 U.S. 872 (1990). However, not much of the *Sherbert* decision survives. In *Sherbert*, the Court reviewed a state decision to deny unemployment benefits to a Seventh Day Adventist because she would not accept a job that required her to work on Saturday—her Sabbath. The Supreme Court used the strict scrutiny test to review this state action, holding that strict scrutiny was the appropriate test whenever a government law, neutral on its face, burdens religious liberty. Even though the unemployment law at issue in *Sherbert* was neutral on its face and was not intended to burden a particular religious practice, the government had to show a compelling reason to deny unemployment benefits under these circumstances. Since the government could not make this showing, its denial of unemployment benefits was unconstitutional.

In contrast, *Smith* held that strict scrutiny was not the appropriate test when reviewing a generally applicable neutral law that burdens religious practices. Thus the *Smith* Court rejected a key portion of the *Sherbert* holding — applying strict scrutiny to some neutral, generally applicable laws that burden religious exercise. The *Smith* Court dismissed the *Sherbert* line of cases as applying only to the denial of unemployment benefits. *Sherbert,* although not overruled, survives only in that narrow category of cases.

You should note that in the period between *Sherbert* and *Smith,* the Court issued several opinions that were difficult to reconcile with *Sherbert's* strict scrutiny test. For example, in *United States v. Lee,* 455 U.S. 252 (1982), the Court rejected the argument that the Free Exercise Clause was violated by requiring the Amish to pay Social Security taxes. And in *Goldman v. Weinberger,* 475 U.S. 503 (1986), the Court rejected the argument that the Free Exercise Clause was violated by not permitting a Jewish soldier to wear a yarmulke. So, while *Smith* is significant in changing the test used to decide whether a generally applicable, neutral law violates the Free Exercise Clause, the Court never fully applied its *Sherbert* decision even before *Smith* was decided.

186.  This question asks whether government may accommodate religious practices without violating the Establishment Clause. Stating the proper test for such an analysis requires some historical context. Thus, the next three paragraphs, which take us on a bit of a detour, are intended as doctrinal background to aid in your studying, and are not part of the answer proper.

The modern era of Establishment Clause analysis begins with the so-called *Lemon* test, named after the case *Lemon v. Kurtzman*, 403 U.S. 602 (1971). There, the Court framed a three-part test for determining whether challenged government action is constitutional:

> First, the statute must have a secular legislative purpose; second, its principal or primary effect must be one that neither advances nor inhibits religion; finally, the statute must not foster "an excessive government entanglement with religion."

*Id.* at 612-13. Over time, several members of the Court have criticized this test, even suggesting that it be abandoned. One such criticism is that the second and third steps sometimes place government in an unacceptable bind. For example, consider a state that wants to provide books and other materials to all elementary schools, public and private. On the one hand, to ensure that the materials do not "advance" religion, the government must monitor whether private religious schools use the materials to further their religious mission. On the other hand, such monitoring could constitute "an excessive government entanglement with religion." *See Aguilar v. Felton*, 473 U.S. 402 (1985), *overruled by Agostini v. Felton*, 521 U.S. 203, 218 (1997). Despite such criticism, the *Lemon* test has not been abandoned. *See Lamb's Chapel v. Center Moriches Union Free Sch. Dist.*, 508 U.S. 384, 398 (1993) (Scalia, J., concurring in the judgment) ("Like some ghoul in a late-night horror movie that repeatedly sits up in its grave and shuffles abroad, after being repeatedly killed and buried, *Lemon* stalks our Establishment Clause jurisprudence once again.")

The continuing vitality of *Lemon* has not stopped some justices from proposing their own tests. For example, Justice O'Connor has advocated a so-called endorsement test, which simply states that the government violates the Establishment Clause "if it endorses or disapproves of religion." *Allegheny County v. ACLU*, 492 U.S. 573, 625 (1989) (O'Connor, J., concurring in part and concurring in the judgment). Whether the challenged government action endorses or disapproves religion is judged from the perspective of a reasonable observer who possesses knowledge of the context and history of the action. While various members of the Court have joined opinions where Justice O'Connor applied the endorsement test, her approach never commanded a majority of the Court.

393

While the *Lemon* test nominally stands as the Court's official Establishment Clause test, Justice O'Connor's endorsement test has influenced *Lemon*'s continuing evolution and application. Indeed, an opinion authored by Justice O'Connor sets forth the current *Lemon* formulation, which requires the government to show that (1) the challenged action has "a secular legislative purpose," and (2) the "principal or primary effect" of the challenged action "neither advances nor inhibits religion." *Agostini v. Felton*, 521 U.S. 203, 218 (1997). In determining the primary effect of the challenged government action, the Court considers whether a "reasonable observer" with knowledge of the "history and context" of the challenged government action, would perceive the government as endorsing religion. *Zelman v. Simmons-Harris*, 536 U.S. 639 (2002). As part of this endorsement inquiry, the Court also considers whether the challenged government action entails excessive entanglement between government and religion. *Agostini*, 561 U.S. at 233. While this test differs substantially from the Court's original formulation, we will refer to this current formulation as the non-endorsement *Lemon* test.

As to the question you are asked to answer, the first part of the *Lemon* test should be satisfied. In *Corporation of the Presiding Bishop of the Church of Jesus Christ of Latter-Day Saints v. Amos*, 483 U.S. 327 (1987) (upholding federal law that exempted religious organizations from the federal ban on religious discrimination in employment), the Court explained that the government's purpose must be secular and not to promote or aid religion. Thus, government may seek to simply avoid interfering with religion, as by exempting religious activity from a generally applicable law. As that is all the Town of Paulsville seeks to do here, the ordinance serves a permissible secular purpose.

Next, we must determine whether the religious use exception has the effect of advancing religion. Or, whether a reasonable observer, viewing the exception in context, would see the Town as endorsing religion. In this case, the question would likely be framed as follows: Would the reasonable observer view the challenged ordinance as a law targeting drunk driving, which merely exempts non-threatening practices such as religious use; or, would such an observer view the ordinance as endorsing the religious practice of sacramental use of alcohol? The former view would likely prevail for two reasons. First, the Town exempts *several* non-threatening uses of alcohol, not only religious uses. In *Texas Monthly, Inc. v. Bullock*, 489 U.S. 1 (1989) (striking down state law that exempted only religious publications from a generally applicable sales tax), a majority of justices noted that such a generally applicable exemption would negate an inference of endorsement.

Second, given that the law arose from a notorious string of drunk driving incidents, and that the law is framed as a general prohibition of alcohol consumption, a reasonable observer familiar with this context would likely view the law as safety-based, not as religious endorsement. This is similar to *Corporation of the Presiding Bishop of the Church of Jesus Christ of Latter-Day Saints v. Amos*, 483 U.S. 327 (1987), where the Court upheld a federal employment discrimination law that exempted religious organizations from its ban on religious discrimination. There, the reasonable observer would view the law as a general anti-discrimination law with a religious exemption, and not as a law that endorsed religion. This was quite different from *Thornton's Estate v. Caldor, Inc.*, 472 U.S. 703 (1985), where the Court struck down a state law prohibiting employers from firing employees who, for religious reasons, refused to work on the Sabbath. The Court viewed the law as promoting religion by giving individuals the absolute right not to work for religious reasons. The same would be true if the Town of Paulsville had enacted an ordinance that simply protected religious consumption of alcohol from any legal consequence, civil or criminal. Such a law would appear to endorse sacramental use of alcohol. The Paulsville ordinance described above, however, places religious use of alcohol at its periphery, leaving the likely perception that the Town is promoting road safety, not religion.

187.  While government may accommodate religious practices if it does not have the purpose or effect of endorsing religion, a different test applies if government prefers one denomination over others. In that case, government action must survive strict scrutiny: the government must have a compelling purpose, and its action must be narrowly tailored to that purpose. *Larson v. Valente*, 456 U.S. 228 (1982). Here, if the Town's purpose is still public safety by preventing drunk driving, it is unclear how discriminating among religions serves that purpose in any way. If sacramental use of alcohol by Roman Catholics does not threaten the Town's public safety interest, there is no reason such use by other denominations would do so. So, even if preventing drunk driving deaths is a compelling government interest, doing so by discriminating among religious denominations is not narrowly tailored to that interest.

188.  **Answer (B) is the best answer.**

**Answer (D) is incorrect** because government can use overtly religious imagery without endorsing religion. For example, in *Allegheny County v. ACLU*, 492 U.S. 573 (1989), the Supreme Court upheld a seasonal display that included a menorah adjacent to a Christmas tree, but struck down a crèche displayed on the steps of the town hall. The Court explained that the circumstances of the display, taken as a whole, determine whether the government has the impermissible effect of endorsing religion. Thus, **Answer (D) is incorrect** because it assumes that government use of overtly religious images or symbols, standing alone, violates the Establishment Clause.

**Answer (A) is incorrect** because it states the incorrect test for determining whether the seal violates the Establishment Clause. As discussed above in Question 186, the Court applies a modified version of the so-called *Lemon* test in deciding Establishment Clause questions. The test requires the government to make two showings: (1) the challenged action has "a secular purpose," and (2) the "principal or primary effect" of the challenged action "neither advances nor inhibits religion." *Agostini v. Felton*, 521 U.S. 203, 218 (1997). The primary effect of the challenged government action is gauged from the perspective of the "reasonable observer" who has knowledge of the "history and context" of the challenged government action; the question is whether such an observer would perceive the government as endorsing religion. *Zelman v. Simmons-Harris*, 536 U.S. 639 (2002). As part of this inquiry, the Court also considers whether the challenged government action entails excessive entanglement between government and religion. *Agostini,* 521 U.S. at 233.

Answer (C) is correct to note that excessive entanglement is part of the analysis. Answer (C) is ultimately incorrect, however, because the seal does not lead to such entanglement. Excessive entanglement means that government and religion would be impermissibly involved in an ongoing relationship where government would involve itself in the operations of religious organizations. Here, the city has never had such involvement with religious organizations, and simple use of the seal does not anticipate any such involvement. Thus, **Answer (C) is incorrect**.

The strongest basis for attacking the seal is that it has the effect of advancing religion because the reasonable observer would view the seal as endorsing religion. Under the stated facts, the case can be argued both ways. On the one hand, several aspects of the seal may appear to endorse religion. Half of the images on the seal are clearly religious in origin, and would likely be recognizable by a reasonable observer familiar with the city. Further, a reasonable observer familiar with the seal's history would know that it was designed by a student from a religious school. On the other hand, the two religious images on the seal are mixed with two secular images. *See Allegheny County,* 492 U.S. at 614 (mixing of religious and secular images may negate appearance of government endorsement of religion). Further, a reasonable observer familiar with the seal's history would know that (1) the contest was open to *all* elementary school students in the city, and (2) that the designer chose the specific items because they represented her image of the city, not because of their religious origin. Which view one believes a reasonable observer would take will decide the seal's constitutionality.

To be sure, whether the seal would be viewed as endorsing religion is a close call, and we do not suggest that one view of the issue is better than the other. But, compared to the other three answers, **Answer (B) has the strongest support under current doctrine, and thus is the best answer**.

**Note:** The facts of the preceding question are loosely based on the case *Harris v. City of Zion,* 729 F. Supp. 1242 (N.D. Ill. 1990), *aff'd in part and rev'd in part,* 927 F.2d 1401 (7th Cir. 1991), *cert. denied,* 505 U.S 1218 (1992).

189.   **Answer (C) is the best answer.** To understand this answer, we must first look at the two recent Supreme Court cases on government displays of the Ten Commandments.

In *McCreary County v. ACLU,* 545 U.S. 844 (2005), the Court, by a 5-4 vote, held that the display of the Ten Commandments in two Kentucky courthouses violated the Establishment Clause. The displays included the text of the Commandments that included references to "God" as found in the King James Version of the Bible. The Court described the circumstances of each display:

In the summer of 1999, petitioners McCreary County and Pulaski County, Kentucky (hereinafter Counties), put up in their respective courthouses large, gold-framed copies of an abridged text of the King James version of the Ten Commandments, including a citation to the Book of Exodus. In McCreary County, the placement of the Commandments responded to an order of the county legislative body requiring "the display [to] be posted in 'a very high traffic area' of the courthouse." In Pulaski County, amidst reported controversy over the propriety of the display, the Commandments were hung in a ceremony presided over by the County Judge-executive, who called them "good rules to live by" and who recounted the story of an astronaut who became convinced "there must be a divine God" after viewing the Earth from the moon. The Judge-executive was accompanied by the pastor of his church, who called the Commandments "a creed of ethics" and told the press after the ceremony that displaying the Commandments was "one of the greatest things the judge could have done to close out the millennium."

After the ACLU filed lawsuits challenging both postings, the counties directed expansion of the displays to include other items, all of which either had a religious theme or were excerpted to highlight a religious element. The asserted purpose of the displays was "to demonstrate that the Ten Commandments were part of the foundation of American Law and Government. . . ."

When the district court held this second display violated the Establishment Clause, the counties created yet a third display. This display again included the Ten Commandments, as found in the King James Version of the Bible. Also included in the display were framed copies of the Magna Carta, Declaration of Independence, and various other historical documents. Each document had attached to it a statement about its historical and legal significance. Again the asserted purpose was to show that the Ten Commandments were part of the foundation of American law.

The Supreme Court easily concluded that the first set of displays had a forbidden religious purpose. Each display consisted solely of the text of the Ten Commandments, including its references to a monotheistic god, and contained no secular items that might "counter the religious implication" of the bare text. Further, the ceremony unveiling one of the displays included a pastor remarking on "the certainty of the existence of God." Consequently, "[t]he reasonable observer could only think that the Counties meant to emphasize and celebrate the Commandments' religious message."

The Court next considered whether the inclusion of secular items in the second and third set of displays cured the impermissible endorsement of the first set of displays. The counties argued that second and third displays should be judged in isolation, without considering the content of, or circumstances surrounding, the first set of displays. The Court rejected this argument, explaining that "reasonable observers have reasonable memories, and our precedents sensibly forbid an observer 'to turn a blind eye to the context in which [the] policy arose.'" Given the religious origins of the first displays, the Court concluded that the reasonable observer would see the same motivation behind the second and third displays, even with the inclusion of secular texts. For the second display, the counties' "unstinting focus was on religious passages" of the secular texts, belying the claim of secular motive. For the third display, the haphazard "selection of posted material [did not] suggest a clear theme that might prevail over evidence of the continuing religious object." Thus, all three displays violated the non-endorsement *Lemon* test by not having a secular purpose and endorsing religion.

In *Van Orden v. Perry*, 545 U.S. 677 (2005), the Court upheld a display of the text of the Ten Commandments located on the 22-acre grounds surrounding the Texas State Capitol. The Ten Commandments monument was installed in the 1960s, and the area currently includes "17 monuments and 21 historical markers commemorating the 'people, ideals, and events that compose Texan identity.' " This monument also included the words of the Ten Commandments and its references to God. While Chief Justice Rehnquist wrote a plurality opinion (joined by three justices) upholding the display, we focus here on Justice Breyer's opinion concurring in the judgment for three reasons: first, his opinion stated the narrowest grounds for the decision; second, he applied the prevailing non-endorsement version of the *Lemon* test; and third, he provided the necessary fifth vote for the decision.

Justice Breyer gave three reasons for concluding that the Texas monument had a permissible secular purpose. First, the display was donated by a private group with an avowed secular purpose. Second, the context of the surrounding monuments and historical markers was important to Justice Breyer because it indicated that the state was attempting to convey a moral message, rather than a specific religious one. Third, the monument had been on display for over forty years without legal challenge, suggesting that few individuals concluded that this monument amounted to a government effort to favor religion over non-religion or to favor a particular religion.

*McCreary* and *Van Orden* illustrate how context-sensitive the endorsement test can be. The Justices must reconstruct the history and context of a religious display, and then view that reconstruction through the eyes of the imaginary reasonable observer. So, it is not surprising that display of the same religious item — here, the text of the Ten Commandments — was held permissible when enshrined in one context but unconstitutional when transplanted to another context. And that explains Justice Breyer's crucial vote switch between the two cases. Looking through the reasonable observer's eyes, he saw the government's purpose as religious in the *McCreary* displays, while he saw a secular purpose in the *Van Orden* display.

**Answer (C) is the best answer** because the facts suggest that the Battle Hymn of the Republic display is intended for a secular purpose, to celebrate human freedom. However, it is a close call. The language of the verse refers to Christ and God, and the mayor wants only that verse displayed. She also ties freedom to God—a monotheistic God associated with Christianity. Yet, in *Van Orden* the monument also referred to God. Additionally, as in *Van Orden,* the mayor's purpose in this question seems to convey a moral, rather than a religious message. A reasonable observer, knowing the history of what the mayor saw and what she intends to convey, likely would see this as an attempt to celebrate human freedom by quoting a song associated with the emancipation of slaves, rather having a purpose to promote Christianity or monotheism. But this will all depend on how the justices see the context and history of the display. If certain Justices see this as suggesting too strongly a religious theme and tied too directly to a particular religion, rather than seeing the display as a general declaration that human freedom is worth fighting for, then the Court may find that the display violates the Establishment Clause. If so, then Answer (A) would replace Answer (C) as the correct answer.

**Answer (B) is incorrect** because Establishment Clause jurisprudence and these Ten Commandment cases do not require that other items be displayed with the religious item. Including non-religious items may help persuade the Court that the display is not an impermissible endorsement of religion, but it is not required. However, as City Attorney, you may want to suggest this approach to the mayor.

**Answer (D) is incorrect** because it is too broad a statement. Government invocation of the image of God does not necessarily violate the Establishment Clause. Indeed, the Supreme Court begins every session asking God to "save this honorable Court." But such invocation may violate the Establishment Clause, as when the government sponsors public school prayer.

190. **Answer (C) is the best answer.**

The Supreme Court has explained that in the public school setting "government may not coerce anyone to support or participate in religion or its exercise, or otherwise act in a way which 'establishes a [State] religion or religious faith, or tends to do so.' " *Lee v. Weisman*, 505 U.S. 577, 587 (1992). The Court has held that this rule bars prayer at both a high school graduation, *Lee*, 505 U.S. at 587, and a high school football game. *Santa Fe Indep. Sch. Dist. v. Doe*, 530 U.S. 290 (2000). In both of these cases, the Court concluded that the government had effectively coerced participation in religious activity (*i.e.*, prayer). **Answer (D) is incorrect** because it mistakenly assumes that strict scrutiny is the correct test.

**Answers (A) and (B)** offer two reasons why the prayer would *not* be considered government coercion of religious practice. First, Answer (A) correctly states that private religious speech does not violate the Establishment Clause. The question, then, is whether students writing the prayer recited by Principal James make it private prayer. Several factors favor finding the prayer to be public speech. The agenda for each of the awards ceremonies was set by school officials, which means that public officials decided to include a prayer at each event as was the case in *Lee* and *Santa Fe*. The fact that a public official delivered the prayer also supports the conclusion that the prayer is public speech. The mere fact that students composed the prayer would not overcome these factors. *See Santa Fe,* (student written and led prayer at high school football games was publicly endorsed religious speech).

**Answer (B)** offers a second reason to find no government coercion of religious practice: No student was coerced to pray because the ceremonies were optional. The Court rejected a similar argument in *Lee* and *Santa Fe*, where attendance at both graduation and football games was optional. In those cases, the Court held that "the government may no more use social pressure to enforce orthodoxy than it may use more direct means." *Lee*, 505 U.S. at 594. This social pressure has two parts. First, the student feels pressure to attend the event at which prayer is said. In *Lee*, high school graduation is a significant event which most students want to attend with their peers. In *Santa Fe*, "[h]igh school home football games are traditional gatherings of a school community." *Santa Fe*, 530 U.S. at 312. The Senior Day awards ceremonies fall somewhere in between. Like graduation, they recognize various forms of achievement; like football games, they are a community gathering of friends and family. Thus, it is likely that Senior Day is an event for which students may not have a meaningful choice between attending and avoiding unwanted religious exercise.

The second aspect of social pressure is whether those students who attend will be coerced into religious practice. In *Lee*, the Court explained that such coercion is present in gatherings of high school students. Social pressure to conform means that students who object to religious practice will either participate or remain silent, for no socially conscious teenager would affirmatively disrupt the gathering to indicate her objection to the prayer. And, if the student remains silent, she risks giving the appearance that she assents to the prayer occurring around her. This puts the student in an unacceptable position: either pray, or stay silent and appear to agree with the prayer. The same analysis would apply here. At Senior Day, we have no reason to believe that the social pressure to conform would be any less than at graduation or a football game.

In sum, the mere fact that attendance at Senior Day is optional does not negate coercion. Thus, **Answer (B) is incorrect**. Because of the social pressure to attend Senior Day, and to conform to the group's behavior once there, students are effectively coerced into religious practice. Thus, **Answer (C) is the best answer**.

191.  The teacher would be allowed to require the singing of all three verses because the Battle Hymn of the Republic is closely associated with patriotism and the struggle to end slavery in the United States, and it is not associated with religious principles. Unless you are given additional facts, this singing would not violate the non-endorsement *Lemon* test because the public school has a secular purpose (teaching a patriotic song to its choir) rather than a religious purpose. Further, given the history and context of this song, requiring the choir to sing it does not endorse religion generally or one religion in particular. Just as having some religious content in displaying the Ten Commandments did not make the display unconstitutional in *Van Orden v. Perry*, 545 U.S. 677 (2005), it is unlikely the teacher is violating the Establishment Clause by requiring this song even with its religious references.

However, because this involves a public high school, we must also ask if the students are being coerced '' to support or participate in religion or its exercise, or otherwise act in a way which 'establishes a [State] religion or religious faith, or tends to do so.' " *Lee v. Weisman*, 505 U.S. 577, 587 (1992). The facts do not support this conclusion.

Unlike school prayer at issue in *Lee* and in *Santa Fe Indep. Sch. Dist. v. Doe*, 530 U.S. 290 (2000), the activity of singing in a public school choir is not a religious activity equivalent to prayer, and it is not done to bring solemnity to an important occasion such as graduation. It is a regular part of the curriculum. Of course, one could imagine a choir teacher violating the Establishment Clause if all the songs chosen were from a certain religious tradition. But nothing in these facts suggests that the students are being coerced into participating in a religious ceremony or exercise.

An interesting case on a similar issue involved requiring public school students to recite the Pledge of Allegiance, which contains the words "under God." *Elk Grove Unified School District v. Newdow*, 542 U.S. 1 (2004), was dismissed by the Supreme Court for lack of standing. For those who like to read Supreme Court tea leaves, however, a three-Justice dissent in *Newdow* provides much food for thought. Chief Justice Rehnquist, joined by Justices O'Connor and Thomas, concluded not only that the child's father had standing, but that the school district's practice of non-mandatory Pledge recitation does not violate the Establishment Clause. Those justices believed that voluntary recitation of the Pledge was a patriotic recognition of God's role in public life, and that the practice neither endorses religion nor coerces schoolchildren to pray. Given that Justice Scalia, who had recused himself due to his prior public comments on the case, would most likely join these three justices, the Court likely had four solid votes to uphold the Pledge. Since then, however, both Chief Justice Rehnquist and Justice O'Connor have left the Court. The question is whether their replacements, Chief Justice Roberts and Justice Alito, and any of the five remaining justices — Stevens, Kennedy, Souter, Ginsburg, or Breyer — will vote to uphold the Pledge.

Another recent noteworthy "no decision" is *Bunting v. Mellen*, 541 U.S. 1019 (2004) (denying certiorari), which raised an interesting wrinkle on the school prayer issue. In that case, cadets at the Virginia Military Institute challenged the school's practice of saying a prayer before dinner. The federal district court and court of appeals both held that the prayer practice violated the Establishment Clause, and the court of appeals denied a request for rehearing *en banc*. *See Mellen v. Bunting*, 181 F. Supp. 2d 619 (W.D. Va. 2002), *aff'd in part, vac. in part*, 327 F. 3d 355 (4th Cir. 2003), *rehearing en banc denied*, 341 F.3d 312 (4th Cir. 2003). The Supreme Court then denied certiorari, leaving the lower court rulings in place, with two Justices taking the unusual step of writing opinions explaining their vote (opinion of Stevens, J., with whom Ginsburg and Breyer, JJ., join, respecting denial of cert.) (certiorari was inappropriate because the case was likely moot); (Scalia, J., with whom Rehnquist, C.J., joins, dissenting from denial of cert.) (court should take the case and resolve the important issue raised). *Bunting* raises a key factual difference from *Lee v. Weisman*, 505 U.S. 577 (1992) (prayer at high school graduation violated Establishment Clause), and *Santa Fe Independent School District v. Doe*, 530 U.S. (2001) (prayer at high school football game violated Establishment Clause). *Lee* and *Santa Fe* both involved high school students, who the Court considered incapable of resisting the peer pressure to join in group prayer. *Bunting*, however, involved college students, all of whom are old enough to live away from home, vote, and serve in the military. So, *Bunting* raises the question whether the peer pressure rationale of *Lee* and *Santa Fe* extends to those beyond high school age. How would you answer this question? Do you see any other differences between *Bunting* and the high-school-prayer cases? Compare your answer to those in the lower court opinions cited above. *See also Chaudhuri v. Tennessee*, 130 F.3d 232 (6th Cir. 1997), *cert. denied*, 523 U.S. 1024 (1998) (prayer at college graduation); *Tanford v. Brand*, 104 F.3d 982 (7th Cir. 1997), *cert. denied*, 522 U.S. 814 (1997) (same).

192.    In *Rosenberger v. Rector and Visitors of Univ. of Virginia*, 515 U.S. 819 (1995), the Supreme Court held that a university would not violate the Establishment Clause by paying the publishing costs of its student-run publications, including publications expressing a religious message. (The university had excluded religious student publications from such a subsidy on the ground that including such publications would violate the Establishment Clause.) The Court explained that such payments did not have either the purpose or effect of advancing religion. The university's purpose was to support a rich exchange of ideas among the student body by subsidizing the publishing costs of student publications. Here, the same is true. The high school's purpose is to foster a rich extra-curricular life through funding the advertising and meeting costs of its student organizations.

In *Rosenberger*, the forbidden effect was also absent, as several aspects of the funding separated the university from endorsement of religion. First, the program was even-handed, treating both religious and secular publications the same. Second, the funds went directly from the university to the publisher, so that the university did not appear to directly fund religious activity. Third, the funds were used for a common, secular purpose — printing and circulating published matter. Fourth, any religious speech or activity was that of the private individuals who contributed to the student publication and not of the university's public officials. Each of these factors apply to the Jefferson High School Student Activity Fund. The program applies evenhandedly to all student organizations; the funds are disbursed directly to the relevant vendor (and not the organization or its members); the fund pays for secular activities (fliers, refreshments, *etc.*); and any religious activity is that of the organization's private members and not of Jefferson High School officials.

Because disbursement of funds to religious student organizations has neither the purpose nor effect of advancing or inhibiting religion, the practice does not violate the Establishment Clause.

# PRACTICE FINAL EXAM: ANSWERS

193. **Answer (D) is the correct answer.**

   **(A) is incorrect** because Disposal satisfies the three standing requirements: injury, causation, and redressability. First, Disposal is threatened with a concrete injury because the import ban would cause economic harm by barring Disposal from doing certain business. Further, this injury is actual and imminent as the Illanoy Attorney General has specifically directed Disposal to end importation of out-of-state hazardous waste. (The fact that enforcement is imminent means that **answer (B) is incorrect**, as the lawsuit is ripe for judicial consideration). Second, the injury is caused by the defendant's conduct, as it would be the Attorney General's enforcement of the statute that would cause Disposal's harm. Third, an injunction against enforcement would redress Disposal's injury as it would allow continued importation of out-of-state waste. Thus, Disposal has standing.

   **Answer (C) is incorrect** because Disposal's lawsuit falls within the exception to Eleventh Amendment immunity created by *Ex Parte Young*, 209 U.S. 123 (1908). In *Young*, the Supreme Court held that a private plaintiff may bring a federal court lawsuit against a state official seeking purely prospective, non-monetary relief. Here, Disposal seeks just such relief. Specifically, Disposal does not seek any money from either Illanoy or its Attorney General, but rather an order preventing prospective enforcement of the state's import ban. The Eleventh Amendment does not bar this suit.

   **Answer (D) is correct** because none of the preceding arguments prevent a federal court from hearing Disposal's lawsuit.

194. **Answer (D) is correct** because a court order against the Governor and Attorney General will not stop private lawsuits, and so the judicial remedy will not redress the plaintiff's alleged harm. The Act gives neither the Governor nor the Attorney General power to enforce the Act's liability provision, to stop private litigants from filing suit, or to direct state courts to not hear such suits. Further, an injunction against the Governor and Attorney General would not bind private plaintiffs, as they are not a party to the lawsuit. Thus, an injunction against these defendants would be utterly useless, in no way redressing the threatened injury of private lawsuits.

**Answer (A) is incorrect** because the Supreme Court has allowed third-party standing for abortion providers to litigate the constitutional rights of their patients. In *Singleton v. Wulff*, 428 U.S. 106 (1976), the Court explained that women seeking an abortion faced an obstacle to litigating their own rights. Because abortions are a private matter, most women will not want to publicize their choice through proceedings in open court. Thus, the Court held that abortion providers may litigate those rights.

**Answer (B) is incorrect** because The Pregnancy Assistance Center is threatened with a concrete injury — substantial civil liability. A closer question is whether The Pregnancy Assistance Center's injury is "actual or imminent, not 'conjectural' or 'hypothetical,'" *Lujan v. Defenders of Wildlife*, 504 U.S. 555 (1992), because The Pregnancy Assistance Center has not yet been sued under the Act. The Supreme Court has held that a party need not wait for liability to bring suit challenging the constitutionality of the statute. For example, the Court has heard abortion providers' pre-enforcement challenges to abortion laws requiring parental consent or notification. *See, e.g.*, *Lambert v. Wicklund*, 520 U.S. 292 (1997); *Bellotti v. Baird*, 428 U.S. 132 (1976). The Pregnancy Assistance Center should be allowed to make such a challenge. Thus, **answer (C) is also incorrect**.

Note that standing would also fail for lack of causation, because neither the Governor nor the Attorney General plays any role in enforcing the Act. Only private parties — the parents of a minor who seeks an abortion — can sue for damages. Thus, The Pregnancy Assistance Center's threatened injury — civil liability from private lawsuits — is not caused by any actions of the defendants.

195.  **Answer (D) is the best answer.**

We begin with whether the subject judicial ethics provision is content-based. The answer is a straightforward "yes." To apply the prohibition, one needs to parse the content of the candidate's speech. If the words reveal her party affiliation, the prohibition is triggered. This logical conclusion is consistent with the Supreme Court's recent decision in *Republican Party of Minnesota v. White*, 536 U.S. 765 (2002). There, the state's judicial ethics rules prohibited "a candidate for judicial office, including an incumbent judge," from "announc[ing] his or her legal views on disputed legal or political issues." As here, the Court easily concluded that the ethics provision was content-based.

As a content-based speech regulation, the party-affiliation provision receives strict scrutiny: the provision must be narrowly tailored to serve a compelling government purpose. (**Answer (B) is incorrect** because it assumes that regulation of political speech is unconstitutional *per se*.) First, consider the government's purpose. The commentary explains that the provision is meant to preserve judicial impartiality. In *White*, the Court explained that judicial "impartiality" is a vague term that has several meanings, and that only two of those meanings might serve as a compelling interest. First, government has a compelling interest to ensure that its judges show "lack of bias for or against either *party* to the proceeding." For example, a judge who might rule on product liability issues must not favor or disfavor a particular manufacturer in reaching her decisions — she must treat all manufacturers the same. Second, the Court considered, but did not decide, whether government has a compelling interest that its judges be open-minded. By open-minded, the Court meant that a judge is "willing to consider views that oppose his preconceptions, and remain open to persuasion, when the issues arise in a pending case." The Court did not decide whether the government has a compelling interest in an open-minded judiciary, holding instead that the Minnesota announce clause was not narrowly tailored to that interest. Because Texana can point to a compelling interest in at least one form of impartiality, **Answer (C) is incorrect**.

The next question is whether Texana's party-affiliation ban is narrowly tailored to either conception of impartiality. First, consider impartiality towards specific parties. In *White*, the Court held that Minnesota's prohibition was not narrowly tailored to this interest because "it does not restrict speech for or against particular *parties*, but rather speech for or against particular *issues*." On this view, Texana's party-affiliation ban is even less well tailored than Minnesota's prohibition. Unlike a candidate's statement of "his or her legal views on disputed legal or political issues," mere revelation of party affiliation is a very weak signal of a candidate's specific substantive beliefs. In reality, political parties have expressed views on a wide variety of issues, and, most importantly, *one need not agree with all of a party's views to be a member of that party*. For example, there are pro-choice Republicans and pro-life Democrats. So, party affiliation is not only a weak signal of a candidate's views on *issues*, but reveals no information about his or her view of *specific parties*. Thus, as in *White*, the ethics rule is not narrowly tailored to ensuring impartiality toward specific parties.

Next, we must consider open-mindedness. In *White*, the Court concluded that "the announce clause is so woefully under-inclusive as to render belief in that purpose a challenge to the credulous." This was because Minnesota banned only a small amount of candidate speech that bears on open-mindedness. For example, the prohibition did not apply to speech before a person became a judicial candidate, such as law review articles, books, CLE presentations, adjunct lectures, or bar speeches. The same is true of Texana's party-affiliation ban. Not only is party affiliation a weak signal of one's views, but it is only a small star in the constellation of speech relevant to open-mindedness. Thus, the party-affiliation ban is not narrowly tailored to achieving open-mindedness.

Because the party-affiliation ban is not narrowly tailored to either definition of impartiality, **Answer (D) is the best answer**.

**Answer (A) is incorrect** because it inaccurately describes the party-affiliation ban. While the ban is content-based, because it defines the regulated conduct by reference to the content of the candidate's speech, it does not discriminate among various viewpoints that the candidate might express. For example, a rule banning judicial candidates from criticizing rulings of the state supreme court would discriminate between those who support and oppose various precedents. The party-affiliation ban makes no such distinction.

196. **Answer (C) is the correct answer.**

The first question is the applicable constitutional test for analyzing the Program. In *Zelman v. Simmons-Harris*, 536 U.S. 639 (2002), the Court explained that the Establishment Clause "prevents a State from enacting laws that have the 'purpose' or 'effect' of advancing or inhibiting religion." Based on this test, we can eliminate Answers (A) and (D). **Answer (A) is incorrect** because it mistakenly assumes that any allocation of public funds to a religious organization violates the Establishment Clause. **Answer (D) is incorrect** because it mistakenly assumes that the applicable test is strict scrutiny.

Under the test set forth in *Zelman*, the first question is whether the Program's *purpose* is to advance or inhibit religion. From the information we have in the question, this is not so. New Island is trying to ensure the viability of *all* its homeless shelters during an economic downturn. The State is doing so to both care for the homeless and prevent the secondary effects of a neglected homeless population. Neither purpose has anything to do with religion.

Next, we must ask whether the Program has the *effect* of advancing or inhibiting religion. Under this test, the Court asks whether a reasonable observer would conclude that the challenged government action (here, the Program) is intended to endorse a religious sect or religion more generally. The Supreme Court decisions applying this test in the education context illustrate the rule's reach. There, the Court's "decisions have drawn a consistent distinction between government programs that provide aid directly to religious schools, and programs of true private choice, in which government aid reaches religious schools only as a result of the genuine and independent choices of private individuals." *Zelman*, 536 U.S. at 649. Three important factors mark these cases: (1) the government funds are equally available to religious and secular organizations, (2) receipt of aid is the result of the choices of private individuals, and (3) the government has not given private actors any incentive to choose a religious organization over a secular one. In *Zelman*, a city offered school vouchers to families that chose to send their child to private school. The vouchers covered all private schools, both religious and secular, and a religious school received public funds only if parents (who are private actors) made the independent decision to send their child to such a school. Further, the voucher program in no way encouraged families to choose religious schools. The Court has applied this principal to other programs that award public funds based on the independent schooling decisions of private actors. *See Mueller v. Allen*, 463 U.S. 388 (1983) (state tax deduction for private school tuition); *Witters v. Washington Dept. of Servs. for Blind*, 474 U.S. 481 (1986) (tuition aid); *Zobrest v. Catalina Foothills Sch. Dist.*, 509 U.S. 1 (1993) (sign-language interpreters in federal program work with deaf children in private schools); *Agostini v. Felton*, 521 U.S. 203 (1997) (federal program providing public teachers to teach disadvantaged children in private parochial schools).

The Program has the same hallmarks as the education programs upheld by the Court. First, the Program makes public funds equally available to religious and secular organizations, as an organization only need operate a homeless shelter to be eligible for funds. Second, receipt of funds depends *solely* on the choices of private actors — homeless individuals seeking a shelter's services — and the amount of funds received depends solely on the number of homeless served. Third, nothing in the Program gives the homeless an incentive to choose a religious shelter over a secular one. Because the Program is one of "true private choice," it does not have the effect of endorsing religion and thus does not violate the Establishment Clause. Thus, **Answer (C) is correct**.

The percentage of homeless shelters run by religious organizations does not change the analysis. In *Zelman*, 82% of the schools participating in the voucher program were religiously-affiliated, while only 60% of the shelters in the New Island Program are religiously-affiliated. As long as the public funds are allocated based on true private choice, these percentages are beside the point.

**Answer (B) is incorrect** because it mistakenly assumes that the manner in which a religious organization uses public funds is relevant to the constitutional question. As long as the funding program allocates funds based on independent choices of private actors, the Establishment Clause does not require that public funds either be strictly segregated for non-religious use, or that the funds not have the effect of freeing up other funds for religious purposes.

197.  **Answer (C) is the best answer.**

By its terms, the statute is limited to crimes that occur in public roadways. While the Court has never precisely defined the term "channel of interstate commerce," it should extend to a state's public roadways. For example, in *United States v. Lopez*, 514 U.S. 549 (1995), the Court cited *United States v. Darby*, 312 U.S. 100 (1941), and *Heart of Atlanta Motel, Inc. v. United States*, 379 U.S. 241 (1964), as cases where Congress had regulated the channels of interstate commerce. *Darby* involved a federal law that prohibited the shipment in interstate commerce of lumber produced by workers not paid a specified minimum wage. *Darby* supports the argument that the channels of interstate commerce continue to their headwaters, at the point of manufacture where the workers produce the goods shipped. By implication, all public roadways in between would be part of the channels. Similarly, *Heart of Atlanta* involved a Georgia hotel "readily accessible" to state and interstate highways, but not directly abutting such roads. Presumably, if the hotel was in the channels of interstate commerce, so were the public roadways connecting the hotel to the state and interstate highways.

Just as in *Darby* and *Heart of Atlanta*, the public roadways regulated by the statute in this question are within the channels of interstate commerce. Such thoroughfares provide the pathways for residents to get to interstate roadways, for interstate deliveries to reach local residents (e.g., deliveries by U.S. Postal Service or private overnight service), and for interstate suppliers to reach local businesses (as in *Katzenbach v. McClung*, 379 U.S. 294 (1964), where the local restaurant — Ollie's Barbecue — received deliveries from out-of-state suppliers). Just as blood flows from the body's main arteries to one's extremities through ever-narrowing branches and capillaries, goods and services (the lifeblood of commerce) flow through interstate highways and railways to remote corners of the United States through ever-narrowing state and county roadways. Because Congress should have an interest in keeping these pathways free from violent crime, **Answer (C) is the best answer**.

While arguable, **Answer (D) is weaker than answer (C)** because it likely conflicts with the Court's reasoning in *United States v. Morrison*, 529 U.S. 598 (2000). One can find support for answer (D) in *Heart of Atlanta*, where the Court explained that race discrimination in public accommodations affected interstate commerce by discouraging interstate travel by African-Americans. But both *Lopez* and *Morrison* explained that aggregation of economic affects on interstate travel was allowed in *Heart of Atlanta* because the case involved commercial or economic activity — the business of public accommodations. When the regulated activity is not commercial or economic, aggregation has not been allowed. So in *Morrison*, the Court rejected the government's argument that gender-motivated violence discouraged interstate travel by women. Because gender-motivated violence is not commercial or economic activity, the Court refused to aggregate that activity's effect on interstate travel. The same reasoning applies to this statute. Drive-by shootings are not commercial or economic activity, and so the Court would not aggregate the effects of that activity on interstate travel. Thus, **Answer (D) is not the best answer**.

**Answer (A) is not the best answer** because the Court has stated that Congress may regulate even violent crime that is targeted at the channels and instrumentalities of interstate commerce. In *Morrison*, the Court stated that Congress may not regulate violent crime that is not so targeted, implying that the involvement of channels or instrumentalities of interstate commerce is enough to give Congress jurisdiction.

While an accurate statement of the law, **Answer (B) is not the best answer** because it does not apply to this case. It is true that the Court never allowed aggregation of non-economic activities under the substantial effects test. But, once one concludes that the statute can be upheld as a regulation of the channels of interstate commerce, it does not matter whether the statute would also pass the substantial effects test.

198.    **Answer (D) is the correct answer.** This question asks you to apply *Gonzales v. Raich*, 545 U.S. 1 (2005), to determine whether Congress can regulate a non-economic activity that does not involve the channels or instrumentalities of interstate commerce. As explained in the answer to Question 50, *Raich* held that the Commerce Clause reaches regulation of an intra-state, non-economic activity when Congress has a rational basis for concluding that such regulation is necessary to the successful regulation of a larger interstate economic activity. In *Raich*, Congress could regulate the personal cultivation and consumption of medical marijuana because Congress had a rational basis for concluding that such regulation was necessary to effective regulation of the interstate drug trade. Specifically, failure to control medical marijuana might allow diversion of such drugs to illegal uses, which would undermine the effectiveness of the comprehensive federal drug control laws. **Answers (A) and (B) are incorrect** because they contradict this holding in *Raich*.

Here, Congress has set forth a rational basis for regulating an intra-state, non-economic activity. Sam's smoking is likely not an economic activity, as that conduct — standing alone — does not involve commercial or economic activity. The law that criminalizes his smoking, however, is part of a comprehensive regulation of a larger economic activity — the interstate market in tobacco products. Further, Congress has articulated a rational basis (similar to that in *Raich)* for including the non-economic activity in its larger regulation: Possession and use of tobacco products near children makes those products more accessible to children and socializes children to be positively disposed toward tobacco. Similar to *Raich*, Congress concluded that it would undermine the Act's comprehensive scheme to permit certain intra-state non-commercial activity — here, tobacco possession in or near a child-related facility. Thus, **Answer (D) is the best answer**.

**Answer (C) is incorrect** because child-related facilities are not in the channels of interstate commerce. While some schools, day care facilities, children's hospitals, and orphanages are surely located near channels of interstate commerce, like the schools in *United States v. Lopez*, 514 U.S. 549 (1995), such facilities are not inherently part of the channels that move goods and people from state to state.

199. **Answer (C) is the best answer** because Congress may not use its Spending Clause power to condition federal funds on a state taking action barred by the Constitution. In *South Dakota v. Dole,* 483 U.S. 203 (1987), the Court explained the four-part test for Congress' power to condition state receipt of federal funds. First, the condition must promote the general welfare. Second, federal law must unambiguously set forth both the terms of the condition and the federal funds to be withheld. Third, the condition must be rationally related to the purpose for which the federal funds have been allocated. And fourth, the condition must not require the state to take action independently barred by the Constitution. The fourth part is referred to as the "no independent bar" requirement. As Answer (C) correctly states, the condition described above — enacting a law that bans virtually all abortions — would violate an independent provision of the Constitution — the Due Process Clause of the Fourteenth Amendment. (The Court held in *Planned Parenthood v. Casey*, 505 U.S. 833 (1992), that states may not prohibit pre-viability abortions.) By requiring states to prohibit all abortions (including pre-viability abortions), the condition requires the states to violate the Fourteenth Amendment's Due Process Clause. Thus, the condition is invalid.

**Answer (A) is incorrect** because it rests on an argument the Supreme Court rejected long ago. The argument is that Congress may not use its Spending Clause power (via conditional spending) to encourage states to take action that Congress could not constitutionally take itself. Here, the argument goes, if Congress cannot regulate abortions directly (because abortion is a non-economic activity beyond the reach of the Commerce Clause), it may not do so indirectly by using its Spending Power to encourage states to do so. In *Dole*, the Court rejected this argument, holding that Congress may impose conditions that lie beyond the scope of its enumerated powers. Thus, it is irrelevant whether Congress could regulate abortion itself.

**Answer (B) is incorrect** because it is incomplete. Recall that the first limit on conditional federal spending is that the condition must be rationally related to the purpose for which the federal funds have been allocated. That is arguably the case here — regulation of abortion (a medical procedure) is arguably related to health care, which is the purpose for the federal funds at issue. However, as discussed above, the condition fails the fourth requirement because it asks states to take action barred by an independent provision of the Constitution.

**Answer (D) is incorrect** for the same reason stated for **Answer (A).** Even if the Fifth Amendment Due Process Clause would prevent Congress from banning pre-viability abortions, Congress may use its Spending Power to encourage states to take action Congress cannot itself take. As explained above, however, the Due Process Clause of the Fourteenth Amendment bars states from prohibiting pre-viability abortions, and thus the condition is invalid.

200. **Answer (C) is the best answer.** Once again, the issue is whether Congress is commandeering the states. The registration provision in this question is similar to the law upheld in *South Carolina v. Baker*, 485 U.S. 505 (1988). There, Congress had repealed the federal tax exemption for interest on state bonds that were not in registered form. The state argued that the economic impact of the federal tax would force states to issue registered bonds, which would effectively commandeer states into passing and administering laws necessary to issue such bonds. The Court rejected this argument, explaining that commandeering occurs only when Congress directs "the manner in which States regulate private parties," and not when Congress applies a general regulation to both states and private parties alike. Here, the Act does not direct states to take any actions regarding lawyers in private practice. Rather, the Act is a generally applicable law that merely asks the states, as one of many organizations that employs lawyers, to register their own lawyers. Thus, **Answer (C) is the correct answer**, and **Answers (A) and (B) are incorrect**.

**Answer (D) is an incomplete statement of the law**. The answer correctly states one test for determining whether a statute falls within Congress' Commerce Clause power. But, even if Congress may reach the regulated activity under the Commerce Clause, Congress may not do so by commandeering the states to regulate. For example, in *New York v. United States*, 505 U.S. 144 (1992), no one denied that Congress could regulate the interstate business of low-level radioactive waste disposal. But, Congress could not do so by commandeering the states into making such laws. The Court explained that while Congress' objective (i.e., regulation of radioactive waste) might be constitutional, its chosen means (i.e., commandeering the states) violated the Tenth Amendment. **Answer (D) is not the best answer** because it does not recognize this means-end distinction.

201. **Answer (D) is the best answer.** The attorney occupation tax is similar to another federal provision reviewed in *South Carolina v. Baker*, 485 U.S. 505 (1988). As noted above, Congress repealed the federal income tax exemption for interest on unregistered state

bonds. The state argued that interest on its bonds was immune from federal taxation. In rejecting this argument, the Supreme Court explained the scope of state immunity from federal taxation. First, the federal government is generally prohibited from collecting a tax directly from the states. (The Court noted that there were some limited circumstances where Congress might do so, but refused to elaborate.) Here, the Act is not collecting any tax directly from state coffers. Rather, the Act imposes a tax on third parties who have dealt with the state — specifically, lawyers employed by the state.

Consequently, the Act's occupation tax falls into a second category for federal taxes on those who have contracted with the states. In addition to state employees, this category includes those who sell or lease land to a state, contractors on state construction projects, and those who receive interest on state bonds. Congress may impose a nondiscriminatory tax on those in this second category. For example, in *Baker*, Congress imposed similar tax treatment on unregistered state bonds and unregistered federal and private bonds. Here, Congress has done the same with its attorney occupation tax. State lawyers must pay the same attorney occupation tax as lawyers in private or federal government practice. Thus, state lawyers are not immune from the occupation tax, and **Answer (D) is the best answer**. (And, consequently, **Answer (A) is incorrect**.)

**Answer (C) is not the best answer** because it mistakenly assumes that Congress may impose a tax on third parties who deal with the government regardless of whether the tax is discriminatory. *Baker* makes clear that discriminatory taxes are invalid. **Answer (B) is incorrect** because it is irrelevant to the issue of tax immunity whether the third parties perform traditional government functions.

202.  **Answer (B) is the best answer.** The Supreme Court has been reluctant to find new substantive rights contained within the Due Process Clause of the Fourteenth Amendment. It does not want to sit as an unelected super-legislature deciding what social and economic paths the country should take. Therefore, although the modern Court, since *Griswold v. Connecticut*, 381 U.S. 479 (1965), has found substantive content in the Fourteenth Amendment's Due Process Clause, it has done so in very few cases. It has never held that the fundamental right of privacy extends to protection of personal autonomy. Because of this, **Answer (C) is incorrect**.

Nevertheless, considering the language used in several opinions, such as the joint opinion in *Planned Parenthood v. Casey*, 505 U.S. 833 (1992), and the majority opinion in *Lawrence v. Texas*, 539 U.S. 558 (2003), the Court might find the facts of this question so distasteful and so against our concept of ordered liberty that it concludes that personal autonomy is a fundamental right, at least under the facts of this case. The Court might find that personal liberty must include a prohibition against the government forcing us to discover our personal genetic code and all that comes from that discovery — such as fear of early death and disease, fear of procreation, and possible loss of insurance coverage, etc. But, for the Court to declare this law unconstitutional, it will have to expand the matters considered to be fundamental rights protected by the Due Process

Clause, and only if it does so will Answer (C) be correct. Under current law, however, this is not a fundamental right, and **Answer (C) is not the best answer**.

**Answer (A) is incorrect** because the Court has held, since 1937, that the Due Process Clause has content and is not limited to issues of procedural fairness.

**Answer (D) is incorrect** because the Court has never held that the Ninth Amendment is an independent source of rights protected by the Constitution.

203.   **Answer (A) is the best answer, but Answer (C) is a credible choice,** in light of the Court's decision in *Lawrence v. Texas*, 539 U.S. 558 (2003). Prior to *Lawrence*, Answer (A) would clearly be the best choice because the Court's decision in *Bowers v. Hardwick*, 478 U.S. 186 (1986), provided a forceful argument that sexual liberty is not included within the fundamental right of privacy. *Lawrence* overruled *Bowers* and suggested strongly in dicta that the fundamental right of privacy may well include the concepts of personal autonomy and the freedom to make intimate, sexual choices without state interference. However, *Lawrence* did not explicitly expand the fundamental right of privacy to include the personal, autonomous choices of who we live with and how we structure our intimate relations. Thus, it is logical to conclude that the cohabitation statute would receive the constitutional scrutiny applied to non-fundamental rights. This favors Answer (A).

The consequences of extending *Lawrence* to all intimate associations may give the Court considerable pause before doing so. For example, if *Lawrence* were so extended, could a state constitutionally continue its ban on same-sex marriage? The Court's possible reluctance to accept such results also argues for Answer (A) as the best choice.

Moreover, the statute at issue in this question is not aimed at an unpopular minority who is stigmatized by the very existence of the statutory prohibition, as was the case in *Lawrence*. Much of the Court's reasoning in *Lawrence* focused on the harm done to the homosexual community by the Texas sodomy law. In today's world, it is unlikely that cohabiting adults are unpopular or subject to ridicule. This also distinguishes this question from the facts in *Lawrence*, and reinforces the conclusion that Answer (A) is the best choice.

**Answer (B) is incorrect** because it suggests that laws that regulate intimate conduct are unconstitutional only if they involve homosexual conduct. While the decision in *Lawrence v. Texas* focused on the harmful effects the Texas sodomy statute had on intimate, personal choices available to homosexuals, its reasoning is grounded on the broad concept that the government should only interfere with such intimate choices if it has legitimate reasons for doing so. This is because such intimate choices involve the very essence of human freedom. Therefore, a law that so interferes without a legitimate purpose would be unconstitutional under *Lawrence,* without regard to whether it discriminates against homosexuals, making Answer (B) incorrect.

Please note that the statute in the question appears to violate the Equal Protection Clause because it allows homosexuals to cohabit but not heterosexuals. But that was not one of your choices.

**Answer (C) is incorrect, but it is a very credible choice**, as discussed in Answer (A). Moreover, if the Court concluded that the purpose of the legislation — to encourage marriage — is not legitimate, then the Court could follow its holding in *Lawrence* and declare the statute unconstitutional because it regulates intimate relationships for no legitimate reason. However, it seems unlikely that the Court would hold that the encouragement of marriage was an illegitimate purpose.

**Answer (D) is incorrect** because the conclusion it reaches is not based on constitutional jurisprudence and is silly. Nothing in the Constitution or in the Supreme Court's decisions makes favoring marriage unconstitutional or suspect.

204.   **Answer (C) is the best answer**, because it takes into account the most recent decisions by the Supreme Court that refuse to extend the reasoning found in earlier cases. These more recent cases limit the application of the "public function" rule and reduce the likelihood that involvement with a state will convert private activity to state action.

As to the "public function" rule, earlier cases, such as *Marsh v. Alabama*, 326 U.S. 501 (1946), strongly suggested that, when a private actor performs significant public functions, the private actor will have to act so as not to violate the Constitution. This broad rule was limited in *Jackson v. Metropolitan Edison Co.*, 419 U.S. 345 (1974), to apply only when the private party is performing functions that are "traditionally exclusively" handled by the government. Although we view firefighting as exclusively handled by the government, this is not true. Indeed, volunteer fire departments are very common, and the facts are constructed to tell you that Chicago did not always have a city fire department. Therefore, under the *Jackson* test, Fire Safety likely would not be seen as performing a public function under the contract because firefighting is not traditionally exclusively handled by the government. **This analysis also makes Answer (A) not the best answer.**

It is, of course, debatable whether the long history of Chicago having a government-controlled fire department makes firefighting traditionally exclusively handled by Chicago's government. If so, then the work of Fire Safety under the contract would be seen as a public function, forcing Fire Safety to abide by the Constitution and thus helping the employee's chances of succeeding. This also **would make Answer (A) the best answer**. Remember, state action decisions are fact bound, and so an answer may change if one particular fact — such as the modern history of the Chicago Fire Department — is particularly important to a particular court.

As to whether Fire Safety's involvement with the state converts its private activities to state action, *Blum v. Yaretsky*, 457 U.S. 991 (1982), and other cases appear to limit the Court's holding in *Burton v. Wilmington Parking Authority*, 365 U.S. 715 (1961), so that a contractual relationship with the government is not likely to be seen as sufficiently interdependent and symbiotic to convert private behavior to state action. Moreover, unlike the facts in *Wilmington Parking Authority*, the city is not acting outside its traditional role in its relationship with Fire Safety. It is not acting as an entrepreneur or using Fire Safety to make a profit as were the facts in *Wilmington Parking Authority*. All this argues against a holding that Fire Safety had such a symbiotic relationship with the city that its behavior was state action. **This makes Answer (B) incorrect.**

The Supreme Court's opinions in the state action area are difficult to reconcile; and therefore, it is often the case that two answers are possibly right. The advantage here, however, goes to Answer (C), if for no other reason than it is more specific and relies on more modern authority.

**Answer (D) is incorrect** because a private party may have to follow the requirements of the Fourteenth Amendment depending on whether the party's relationship with the state is sufficiently interdependent, or whether its behavior is deemed a public function, so that its private behavior is converted into state action.

205.   **Answer (D) is the best answer.** This answer recognizes that the President has absolute immunity, but the Secretary of Commerce does not. The Supreme Court has recognized only qualified immunity for other members of the executive branch for official conduct. *See Harlow v. Fitzgerald*, 457 U.S. 800 (1982). The *Harlow* case was a companion to *Nixon v. Fitzgerald*, 457 U.S. 731 (1982), but in *Harlow*, the Court found only a qualified immunity protected these other officials. The Court stated: "[G]overnment officials performing discretionary functions, generally are shielded from liability for civil damages insofar as their conduct does not violate clearly established statutory or constitutional rights of which a reasonable person would have known." This means that the immunity is qualified, because an official would be liable if she violated "clearly established statutory or constitutional rights" known to a reasonable person. Notice the President is immune *even if* he violates these clearly established rights because his immunity is absolute.

    **Answer (A) is incorrect** because the President does have absolute immunity from money damages for official conduct while President. *See Nixon v. Fitzgerald*, 457 U.S. 731 (1982). The Supreme Court based its decision to grant absolute immunity to the President on the President's "unique status under the Constitution," which requires him to be free to discharge his duties without concern for subsequent lawsuits concerning his official conduct. The dissenters in this 5-4 decision contended that this ruling "places the President above the law," but their position was in the minority.

    **Answer (B) is incorrect** because the President's absolute immunity for official conduct extends past his term of office. Indeed, in *Nixon v. Fitzgerald*, the suit was filed against President Nixon after he left office. Nevertheless, the Supreme Court held that his absolute immunity continued in effect.

**Answer (C) is incorrect** because the lawsuit does not involve the political question doctrine. This lawsuit does not involve any of the six factors listed by the Supreme Court in *Baker v. Carr*, 369 U.S. 186 (1962), to decide if the political question doctrine applies.

206.   **Answer (A) is the best answer, at least for now.** In *Missouri v. Holland*, 252 U.S. 416 (1920), the Supreme Court was faced with a very similar fact pattern, and it held that the treaty was not an unconstitutional infringement on a state's sovereignty. Missouri had attempted to enjoin the enforcement of the Migratory Bird Treaty Act of 1918. Prior to this treaty between the United States, Canada, and Great Britain, Congress had attempted to protect migratory birds by statute in a manner similar to how migratory birds would be protected under the treaty. A lower court had struck down this statute as an invasion of the states' sovereignty. Thus, Missouri argued that Congress could not do through a treaty what it was unable to do through a statute. However, the Supreme Court, in *Missouri v. Holland*, held that the protection of migratory birds was a proper subject for a treaty, because birds do not observe national boundaries. Because it was an appropriate treaty subject, it came within Congress's necessary and proper powers. Justice Holmes also noted that Congress and the federal government may acquire authority under a treaty that the national government did not have otherwise under Article I. *Missouri v. Holland* is still good law, and thus would seem to govern the answer to this question. However, given the Supreme Court's recent protection of state sovereignty, one might well question whether *Missouri v. Holland* will survive if challenged in the appropriate case.

**Answer (B) is incorrect** because the factual distinction it makes between the two cases would not matter. The Supreme Court's decision in *Printz v. United States*, 521 U.S. 898 (1997), involved the question of commandeering state resources to implement a federal program. It would not matter under that decision whether the state's resources were being used to register handguns or to perform background checks. This answer is a red herring.

**Answer (C) is incorrect** because it misstates the current state of the law. It claims that *Missouri v. Holland* has been overruled. It has not. It is reasonable to question whether *Missouri v. Holland* would survive if challenged in the appropriate case given the new protection of state sovereignty exhibited by the Supreme Court. But it has not yet been overruled, and thus Answer (C) is incorrect.

**Answer (D) is incorrect** because it ignores the Supremacy Clause of Article VI of the Constitution, which specifically includes treaties as the supreme law of the land. Therefore, if the treaty is constitutional, it is the supreme law of the land and is binding on the states without their approval, just as any act passed by Congress is binding on the states if it is constitutional.

207.   **Answer (B) is the correct answer**. The PUC's collocation requirement is a *per se* taking because it forces existing carriers to endure a physical invasion of their property

by a third party. Specifically, the PUC directs existing carriers to allow a new entrant to locate equipment on their property. The Court held the same type of conduct a *per se* taking in *Loretto v. Teleprompter Manhattan CATV Corp.*, 458 U.S. 419 (1982), where New York City required apartment owners to permit a cable company to locate equipment on their buildings.

**Answers (A) and (C) are incorrect** because a forced physical invasion is a taking without regard to either the government's interest or the regulation's effect on the property's value.

208.  **Answer (D) is the best Answer** because it is in accord with the Court's decision in *Allied Structural Steel Co. v. Spannaus*, 438 U.S. 234 (1978). However, if the *Allied Structural Steel* case did not exist, then Answer (A) would be the best answer.

In *Allied Structural Steel*, the Court faced facts almost identical to those in this question. Minnesota had passed a law requiring employers to pay a "pension funding charge" if they closed a Minnesota office. Allied Structural Steel sued when, after closing its Minnesota operation, it was assessed a $185,000 fee under the law. The Court agreed with Allied Structural Steel that the Minnesota law violated the Contract Clause, making this one of only two times since 1934 that the Court struck down a law under the Clause. In reaching this decision, the Court focused on the fact that this was not emergency legislation and that the law was not "enacted to protect a broad societal interest rather than a narrow class."

Further, the Court emphasized that the state had not previously regulated in this area, so that employers could not have reasonably expected this law. To the Court, it was important that the employer "had no reason to anticipate that its employees' pension rights could become vested except in accordance with the terms of the plan. It relied heavily, and reasonably, on this legitimate contractual expectation in calculating its annual contributions to the pension fund."

Despite this holding, we must not give undue weight to *Allied Structural Steel*. It has not been followed by the Court in any other case. Further, more recent cases have displayed great deference in allowing state regulation that arguably impairs contractual relationships. Nevertheless, *Allied Structural Steel* has never been overruled, and it certainly would apply when, as in this question, the facts follow so closely the data upon which the Court based its decision.

**Answer (A) is incorrect** for the reasons discussed in connection with Answer (D). However, in the absence of the *Allied Structural Steel* decision, Answer (A) would be the best answer because it recognizes the great deference the Court has shown in upholding state regulations that impair contracts.

**Answer (B) is incorrect** because the Constitution explicitly limits the states' power to impair contracts. Further, neither the language of the Eleventh Amendment nor the cases interpreting it stand for the principle that the states cannot be sued to force them to comply with a constitutional provision that expressly limits state power. While recent Supreme Court decisions interpreting the Eleventh Amendment have extended its reach, nothing in these cases supports nullifying the Contract Clause by holding that the Eleventh Amendment makes the Clause unenforceable against the states.

**Answer (C) is incorrect** because the question does not give you enough information to conclude that the state legislation is preempted by the federal legislation. As discussed in Question 89, federal preemption jurisprudence depends on evaluating and comparing state and federal legislation. Without sufficient facts, you cannot make the necessary comparison, and thus Answer (C) is incorrect.

209. **Answer (C) is the correct answer**. The TEAB promotion policy classifies employees based on their ability to see. Because the classification does not involve race, ethnicity, national origin, or gender, neither strict scrutiny nor intermediate scrutiny applies. (Also, there is no indication that this facially neutral law was intended to discriminate based on race, ethnicity, national origin, or gender.) Thus, **Answers (A) and (B) are incorrect**. This leaves rational basis review as the proper standard of review.

**Answer (D) is a red herring** because the undue burden test is not an Equal Protection test. Rather, that test applies to abortion regulations. *See Planned Parenthood v. Casey*, 505 U.S. 833 (1992).

210. **Answer (C) is the best answer**.

**Answer (A) is incorrect** because it suggests that commercial speech must be either false or misleading for the government to regulate it under the First Amendment. If commercial speech is either false or misleading, then the government may regulate or ban that speech in the name of protecting consumers from deception. If, however, commercial speech is neither false nor misleading, the government may still regulate the speech as long as the regulation survives scrutiny under the *Central Hudson* test described in the answer to Question 179.

**Answer (B) is incorrect** because it implies that improving traffic safety is not a substantial government interest. Because traffic safety is akin to the health and safety interest found substantial in Question 179, *see Rubin v. Coors Brewing Co.*, 514 U.S. 476 (1995); *44 Liquormart, Inc. v. Rhode Island*, 517 U.S. 484 (1996), the city should have no problem satisfying this prong of the *Central Hudson* test.

While it may be a close call between **Answers (C) and (D)**, we give the edge to **Answer (C)**. We believe that **Answer (D) is not the better answer** because the city has drawn its regulation quite narrowly to only those lighted displays that pose a threat of driver distraction. The signs must be visible to drivers on public roadways, and the signs must be of a type — lighted and changing display — that poses the threat. Consequently, the ordinance does not appear more extensive than necessary. Further, the ordinance differs from *44 Liquormart, Inc. v. Rhode Island*, 517 U.S. 484 (1996), in another important respect. In *44 Liquormart*, the Court concluded that the government could achieve its purpose — promoting temperance — through non-speech regulations, such as direct regulation of alcohol consumption or a tax on the sale of alcohol. Here, it is the very speech at issue — the lighted signs — that pose the threat to traffic safety, so non-speech regulations would not similarly address the government's interest.

We believe that **Answer (C) is the better answer** because the city arguably offered weak evidence that the ordinance directly advances its interest in traffic safety. Recall from the answer to the prior question that the Court looks at two main factors in deciding this issue. First, a plurality of justices ask whether the government has evidence proving that the challenged action directly advances the government's interest. Second, the Court asks whether activity not covered by the challenged law may undermine the government's interest.

Here, the ordinance is vulnerable under both factors. First, the city's evidence — the Department of Transportation study — is arguably inapposite. The study documents the threat of distraction to drivers on interstate highways, which are high speed roadways. It is not clear whether and to what degree the same threat applies to local roads in a small, rural community. Second, the ordinance allows some commercial lighted displays, such as temperature and time displays, that might pose the same threat. (At least, the question provides no information that the city has evidence that such displays pose little or no threat.) Further, the city allows non-flashing or changing lighted displays, or changing displays that do not involve lights, both of which could distract drivers. And the ordinance does not address lighted non-commercial displays that pose a similar threat, such as holiday and other similar displays visible from public roadways. So while it is a close call whether the ordinance directly advances the city's interest in traffic safety, we believe that this is the city's weakest argument under the *Central Hudson* test.

211. **Answer (C) is the best answer**.

As noted in the answer to Question 84, the first issue is whether the state law discriminates between in-state and out-of-state commerce, or if it is evenhanded. Here, Utep's new speed limit is evenhanded because it applies to *all* vehicles on its roads, regardless of origin or destination. Thus, we must apply the balancing test. **Answer (A) is incorrect** because it mistakenly states that the Utep speed limit discriminates against out-of-state commerce.

The Court applied the Dormant Commerce Clause balancing test to a state highway regulation in *Kassel v. Consolidated Freightways Corp.*, 450 U.S. 662 (1981). There, an Iowa law limited most trucks to 55 feet in length. The Court concluded that this law's burden on interstate commerce greatly outweighed the slight benefit to the state's interest in highway safety. On the burden side, the Court noted that interstate trucking companies would incur millions of dollars in extra cost either using shorter trucks on all routes through Iowa, switching to shorter trucks at the Iowa border, or diverting their longer trucks around Iowa. On the benefit side, the state had little evidence that the banned longer trucks posed a greater safety risk than the 55-foot trucks allowed on the state's highways. And by forcing trucks to divert around Iowa and thereby drive more miles, the law likely increased the out-of-state threat to traffic safety. Further, Iowa law made exceptions to the length limit that mainly benefited in-state economic interests. For example, longer trucks were allowed in Iowa border cities and to carry certain farm equipment and livestock within the state.

The Utep law in this question differs from the Iowa law in *Kassel* in just about every respect. First, the burden on interstate commerce is surely much less. In *Kassel*, the trucking companies had to either switch trucks or drive around an entire state, while here the companies can use the same equipment and drive the same number of miles. While the ten mile per hour reduction in speed will surely increase delivery times, and thereby reduce the number of deliveries, the overall economic burden does not appear as great as in *Kassel*. On the benefit side, the problem tells us that Utep has overwhelming evidence of the safety benefits of the reduced speed limit. This contrasts sharply with *Kassel*, where the state had little evidence of increased safety, and the law may have increased out-of-state traffic accidents. And last, the Utep law has no exceptions that preserve the benefit of an increased speed limit for in-state interests — the law applies to all vehicles on the state's roads. **Answer (C) is the best answer** because it notes that the Utep law strikes a permissible balance between slight burden on interstate commerce and significant benefit to in-state traffic safety. **Answer (B) is not the best answer** because it states the opposite balance of interests.

**Answer (D) is incorrect** for at least two reasons. First, the regulation of state highways is not just a local matter. Recall that *United States v. Lopez*, 514 U.S. 549 (1995), held that the Commerce Clause extends Congress' power to the channels of interstate commerce, which include the roadways on which interstate goods and travelers move. So while states may have concurrent jurisdiction with Congress to regulate such roadways, state regulation may be preempted by federal Commerce Clause legislation. Second, even the state's concurrent power over the channels of interstate commerce must be exercised in a manner that does not unreasonably burden interstate commerce. **Answer (D) is incorrect** because it does not recognize either limitation on the state's power.

212. The promotion policy should easily survive traditional rational basis review. First, protection of physical safety is a recognized legitimate interest. In *New York City Transit Authority v. Beazer*, 440 U.S. 568 (1979), the Supreme Court upheld public safety as a reason for a transit authority policy against hiring methadone users. Second, the classification need only be rationally related to the government's purpose. This test tolerates significant over-and under-inclusiveness. For example, in *Beazer*, it was undisputed that many methadone users were as safe as the average job applicant, and that the Transit Authority could easily identify these safe methadone users. Further, it was uncontested that the Transit Authority did not bar employment of groups that were as unsafe as methadone users (such as former alcoholics and mental patients, diabetics, and epileptics). Yet, the rational relationship test does not require a precise means-end fit. It only requires that the classification have some logical bearing on the government's purpose.

Here, it is not illogical to think that employees who cannot perform job tasks within a department might be unsafe supervisors or managers. The supervisor or manager may be required to train or assist employees in use of the department's equipment. Having never used certain equipment may make the visually-impaired employee unable to perform these functions. Of course, this will not be true for all visually-impaired employees. Moreover, many sighted employees (who are eligible for promotion) may be less qualified supervisors or managers. But, traditional rational basis review allows such over-and under-inclusiveness.

213. When the Court suspects that a group is being targeted out of animus, it requires a tighter relationship between the classification and the government's purpose than under traditional rational basis review. For example, in *City of Cleburne v. Cleburne Living Center*, 473 U.S. 432 (1985), the Court suspected that animus motivated a city's denial of a site permit to a group home for the mentally retarded. This suspicion arose from statements in the public record that local residents opposed the group home based on bias and prejudice against the mentally retarded. Suspicion led the Court to carefully scrutinize, and ultimately reject, the city's reasons for denying the permit: fear that nearby high school students would harass the residents, concerns about civil liability, and safety problems due to the proposed home's location in a five-hundred-year flood plain. The Court noted that none of these concerns were unique to the proposed group home, and that similar concerns had not stopped location of either a hospital (flood plain concerns) or a fraternity (liability concerns) in the same area. This different treatment, though tolerable under traditional rational basis review, did not survive heightened scrutiny.

The Court might apply the same heightened scrutiny to the TEAB promotion policy. The question is whether the Court has any reason to suspect bias or prejudice as the basis for the policy. The only hint of such motivation might be that compensation of TEAB supervisors and managers is linked to productivity. If visually-impaired supervisors and managers are perceived as less productive, the promotion policy might be a covert effort to increase salaries at the expense of TEAB's mission. Further, federal laws such as the Americans with Disabilities Act have documented workplace biases and prejudices against disabled employees. So, some basis for suspicion exists. And, if the Court is suspicious, it may not tolerate the obvious over-and under-inclusiveness of the promotion policy discussed above. Ultimately, however, it is speculative whether the Court will be motivated to apply a heightened form of rational basis review.

**Note:** The facts of Questions 209 and 213-14 are loosely based on the case *Brown v. Sibley*, 650 F.2d 760 (5th Cir. 1981).

214.    The key to this question is the state's definition of "in-state student." The status is defined by duration of residency and not by current residence itself. Indeed, given that Arkabama State University is a residential campus, *all* students — regardless of whether they are deemed in-state or out-of-state — actually reside within the state. Consequently, the University's tuition scheme does not discriminate between residents and non-residents. Rather, it discriminates *among residents* based on the duration of their residency. Thus, the Article IV Privileges and Immunities Clause does not apply to the tuition policy.

**Note**: The Supreme Court has also reviewed durational residency requirements under the Equal Protection Clause and the Privileges and Immunities Clause of the Fourteenth Amendment.

215.    Putting aside the question of whether the Supreme Court would dismiss such a case as involving the political question doctrine, the constitutionality of the War Powers Resolution has been discussed and debated without resolution. Why? As stated previously, the Constitution gives authority to both the President and Congress to handle the nation's military affairs. In analyzing the War Powers Resolution, some have argued that this law amounts to Congress usurping the power the Constitution grants the President both in his role as Commander-in-Chief and through the inherent power of the chief executive to defend the nation. Others argue that the President committing armed forces for a protracted period without a Congressional war declaration or other approval violates separation of powers principles because it takes from Congress its authority to be substantially involved in the decision to go to war. Therefore, whether the terms of the War Powers Resolution could be imposed on the President under the Constitution would depend on whether it was seen as usurping presidential power, making it unconstitutional, or seen as required to protect congressional authority over military matters, making it constitutional.

# TABLE OF CASES

[References are to pages.]

[References are to pages.]

[References are to pages.]

[References are to pages.]

[References are to pages.]

[References are to pages.]

# INDEX

# INDEX

433

**TOPIC**                                                    **QUESTION**